Leed Trinity

The Shape of Fear

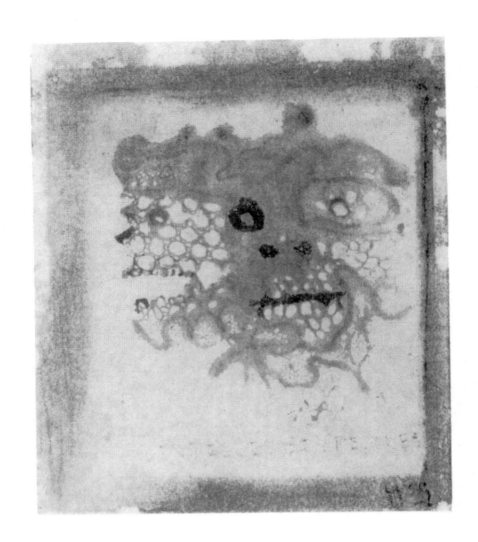

The Shape of Fear

Horror and the Fin de Siècle Culture of Decadence

Susan J. Navarette

THE UNIVERSITY PRESS OF KENTUCKY

Publication of this volume was made possible in part by a grant from the National Endowment for the Humanities.

Editorial and Sales Offices: The University Press of Kentucky 663 South Limestone Street, Lexington, Kentucky 40508-4008

01 00 99 98 5 4 3 2 1

Frontispiece: Victor Hugo, *Dentelles et spectres* (1855-56). Courtesy of Photothèque des Musées de la Ville de Paris

Portions of the Introduction and chapters 1 and 2 of this book were previously published as "The Soul of the Plot: The Aesthetics of Fin de Siècle Literature of Horror" in *Styles of Creation: Aesthetic Technique and the Creation of Fictional Worlds*, ed. George Slusser and Eric S. Rabkin (1992). Reprinted by permission of the University of Georgia Press. Chapter 6 was previously published as "The Anatomy of Failure in Joseph Conrad's *Heart of Darkness*," *Texas Studies in Literature and Language* 35:4. Reprinted by permission of the University of Texas Press.

Library of Congress Cataloging-in-Publication Data

Navarette, Susan J., 1960-
    The shape of fear : horror and the fin de siècle culture of decadence / Susan J. Navarette.
    p.   cm.
    Includes bibliographical references (p.   ) and index.
    ISBN 0-8131-2013-6 (alk. paper)
    1. English fiction—19th century—History and criticism. 2. Horror tales, English—History and criticism. 3. Literature and science—Great Britian—History—19th century. 4. Conrad, Joseph, 1857-1924. Heart of darkness. 5. James, Henry, 1843-1916. Turn of the screw. 6. Decadence (Literary movement)—England. 7. Degeneration in literature. 8. Body, Human, in literature. 9. Fear in literature. I. Title.
    PR878.T3N38   1997
    823'.087380908—dc21   97-34081

Out of the secret places of a unique temperament he brought forth strange blossoms and fruits hitherto unknown; and for him, the novel impression conveyed, the exquisite effect woven, counted as an end in itself—a perfect end.

Walter Pater

Contents

Figures

Acknowledgments

IN THE SEVEN YEARS that it has taken me to discern the outline of *The Shape of Fear*, I have incurred many outstanding debts to many good people whose encouragement and support have proven talismanic, keeping the specters of failure and despair at bay. Regretting that I must avail myself of the same words with which all the world declines a disagreeable invitation—a "man is occasionally grateful when he says 'thank you,'" rues George Eliot's Stephen Guest—I hope that those to whom I am indebted will extend to me yet another kindness in the form of the reassurance that Maggie Tulliver offers to her frustrated suitor when she grants that common words used on an important occasion sometimes prove "the more striking, because they are felt at once to have a particular meaning, like old banners, or everyday clothes, hung up in a sacred place."

The first to receive my thanks ought perhaps to be he who was the first to take an active interest in the project. When I had little more to offer than an unseasoned curiosity about a subject to which he has devoted his best energies, George Slusser gave me generous and unlimited access to the treasures of the University of California at Riverside's Eaton Collection of Fantasy and Science Fiction, of which he has for many years been a most tireless curator. He has long been an enthusiastic and unbiased supporter of good work, no matter where or in whose hands it is to be discovered.

A research fellowship granted by the University of North Carolina at Chapel Hill's Institute for the Arts and Humanities gave me a much needed semester during which I could reconsider my methodology in the company of supportive and commiserative colleagues, each of whom was as grateful as I to find in Ruel Tyson, the director of the institute, someone who recognizes that a devotion to teaching is not exclusive of the need and the desire to occasionally quit the classroom in order to resuscitate intellectual curiosity and vitality. Ralph Cohen awarded me an invaluable resident fellowship at the University of Virginia's Commonwealth Center for Literary and Cultural Change, providing me at a critical period in my writing with a semester's leave during which I rewrote the first and most difficult chapter of *The Shape of Fear*. Research and publication expenses, as well as the costs associated with the reproduction of the illustrations featured herein, were subsidized by grants awarded by the University Research Council and assistance from the Scholarly Publications Committee of the College Endowment Committee, both of the University of North Carolina at Chapel Hill.

To those who have, over the years, read individual chapters of this book at various stages of revision—Edward Wagenknecht, John McGowan, Barton Levi St. Armand, Everett Emerson, Joy Kasson, Beverly Taylor, and James Thompson—I ought perhaps to extend equal shares of sympathy and gratitude. To the latter five individuals in particular I wish to offer a more personal thanks, for they have always enhanced their praise or—when it was warranted—chastened their intelligent censure with a patience and a solicitude that have taught me to regard their conduct as a standard of professionalism and to count their friendship as a privilege.

I am personally obliged to a number of people who provided me with invaluable support and expertise in subjects as esoteric as any with which I occupy myself in the pages of this book. With patience and a creditable appreciation for the absurd, Cynthia Adams, Thomas Nixon, and Hugh Singerline ferreted out the origin and context of many an elusive reference and hermetic fact, and Rebecca Breazeale unearthed from other collections volumes otherwise inaccessible. Mitchell Whichard and his efficient library staff helped me to manage the many books that had to be read before the one book could be written. Rachel Frew, Linda G. Zatlin, Xavier Tricot, Libby Chenault, Mary Snider, Laure Dosogne, Nelly Dosogne, and Jennifer L. Bowden aided me in tracking down and arranging for the reproduction of the prints and line drawings here assembled. Frederick N. Stipe expertly produced the reproductions of the images housed in the University of North Carolina at Chapel Hill's Rare Book Collection. For help in translating many of the idiomatic peculiarities of the French Decadents, I relied upon Mary Snider's interpretive skills. While Nina Wallace graciously assisted in the production and layout of the manuscript, Geraldine Taylor and Linda Horne have been for me the Champollions of that occult grammar known as departmental procedure.

There are those who, though having little to do with the actual writing of the book, yet stand in an important relation to it, much as the outermost of the series of concentric circles bears an essential relationship to a resonating note of origin. Charles T.L. Anderson, A. Reid Barbour, Stephen S. Birdsall, Darryl J. Gless, Rebecca Goz, Barbara Harris, and Linda Wagner-Martin—each according to his or her lights and capacities—worked to ensure that the context remained intact in which *The Shape of Fear* and other such productions were to be conceived of and brought to term. Stephen A. Navarette assured me that sufficiency would not be wanting should self-reliance have proven insufficient unto the day. When it was most difficult for her to do so, Jennie Marciano traced an Ariadne's thread that showed me the way.

I would be a most insensible teacher were I to forget my debt to my students at the University of North Carolina at Chapel Hill, who for several years now have endured my folly with good-natured patience, offered me fresh perspectives from which to reconsider it, and even remembered on occasion to ask after it with affectionate interest. The informed solicitude shown me by two of my former students in particular—Mary Moore Parham and Sarah Spencer White—has served as an affirmation of the powerfully reciprocal nature of teaching.

Finally, this study owes much of the most essential part of its being to several people whose constancy and commitment are insinuated in every line of its prosings. Christine J. Navarette and Alfred J. Navarette have expressed their support in ways that I would not presume to detail, lest in the naming I diminish the scope and degree. Their influence being profound—like Blaise Pascal's sphere, its center is everywhere present, its circumference nowhere—my debt to them is, in kind, immeasurable. There is another person without whose care and oversight my speculations would never have resolved themselves into *The Shape of Fear*. David C. Cody has shared with me, generously and without reservation, invaluable sources, astute observations, and his editorial expertise. He has taken as great an interest in the genesis of this book, lavished as much careful attention upon its evolution, and borne its fearful conceits ever as fully as its author could have done.

To Christine, Alfred, Stephen, and David—each tolerating patiently and encouraging my fitful engagement with George Santayana's proposition that in order to be happy one must take the measure of one's powers, taste the fruits of one's passion, and learn one's place in the world—I lovingly inscribe this book.

Introduction

Ego-maniacs, Decadents and Aesthetes have completely gathered under their banner this refuse of civilized peoples, and march at its head.

Max Nordau, *Degeneration* (1895)

A disconcerting discovery lies in wait for the amateur explorer of any
recent literary period—its refuse.

Walter de la Mare, *The Eighteen Eighties* (1930)

THE SHAPE OF FEAR FOCUSES ON the literature of horror, which, as Everett F. Bleiler reminds us, emerged in a "shower of different forms, with many different types of association with the supernatural" in England at the turn of the century.[1] More specifically, it concerns itself with the ways in which fin de siècle horror writers created an aesthetic that functioned as a response to and as a restatement of trends in contemporary scientific theory that, taken as a whole, permitted these aestheticians to advance the idea that a period of cultural decline was imminent both in England and on the Continent. Sir Charles Lyell's theory of uniformitarianism, Charles Darwin's theories of evolutionary descent, Thomas Henry Huxley's exploration of the physical basis of life: all of these suggested that a tendency toward a state of decay and final dissolution was inherent in all things. Writing half a century after the English physicist William Thomson, Lord Kelvin, had introduced the notion of heat death with his second law of thermodynamics, William James traced "the curdling cold and gloom and absence of all permanent meaning" to "the popular science evolutionism of our time" and to a "naturalism, fed on recent cosmological speculations" that had described humankind as existing "in a position similar to that of a set of people living on a frozen lake, surrounded by cliffs over which there is no escape, yet knowing that little by little the ice is melting, and the inevitable day drawing near when the last film of it will disappear, and to be drowned ignominiously will be the human creature's portion." Nearly a decade earlier, Huxley had made such soul-sickening prophecies, bred of the science of his day, the subject of his "Prolegomena," the introductory essay written the year after he had delivered his influential 1893 Romanes lecture, "Evolution and Ethics": "Man may develop a worthy civilization, capable of maintaining and constantly improving itself," he announced, but only "until the evolution of our globe shall have entered so far upon its downward course that the cosmic process resumes its sway; and, once more, the State of Nature prevails over the surface of our planet."[2] Distilled in the alembic of a cultural consciousness tempered by an attritive sense of dislocation, futility, and alienation, fin de siècle horror literature—emerging during a decade that H.G. Wells characterized as "a good and stimulating period" for writers of short fiction—is an expression of cultural anguish, because it is the vessel into which various authors poured their most corrosive anxieties and their darkest fantasies about the "true" nature of reality.[3]

The degree of interchange and commerce between individual fields of scientific inquiry in the nineteenth century suggests that scientists sought not only to promote their own disciplines, but also to establish what Elizabeth Knoll sees as the fundamental "methodological unity of the sciences." Knoll suggests that political aims underscored rhetorical strategies, for comparative studies and approaches "gave geological writers a way to make their science sound more familiar, since philology was a more established part of the scholarly curriculum, and it gave philologists a way to affirm that their field was as progressively scientific as the newer geology."[4] In his study of thermodynamics and social prophecy. Greg Myers also draws attention to the "constant movement of commonplaces between" distinct scientific discourses, focusing in particular on the example of nineteenth-century physicists, who were unanimous in wanting to make their field approachable although the "differences in the causes to which they [applied] physics" may have made them seem disunified: "The need to appeal for popular support for the discipline may account for some of the physicists' emphasis on the moral and social relevance of physics and for their use of concepts familiar from other fields to explain new concepts."[5] Such exchanges were not restricted to the fields of geology and philology. The investigations of physicists such as Balfour Stewart (who put forward the "elementary treatise" on the conservation of energy) and William Thomson, for example, provided criminal anthropologists with one way of expressing the etiology of genius and insanity, for, as the Italian criminologist Cesare Lombroso would argue in *The Man of Genius* (1891), the "law of the conservation of energy which rules the whole organic world, explains to us other frequent abnormalities, such as precocious greyness and baldness, leanness of the body, and weakness of sexual and muscular activity, which characterize the insane, and are also frequently found among great thinkers."[6] Darwin made no secret of the fact that his methods of biological investigation were indebted to those he had encountered in Lyell's *Principles of Geology* (1830), a work capable, in Darwin's view, of altering "the whole tone of one's mind," to the extent that when observing something "never seen by Lyell, one yet saw it partially through his eyes." "I always feel as if my books came half out of Lyell's brain, and that I never acknowledge this sufficiently," Darwin admitted to his friend Leonard Horner.[7] Linguists remained, however, the most enthusiastic—as well as the most overt—interlopers into the realm of the physical sciences. F. Max Müller publicly acknowledged that his philological studies were of a piece procedurally with those of contemporary biologists and geologists, whereas his colleague August Schleicher suggested that philology could offer practical examples that could provide a means of evaluating the validity of theoretical models, because the "kinship of the different languages may consequently serve, so to speak, as a paradigmatic illustration of the origin of species, for those fields of inquiry which lack, for the present at least, any similar opportunities of observation."[8]

Facilitating the "reciprocal borrowing and contestation" that took place between "critical forms of thought and philosophies of life" throughout the nineteenth century was the emphasis on the "positive basis of knowledge" predominant, as Foucault notes, "in grammar and philology, in natural history and biology, in the study of wealth and political economy."[9] Contemporary scientific writings were unified, that is, not merely by *what* their authors appeared to say, but by *how* they presented their findings. Darwin's reading of the body, for example, allowed him to infer the existence of inner workings unobservable on their own terms. Thus, in *The Expression of the Emotions in Man and Animals* (1872), Darwin observed that the "just perceptible drawing down of the corners of the

mouth," or the "slight raising up of the inner ends of the eyebrows, or both movements combined" followed by "a slight suffusion of tears" told him that "some
melancholy thought passes through the brain."[10] Lombroso classified the criminal type by identifying certain telltale features such as microcephaly, gigantic
bodily stature, or a distorted sense of hearing; his disciple, Max Nordau, worked
zealously to pinpoint those stylistic devices indicative of the literary madness
that would not betray itself physiognomically. Crossing several disciplinary lines,
the philologist George Romanes argued that language, considered paleon-
tologically, "may be regarded as the stratified deposit of thoughts, wherein they
lie embedded ready to be unearthed by the labours of the man of science."[11] The
scientific methodology to be considered here was predicated on the notion that
"exterior" modes—the shape of organic bodies, the physiognomy of "deviant"
types, linguistic or syntactic patterns—serve as indices of interior states or agencies. The semiotic disposition that it betrayed was particularly evident in those
studies emerging within the fields of evolutionary biology, criminal anthropology, and philology, each of which was directly concerned with the attempt to
locate humanity within a universe of animals and things. In a natural world
already entropically inclined, the human situation—and even human identity—
had come to seem even more precarious since Darwin had suggested that certain actions—"the bristling of the hair under the influence of extreme terror, or
the uncovering of the teeth under that of furious rage"—were hardly to be understood "except on the belief that man once existed in a much lower and animal-
like condition."[12]

Important nineteenth-century scientific discoveries and models of inquiry
were transmuted within the works of imagination of people whose intellectual
activities, although undertaken in isolation and "confined," as Walter Pater would
suggest, "to [their] own circle of ideas," nevertheless disclosed shared assumptions, expectations, and motivations common among artists and philosophers
who "breathe a common air, and catch light and heat from each other's
thoughts."[13] More specifically, the body-as-text analogy central to the writings of
evolutionists and anthropologists emerges in many turn-of-the-century horror
stories, which express the pervasive fear that the otherwise pleasant-looking
human body might camouflage "horrors," spiritual and material. Drawing upon
a popular scientific methodology in which distinctive surface patterns and structures were read as a means of understanding occult mechanisms and processes,
fin de siècle horror writers created texts that not only emphasized themes of
madness, alienation, and degeneration, but also were themselves stylistically
and linguistically degenerative, as well as structurally unstable. They depend for
their final effect on the degree to which they are able to generate anxiety through
semantic, structural, and stylistic patternings—diction, word tonalities, syntactic
textures, linguistic disruption, stylistic decomposition, hesitancy, and instability—and thereby duplicate the process by which evil bursts through the calm
surfaces of daily living.

Conjoining the aesthetics of "horror," "decadence" (both cultural and stylistic), and the methodology of scientific theory, *The Shape of Fear* diagnoses the form and the function of certain hybrid literary monstrosities and contextualizes the structural, stylistic, and thematic systems developed by writers seeking to record and to reenact in narrative form what they understood to be the entropic, devolutionary, and degenerative forces prevailing within the natural world. Like Terry Heller's *The Delights of Terror* (1987) or Eve Kosofsky Sedgwick's *The Coherence of Gothic Conventions* (1986), *The Shape of Fear* attempts to construct a poetic based upon underlying structural principles that engender both meaning and horror. Its primary interest, however, is to reconstruct some portion of the *histoire de mentalité* betrayed by the defining themes and verbal patternings symptomatic of these stories, themselves woven together out of reticulated strands drawn from the graphic arts, the sciences and pseudosciences, philosophy, aesthetics, and literature. In this way *The Shape of Fear* undertakes what Richard Altick describes as "an informed exercise of the historical imagination."[14]

Primary emphasis is given to the literary detritus or "refuse" (which we might think of as "hybrids" or variations within a genre) that, although it has a great deal to say about the culture that produced it, has itself long suffered under what E.P. Thompson calls "the enormous condescension of posterity."[15] The works of largely ignored authors such as Walter de la Mare, Vernon Lee, and Arthur Machen are here given pride of place, although the works of "major" authors—Henry James and Joseph Conrad, for example—are also discussed. (This book borrows its title from one such forgotten story. Tim O'Connor, the central character in Elia Wilkinson Peattie's "The Shape of Fear" [1898], is convinced that because it is compounded of suppressed regrets, desires, and obsessions, "Fear has a Shape" unique to the one who feels it.)[16] The first four chapters feature horror stories in which the human body is treated as a deceptive text whose ostensibly "normal" and "healthy" surface masks the degenerative, devolutionary tendencies to which any organism is prone. These stories center on a "family" of protagonists: decadent "gentlemen," an aborted fetus, beatific children, and beautifully preserved women. The two chapters of part 2 are devoted to stories that treat language (cited by nineteenth-century philologists and biologists as the *differencia specifica* of humanity—*"our Rubicon,"* as Müller saw it, *"which no brute will dare to cross"*) as an organic body poised to revert to a primitive condition of structure that the philologist Romanes designated "the undifferentiated protoplasm of predication."[17] A casual preview of the table of contents will readily disclose that this study does not aim at breadth, nor does it seek to establish the sort of taxonomies or propose the sort of "subject headings" for fin de siècle horror that might encourage a false sense of homogeneity or delimiting consistency within the field. Recognizing that opting for encyclopedic inclusivity would have entailed the sacrifice of more culturally informed readings of a limited number of texts, I preferred to pursue what struck me from the start as the sort of archaeology that reconstructs a mosaic pieced together out of the tesserae of cultural and historical associations. Such a critical approach facilitates a depth of analysis that stories conventionally dismissed as sports (when, that is, they are taken up at all) not only permit but require if they are to be understood as having been conceived of not in vacuo but rather in relation to degenerative prophecies of Victorian science that had as their own genesis the most sophisticated tendencies discernible in nineteenth-century thought.

Part 1

Let us begin with that which is without—our physical life.

Walter Pater

1

Rictus Invictus

. . . loathsome sight,
How from the rosy lips of life and love
Flash'd the bare-grinning skeleton of death!

> Alfred, Lord Tennyson, *Idylls of the King* (1859)

Camilla: You, sir, should unmask.
Stranger: Indeed?
Cassilda: Indeed it's time. We all have laid aside disguise but you.
Stranger: I wear no mask.
Camilla: *(Terrified, aside to Cassilda)* No mask? No mask!

> Robert W. Chambers, fragment from
> *The King in Yellow* (n.d.), act 1, scene 2

"What of Art?" she asked.
"It is a malady."

> Oscar Wilde, *The Picture of Dorian Gray* (1891)

THREE YEARS AFTER THE DEATH of Victor Hugo in 1885, the first exhibition of his graphic works was held at the Galerie Georges Petit in Paris. Among the works there assembled were drawings that Hugo had produced during his stay in the Channel Islands, to which he had retreated upon his exile from France in 1851. The nearly twenty years he spent there, first in Jersey and then in Guernsey, proved unusually fertile in an artistic sense, and when he was not absorbed in intense literary work, Hugo devoted himself to the graphic arts. It was during this period that he "discovered" an artistic technique involving and exploiting an inherent degree of chance or risk.[1] He began to generate forms and images by folding paper in half and blotting it with ink, or by stamping it with cutouts or objects dipped in ink. He employed the former method, for example, in *Tache d'encre sur papier plié et personnages* (1853-55) (fig. 1), in which he drew out or encouraged the appearance of the faces and grotesques that he saw lurking within the aleatory shapes. Born of the interaction of imagination and technical ingenuity, and involving, as he himself put it, "all sorts of queer mixtures that eventually render more or less what I have in my eye and above all in my mind," Hugo's images are projections from within, their curves, dimensions, and contours roughly approximating the features of subconscious phantoms and the internal landscape they haunt.[2]

Most of the drawings that Hugo produced during this period are dominated by fluid, amorphous masses from which shadowy patterns, forms, and structures surface, hinting at meanings unsettling and often ominous. The French littérateur Théophile Gautier referred to them as "dark and savage fantasies" imbued with the "chiaroscuro effect of Goya" and "the architectural terror of Piranesi."[3] A unique series of *Dentelles* (1855-56) contain eerie images created when Hugo dipped a piece of finely patterned lace in ink, pressed it between two leaves of paper, and then enhanced the impression with ink blots. The resultant image would depend on how much of the lace had been treated with ink and on how much pressure had been exerted when the lace was pressed onto the paper. The effect is eerie, for the technique reproduces the highly structured nature of the fabric but also (because the inked pattern is fragmentary) suggests that it is in the process of decomposition.

Of this select group of blottesques, three in particular merit close scrutiny: a *carte de voeux* (fig. 2)—the earliest and best known of the *Dentelles*—and two of the *Dentelles et spectres* (frontispiece and fig. 3), so called because in them Hugo conjures up the toothy, grinning skulls that he discovered staring out at him, latent within the filaments of the design. All three pieces are linked by the organicism that Hugo perceived and emphasized within the lacy figurations. The *carte de voeux* (bearing the handwritten date along the bottom of the card—"1er janvier 1856"—that has allowed scholars to roughly date its companion pieces) is richly evocative. In it, the first letter of Hugo's last name descends from a fretted image that hovers, wraithlike, in the muted upper half of the card: although so much more substantial than the shadowy entity out of which they materialize, the

Figure 1. Victor Hugo, *Tache d'encre sur papier plié et personnages* (1853-55). Courtesy of Bibliothèque Nationale de France, Paris

letters "H-U-G-O" are inextricably tied to an "ancestral" point of origin, however ephemeral or skeletal it may appear, and thus connect the artist himself, by extension, to the reticulated specters of his art.

The lace of the *Dentelles et spectres*, in particular, seems to evoke the physiological qualities of the human body whose grinning skull it discloses. Hugo emphasized and highlighted the amorphousness latent in the fragile, delicately delineated lines that blur and melt in the midst of their own surcharged intricacy, the signature of the fabric's complexity but also the signifier of its imminent dissolution. Like the human body (which in its healthy state displays a pleasing symmetry but upon its demise reverts to an amorphous chaos, undifferentiated and atomized), lace is characterized by an ornamental design often predicated upon the ordered repetition of symmetrical patternings. It is also, however, an open-work material reminiscent of a skeletal structure from which the flesh has been eaten away ("burnt-out" or "etched," to use the argot of the lace-makers). The lace of Hugo's *Dentelles et spectres* thus functions as a medium revealing underlying structures that (when fleshed out again with haunting images drawn from Hugo's own reservoir of sublimated horrors) metamorphose into blotted phantoms. The phantoms, turning their gaze upon the viewer, reveal a skeletal rictus with teeth (the French *dentelle* means "little tooth") prominently displayed. Viewed in evolutionary terms, lace might be thought of as the Roderick Usher of its species: easily thrilled by external stimuli (the slightest of breezes disturbs it; too strong a light foxes it), easily torn asunder, its complexity quick with dissolution. Its defining quality—its fragile beauty—also poses the greatest threat to its material integrity. It is worth noting that because Hugo utilized the same wisp of lace for the dozen or so *Dentelles* that he generated, the demise of the fabric signaled the extinction of this particular subspecies of graphic works.[4]

Working in little—the largest of the *Dentelles* measures 38 by 13 centimeters, whereas the *Dentelles et spectres* are even smaller, measuring only 6.5 by 6 centimeters—Hugo brings to light webbed networks of association and meaning in which each mesh draws in all the rest, and thus he compels his viewer to confront the skeletal figures that would otherwise lurk undetected within the larger patterns that constitute the fabric as a whole. He resurrects in this body of work his belief, voiced some twenty years earlier, that "what we call the ugly . . . is a detail of a great whole which eludes us, and which is in harmony, not with man but with all creation."[5] Moreover, he exploits the innately conflictive nature of his medium (lace is, after all, "fretted," containing both ornamental patterns and cankerous spots in which it is simultaneously made and unmade) and renders explicit what is often ignored (the unstable and therefore unnerving character of a fabric prized for its attenuated beauty). In so doing, Hugo recasts his medium as "the thread"—to invoke the metaphor he introduces in the preface to *Cromwell* (1827), his disquisition upon "the grotesque"—"that frequently connects what we, following our special whim, call 'defects' with what we call 'beauty'"—a condition synonymous, in Hugo's view, with "originality" and "genius":

Figure 2. Victor Hugo, *Carte de voeux* (1856). Reproduced by courtesy of the Director and University librarian, the John Rylands University Library of Manchester, England

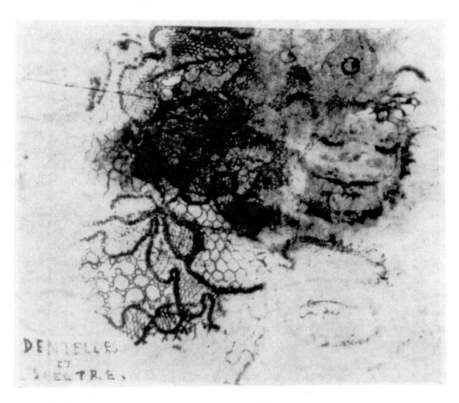

Figure 3. Victor Hugo, *Dentelles et spectres* (1855-56)

Defects—at all events those which we call by that name—are often the inborn, necessary, inevitable conditions of good qualities.

Scit genius, natale comes qui temperat astrum.

Who ever saw a medal without its reverse? a talent that had not some shadow with its brilliancy, some smoke with its flame? Such a blemish can be only the inseparable consequence of such beauty.[6]

The lace, suggesting the connection between Hugo's own genius and his troubled unconscious, also functions as a "medium" in another sense of the word, for it becomes a channel through which an ominous thing intrudes upon the viewer's field of vision. When we examine lace closely, our eyes stumble across an uneven terrain wherein accretion leads on to black holes of emptiness defined by the edges of grotesques and arabesques. A multitude of tiny abysses mushrooms in the midst of a complex design. M.R. James gave us a way to visualize this very phenomenon in "Mr Humphreys and His Inheritance" (1911), in which, poring over a sheet of paper bearing his original plan for a maze, the eponymous character stumbles across a "hitch" that he had not noticed before: "an ugly black spot about the size of a shilling." As he stares into the hole—"but how should a hole be there?" he wonders—he is unexpectedly overwhelmed by feelings of hate, then of anxiety, then of horror at the notion that "something might emerge from it" and rise to the surface. And, of course, something does emerge:

> Nearer and nearer it came, and it was of a blackish-grey colour with more than one dark hole. It took shape as a face—a human face—a *burnt* human face: and with the odious writhings of a wasp creeping out of a rotten apple there clambered forth an appearance of a form, waving black arms prepared to clasp the head that was bending over them.[7]

Hugo's blottesques in general—and his *Dentelles* in particular—are similarly transgressive (like the hole in Mr. Humphreys's plan, which, as we discover, runs down through paper, table, and floor into the "infinite depths" of the abyss), defined by the violation of demarcating borders: those, for example, that separate complexity of design and amorphousness, ornament and decomposition, and, finally, the visible and invisible worlds. The reality that they disclose is deeply imbued with the "sadness" that William James, in *The Varieties of Religious Experience* (1902), detected "at the heart of every merely positivistic, agnostic, or naturalistic scheme of philosophy." "Let sanguine healthy-mindedness," he wrote, "do its best with its strange power of living in the moment and ignoring and forgetting, still the evil background is really there to be thought of, and the skull will grin in at the banquet": "Back of everything is the great spectre of universal death."[8] It is precisely the "evil background" ignored by the sanguine, healthy-minded that becomes the point d'appui for Hugo's *Dentelles*, which depict the moment at which the mask begins to slip, revealing the power of the unconscious (just as M.R. James's story reveals the power of the living past) and a vital source of his creative impulse. What is made suddenly manifest in the *Dentelles* is not the "unconquerable soul" that seems, for the protagonist of William Ernest Henley's vigorously optimistic "Invictus" (1888), to be a talisman against the looming "Horror of the shade," but the grinning bare skeletal truth of things, the always-denied triumph of the horrific: the rictus invictus.

Because the sheer number of drawings displayed there suggested that Hugo's acuity was as compellingly visual as it was literary, the 1888 exhibition at the Galerie Georges Petit proved enormously important to students of Hugo's work, prompting a reevalution of what the Belgian symbolist Emile Verhaeren called "l'imagination hugonienne."[9] The exhibition also served as a confirmation of a belief that many of those in attendance had long maintained: that Hugo, "poëte sacré" (the phrase belongs to Auguste Vacquerie, Hugo's friend and spokesperson) and "dessinateur de génie" (the designation of the painter Benjamin Constant), was quite simply "le Maître." Stéphane Mallarmé made that role explicit in a letter in which he invited the Provençal poet Théodore Aubanel to reside as his guest in a room that he had carefully decorated with "an old lace thrown over the bed, and simply, together with the portrait of Hugo, the portraits of friends who deserve to be here."[10] The exhibition also revealed that in the *Dentelles* Hugo had discovered an idiom that rendered the pieces assembled there consonant with two distinct cultural moments—that in which they had been engendered and that in which they were finally disclosed to the gaze of the public. When he identified the "strange originality" and "unlooked for effect" of Hugo's drawings, which had been born of "the transformation of a blot of ink" and which revealed images "striking, mysterious . . . sometimes sublime, sometimes familiar, always wonderful," Gautier spoke for viewers such as Edmond de Goncourt, who took particular note of the exposition in his *Journal*, and Joris-Karl Huysmans, who wrote in praise of "these painted tempests . . . considerably quieter, however, than the hurricane of his sentences" that assail one with an "obsessive fear."[11] All of these aesthetes shared a way of looking at things that was predicated on the notion that the outward and the sensible always bodied forth, however imperfectly, the inward and the ineffable: "a dream of form in days of thought" was how Oscar Wilde expressed this dialectic in *The Picture of Dorian Gray* (1891).[12]

Perhaps because he was so fervent an admirer of Hugo's work, Gautier went to the heart of the master's otherworldly visions when he alluded to the curious shape that they assumed: "behind the reality he introduces the fantastic like a shadow behind the body, and one never forgets that in this world every figure, beautiful or deformed, is followed by a black spectre like a shadowed page."[13] It was a glimpse of this same crepuscular reality that Nathaniel Hawthorne (a contemporary of Hugo who was similarly intrigued by the notion of an intermediate world of shadows in which things otherwise unseen might be made partially manifest) had hoped to afford his reader when, in a notebook entry of August 14, 1835, he recorded the germ of "a grim, weird story" wherein the "figure of a gay, handsome youth, or young lady" might "all at once, in a natural, unconcerned way, [take] off its face like a mask, and [show] the grinning bare skeletal face beneath."[14] In *Tess of the d'Urbervilles* (1891), Thomas Hardy presents his reader with a heroine who, moments before she disfigures the beautiful face that has brought her such woe, presses her hand "to her brow, and [feels] its curve, and the edges of her eye-sockets perceptible under the soft skin," and, with a prescience symptomatic of what her husband terms "the ache of modernism," thinks with longing of the time when "that bone would be bare" and when her corporeal frame would thus more truly cohere with her blighted condition.[15] The jungle that looks "like a mask—heavy like the closed door of a prison," with its "air of hidden knowledge, of patient expectation, of unapproachable silence," whispers to Conrad's Kurtz of things "of which he had no conception," but which he approximates by means of a series of heads on stakes—all the faces but one turned in toward his house, and that one (correspondent, presumably, with the rest) "black, dried, sunken, with closed eyelids . . . and with the shrunken dry lips showing a narrow white line of teeth, . . . smiling too, smiling continuously."[16]

Similarly populated with apparently robust individuals who nevertheless turn upon the viewer a death's-head stare, the imaginary worlds of the symbolist artists James Ensor, Félicien Rops, and, in his late "sick" phase, the Viennese artist Anton Romako remind us that Hugo and Hawthorne, as well as their late-nineteenth-century heirs presumptive, were not merely appropriating the image of "the skeleton at the feast" from a momento mori tradition that dates back to antiquity, but taking inspiration from an evolving scientific discourse that increasingly recast the physical world itself as a Melvillean pasteboard mask. Rops's coquettes romp at masked balls, seducing with fleshless grins (fig. 4), while the subject of Romako's *Portrait of Isabella Reisser* (1885) (fig. 5) although nominally alive, maintains a cadaverous presence, her strange beauty erotically engaged with the specter figured forth in eyes that stare without speculation, in teeth prominently outlined and curiously fetishized, in the hard angularity of a waist cinched to achieve the wasted proportions of the dead, and in wrists decoratively manacled with coiled snakes. Ensor's is the only speculative stare in his *Ensor Surrounded by Masks* (1899) (fig. 6), which depicts a world overrun with figures whose masquerade of life reveals more than it conceals about the parade of death in which they are taking part. This death-in-life theme defines Ensor's corpus, and nowhere does it figure more vividly than in three self-portraits: *Death's Head* (1886), *Skeleton Painter* (1896), and *My Portrait Skeletonized* (1889) (figs. 7, 9, and 11a and 11b). Because two of these self-portraits (*Skeleton Painter* and *My Portrait Skeletonized*) were preceded by photographs (figs. 8 and 10) in which the artist stands in for the reliqued figure, it has been suggested that, in replacing "his own head with a skull," Ensor is "[anticipating] the future."[17] Such a reading, however, treats Ensor's work as a mere redaction of the traditional "skeleton at the feast," in which a corpse image (artfully devised in wood or silver, and sometimes articulated) served both as an emblem of the inexorable approach of death and as a spur to good living, reminding the celebrants among whom it was circulated that "What this is, we soon shall be; / Then be merry whilst you may."[18] However sobering (or, conversely, stimulating) the revelers find the truth that is conveyed by the relic referred to in Petronius Arbiter's *Satyricon* (in which the original version of these lines appears), there is nothing deceptive or counterfeit about the "memento" of a future condition. The photographs, on the other hand, emphasize what Ensor's self-portraits were intended to make clear even had there been no such accompaniments: that it is in the *present* that the artist is thus anatomized.

The horror of the self-portraits resides not merely in what is represented— an undead but ever-dying character—but in the presentation of the representation, for this is a composition depicting the artist's own ongoing decomposition. It rests, in other words, in the unveiling of what Symons, in his exposition of the Decadent style of literature, had identified as "*la vérité vraie*, the very essence of truth—the truth of appearances to the senses, of the visible world to the eyes that see it; and the truth of spiritual things to the spiritual vision."[19] The Decadents in whose behalf he spoke anticipated in their writings the possibility that the two truths that made up the whole might be inversely related—that the visible symbol might serve as the inverted representation of the invisible ideal that it prefigures. They acquired their idiom within a changing intellectual landscape mapped out not merely by their romantic precursors—by the Hugos and the Hawthornes— but also by those whose occupation it was to read and decipher surface configurations (geological formations, bodily types, word patterns) and were therefore increasingly drawn to conclusions as startling as that which Charles Darwin had reached when he realized with wonder that "the peaceful woods & smiling fields" that presented themselves to his view served but to camouflage "the dreadful but quiet war of organic beings" engaged in "a contest & a grain of sand turns the balance."[20] This—a March 1839 notebook entry that might be mistaken for the rough sketch of a horror story—was penned less than a year after he had reminded himself (again in his notebook) that "when we talk of higher orders, we should always say, intellectually higher," for "who with the face of the earth covered with the most beautiful savannahs & forests dare to say that intellectuality is [the] only aim in this world."[21] The revelation of hidden and previously unanticipated realities—the cryptic "slow force cracking surface," for example, to which he referred in an entry dating from 1838—struck him as being "truly poetical."[22] In 1838 Darwin could cite as a reference and tentative point of departure Wordsworth's belief that poetic expression would provide a way to read "the countenance of all Science," with science itself assuming "a form of flesh and blood," transmogrified into a "Being" whom the poet, lending "his divine spirit to aid [in] the transfiguration," would then "welcome . . . as a dear and

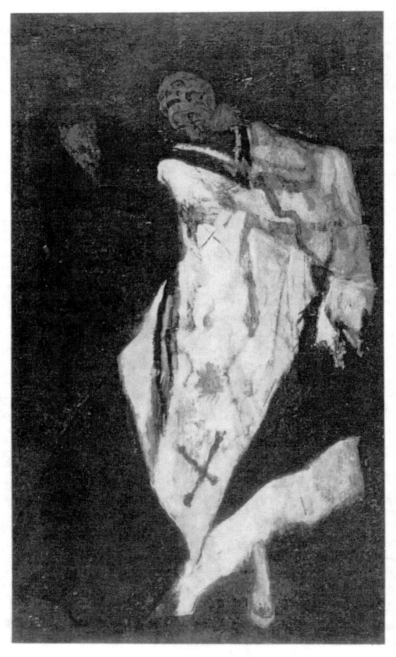

Figure 4. Félicien Rops, *La mort au bal* (c.1865-75). Courtesy of Kröller-Müller Museum, Otterlo, the Netherlands

Figure 5. Anton Romako, *Portrait of Isabella Reisser* (1885)

Figure 6. James Ensor, *Ensor Surrounded by Masks* (1899). Photograph courtesy of Menard Art Museum, Aichi-pref, Japan. © 1997 Estate of James Ensor/licensed by VAGA, New York, N.Y.

Figure 7. James Ensor, *Death's Head* (1886). Photograph courtesy of Musée du Louvre, Paris. © 1997 Estate of James Ensor/licensed by VAGA, New York, N.Y.

Figure 8. James Ensor, photographed in his studio, in Ostend (c. 1893) (photographer unknown). Photograph courtesy of Musées royaux des Beaux-Arts de Belgique, Brussels

Figure 9. James Ensor, *Skeleton Painter* (1896). Photograph courtesy of Koninklink Museum Voor Schone Kunsten, Antwerp. © 1997 Estate of James Ensor/licensed by VAGA, New York, N.Y.

Figure 10. James Ensor, photographed in front of the Rousseau house (photographer unknown). Photograph courtesy of Musées royaux des Beaux-Arts de Belgique, Brussels

Figure 11a (left). James Ensor, *My Portrait Skeletonized* (1889), first state. Photograph courtesy of Museum of Fine Arts, Wapenplein, Belgium. © 1997 Estate of James Ensor/ licensed by VAGA, New York, N.Y.   Figure 11b (right). James Ensor, *My Portrait Skeletonized* (1889), second state. Photograph courtesy of Museum of Fine Arts, Wapenplein, Belgium. © 1997 Estate of James Ensor/licensed by VAGA, New York, N.Y.

genuine inmate of the household of man."[23] Less than a year later, although he
had not altogether abandoned his anthropocentric metaphor, Darwin had begun to see more plainly the full implications of the evolutionary insights that
would serve as the basis for his life's work—work that cost him dearly in psychic
terms, because he knew that his revelations would surely hasten the erosion of
some of his culture's most cherished beliefs and expose him as well to the charge
of being fully gripped by what John Ruskin vilified as "the universal instinct of
blasphemy in the modern vulgar scientific mind," an instinct "above all manifested in its love of what is ugly, and natural enthralment by the abominable": "If
only the Geologists would let me alone," he would gripe in a letter to his friend
Henry Acland, "I could do very well, but those dreadful Hammers! I hear the
clink of them at the end of every cadence of the Bible verses."[24] Less than a year
later, Darwin was more inclined to share the view that Ruskin had expressed
metaphorically when he deplored humanity's having "been hitherto taught, not
by portraits of great men, but by the skulls of cretins" housed in "the natural
history museum of Oxford," the same view that Hugo had rendered graphically
in his L'Ombre du mancenillier (c. 1854) (fig. 12), in which the artist visualizes an
otherwise inviting manchineel tree whose branches—looking as though they offer nothing more threatening than a protective shield from a blinding noonday
sun—harbor more "shade" than shadow in their leafy depths.[25] Nature, monstrous nature, still seemed to possess the "smiling" face of a beckoning fair one,
but the mask had begun to slip.

In speaking of the "material revolution" that "the labours of Men of science"
promised (or threatened) to instigate, and of the consequent need of the poet to
reinvest a world made "manifestly and palpably material" with "sensation,"
Wordsworth anticipated the continued rise of scientific materialism, although
even his poetic insight could not have forewarned him that nineteenth-century
scientific discovery and discourse would eventually dispense altogether with the
poet's intuitive services, adopting instead a rationalistic and positivistic system
predicated on the belief that exterior forms serve as indices of and conduits to
interior (and hitherto occult) processes, agents, and states of being.[26] A point of
view that had begun to coalesce much earlier had become dominant by the
century's close, when the German philologist F. Max Müller prefaced the 1890
edition of The Science of Language (which had made its first appearance as a
series of lectures delivered at the Royal Institution in 1861 and 1863) by asking
whether any of his readers could still doubt what an earlier generation had "by
no means accepted as a matter of course"—that the "principle of Geology" that
he applies to "the Science of Language" hinges on the notion that "we must
begin with what is known and then proceed to what is unknown."[27] Within such
a program, the scientist seemed an adventurer/sleuth/metaphysician, a role
that the physicist John Tyndall made explicit when he described his attempts "to
show the tendency displayed throughout history, by the most profound investiga-

tors, to pass from the world of the senses to a world where vision becomes spiritual." The scientist's quest for knowledge assumed epic proportions, because it subsumed that of "the explorer [who] emerges with conceptions and conclusions, to be approved or rejected according as they coincide, or refuse to coincide, with sensible things"—and carried with it dangers just as nightmarish as those that beset the heroes of legend.[28]

Although it began by reading "surface" truths, then, nineteenth-century scientific discovery ended by probing hitherto unsuspected depths in both the physical universe and the human psyche, those caverns that had formerly seemed measureless to man. With nature as the scientist's guide, the quest led, as Huxley had prophesied that it might, not to the heights but to the edge of a country as mysterious as Africa seemed to the first European explorers, with the scientist/ explorer himself suffering some diminution in stature in consequence of having to "follow humbly" as "a little child . . . wherever and to whatever abysses nature leads."[29] The material world stood now revealed in all its tenuity as a merely Carlylean corporeality, and nature itself seemed imbued with "the deep cunning which hides itself under the appearance of openness, so that simple people," as George Eliot knew, "think they can see through her quite well, and all the while she is secretly preparing a refutation of their confident prophecies."[30] The extremity of distaste suffered by those whose sensibilities were affronted by the sight (or impression, at least) of nature all indecorously unveiled is notoriously registered in Ruskin's response (composed on January 13, 1886, and published six days later in the *Pall Mall Gazette*) to the list of the "best hundred books" that Sir John Lubbock had put forward in a lecture at the Working Men's College. "MY DEAR SIR,—" Ruskin begins, "Putting my pen lightly through the needless—and blottesquely through the rubbish and poison of Sir John's list—I leave enough for a life's liberal reading."[31] The "rubbish and poison" included Darwin's *Origin of Species*, effaced because "it is every man's duty to know what he *is*, and not to think of the embryo he was, nor the skeleton that he shall be. . . . Because, also, Darwin has a mortal fascination for all vainly curious and idly speculative persons, and has collected, in the train of him, every impudent imbecility in Europe, like a dim comet wagging its useless tail of phosphorescent nothing across the steadfast stars."[32] The Darwinian "theory" born of this fascination, continues Ruskin, is "mischievous" in the avidity with which it licenses its immodestly roving speculations to go before, behind, above, below the body of nature: "not only in looking to the past germ instead of the present creature,—but looking also in the creature itself—to the Growth of the Flesh instead of the Breath of the Spirit. The loss of mere happiness, in such modes of thought, is incalculable. When I see a girl dance, I thank Heaven that made her cheerful as well as graceful; and envy neither the science nor sentiment of my Darwinian friend, who sees in her only a cross between a Dodo and a Daddy-long-legs."[33]

Ruskin might have been less harsh had he known that the subject of his imprecations—and, more generally, those whose training had enabled them to

Figure 12. Victor Hugo, *L'Ombre du mancenillier* (c. 1854). Photograph courtesy of Bibliothèque Nationale de France, Paris

anticipate or accept the surprises that came with the new scientific discoveries—
was not himself immune to the sort of intense anxiety that often gripped the
"best and most cultivated minds" of the day—some of whom, according to the
Hungarian journalist Max Nordau, came to view science as having "deceived
them" because it had "not done for them what it had promised to do."[34] Darwin
found disheartening the startling implications of the discoveries of the physicists
whose speculations had prompted him to entertain a "pet horror" in which he
conceived of a Wellsian future as "the progress of millions of years, with every
continent swarming with good and enlightened men, all ending in this [the heat-
death of the world], and with probably no fresh start until this our planetary
system has been again converted into red-hot gas. *Sic transit gloria mundi*, with
a vengeance."[35] And he was troubled by the implications of his own investigations—was disconcerted, for example, even by the illusory quiet he encountered
in the present, in the typical English landscape, compact of ephemerality and
desperate struggle. The previously mentioned passage from one of Darwin's
early notebooks merits comment not least because it conjoins the beauty of a
picturesque landscape—the "peaceful woods & smiling fields"—with shocking
realities and an anxiety deriving from the knowledge that an underlying struggle—
a "dreadful but quiet war"—may be embodied in an apparently pastoral image.

The same "unceasing struggle for existence" was apparent to Huxley in
"the flowing contours of the downs" that made up "the whole country-side visible
from the windows of the room in which" he wrote the "Prolegomena."[36] Huxley's
downs, like Darwin's patch of woodland or Matthew Arnold's memorable stretch
of Dover beach or Hardy's Vale of Blakemore ("or Blackmoor aforesaid— . . .
known in former times as the Forest of White Hart," with "traces of its earlier
condition . . . to be found in the old oak copses and irregular belts of timber that
yet survive upon its slopes"), reveal a world in which fixity proves illusory and
stability chimerical.[37] "Turn back a square foot of the thin turf," Huxley urged:
"the solid foundation of the land, exposed in cliffs of chalk five hundred feet high
on the adjacent shore, yields full assurance of a time when the sea covered the
site of the 'everlasting hills'; and when the vegetation of what land lay nearest,
was as different from the present Flora of the Sussex downs, as that of Central
Africa now is."[38] Huxley speaks not merely of impermanence and disequilib-
rium, but of a landscape counterfeited: although it had once been plausible to
assume that truth was beauty and beauty truth, the new sciences revealed that
even all that seemed benign or beautiful merely masked—was in reality symptomatic or premonitory of—extensive processes of decay, so that rioting nature
itself became in fact a vast memento mori, a continual reminder of the forces in
nature that were degenerative and decompositive.[39]

And if, as Huxley speculated in the "Prolegomena," "man, physical, intellectual, and moral, is as much a part of nature . . . as the humblest weed," then the
human body too seemed destined to bear the figurations of "the cosmic process" of which it was a "product."[40] The grammar of those engaged in the ongo-

ing discussion of devolution and degeneration regularly troped the body as a text scripted with ciphers that stood for the reversionary tendencies lying dormant within the natural world: the "silent laws," as Cesare Lombroso viewed them, "which never cease to operate and which rule society with more authority than the laws inscribed on our statute books."[41] Recapitulation (a variety of "degeneration theory") in particular focused typically on the body of the "born criminal," its contours determined, it was thought, by an ancestral past that found fresh expression in the physiognomical, phrenological, and, by extension, behavioral traits of its hapless heirs. The French psychiatrist Jean Esquirol described that primitive past as a "fatal heritage . . . painted upon the physiognomy, on the external form, on the ideas, the passions, the habits, the inclinations of those who are the victims of it," whereas Havelock Ellis spoke of the criminal physiognomy as having been "branded by the hand of nature."[42] In his influential *Traité des dégénérescenses physiques, intellectuelles et morales de l'espèce humaine* (1857), the French psychologist Bénédictin Augustin Morel referred to the "typical stamp" and "typical impress" of "degenerations," which impelled the scientist "to confide to the engraver the care of giving a very exact idea of the different types of degenerated beings."[43] In the notorious 1895 study of degeneration upon which his fame chiefly rested, Nordau too characterized the "deformities" by which degeneracy "betrays" itself as "stigmata" and "brandmarks"— although he considered these to be "unfortunate" terms "derived from a false idea, as if degeneracy were necessarily the consequence of a fault, and the indication of it a punishment" (16-17).[44]

The physiognomist thus becomes the privileged reader of the body/text of the criminal, who was thought to be incapable of realizing the significance (and signification) of his or her own body—and equally unaware of the fact that the criminal acts that he or she was impelled to commit were themselves prefigured therein.[45] The bearer of the anatomized word *required* a reader, someone to take in the impression conveyed by the body thus stigmatized, thus textualized, in order that that body might be identified, controlled, disciplined, and perhaps punished. Moreover, he or she required a knowing reader capable of interpreting what the French neurologist Guillaume Duchenne de Boulogne described in his *Mécanisme de la physionomie humaine* (1862) as "ce langage de la physionomie . . . le langage universel et immuable" [this language of facial expression . . . the universal and immutable language], and not merely the "ordinary observer" receptive only to what Ellis identified as the expression or "mimique": a countenance "sad or merry, angry or good-tempered, cowed or elate," just as the legal and scientific apparatus required a reliable lexicon upon which to base their interpretations.[46] One who understood, as the American phrenologist and editor of the *American Phrenological Journal and Miscellany* Orson S. Fowler did, that "shape is as structure, and structure as character, and therefore shape as character" would also be prepared to decipher—"by universal observation"—hieroglyphic bodily inscriptions: "the shape of the jaws, or the cut of the ears, or

the lines of the forehead" were among those that Ellis identified.[47] Like the pale-
ontologist who studied fossil remains, or the geologist who surveyed topographi-
cal patternings, or the philologist who traced word morphologies, the criminal
anthropologist recognized what Nancy Stepan terms the "law of physique" as a
reflection of a biological imperative that was the only law that the degenerate
could not help but obey and the only law by which he could be judged.[48] In this
sense nineteenth-century recapitulation functioned as a semiotic science that
studied "external differences" and "surface . . . drapery" in order to discern the
underlying "constituent form, . . . the true figure": what the naturalist Comte de
Buffon saw as "the internal differences" where the meanings were.[49]

To writers such as Lombroso and Nordau, however, the success of such
"scientific" attempts to detect degeneracy was threatened by the fact that some
forms of retrogression did not seem to betray themselves outwardly.[50] What
was the reader to do in those cases in which reversionary tendencies disguised
themselves or failed in some other fashion to announce themselves extrinsi-
cally? Such, according to Lombroso, were the facts in the case of the rare individual whose pleasing aspect merely masked an underlying psychosis and a
spiritual deformity, just as Darwin's "smiling fields" belied the "dreadful but quiet
war" raging beneath the surface.[51] This threat to the semiotics of physiognomy
was the "man of genius," whose appearance, Lombroso believed, was a sign that
a culture has reached its peak and begun to decline, following one of the "reactionary curves" that, as he later argued in "Atavism and Evolution" (1895), the
most advanced peoples must inevitably describe.[52] Granting that not every genius was insane, Lombroso nevertheless accepted as "not devoid of solid foundation" the conclusions put forward by his contemporaries who branded genius
itself as "always a neurosis, and often a true insanity."[53] Genius, he insisted, was
by its very nature excessive, a teratological distortion of "normal" cerebration,
as pathological in its own way as common criminality or brute savagery, and as
consequential: "Just as giants pay a heavy ransom for their stature in sterility
and relative muscular and mental weakness, so the giants of thought expiate
their intellectual force in degeneration and psychoses" (vi). The "point of greatest strain and achievement" lying "naturally near to the danger line of accident
and disaster," genius was increasingly represented as a fragile, unsustainable
state of evolutionary decadence—as a hyperevolved complexity continually eva-
nescing into confusion, madness, and bizarrerie.[54] In 1891 a conceit that had
already become something of a philosophical commonplace found perhaps its
most vivid expression in Herman Melville's *Billy Budd, Sailor,* in which the surgeon, considering the display of "a transient excitement" and "unwonted agitation" so at variance with Captain Vere's "normal manner," wonders "Who in the
rainbow can draw the line where the violet tint ends and the orange tint begins?":

Distinctly we see the difference of the colors, but where exactly does the
one first blendingly enter into the other? So with sanity and insanity. In

pronounced cases there is no question about them. But in some supposed cases, in various degrees supposedly less pronounced, to draw
the exact line of demarcation few will undertake, though for a fee becoming considerate some professional experts will.

The American physician John F. Nisbet, writing nearly a decade after
Melville's meditation on the confluence of madness and divinest sense, put the
matter more prosaically when he spoke of sanity as frequently merging "into
insanity, and insanity into genius," but both men had been anticipated by Darwin when, in a somewhat cryptic notebook entry of June 1838, he wondered
whether the "doctrine of monsters" was not "preeminently worthy of study on
the idea of those parts being most easily mostrified [sic], which last produced—
insane men in civilized countries."[55] In this sense insanity acquired a certain
cachet, because "a simple organism with less differentiation of tissue and less
complexity of structure"—a savage or a child, as Henry Maudsley suggested—
could aspire only to "imbecility, or idiocy," although he conceded that accompanying the ganglionic and neural complexity characteristic of the "mental organi-
zation" of the cultured individual was a "correlative degeneration" and "increase
of insanity," the "penalty which an increase of our present civilization necessarily pays."[56] Genius represented the quintessentially devolutionary state, not only
because a sufficiently advanced civilization alone could aspire to this plateau of
derangement, but also because, there being "infinite varieties shading insensibly
one into another[,] . . . the extremest cases of madness" had their origin in "the
highest level of mental soundness."[57] (And all this, of course, was in the service
of orthodoxy, conservatism, and conformity.)

Congruencies might exist between outward form and the inward condition
it clothed—deformation translating deformation—as in the case of the subversive
Arthur Schopenhauer, whose countenance was, according to Lombroso,
inscripted with the "various characters of degeneration"—"large ears, very promi-
nent eyes, thick lips, a short, up-turned nose" (148). Lombroso's disciple discovered "in astonishing completeness, all the physical and mental marks of degeneration" gathered together in the features of the symbolist poet Paul Verlaine,
who, with his "wholly bald and huge long skull, misshapen by enigmatic bumps,"
seemed to Nordau to answer "exactly, trait for trait, to the descriptions of the
degenerate given by the clinicists" (119). He was apparently not alone in his
opinion, which, according to Ellis, was shared by those for whom Verlaine's
"very remarkable head"—with its "projecting orbital arches and acrocephalic
occiput," called by some "Satanic"—announced "the monstrous alliance of the
most eminent faculty of man, genius, with the most pronounced tendencies to
crime."[58] Arthur Conan Doyle's characterization of the criminal genius Professor Moriarty—Sherlock Holmes's nemesis, who, with his "clean-shaven, pale,
and ascetic-looking" countenance, retains "something of the professor in his features"—makes clear that not only anthropologists but writers of popular fiction

as well had acquired the criminological idiom by the century's close. Professor Moriarty's degeneracy—the consequence of "hereditary tendencies of the most diabolical kind" and the "criminal strain [that] ran in his blood, which, instead of being modified was increased and rendered infinitely more dangerous by his extraordinary mental powers"—is betrayed by the forehead that "domes out in a white curve" and by the face that "protrudes forward and is forever slowly oscillating from side to side in a curiously reptilian fashion."[59] In his *Chronicles of the House of Borgia* (1901), Frederick Rolfe also strikes the anthropologist's stance when he cites the case of the "mattoid" Savonarola who bore the vestitures of his own conflicted nature: in "the mould of the animal-man . . . [he] had the long head with immense hinder development, the great thick nose, the enormous lower lip, coarse mouth, heavy jowl, of a ram" as well as "the little lateral muscles of the nose-root . . . , a sign which is unmistakable," although his "narrow temples with their overhanging brows pointed in the middle, struck the note of ideality."[60]

It was not always sufficient, however, merely "to measure the cranium of an author, or to see the lobe of a painter's ear" in order to detect degeneracy (Nordau 17). Sometimes, as has been suggested, the mind of a "giant of thought" resided in an ordinary-looking body, and the absence of telltale signs threatened the viability of the whole interpretive apparatus, given that "literary madness"—"one of the teratologic forms of the human mind"—was not only, in Lombroso's view, "a curious psychiatric singularity, but a special form of insanity, which hides impulses the more dangerous, because not easy to perceive" (vi, xi, 1). And so, by necessity, they went a step further. Lombroso announced that the revelatory physical signs of degeneration might very well be "masqued by the vivacity of the countenance and the prestige of reputation" (6) of such notorious individuals as Gautier, Huysmans, and Wilde, each of whom Nordau viewed as a *"morbid deviation from the original type,"* a "repulsive *lusus naturae*" (16, 24) despite the fact that they were not visibly deformed. The asymmetry of face and cranium of the born criminal might be readily apparent, but the "physiognomy of mental disease" would appear "very striking" and "highly diagnostic" only to "an experienced eye" (the phrasing is Morel's), which could detect the abnormal mental stigmata—what Nordau later enumerated as the atrophied sense of morality, the "unbounded egoism," "impulsiveness," "emotionalism," "excitability," "pessimism," and "contempt for the world and men"—characteristic of the "higher degenerate" (Nordau 18-20, 23).[61] And just as regressive impulses were anatomized in the born criminal, so psychical atavisms were understood to be literalized in the expressions of what Nordau termed "written and painted delirium" (559)—the symbolism, special words, assonances, alliteration, aphorisms, and the "Biblical" style—which he identified as symptomatic of such psychical aberrations as apathy, originality, eccentricity, and morbid vanity, all characteristic of the man of genius.

The German philologist August Schleicher had already argued that any classification predicated on morphological structure alone was bound to be inadequate. Language, a "finer, higher criteria, exclusively proper to man," served to distinguish not only humans from animals but also superior human races from inferior ones. "For us then," he insisted, "the externally observable form of the cranial, facial, and bodily skeleton is markedly less important for the human than that no less material, though infinitely finer, bodily characteristic, of which the symptom is language. . . . The whole higher activity of human life is inseparable from language, and it is for language above all that humanity merits attention."[62] Müller went even further, asserting that the science of language should serve as the basis for a science of human psychology, because—the word being "the thought incarnate"—language itself becomes "the primeval and never-ending autobiography of our race": "Not till we understand the real nature of language," he announced, "shall we understand the real nature of the human Self."[63] Because language was the *differencia specifica* of humanity (specially) and of the individual (psychologically), it could serve as what Lombroso called the "principal trace of the delusions of great minds"—delusions discernible "in the very construction of their works and speeches, in their illogical deductions, absurd contradictions, and grotesque and inhuman fantasies" (322). Nordau saw the Parnassian idiom, for example, with its emphasis upon "the intrinsic value of beauty in the sound of words, . . . the sensuous pleasure to be derived from sonorous syllables," as originating in "a kind of disorder and permanent chaos" that already exist "in the brain of the poet," and thus "the exaggeration of the importance of rhyme is only a consequence of this state of mind" (270). He identified individual dialects as well, speculating that Maurice Maeterlinck's "idiotic sequences of words" demonstrated "the workings of a shattered brain"; that Emile Zola's "endless descriptions [delineated] nothing but his own mental condition"; and that from "the first to the last page . . . [Friedrich] Nietzsche's writings" pictured forth for the careful reader "a madman, with flashing eyes, wild gestures, and foaming mouth, spouting forth deafening bombast" (227, 495, 416). Wagner's graphomania, he insisted, was traceable in the "whole half-pages printed in spaced letters" (182)—an incontrovertible sign of his psychosis, and a fortuitous one given that "the commonest variety" of graphomaniac, according to Lombroso, has "true negative characteristics—that is to say, the features and cranial form are nearly always normal" (209).

Although he was the great popularizer of these methods of diagnosis, Nordau was not alone in adopting them. As early as 1827, Sir Walter Scott had discerned a connection between "the grotesque in the compositions" of E.T.A. Hoffmann (reminiscent, he thought, of "the arabesque in painting") and an imagination "strained to the pitch of oddity and bizarrerie" and nerves strained to a "morbid degree of acuteness": "Thus was the inventor, or at least first distinguished artist who exhibited the fantastic or supernatural grotesque in his compositions, so nearly on the verge of actual insanity" that the critic of his oeuvre "cannot help considering his case as one requiring the assistance of medicine rather than of criticism."[64] In a review that appeared in a July 1853 issue of the

New Monthly Magazine, similarly, the English novelist and critic William Harrison Ainsworth decried *Moby-Dick* as stylistically "maniacal—mad as a March hare—mowing, gibbering, screaming, like an incurable Bedlamite, reckless of keeper or strait-waistcoat."[65] The capriccios and lavish prodigalities characteristic of Horace Walpole's "literary luxuries" were symptomatic, in Thomas Babington Macaulay's estimation, of an "unhealthy and disorganized mind," its "whims and affectations . . . covered by mask within mask" of conventional behavior, whereas as late as 1930 Symons was ascribing pathogenic qualities to the stylistic excrescences he found in his own works and in those of his contemporaries—in his *Confessions: A Study in Pathology,* for example, associating the otherwise "wonderful prose" of Gérard de Nerval (who numbered one of that group of literary malcontents which most frequently provided Nordau with grist for his inquisitorial mill) with "a madman's vision."[66] Less diagnostic than these, perhaps, and less castigatory as well, is Pater, who cast style as a mold bearing the contours of the individual mind to which it belonged:

> In this way, according to the well-known saying, "The style is the man," complex or simple, in his individuality, his plenary sense of what he really has to say, his sense of the world. . . . Style in all its varieties, reserved or opulent, terse, abundant, musical, stimulant, academic, so long as each is really characteristic or expressive, finds thus its justification, the sumptuous good taste of Cicero being as truly the man himself, and not another, justified, yet insured inalienably to him, thereby, as would have been his portrait by Raffaelle, in full consular splendour, on his ivory chair.[67]

Even when effaced anatomically, then—even when there was no sign of the expected monstrous alliance of bodily form and inward deformity—genius might well betray itself in literary texts that themselves became what Lombroso termed "monuments of phrenopathic poetry" (320). Pater saw in "the matter of [the] imaginative or artistic literature" of his day a "transcript, not of mere fact" but of "soul-fact," limned in a style expressive of "some pre-existent adaptation, between a relative, somewhere in the world of thought, and its correlative, somewhere in the world of language—both alike, rather, somewhere in the mind of the artist, desiderative, expectant, inventive—meeting each other with the readiness of 'soul and body reunited.'"[68] To fix the essential nature of the conjunction between language and thought, then, was to fix the personality—or pathology—of the individual in whose imaginative alembic thought and word had originally coalesced. Individual works of art and literature could thus be treated as narratives of disease in which "soul and body reunited" by means of "a *physiological* language" (Lombroso 217) that expressed the deviance of its maker much as Hugo's attenuated lace incorporated delitescent horrors—and as an atavistic past lived on in the body of the born criminal.[69]

Increasingly for both the anthropologist and the aesthetician, the act of ana-
lyzing a literary text became also a diagnosis of the mental condition and sensibility out of which it had emerged.[70] Armed with the "torch of [Lombroso's]
method" and with the certain knowledge that degenerates "are often authors
and artists . . . who satisfy . . . with pen and pencil" the unhealthy impulses that
others satisfied with "the knife of the assassin or the bomb of the dynamiter,"
Nordau (apparently innocent of ironic intent) undertook in *Degeneration* (1895)
the creation of "a really scientific criticism" of the "vast and important domain
. . . of art and literature" that Lombroso and his disciples had left unexplored
("Dedication"). As Lombroso had sought to predict future crimes on the evidence of present anomalies—mancinism or the downy face or the receding forehead—so Nordau attempted to associate aesthetic excesses with artistic aptitude, positing, for example, that because "their predominant attribute" was "the
colour-sense," painters would be "decorative," whereas poets would be "rich in
rhyme, brilliant in style, but barren of thought"; "sometimes," he added, "they
will be 'decadents'" (24).[71]

In fact, he might have noted that they would almost always be "decadents," for he
found "in the tendencies of contemporary art and poetry" a "*fin-de-siècle* disposition" born of "the confluence of two well-defined conditions of disease . . . viz.
degeneration (degeneracy) and hysteria," and he tended to see the dominant
literary movements of his day—naturalism, neomysticism, and impressionism,
for example—as so many expressions of the "twilight mood"—the decadence—of
the "civilized world" (15, 43). Complexities of style were often perceived as being
symptomatic of the complexities of the cultural moment, and thus the critic Walter
Bagehot found it "singularly characteristic of this age that the poems which rise
to the surface should be examples of ornate art, and grotesque art, not of pure
art."[72] The French critic Paul Bourget might wonder at the kraken-like emergence of Decadence, which he referred to as "this delicate monster" that "has
never more energetically yawned its distress than in the literature of our century
in which so many conditions of life are perfectioned," all the while fully compre-
hending that "this very perfecting, in complicating our souls as well, makes us
inept for happiness."[73] Lacking Bourget's ingenuousness, Nietzsche readily comprehended that the "more energetically and boldly [a society] advances, the richer
it will be in failures and deformities, the closer to decline" and "exhaustion."[74]
Just as only a civilization sufficiently evolved could aspire to the insanity of genius—the one, as Maudsley had postulated, blending by nearly imperceptible
degrees into the other—so only such a civilization could discover the literary and
artistic Decadence that was the aesthetic correlative of genius: excessive, transgressive, without restraint, "the last pronouncement of the Word," as Gautier
saw it, "summoned to express everything and then pushed to its extreme"—an
extreme, it should be noted, that Nordau viewed as capable of catapulting the
human mind back to "its brute-beginnings" (485).[75]

By his very nature the Decadent artist functioned as the transmitter of the most virulent form of the literary disease that found its natural expression in what Gautier called "the necessary and fatal idiom of peoples and civilizations whose natural life has been replaced by an artificial one."[76] With its emphasis on postpositive constructions or on damasked layers of meaning or descriptions vermeiled and repoussé (of the sort with which Wilde amuses himself in the idiosyncratic chapter 11 of *Dorian Gray*), the Decadent style remakes the body of its maker, whose elegant deportment, "vivacity of countenance and . . . prestige of reputation" obscure the pronounced powers of cerebration that render him "a solitary, a nerve-sufferer, and almost a madman" (Lombroso 6, 232). To Lombroso, even the love of heavily ornamented forms so characteristic of the Decadent style seemed a symptom of insanity, for he had noted that monomaniacs showed "a singular predilection for arabesques and ornaments which tend to assume a purely geometric form, without loss of elegance" (200). It was no accident, he therefore thought, that Edgar Allan Poe, the tutelary deity of the French Decadents, had called his collection of stories *Tales of the Grotesque and Arabesque* (1839). It seemed to Lombroso, that is, that in deliberately choosing a title that would "exclude the human countenance," Poe had sought to create the impression that his compositions were *"extra-human."* Although nineteenth-century aestheticians understood the arabesque to have been born out of the Islamic injunction (by no means unambiguous) that seemed to forbid the representation of human beings, Lombroso pointed out that it nevertheless suggests "the human figure" (318), so that metaphorically Poe was in fact shadowing forth the crucial fact that his emphasis on what he termed his "matured purpose and very careful elaboration" seemed intended to hide. Which is to suggest, as Baudelaire did, that the "man is found in his work. The characters and incidents are the framework and drapery of his memories."[77] In the same fashion, the complexities of the Decadent style in essence serve as a surrogate for or signifier of the very decompositive elements that—superficially at least—they would seem to deny or occlude. As Rae Beth Gordon notes in her study of ornament, fantasy, and desire in nineteenth-century French literature, "one of the primary functions of ornament is to carry meaning and intent that have been suppressed or excluded from the central field," with the ornamental itself serving as "the site of the emergence of desire repressed elsewhere in" the texts of fin de siècle writing that it invades.[78]

It seems probable that members of this stigmatized group derived a good deal of ironic satisfaction from the knowledge that the motivation underlying their challenge to bourgeois respectability would be so grossly misconstrued by the self-anointed experts who thought of themselves as possessing the requisite "experienced eye." And yet, to read what the Decadents had to say for themselves is to be struck by the similarities in approach and attitude between the excoriator and the excoriated—leading one to conclude, as Barbara Spackman does in her study of the fin de siècle rhetoric of sickness, that "Nordau is perhaps not so 'stupid' as he might seem."[79] Those who attacked Decadence and those who gathered under its banner, after all, phrased their respective descriptions of the Decadent style in roughly the same terms. Although many of those who called themselves Decadent defined the term in very different ways, Decadent literature in general was understood by both sides as a celebration of and an evocation of the variety of beauty bred of disease—what Baudelaire called "la phosphorescence de la pourriture" [the phosphorescence of decay] and the American poet Francis Saltus Saltus (brother of the novelist Edgar) in his turn described in "An Answer" (1873) as the "bluish touch" flush with the "beauty" "from horrors brought forth."[80] Decadent texts are further characterized by a so-called morbid attention to form and a predilection for a perversity that arises out of the conjunction of ingenious, complicated, and "jeweled" language and the repulsive and sometimes morally repugnant ideas conveyed by that language. In his preface to Les fleurs du mal (1857), for example, Gautier defined the "new" style—he resisted the standard nomenclature—as one that strives to take "colours from all palettes, notes from all keyboards" in order to convey "in . . . new forms and words that have not yet been heard" the (distinctly pathological) monstrosities of the coming age: "the subtle confidences of neurosity, . . . the confessions of aging lust turning into depravity, and . . . the odd hallucinations of fixed ideas passing into madness."[81] Nordau is really paraphrasing Gautier when he provides his exposition of the "'decadent' language," which is itself, he claims, an extension of a "mystically degenerate mind, with its shifting nebulous ideas, its fleeting formless shadowy thought, its perversions and aberrations, its tribulations and impulsions. To express this state of mind, a new and unheard-of language must in fact be found, since there cannot be in any customary language designations corresponding to presentations which in reality do not exist" (300). Incriminating as he intends to be, Nordau probably comes closer to an understanding of the true motivation behind the Decadent's devotion to form and technique than T.S. Eliot did when, writing about Baudelaire, he observed that "the care for perfection of form, among some of the romantic poets of the nineteenth century, was an effort to support, or to conceal from view, an inner disorder."[82] As Symons announced in his study of the Decadent movement, "Healthy we cannot call it, and healthy it does not wish to be considered."[83] Acutely conscious of language, the Decadent infects his creation with his neurosis not by describing his emotional state but by succumbing to or indulging in what was satirized as "an attack of nerves on paper."[84]

The Decadent story, poem, or text, then, conveys beauty, disease, or tension not in any traditional sense—strictly by means of characterization or plot, for example—but rather in the contours, shadows, and rhythms created by a language that exposes the reader to a hidden malady: what Renée A. Kingcaid has called "language in its high neurotic mode."[85] Nordau referred to the typically Decadent text as "psycho-physiologically accurate" (a "commonplace" expression, he claimed, by the time he invoked it) in the sense that within it are encoded the psychological and physiological characteristics of its maker (324).

By permitting the stylized expression of intense emotions, and by channeling nervous energy into syntactic patternings, the text makes possible the "self-deliverance of the artist" (Nordau 324) in much the same way that a patch of linen, embroidered "with coloured threads pulled from her clothing," was worked with the "faithful representations of [the] delusions" of a woman living in isolation whose case Lombroso recounted: "Her autobiography is, so to speak, traced in this embroidery; in every piece of work she has represented herself" (184). In *The Picture of Dorian Gray,* Basil Hallward contends that his is an age in which men treat art "as if it were meant to be a form of autobiography," a notion that Wilde adapts in the preface to the work when he writes that the "highest as the lowest form of criticism is a mode of autobiography" (Wilde 57, 48). One arrives at meaning in isolated works of fin de siècle literature, in other words, by reading the deliberately encoded signs and stigmata, as well as accompanying themes and ideas, just as Lombroso searched for physical traits, and Nordau for psychological ones, in order to read the represented body—and, by extension, to discern the real nature of the human—and the individual—self.

Decadence, both cultural and stylistic, emerges in many works of fin de siècle horror that explore the dynamic between external forms and internal (psychological, metaphysical, structural) disorders. Like the Gothic romance itself, which Maurice Lévy described as "an 'imaginative compensation,' an 'expression' of the anguish engendered by the historical context," these later stories attempt to discover the sources of the psychological fears and sense of cultural anxiety that impelled their writers to experiment with this "underground" genre.[86] Many late-nineteenth-century stories of horror and the supernatural are Decadent in the sense that their defining themes and leitmotivs are drawn from popular reinterpretations of scientific theories that served to undermine the faith of so many eminent Victorians in the inherent stability and continued advancement of human society—theories, for example, like that informing the new biology, which came to seem as deceptive (in its own way) as the elusive processes it had disclosed. It thus lay open to the charge that it had not "done" what it had seemed to promise—in Darwin's grandfather's day, for example—that it would do. Huxley made it his business to emphasize that "evolution," a term that Victorians tended to think of as synonymous with "progress" and "advancement" (the staunchly optimistic attitude underlying Ramsay MacDonald's prewar credo in praise of humanity's movement "Up and Up and Up, and On and On and On," a more tempered if equally progressive version of which is to be found in Tennyson's oft-recalled aphorism that "men may rise on stepping-stones / Of their dead selves to higher things"), was not inevitable or perpetual, in that *devolution* in the sense of degeneration, retrogression, and decay was also possible: "every cosmic magma predestined to evolve into a new world," Huxley urged, "has been the no less predestined end of a vanquished predecessor."[87] By the latter part of the century, dissolution seemed so integral a part of the natural cycle, so fully ingrained in what Huxley termed the "cosmic forces, whose ends are not [man's] ends," as to prompt the realization that evolution and its morbid opposite were really two phases of the same process: it could then be argued that in devolution the traditional signposts of advancement—heightened beauty or increased complexity of form—might in fact signify imminent reversion.[88] "The theory of evolution encourages no millenial anticipations," Huxley gruesomely reminded readers of his "Evolution and Ethics": "If, for millions of years, our globe has taken the upward road, yet, some time, the summit will be reached and the downward route will be commenced. The most daring imagination will hardly venture upon the suggestion that the power and the intelligence of man can ever arrest the procession of the great year."[89] Huxley's vision of the future of the universe—which echoed Darwin's version of the shape of the past—was absorbed into the late-ninteenth-century stories that take as their subject the disclosure of corruption and that consequently present an image of a world populated with beings who might have looked like Wells's Eloi but who thought and behaved as his Morlocks did.

H.P. Lovecraft's later assertion that the "most terrible conception of the human brain" is the possibility of "a malign and particular suspension or defeat of those fixed laws of Nature which are our only safeguard against the assaults of chaos and the daemons of unplumbed space" is merely a recapitulation of the anxiety felt by his Victorian precursors, whose worldview, in the face of assaults by the new sciences—present in embryonic or even explicit form in the writings of Darwin, as in those of his mentor, Lyell, or of his contemporary Lord Kelvin—gradually lost its coherence.[90] The selfsame anxiety nourished William Hope Hodgson's massive, fascinating, almost unreadable, and Wells-indebted *The Night Land* (1912), a horror fantasy set in a distant twilight future, after "the sun had lost all power to light": a time when the world had grown "very dreadful . . . full of lawlessness and degeneracy," when "unmeasurable Outward Powers" had allowed "to pass the Barrier of Life some of those Monsters and Ab-human creatures . . . so wondrously cushioned from us at this normal present," and when the remaining "sound millions" had banded together in a foredoomed attempt to protect themselves against "the Forces of Darkness" plotting "the End of Man" by retreating to the "Great Redoubt," a pyramid circuited by a vast "electric circle" powered by the fast-fading "Earth-Current."[91] *The Night Land,* and works like it, are fueled by the fear that traditional systems of belief—once considered fixed and stable—were in fact subject to the same forces of decay that had undermined the faith in the innate biological superiority of humanity and in the finely balanced (and divinely sanctioned) workings of a Newtonian universe. In one of his lectures on Darwin's philosophy of language, Müller offered one expression of this fear when he identified his own historical moment as "the eve of a storm which will shake the oldest convictions of the world, and upset everything that is not firmly rooted." Just as Darwin's examination of an ostensibly peaceful landscape left him with a sense of intense anxiety, so Müller found himself in a universe in which imminent dissolution seemed to threaten protective boundaries and chaos seemed to underlie surface stability: "There is everywhere the same desire to explain the universe, such as we know it, without the admission of any plan, any object, any superintendence; a desire to remove all specific barriers, not only those which separate man from the animal, and the animal from the plant, but those also which separate organic from inorganic bodies; lastly, a desire to explain life as a mode of chemical action, and thought as a movement of nervous molecules."[92]

The much-feared suspension of the fixed laws of nature was reflected in a corresponding suspension of the fixed laws of narrative structure, linguistic and semantic stability, and authorial credibility in Decadent horror stories situated within the larger context of late Gothic. The germ of this attitude lurked in the Gothic and romantic fantasies of authors such as Walpole and Hoffmann, but these Decadent horror stories may be distinguished from their early Gothic precursors in the sense that their creators, adopting Poe's dictum that true "terror is not of Germany, but of the soul," developed a self-consciously Decadent style that, in its pursuit of irregularly beautiful forms, verbal *ornatus*, and miasmic atmospheres, proved to be the medium best capable of embodying the symptoms of internal madness and degeneration—what a gloating Gautier had envisioned as "the larvae of superstitions, the haggard phantoms of insomnia, nocturnal terrors, . . . obscure phantasies at which the daylight would stand amazed, and all that the soul conceals of the dark, the twisted, and the vaguely horrible, at the bottom of its deepest and furthest recesses."[93] Such a style generates in the reader a *frisson nouveau* (the term Hugo gave to the emotion he sought to evoke in his blottesques): the instinctive, visceral shudder provoked by the presence of something monstrous or uncanny expressed in the very lines and proportions of a text or an image. Those experimenting with Decadence and horror learned to create what Lovecraft, an admirer and on occasion an imitator of fin de siècle horror writers such as Matthew Phipps Shiel, Arthur Machen, and Wilde, described as "the actual anatomy of the terrible or the physiology of fear." The physiology of fear was constructed, he wrote, out of "the exact sort of lines and proportions that connect up with the latent instincts or hereditary memories of fright, and the proper colour contrasts and lighting effects to stir the dormant sense of strangeness."[94] We might think of Lovecraft's analysis as a macabre inversion of William Hogarth's theory of the "line of beauty," which, though "drawn on the surfaces only of solid or opake bodies" yet conveys "as accurate an idea as is possible, of the *inside* of those surfaces"—a definition remade yet again in the neo-Platonism of Wilde's *The Picture of Dorian Gray*, in which, we are told, "the mere shapes and patterns of things" become refined, and gain "a kind of symbolical value, as though they were themselves patterns of some other and more perfect form whose shadow they [make] real" (75).[95]

Once again, however, nineteenth-century scientific investigation provides a more provocative analog to Lovecraft's allusion to latent instincts and hereditary memories of fright, for Darwin (although he did not define it in these terms) had also invoked a kind of "physiology of fear" in his *Expression of the Emotions of Man and Animal*, in which he fixed on fear as the emotion that promised to deliver the richest source of evidence concerning the instinctive (as opposed to the conscious and reasoned) origins of expression. Unlike other feelings that would evince only a diffusive action "too general to throw much light on special expressions," fear, "'when strong'" (here Darwin quotes from Herbert Spencer's *Principles of Psychology* [1855]) "'expresses itself . . . in a general tension of the muscular system,'" which in turn represents the "'weaker forms of the actions that accompany the killing of prey.'" Anyone viewing such a display tends, Darwin suggests, to react instinctively; indeed, only a few such facial cues are required to prompt the observer's full-blown response to the immediately recognizable evocation of horror and pain, for "from the power of the imagination and of sympathy we put ourselves in the position of the sufferer, and feel something akin to fear."[96] In other words, certain envisaged lines, features, and patterns lend themselves to such decipherment. Moreover, Darwin notes that the face itself is prepared, physiologically, to evince horror, equipped as it is with what Duchenne de Boulogne (a pioneer in the study of electrophysiology, the forerunner of neurology) called the "muscle of fright, of terror," which, he claimed, when "tonically contracted by fear," evokes that very emotion, and in so doing gives rise to the expression "of the damned" (fig. 13).[97] Darwin saw underlying physiological structures and systems, then, as providing for the bodily transcription of fear. In this sense the human body (and not just the body of the born criminal) is precisely analogous to certain literary texts, the underlying structures of which (syntactic, narrative, structural) script a fear that elicits a visceral shudder and brings to the surface the reader's own sublimated impulses and instinctual memories.

In the pursuit of a revised Decadence, the creators of fin de siècle horror became anatomists of the imagination, producing horror stories that served as apt metaphors not merely for the society that produced them but for the concept of horror itself, which was represented far more realistically than even Darwin (whose research had helped to develop models for the scripting of the body, both literally and textually) could have imagined. For all his emphasis on the need to read plainly anatomized fear, and for all his denigration of painters for their reliance upon "accessories which tell the tale" of the starker emotions, Darwin himself romanticized certain sorts of fear, availing himself of stock expressions and traditional rhetorical strategies. "[See] what a change!" he wrote, is effected in the face of a woman whose child is threatened: "how she starts up with threatening aspect, how her eyes sparkle and her face reddens, how her bosom heaves, nostrils dilate, and heart beats; for anger, and not maternal love, has habitually led to action."[98] This sort of inflated, formulaic rhetoric, once functional because psychophysiologically accurate in its own right and thus capable of creating a vivid picture in the mind's eye, was rejected by the creators of the Decadent horror story in favor of stylized descriptions of horror. Highly polished and carefully wrought, the surface beauty and seductive charm of their fearful conceits serve to veil the corrupting and corrosive anxieties, truths, and even abysses that lurk beneath. One took a chance, of course, in exposing oneself to such literature: in his analytical "On Some Technical Elements of Style in Literature," Robert Louis Stevenson demystified "beauty, fitness, and significance" as hollow virtues lying "wholly on the surface" of our "arts and occupations," suggesting that "to pry below is to be appalled by their emptiness and shocked by the coarseness of the strings and pulleys." Speaking less prosaically than Stevenson of the gross materialities underlying the aesthetics of creation, Wilde contented himself with a cryptic warning in his preface to *The Picture of Dorian Gray* (which explores the intimate connection between surface beauty and inner corruption): "Those who go beneath the surface [of art] do so at their peril" (3).[99] In this sense Decadent horror writers saw themselves not as fantasists but as true realists who depicted not the crude verities of a Thackeray or an Eliot—"the sweepings of a Pentonville omnibus" were all that Wilde could discern in the latter's novels—but rather what Pater had sought to capture in a style that could deliver "that finest and most intimate form of truth, the *vraie vérité*."[100] Pater described the distinctive "style" of his period as "the special and privileged artistic faculty of the present day": "an instrument of many stops, meditative, observant, descriptive, eloquent, analytic, plaintive, fervid."[101] In its ability to permit a glimpse of transcendent realms of meaning—to permit the disclosure, in fact, of subterranean horrors—the Decadent style functioned as another of those "delicate instruments" that Pater admired Leonardo da Vinci for having created—the beautiful women in his paintings who, in confronting viewers with otherwise occulted realities, made them

> aware of the subtler forces of nature, and the modes of their action, all
> that is magnetic in it, all those finer conditions wherein material things
> rise to that subtlety of operation which constitutes them spiritual, where
> only the finer nerve and the keener touch can follow. It is as if in certain
> significant examples we actually saw those forces at their work on human flesh. Nervous, electric, faint always with some inexplicable faintness, these people seem to be subject to exceptional conditions, to feel
> powers at work in the common air unfelt by others, to become, as it
> were, the receptacle of them, and pass them on to us in a chain of secret
> influences.[102]

And just as it was the linguistic equivalent of these delicate instruments that had introduced "powers" and "secret influences" into the realm of the living, so the Decadent style was also the author's equivalent of the microscope, an instrument that by midcentury had fully exposed the otherwise hidden realms of the microbe and the bacterium and had thus made possible the disclosure of what Huysmans called "la souveraine horreur."[103]

Oscar Wilde's Basil Hallward is a searcher after verities (he affiliates himself with realism rather than with aestheticism) who plumbs horrific depths, at least in his portrait of Dorian Gray, which he calls the "best work of [his] life." Hallward has learned to "recreate life in a way that was hidden from [him] before" (56), for his idealized subject's presence is felt, in that particular canvas and even more pervasively in others in which he does not figure at all, "in the curves of certain lines, in the loveliness and subtleties of certain colours. That is all" (56).[104] Hallward's masterpiece is one of the two poisonous texts in *The Picture of Dorian Gray*, both of them exercising a fatal influence over those who come into contact with them. The portrait is also one of a long line of similarly poisonous texts, beginning with the sorcerers' books of the medieval period and including such fictional nineteenth- and twentieth-century incarnations as Merlin's book of magic (with, as Tennyson imagined it, "every page having an ample marge, / And every marge enclosing in the midst / A square of text that looks a little blot, / The text no larger than the limbs of fleas; / And every square of text an awful charm"); Chambers's aforementioned *The King in Yellow*; Lovecraft's *Necronomicon*; the purulent wallpaper of Charlotte Perkins Gilman's fevered fiction; the written statement of Henry James's governess (its quaint antiquarianism, conveyed by "old, faded ink, and . . . beautiful hand," challenged by the term—"outbreak"—that describes the anticipated effect of its release from "a locked drawer" in which it has been quarantined "for years"); the full statement of Henry Jekyll, which cannot be disclosed until after the sealed narrative of Hastie Lanyon has been read, and only then by J.G. Utterson, for whose hands "ALONE" it is intended and in case of whose "predecease" it is "to be destroyed unread"; and Kurtz's deceptively alluring essay written on behalf of the International Society for the Suppression of Savage Customs in Conrad's *Heart of Darkness*.[105] The line extends, as well, to such real-life examples as Huysmans's *À rebours* (1884) (which served as the fatally influential urtext for many of the most jaundiced books of the nineties) and Pater's "Conclusion," which George Eliot decried as "quite poisonous" and in which John Wordsworth, grandnephew of the poet, discerned "dangers" that he reproved Pater for having made accessible to "minds weaker than your own."[106] One might even include in this context the letters for which Huysmans and Pater, as some of Wilde's supporters darkly hinted, had been indirectly responsible: those, that is, that Lt. Col. Henry Isaacson, the governor (and "'mulberry-faced Dictator,'" according to Wilde) of Reading Prison, gave his notorious ward special permission to compose in the latter days of his incarceration. Regarded as potentially contaminatory, Wilde's letters could not be circulated even among his friends until, as Richard Ellmann reminds us, they had been "collected and inspected, and the writing materials removed," a perception of their dangerous nature apparently shared even by his supporters, to judge by the amount of bowderlization that was deemed necessary before Wilde's epic letter, *De Profundis*, could see the light (Robbie Ross, Wilde's editor in this case, going so far as to change the title from its original *In Carcere et Vinculis*).[107] The narrator of Chambers's "The Yellow Sign" (1895) gives us an insight into what happens when one encounters one of these contagious texts—in this case the play *The King in Yellow* with its poisonous, mottled, yellow, serpent-skin binding: "Oh the sin of writing such words,—words which are clear as crystal, limpid and musical as bubbling springs, words which sparkle and glow like the poisoned diamonds of the Medicis! Oh the wickedness, the hopeless damnation of a soul who could fascinate and paralyze human creatures with such words,— words understood by the ignorant and wise alike, words which are more precious than jewels, more soothing than Heavenly music, more awful than death itself."[108]

Critical attention has tended to focus on what is actually the lesser of the two occult texts that figure in Wilde's story—the infamous "yellow" book with which Lord Wotton continues his protracted seduction of Dorian. In a scene recalling that in which the Seven Deadly Sins pass ethereally before Marlowe's Faustus, Dorian (himself a decadent Faustus) becomes "absorbed" in this "strangest" of books, with its "exquisite raiment," its "delicate sound of flutes," and "the sins of the world" that pass "in dumb show before him," making real to him things of which he had only "dimly" or "never" dreamed (109). Traditionally thought of as the font and inspiration of Dorian's excesses, this unnamed book, with its "mere cadence of sentences" and its "music . . . of complex refrains and movements elaborately repeated" (141), infects Dorian with the thought that evil exists simply as "a mode through which he could realize his conception of the beautiful" (157).

Yet Dorian insists that "all his misery" originates in "the fatal portrait" (166) itself, and not in his exposure to a breviary detailing the requisite sins and obsessions of the cultivated sensualist (although it is true enough that at various points in his story this "multiform creature" blames his undoing on Basil, book, *and* portrait). With its "curious jewelled style," its "elaborate paraphrases," and its "monstrous" metaphors, the story's poisonous book provides Dorian with a role model in its account of a "certain young Parisian" (141) whose behavior subverts bourgeois standards of conduct. By Lord Henry's reckoning, such a book possesses the only sort of "immorality" that can inhere in a work of art, since it exerts a pernicious influence on the reader: "He does not think his natural thoughts, or burn with his natural passions. His virtues are not real to him. His sins, if there are such things as sins, are borrowed. He becomes an echo of someone else's music, an actor of a part that has not been written for him" (61). Conversely, the portrait merely hints at what Dorian himself is capable of doing by alluding in its very lines and contours to the apparently monstrous but otherwise only obliquely referred-to acts that he has already committed. William E. Buckler would have it that the yellow book performs a commensurate function

Figure 13. Duchenne de Boulogne, *L'Effroi* (1854). One of a series of photographs commissioned by the electroneurologist Guillaume Duchenne de Boulogne for his *Mécanisme de la Physionomie Humaine* (1862). This particular image was reprinted in Darwin's *The Expression of the Emotions in Man and Animals* (1872). Photograph by Adrien Tournachon. Courtesy of Ecole nationale supérieure des Beaux-Arts, Paris

because it "provides [Dorian] with instruction in advanced ways of attaining what he is already determined to seek": having "produced in the mind of the lad . . . a malady of dreaming" (141), it merely catapults him, Buckler suggests, into the life of hedonism and iniquity that he is in any event poised to undertake.[109] Although book and portrait draw roughly the same response from Dorian—each simultaneously repulses and fascinates him—the book contains "the story of his own life, written before he had lived it"(142); the story that the portrait limns, however, cannot develop further before Dorian himself advances further in his process of "self-development" (61). The book is thus a "prefiguring type of himself" (142), whereas the portrait is a "diary of [his] life from day to day" (162), which cannot narrate the story it records before Dorian himself furthers the plot.[110] It is therefore more truly one of those works of art that, as Wilde suggests both in the preface and elsewhere in his narrative, "mirrors the spectator, and not life" (48), and thus Basil conflates the two—simulacrum and original—when he announces early on that "as soon as you are dry, you shall be varnished, and framed, and sent home. Then you can do what you like with yourself" (69).[111] Unlike a more conventional author who shapes his plot to fit his thematic ends, Dorian sits mesmerized before his canvas, reading a story that he can neither predict nor premeditate, trapped as he is in his deterministic tragedy in which even an act of premeditation would translate into but another predetermined act, the ultimate consequences of which only the portrait—a text that envisages no outcome, no closure—can reveal. We see how fully Dorian is imprisoned in his own fictive world—his fatal text, we learn, "never leaves the room in which it is written" (134)—when he attempts to touch up the portrait by sparing the virtue of Hetty Merton, the country girl whom he would otherwise have seduced. He does, of course, reshape the portrait, but not as he had planned.

Having resolved upon a life of "infinite passion, pleasures subtle and secret, wild joys and wilder sins," Dorian is pained initially to consider the "desecration that was in store for the fair face on the canvas" (126). His regret, however, is transformed into a curious pleasure as he anticipates the growing fascination that the painted image—an ever-decomposing object of contemplation—will hold for him. Even his utter inability to comprehend the subtle means by which the canvas physically enacts his morbid metamorphosis provides him with a peculiar *frisson*: "Was there some subtle affinity between the chemical atoms, that shaped themselves into form and colour on the canvas, and the soul that was within him? Could it be that what that soul thought, they realized?—that what it dreamed, they made true? Or was there some other, more terrible reason? He shuddered, and felt afraid, and, going back to the couch, lay there, gazing at the picture in sickened horror" (118-19). Once again, Lord Henry, with his typically Mephistophelean prescience, captures the quintessence of Dorian's experience when he speculates that a certain kind of tragedy transforms the actors into the "spectators of the play": "We watch ourselves, and the mere wonder of the spectacle enthralls us" (123). As a reader of his own story, Dorian is as scrupulous as

he is avid (he abruptly quits both house and guests in Nottinghamshire to escape
to his boyhood "playroom," which is also the room in which the final scene of his
own somber tragedy will play itself out), and as he reads he grows "more and
more enamoured of his own beauty, more and more interested in the corruption
of his soul" (143). Although thrilled by the "very sharpness of the contrast," he
yearns for that which is always denied him: the opportunity to witness the slip-
ping of the mask. Spurred by the hope "that some day he would see the change
taking place before his very eyes" (126), he examines the portrait "with minute
care, and sometimes with a monstrous and terrible delight," searching for "the
signs of sin or the signs of age" (143).[112] The "signs of age" for which Dorian
searches so avidly are the signs of his own encroaching decrepitude, although
we have just learned that his friends and acquaintances "wondered how one so
charming and graceful as he was could have escaped the stain of an age that
was at once sordid and sensual" (142). So far from escaping such staining, however, Dorian gradually becomes the visible emblem of his fin de siècle, *fin du
globe* age, serving as well as an ironic embodiment of Basil's vision of him as
"the visible incarnation of [an] unseen ideal" (132). And as the novel progresses,
he becomes the quintessential hypocrite, a whited sepulchre, a perverse avatar
of "the Bride of Christ, who must wear purple and jewels and fine linen that she
may hide the pallid macerated body that is worn by the suffering that she seeks
for, and wounded by self-inflicted pain" (151). He is the "complex multiform creature . . . whose very flesh was tainted with the monstrous maladies of the dead"
(154), and his "charming boyish smile" (153) elides (and, as a perfect counterfeit,
serves to *reveal*) "the face of [his] soul" (164), which has been eaten away by
"leprosies of sin" so virulent that the "rotting of a corpse in a watery grave was
not so fearful" (164). He is also related to the youthful Satan who appears in
X.L's "Aut Diabolus aut Nihil" (1888), another period work with which *The Picture of Dorian Gray* seems to share a good deal in common. "Sa Majesté," as he
is called by his devotees (a group of twelve "men of culture and refinement"), is
"apparently twenty, tall, as beardless as the young Augustus, with bright golden
hair falling from his forehead like a girl's." When he makes his appearance "in
evening dress," his cheeks are "flushed as if with wine or pleasure," and his eyes
gleam with "a look of inexpressible sadness, of intense despair" (and we might
recall here the look of "infinite pity" reflected in Dorian's eyes as he blackmails
his former friend and cohort, Alan Campbell, into changing Basil "and everything that belongs to him into a handful of ashes" to be scattered in the air [172-
73]).[113] Dorian is the boyish variant of the well-heeled devil whom Rops, in *The
Sphinx* (1879) (fig. 14), depicts as eavesdropping upon the fevered outpourings
of a woman who presses herself upon the stony Sphinx whom she supplicates
(just as Dorian fantasizes about secreting himself in a confessional and listening
to "men and women whispering through the worn grating the true story of their
lives" [146]). In his "Instrumentum Diaboli," his commentary on *The Sphinx*
and Rops's other *sataniques*, Huysmans makes explicit the manner in which

this fin de siècle fiend is representative of the conceits not merely of Dorian or
Rops but also of the age itself (in its position as frontispiece, *The Sphinx* served
as the gateway to J. Barbey d'Aurevilly's collection of diabolical "tragedies"—the
"true stories of this age of progress," as their author calls them—titled *Les
Diaboliques* [1886]).[114] Whereas the Satan of old took "horrible and grotesque
shapes," Rops's Satan "is thoroughly modern, up-to-date in every way," "Satan
in a black dress suit," "the modern, the real twentieth century polished Satan, a
gentleman in evening dress, quiet and polite, patient and persistent."[115] And as
the portrait is "a visible symbol of [Dorian's] degradation of sin" (119), as Dorian
becomes what Lord Henry speculates he might be—the "visible symbol" of their
century (65)—so the portrait is by extension the visible symbol of what the cynical Dorian characterizes as "the native land of the hypocrite" (160).

Dorian's picture is far more enthralling, and therefore far more poisonous,
than the story's (ultimately tame) yellow book could ever aspire to be because it
functions as an idiosyncratic revelation of aging lust turning into depravity, embodying the unique stigmata of his own spiritual degeneracy and providing Dorian,
by extension, with his most compelling excuse for announcing to the incredulous
Duchess of Monmouth that "Art . . . is a malady" (193). The focus is on his face,
the wonderful beauty of which Lord Henry earlier described as "a form of Genius— . . . higher, indeed, than Genius" (64). Yet there is also another whose
secret the portrait betrays; one who knows better than anyone else that it is not
only the sitter—"merely the accident"—who is revealed on the canvas, but the
painter—another spectator—who, "on the coloured canvas, reveals himself" (52).
The portrait is psychophysiologically accurate in the sense that it embodies its
maker's "genius" even more certainly than it does Dorian's. Basil has managed
to do what Lord Henry covertly longs to do—to "project one's soul into some
gracious form, and let it tarry there for a moment" [74-75])—and thus he initially
refuses to exhibit the picture at the Grosvenor, or anywhere else for that matter,
claiming that there "is too much of [himself] in the thing." Basil is as secretive as
Dorian because he is as convinced as his idealized subject comes to be that the
fearful image is inscripted with the very "secret of [his] own soul" (52), which he
will not bare to the "shallow, prying eyes" of the world (56). Once separated from
his creation, however, the painter is able to shake off "the intolerable fascination
of its presence," and, having forcibly rid himself of the belief that "every flake and
film of colour seemed to [him] to reveal [his] secret" (133), he permits himself to
entertain the notion of exhibiting the portrait in Paris. For Dorian, however, who
remains to the end held in thrall by this auto-icon, the prospect that the "world
was going to be shown his secret" and that people might be permitted "to gape at
the mystery of his life" (131) is insupportable.

Once beyond the pale of the portrait's provocative sphere of influence, Basil
loses some part of the visionary aptitude that has allowed him to discern Dorian's
presence most palpably when "no image of him is there" (56). He persuades
himself that the truths the portrait reveals are less searing than they really are,

and in convincing himself that "art conceals the artist far more completely than it ever reveals him" and that "form and colour tell us of form and colour—that is all" (133), Basil becomes a resistant reader, for the latter hypothesis in particular proves a pallid substitute for his earlier admission that Dorian is insinuated "in the curves of certain lines, in the loveliness and subtleties of certain colours. That is all" (13). Although he is a capable physiognomist—he admits to having spurned a would-be sitter because there "was something in the shape of his fingers that [he] hated" (130)—he loses the ability to read Dorian aright, refusing to believe "anything against" a boy with such a "pure, bright, innocent face" and "marvellous untroubled youth" (159). Taking refuge in Lombrosian hermeneutics, Basil insists that "if a wretched man has a vice, it shows itself in the lines of his mouth, the droop of his eyelids, the moulding of his hands even" (159). Yet he is not so resistant a reader as to blind himself to the truth, and when brought into the portrait's subversive presence, Basil readily falls victim to his old morbid fascination: recognizing the brushwork but not the subject of his canvas, he deduces that the surface could only be "quite undisturbed, and as he had left it" because it was "from within, apparently, that the foulness and horror had come." "Through some strange quickening of inner life the leprosies of sin were slowly eating the thing away" (164). The portrait bears ironic witness to his belief that "sin is a thing that writes itself across a man's face. It cannot be concealed" (159)—ironic because Dorian discovers in the end that his beauty, all ivory and rose leaves, "had been to him but a mask" (212), and more ironic still because Wilde had elsewhere noted that "a mask tells us more than a face."[116] Basil suffers an emblematic death at the hands of his own creation—his naive conception of narrow correspondences and physical equivalencies ruptured, violently replaced by one predicated on contrarities, contradictions, and inversions—moments before the embodied self rises up to kill him, thus confirming Dorian's suspicion that there "is something fatal about a portrait. It has a life of its own" (135).

In its guise as a literary work of art, *The Picture of Dorian Gray* also assumed something of a life of its own, and one as destructive in its own way to its maker as Basil's portrait proves to be. That it would eventually be hauled up before, interrogated, and even tortured to elicit the desired confession by those seeking information concerning the life and convictions of its creator—who was thus forced to defend himself against the charge of having produced a beautifully scripted confession of his own criminal intent—should not perhaps have come as a surprise to Wilde, who had admitted that his sui generis creation "contains much of me in it," an opinion that Lord Alfred Douglas's mother, Lady Queensberry, apparently shared, as her distressed complaint to her son suggests: "If Mr Wilde has acted as I am convinced he has the part of a Lord Henry Wotton to you I could never feel differently towards him than I do, as the murderer of your soul."[117] James Joyce also suspected as much when he credited (or charged) Wilde with having had "some good intentions in writing it—some wish to put himself before the world—," although Wilde had never masked the criminality of his artistic and theoretical explorations, as his *Intentions* (1891) had made flamboyantly clear.[118] Since neither the "Criminal Investigation Department" nor "the Treasury" nor "the Vigilance Society" chose to prosecute it (or him) as one would any common criminal, *Dorian Gray* was brought before the jury in Wilde's infamous first trial of 1895 as a sort of witness for the prosecution. Although Justice Sir Arthur Charles, the judge in the case, dismissed the notion that an author could be confounded "with the characters of the persons he creates," Lord Queensberry's counsel, Edward Carson, devoted an extensive part of his cross-examination during the first trial to "reading" Wilde's story in order to reveal what the jury could not have determined simply by viewing or conversing with a man charged with authoring what the editor of the *Daily Chronicle* had reviled as "a poisonous book, the atmosphere of which is heavy with the mephitic odours of moral and spiritual putrefaction," leaving behind a "contaminating trail."[119] Having learned in the crucible of his experience that society "never forgives the dreamer," Wilde sought to discover whether it might indeed be the case that it "often forgives the criminal" (as he had once believed).[120] In the end, desperate to escape his confinement, Wilde, betraying his own earlier self, proclaimed himself a criminal, but with none of the winning effrontery accompanying his earlier pronouncements that "lying and poetry are arts" requiring "the most disinterested devotion"; that pen, pencil, and poison are not antithetical on moral or aesthetic grounds (we might recall here Nordau's correlation of pen, pencil, and bomb); that "all the arts are immoral"; that "an intense personality" is "created out of sin"; and that crime, because it seems "under certain conditions" to have "created individualism," and art, because it is *"the most intense mode of individualism,"* together render the artist criminal by nature as well as by art.[121] Addressing himself to the home secretary (Sir Matthew White Ridley), Wilde "humbly" urged that he sought, not "to palliate in any way the terrible offenses of which he was rightly found guilty,"

> but to point out that such offenses are forms of sexual madness and are recognized as such not merely by modern pathological science but by much modern legislation, notably in France, Austria, and Italy, where the laws affecting these misdemeanors have been repealed, on the ground that they are diseases to be cured by a physician, rather than crimes to be punished by a judge. In the works of eminent men of science such as Lombroso and Nordau . . . this is specially insisted on with reference to the intimate connection between madness and the literary and artistic temperament, Professor Nordau in his book on "Degenerescence" published in 1894 having devoted an entire chapter to the petitioner as a specially typical example of this fatal law.
>
> The petitioner is now keenly conscious of the fact that while the

three years preceding his arrest were from the intellectual point of view
the most brilliant years of his life . . . , still that during the entire time he
was suffering from the most horrible form of erotomania, which made
him forget his wife and children, his high social position in London and
Paris, his European distinction as an artist, the honour of his name
and family, his very humanity itself, and left him the helpless prey of
the most revolting passions, and of a gang of people who for their own
profit ministered to them, and then drove him to his hideous ruin.

It is under the ceaseless apprehension lest this insanity, that displayed itself in monstrous sexual perversion before, may now extend to
the entire nature and intellect, that the petitioner writes this appeal which
he earnestly entreats may be at once considered. Horrible as all actual
madness is, the terror of madness is no less appalling, and no less
ruinous to the soul.[122]

Part of what makes this letter a horror story in its own right is the knowledge (accessible to all but a wretchedly broken man) that Nordau had not earned
his place beside "Napoleon," "Nero," and "Narcissus," in Oliver Herford's *An
Alphabet of Celebrities* (1899) by being less notorious than Wilde himself had
been—by making his theories of art and criminality, that is, less accessible than
Wilde's had been to people like Carson, who found in them both a motivation for
purging society of the poisonous presence that Wilde's was perceived to be (vide
the critic Sidney Colvin's characterization of "Oscar Wilde-ism" as "the most
pestilent and hateful disease of our time"), and a means of doing so.[123] Wilde's
petition to be released from prison was denied, but he was granted writing materials and greater access to books—although the texts he produced while incar-
cerated, as we have had occasion to note, were as jealously guarded as was their
creator himself, exposure to either clearly regarded as equally threatening to the
health and well-being of society.

As a prosecutable criminal and a witness for the prosecution; as the secre-
tion of a hidden life whose morbid secrets it betrays; as one of those "self-assert-
ing organisms" (one anonymous reviewer's term for works like *Dorian Gray*)
"spawned from the leprous literature of the French Décadents" (another anonymous reviewer's description of the same): *The Picture of Dorian Gray* is the
animated heir of an era in which, as Bruce Haley reminds us, health and disease
were increasingly viewed as being "transmittable states of an organism's character or spirit; in the creative process they are passed from the character of the age
to that of the artist and thence to the character of the work and finally, as the
work finds its audience, back into the character of the age."[124] As a Lombrosian
phrenopathic monument, fully invested with and reciprocally corruptive of the
life of its day, it served as a literary counterpart to those more conventional
monuments that, as Ruskin had argued, may be taken as the architectural "expression of national life and character": because "on these inner and great ques-

Figure 14. Félicien Rops. *Le Sphinx* (1879). Courtesy of Musée d'Orsay, Paris

tions depend all the outer and little ones," with "certain right states of temper
and moral feeling" producing "all good architecture, without exception" and all
bad architecture indicative of "concealed national infidelity, and of domestic corruption."[125] Although Wilde, in defense of his work, maintained that the "superior pleasure in literature is to realize the non-existent"—that "life by its realism is
always spoiling the subject-matter of art"—Pater took note of the "pleasant ac-
cessory detail, taken straight from the culture, the intellectual and social interests, the conventionalities, of the moment" that invest *The Picture of Dorian
Gray* with "the better sort of realism, throwing into relief the adroitly-devised
supernatural element."[126] The "rage" that it provoked—part of the "contaminating trail" that it left behind—was like the rage of Caliban. Frustrated by what they
did see, enraged by what was occulted, readers found in these representations
the image of what H.G. Wells would later describe as "a mild and massive Sphinx
of British life," "an amoeboid Sphinx" beneath the "tranquil-looking surfaces" of
which "many ferments were actively at work," while "its serene and empty visage masked extensive processes of decay."[127]

Wilde spoke perhaps more truly than he knew when, with thinly veiled self-
delight, he confided to Beatrice May Allhusen that *The Picture of Dorian Gray*
is "rather like my own life—all conversation and no action," for the novel is rich in
commentary upon the aesthetics of decadence and "fin du globe" tonalities while
it remains relatively free of the decadent gestures, stylistic and thematic, exhibited by other period texts with which it maintains a dialogue.[128] As others have
remarked, it offers a "decadent" treatment of the traditional supernatural motif
of the doppelgänger arising as the spectral, subconscious other—already a familiar figure in such early supernatural fiction as Poe's "William Wilson" (1839),
and reemergent as the latent Darwinian type in later works such as Stevenson's
The Strange Case of Dr. Jekyll and Mr. Hyde (1886).[129] It is also, however, much
more concerned with materialism, physicality, and scientific determinism than
a cursory reading might suggest. In it, Wilde examines many of the "scientific
laws" with which Lord Henry suggests that it is useless to interfere. In a desperate search for some "curious scientific reason" to explain the portrait's chemical
reconstitution of his guilt, for example, Dorian reverses the terms of the argument of materialists such as Huxley who sought a physical basis of life, wondering whether thought might not "exercise an influence upon dead and inorganic
things . . . , atom calling to atom in secret love or strange affinity" (127). And
then, changeable creature that he is, he goes on to assume a materialist stance,
convinced that "there was no mood of the mind that had not its counterpart in
the sensuous life" (147). Arguing much more forcefully for its physical integrity,
Lord Henry, on the other hand, insists that life "is not governed by will or intention. Life is a question of nerves, and fibres, and slowly built-up cells in which
thought hides itself and passion has its dreams" (209). Scientific determinism is
recast as genetic determinism when Dorian redacts a central premise of Morel's
argument from degeneration—to wit, that degeneracy is a condition transmis-

sible, in ever more virulent forms, from the fathers to successive generations of sons—when, wandering through his ancestral picture gallery, he considers the possibility that his "very flesh was tainted with the monstrous maladies of the dead" and dreams of "strange legacies of thought and passion" (154). Degeneration blends into Darwinism when Dorian speculates that, since "every fibre of the body, as every cell of the brain, seems to be instinct with fearful impulses," "the passion for sin" (189) may be genetically encoded; and Darwinism in turn leads on to "the materialistic doctrines of the *Darwinismus* movement in Germany," which delighted in "the conception of the absolute dependence of the spirit on certain physical conditions, morbid or healthy, normal or diseased" (146). The theories of "modern" psychologists such as the medical psychiatrist Jean-Martin Charcot also enjoy some representation, as when Dorian intuits the "myriad lives and myriad sensations" of the sort of "complex multiform creature" (124) occupying the pre-Freudian landscape that he surveys. Like the stories to which the next several chapters of this book are devoted, then, *Dorian Gray* mines scientific theory as it tropes the human body, both as a text of outwardly pleasing aspect (in which ostensibly suppressed maladies and devolutionary promptings are scripted) and as the site of Gothic horrors.

Despite its aphoristic tendencies, however, the novel possesses a well-defined skeletal structure and thus differentiates itself from other "typical" works in which horror and Decadence express themselves through narrative atomization and fragmentation. Moreover, Wilde's use of jeweled language is much more restrained than such language later became in the fevered fictions of, for example, Shiel or John Buchan. Significantly, the most striking of the decorative passages in the novel tend to describe the artistic or intellectual works of others. "Metaphors as monstrous as orchids" characterize the stylistic excesses of the yellow book, about the pages of which clings "the heavy odour of incense" (110); references to the "stiff flowered dalmatic," the "jewelled lantern-shaped monstrance with that pallid wafer," and the "fuming censers" born aloft by the "grave boys, in their lace and scarlet" (146) mark Dorian's ritualized engagement with aestheticism; Lord Henry's "Philosophy" dances like a Bacchante before those upon whom he bestows his extempore (if somewhat Rubáiyátical) utterances: "Her white feet trod the huge press at which wise Omar sits, till the seething grape juice rose round her bare limbs in waves of purple bubbles, or crawled in red foam over the vat's black, dripping, sloping sides. It was an extraordinary improvisation" (79). The "improvisation" is Wilde's as well, for the decorative idiom and ormolu of the day is less natural to him than to those other anatomists of Decadence—Baudelaire, Huysmans, or even the earlier Barbey d'Aurevilly—in whose books we might expect to encounter such gorgeously gilt horrors—a fact not lost on Jorge Luis Borges, who argued that Wilde generally dispensed with the purple passages to which custom had linked his name: "in verse or in prose Wilde's syntax is always very simple."[130] The cultural decadence that provided these other excursions into horror with their subject—overt or covert—called for a correspondingly subtle textual and linguistic analog that only the Decadent style, with its obsessive and sometimes monstrous metaphors, elaborate paraphrases, complex refrains, and exhaustive leptologia, could provide.[131] The Decadent style of literature, Huysmans wrote, was "attacked by organic diseases, weakened by intellectual senility, exhausted by syntactical excesses, sensitive only to the curious whims that excite the sick"—but in it the outward form testified to the presence of the ravaging inward malady.[132] In those late-nineteenth-century works of literature and art that self-consciously employ such a style, it "is simply expression," as Wilde's Lord Henry has it, "that gives reality to things" (94). "Words! Mere words! How terrible they were! How clear, and vivid, and cruel! One could not escape from them. And yet what a subtle magic there was in them! They seemed to be able to give a plastic form to formless things, and to have a music of their own as sweet as that of viol or of lute. Mere words! Was there anything so real as words?" (62): thus Dorian's thoughts shape themselves as he succumbs to his friend's influence as Chambers's narrator succumbs to the power of the words of *The King in Yellow* ("more precious than jewels, more soothing than Heavenly music, more awful than death itself"). Here, too, Dorian would seem to be paraphrasing Müller, who hypothesized that to "examine the influence which words, mere words, have exercised on the minds of men" would be to "write a history of the world that would teach us more than any which we yet possess."[133] In the stories that are subjected to analysis in the remainder of this book, it is the word that is made flesh and the body of the text that betrays the secrets sealed in the text of the body.

Pater's description of one of the defining portraits of Leonardo's artistic corpus is perhaps worth recalling in a discussion that conjoins Decadence, language, and horror. Speculating on the origins of the subtle charms of the Mona Lisa, Pater noted that her troubled beauty was directly related to her enigmatic spirit, "wrought out from within upon the flesh, the deposit, little cell by little cell, of strange thoughts and fantastic reveries and exquisite passions." According to this anatomy, Leonardo's portrait serves as an analog to that of Dorian Gray, for the Mona Lisa's is a beauty "into which the soul with all its maladies has passed!"[134] In both texts, a subtle affinity exists between the soul of the subject and the soul of the plot, and in the fin de siècle stories that follow, the horror embodied in the soul of the plot is wrought out from within, little word by little word, in sentences and images that are symptomatic of the maladies of the soul.

2

Walter de la Mare's "A: B: O."

The Text for the Context

NATURA nihil agit frustra, is the onely indisputable axiome in Philosophy: there are no *Grotesques* in nature: not any thing framed to fill
up empty cantons, and unnecessary spaces: . . . There is [therefore] no
deformity but in monstrosity, wherein notwithstanding there is a kind
of beauty, Nature so ingeniously contriving those irregular parts, as
they become sometimes more remarkable than the principall Fabrick.
To speake yet more narrowly, there was never anything ugly, or misshapen, but the Chaos: wherein not withstanding, to speake strictly,
there was no deformity, because no forme: nor was it yet impregnate
by the voyce of God: Now nature is not at variance with art, nor art
with nature: they being both the servants of his providence: Art is the
perfection of Nature: Were the world now as it was the sixt day, there
were yet a Chaos. Nature hath made one world, and Art another. In
briefe, all things are artificiall, for Nature is the Art of God.

Sir Thomas Browne, Religio Medici (1642)

Legions of grotesques sweep under his hand: for has not nature too her
grotesques—the rent rock, the distorting lights of evening on lonely roads,
the unveiled structure of man in the embryo, or the skeleton?

Walter Pater, "Leonardo da Vinci: (1869)

The plots of God are perfect. The Universe is a plot of God.

Edgar Allan Poe, Eureka (1848)

Beholde, I shewe you a mistery.

The Boke of Common Prayer (1552)

IN "A REVENANT" (1936), AN HOMAGE to Edgar Allan Poe, Walter de la Mare tacitly acknowledges his fascination with the effluvia or the miasma of the Gothic when his narrator, a professor who grudgingly concedes the virtues of Poe's works while decrying his personal failings, observes that

> the most salient, the most impressive feature of Poe's writings . . . is his own personal presence in them. Even in his most exotic fantasies, some of them beautiful in the sense that the phosphorescence of decay, the brambles and briars of the ruinous, the stony calm of the dead may be said to be beautiful; some so sinister and macabre in their half-demented horror that if we ourselves encountered them even in dreams we should awake screaming upon our beds—even here the sense of his peculiar personality is so vivid and immediate that, as we read, it is almost as if the poet himself stood in the flesh before us—.[1]

Although this scarcely amounts to unqualified praise—the "exotic" fantasies and "half-demented" horrors are offered as symptoms of the "peculiar personality" that had conceived them—de la Mare had not always been so laudatory. "Edgar Allan Poe" (1909), an earlier appreciation written in propria persona, echoes Henry James in depicting Poe as a literary seducer of naïfs—"it is in early youth," he admitted, "before experience has taught one to appreciate the charms of so-briety in literature as well as in life, that Poe waylays his victim"—and as some-one whose indiscreet confidences impart a dubious sort of knowledge: "If life on earth be but a brief series of reminiscences, then Poe has whispered in our ear many that might more prudently have been left undisturbed."[2] Perhaps more telling than these explicit reproaches, however, is the fact that "A Revenant" con-tains a coded tribute to Poe, for embedded in the passage cited above is a phrase borrowed from Baudelaire, who identified "la phosphorescence de la pourriture" as the telltale signifier of Decadence in literature.[3] In purloining Baudelaire's phrase, de la Mare invokes the memory of the poet who first translated Poe's works into French not only because Baudelaire sought, as he wrote in his pref-ace to *Histoires Extraordinaires* (1856), to "add a new saint to the martyrology . . . of . . . illustrious unfortunate men, too rich in poetry and passion, who came . . . to serve the harsh apprenticeship of genius among inferior souls," but also because he believed that "no man . . . has told about the *exceptions* in human life and in nature with more magic—the enthusiastic curiosities of convales-cence, the dying seasons charged with enervating splendors, hot, humid and misty weather when the south wind softens and relaxes one's nerves like the strings of an instrument."[4] De la Mare is also reemphasizing, however, the specific predilection that the Decadents had found most admirable in Poe as they developed their own literary aesthetic in which conditions otherwise con-tradistinctive and oppositional were made to coalesce. Such hints and link-ages (an American professor of English characterizes the dead Poe in terms put forth by a French Decadent) suggest that de la Mare approached Poe with a curious admixture of guilty pleasure and skittish attraction. In his popular role as the decorous and conventional singer of the *Songs of Childhood* (1902), however, de la Mare betrayed few of the dark conceits that another self, more private and more given to bizarrerie and the outré, would nurture in some of his horror stories.

Later, during the prime of his own career, de la Mare expressed his thoughts on the obscure literary motives, inclinations, and allegiances of writers of fiction, proposing that they "are nowadays inclined to be reticent. . . . If they have any secrets they keep them dark."[5] His own inner, private life, his own affinities with those other Victorians—those who, as Baudelaire said of Poe, "created in order to show . . . that strangeness is one of the integral parts of the beautiful," or sought to demonstrate that, as Ruskin put it, the beautiful itself is "continually mingled with the shadow of death"—were such secrets: secrets most nearly betrayed in "A: B: O.," one of de la Mare's earliest and only recently exhumed tales of horror.[6] Like the treasure it describes, "A: B: O." lay buried for more than half a century, and it was only just before his death in 1956 that de la Mare, by then a Companion of Honour and possessor of the Order of Merit and obviously less concerned than in earlier years about the effect its publication might have on his reputation, agreed "to sanction [the] ghoulish proceedings" that his friend Edward Wagenknecht had set in motion when he set out to collect and reprint his early stories. During the five decades between its birth and possible first publication—circa 1895—and de la Mare's consenting to its inclusion in a collection titled *Eight Tales* (which appeared eventually in 1971), de la Mare apparently saw his "A: B: O." as something that ought to be kept hidden.[7] In the intervening years, like the disgraced parent of a blighted offspring, he remained silent as to the hiding place of his story of buried corruption. At the last, however, apparently unwilling that any part of his legacy should be lost, he allowed Wagenknecht to raise it from the dead.

Always self-deprecatory, de la Mare professed to believe that his early stories were amateurish, not merely ill-conceived but poorly crafted, and yet "A: B: O." is an accomplished piece of work, full of nervous description and elusive, cryptic dialogue that successfully conveys an atmosphere of delirium, hallucination, and "half-demented" horror. As is the case with a number of de la Mare's early efforts, it is quite self-consciously derivative and "literary" in style. It is more, however, than a literary pastiche revealing the adroitness with which a young writer appropriated images and phrases from the works of precursors as diverse as Jeremy Taylor, Sir Thomas Browne, Hawthorne, Poe, and Pater. "A: B: O." is a quintessential example of a certain sort of fin de siècle conceit that flourished in the twilight of the Victorian era—monstrous offspring such as Wells's *The Time Machine* and *The Island of Dr. Moreau* (1896), Vernon Lee's *Hauntings* (1890), Chambers's *The King in Yellow*, Shiel's *Shapes in the Fire* (1896), X.L.'s *Aut Diabolus aut Nihil and Other Tales* (1894), and Stoker's

Dracula (1897), all of which were published in the 1890s and all of which embodied the conflict between the urge to continue to believe in what John Buchan
referred to as the "old noble commonplaces of love and faith and duty [that] are
always with us" and a gnawing distrust of the literary and cultural past in which
such commonplaces were rooted.[8] To the extent that it reflects its author's interest in and compelling engagement with contemporary scientific theory and evolutionary biology—and with embryology and recapitulation theory in particular—"A: B: O." displays the characteristic indicia of the day. Such historicist
concerns, however, are subsumed within the encompassing semiotic play of a
text that charts the difficulties confronting those who struggle to situate themselves within a universe of signs—barely legible missives, encoded maps, cryptic cognomens, and parabolic pronouncements—that must be read, deciphered,
and analyzed before its monstrous proportions may be apprehended, however
imperfectly, however disastrous the consequences. All of these things make "A:
B: O" valuable both as a text and as a document disclosing not merely anxieties
and horrors, but also the distinctive *mentalité* of an age, expressing itself in
questions and concerns voiced by an apprentice writer who saw himself as a
witness to both the death of one culture and the birth of its successor.

As a horror story, "A: B: O." proceeds swiftly from the merely quaint to the
genuinely horrific, leading us through a series of abominable events that begin
benignly enough when Pelluther, the story's narrator, receives a scrawled message from his friend Dugdale in which he discerns the magical word "Antiquities." With an old map left by Dugdale's great uncle as a guide, the two set about
excavating Dugdale's garden, the site of what they hope will prove to be buried
treasure. After a good deal of digging, hauling, and scraping, the two unearth an
old metal chest that proves to be "cryptic" in more ways than one, for along its
side is inscribed a word that time and soil have partially eroded: only the puzzling fragment "A: B: O." remains. Prying open the lid of the chest, they find
neither gold nor jewels nor pearls of great price, but a shriveled creature wrapped
in yellow cotton wool, its skull and features bearing a "hideous and ungodly
resemblance to the human face."[9] And then, even more horribly, they discover
that although it has been buried for many years, the creature is still somehow
alive—its casket having been provided with a metal pipe that links it to the boss
of a yew tree overhead. Terrified, the two men decide to rebury their "treasure,"
but the creature escapes before they have an opportunity to do so, and when
last seen it is pattering off toward the heart of London. In the end Pelluther
returns to Dugdale's home only to discover that his friend, now hopelessly insane, has taken the place of the homunculus within the chest.

Although this brief synopsis omits a great deal of the story's plot, it suggests that in writing "A: B: O." the young de la Mare had quite consciously appropriated several literary traditions and conventions—primarily, however, in
order to put them to ironic use. With its requisite black cat, yew tree, and late
night dig, for example, "A: B: O." recalls the early Gothic romances of Ann

Radcliffe or "Monk" Lewis. But whereas such romances often contain little more than the sum of their physical horrors (the bleeding nun, the rapist monks), so that once these have been explained away or disposed of in one fashion or another, the reader is left with little but the recollection of a brush with the *unheimlich*, the mystifications of de la Mare's story pale beside a horror whose unveiling has little to do with such gothicized excrescences. Predicated as it is upon the traditional theme of buried treasure, "A: B: O." also emphasizes its own antiquarianism, its obsession with the past and with historiography, as embodied in a map that marks the site of "Antiquities" and in the feckless seekers after forbidden knowledge. Such questers were the favorite protagonists of the writers of the antiquarian ghost stories of the period, most notably M.R. James, whose *Ghost-Stories of an Antiquary* (1904) features the scholars, professors, pedants, curators, and collectors best suited to the tastes of the Cantabridgeans who for years gathered at his hearthside to hear his annual yuletide ghost story. The scholar/narrator of de la Mare's story is first seen poring over a book, although he glances up occasionally at the portrait of the great-grandfather who will preside over the tragedy that is about to occur. Dugdale, the friend whose missive lures him from the cozy sanctity of his study, bears the name of Sir William Dugdale, the Warwickshire antiquary distinguished for his tireless investigations into histories, origins, pedigrees, and precedents, and author of *The Antiquities of Warwickshire* (1656) and *Antiquities of the Inns of court and chancery* (1666).[10] The treasure buried at the heart of de la Mare's story is not the sort for which adventurers and antiquarians usually seek, however—not the gold to which his knowledge of Latin and an agile mind led the scholarly Mr. Somerton in James's "The Treasure of Abbot Thomas" (1904); nor the abundant riches heaped upon Poe's studiously eccentric William Legrand, who successfully decodes a cryptograph of Captain Kidd's devising, recorded on the scrap of parchment to which Legrand is led by the eponymous gold bug. In de la Mare's story, the successful transcription of an ancestral map discloses only a little lower layer of mystification: a palimpsestic reality denominated by the hieroglyphic "A: B: O.," the exact meaning and nature of which remains a matter for almost endless speculation.

History and their own complacent familiarity with an antiquarian tradition lead the two men to anticipate that their map records the burial place of "Old Roman, or Druidical" artifacts, but their treasure proves to be a loathesome "ABOmination," and their experience in the unearthing of it that of the envisioned protagonist of one of Hawthorne's unwritten stories, the germ of which he had jotted down in the early 1840s in one of his notebooks: "A man seeks for something excellent, but seeks it in the wrong way, and in a wrong spirit, and finds something horrible—as for instance, he seeks for treasure, and finds a dead body—for the gold that somebody has hidden, and brings to light his accumulated sins."[11]

Promising, in typically Poesque fashion, to "speak without emotion,"

Pelluther gives the following description of their "treasure": "I saw a flat mal-
formed skull and meagre arms and shoulders clad in coarse fawn hair. I saw a
face thrown back a little, bearing hideous and ungodly resemblance to the human face, its lids heavy blue and closely shut with coarse lashes and tangled
eyebrows" (97). The emphasis de la Mare places on this "ungodly resemblance"
is the first suggestion that the "damnable thing," as Dugdale calls it, may also be
thought of as an "ABOrigine" in the sense of "primitive" or, as the *Oxford English Dictionary* has it, "first or earliest so far as history or science gives record."
De la Mare further hints that the A: B: O. may be a biological throwback or
reversion to type when he describes its face as "thrown back a little," the phrase
suggesting not merely the relation of head to body, but the creature's connection
to the shadowy, hairy ancestor so familiar to later Victorians and Edwardians—
the figure who is featured, for example, on the cover of a child's history of evolution, published in 1911, which tells the story of *Ab, the Cave Man* (fig. 15). The
children of such a figure appear in Wells's "A Story of the Stone Age" (1897):
"Wild-eyed youngsters . . . with matted hair and little broad-nosed impish faces,
covered (as some children are covered even nowadays) with a delicate down of
hair. They were narrow in the loins and long in the arms. And their ears had no
lobes, and had little pointed tips, a thing that still, in rare instances, survives.
Stark-naked vivid little gipsies, as active as monkeys and as full of chatter, though
a little wanting in words."[12]

Various clues point to at least one other possible interpretation of the inscrutable acronym "A: B: O."—one that (as we shall see) is related to the notion of an
aboriginal. As the story unfolds, we come to suspect something more ominous
still, and Pelluther confirms our hypothesis when, far advanced in his adventure,
he has a ghastly epiphany and stammers "abortion—A-B-O, abortion; I knew
then" (104). His friend, who has guessed independently that they have dug up a
"wretched abortion," gives an additional turn of the hermeneutic screw when he
alludes to the gender of the aborted fetus, for his choice of pronoun ("He—he,
Pelluther") tells us that the A: B: O. is also "A BOy."[13]

Wilfully outré as his choice of subject may seem (even to our own case-
hardened sensibilities), de la Mare was not the first author to make human
embryos and aborted fetuses the centerpiece of a fictive creation. In "The Peach
in Brandy," one of the stories collected in Horace Walpole's privately printed
Hieroglyphic Tales (1785), the archbishop of Tuum stifles a violent coughing fit
by gulping down what he takes to be a medicinal fruit—a peach in brandy—little
knowing that the restorative is in fact one of the premature twins that the queen-
mother has just aborted and that her conscientious butler has caught up in a
glass. The five-year-old Queen Grata alerts her mother to the archbishop's unfortunate error in judgment as she cries, "'Mama, mama, the gentleman has eat
my little brother!'"[14] As an image of something begun but not completed, or
completed only imperfectly and in an untimely manner, the abortion held particular appeal for the Decadents, and for Aubrey Beardsley in particular, whose

Figure 15. Fred Stearns, cover of *Ab, the Cave Man* (1911)

illustrations of this period are rife with what (in a letter regarding his forthcoming cover for the April 1896 issue of *The Savoy* [fig. 16]) he referred to as a "little creature . . . *not* an infant but an unstrangled abortion."[15] (It would have been impossible for de la Mare *not* to have seen Beardsley's illustrations, given the notoriety of the artist through his affiliation with the infamous *Yellow Book*, a publication that, despite the brevity of its three-year existence, and despite the fact that much of what it published was quite innocuous, had come to be known as a repository of Decadence.) Embryonic creatures creep into Beardsley's illustrations for *Lucian's True History* (1894) (figs. 17 and 18), and a sultry Madonna smiles lazily upon a human fetus in a drawing called "Incipit Vita Nova" (c. 1893) (fig. 19). Human embryos emerge as well in some of Beardsley's illustrations for *Salome* (1894) (figs. 20 and 21), in a headpiece designed for *St. Paul's* depicts an embryo under glass, the object of study for the genteel young woman seated beside it (fig. 22). Individual vignettes from Dent's *Bon-Mots* series (1893-94) (figs. 23a-23d) feature the embryo in various modes: as the tuxedoed gentleman-manqué, for example; or as a death's-head fetus from out of whose skull ascends a skeletal man—an unveiling of what Pater took to be one of nature's grotesques, "the unveiled structure of man in the embryo, or the skeleton"; or even as the fetus grimly returned by the abortionist to its mother: what one might conceive of as the artistic rendering of the "procured . . . abortion" that Beardsley would later praise "Good old Collins" for having "managed" for him.[16]

Judged within the larger context of his graphic work, Beardsley's homunculi allude to what Ewa Kuryluk, in her study of the grotesque iconography of the fin de siècle, identifies as "the deadly secrets and dangers of sex."[17] The artist himself identified the "masks of . . . apes, . . . of men and women, of little embryons" as being among those donned by the guests who sup with the "frockless Venus and Tannhäuser" in one of the many preambles to sexual play featured in *Under the Hill* (1896), his mock-erotic version of the medieval legend.[18] Seated in the leaden coffin that once contained the abortion, Dugdale identifies the "pestilent secret sin" that they have uncovered as "a sin perhaps of yours and of mine," an observation that refers less to the disclosure of and consequent retribution for ancestral misconduct—the proverbial sins of the fathers visited upon the sons—than to the manner of its unveiling. For Pelluther's and Dugdale's own obsession with the past, expressed in their compulsive curiosity and their frenzied digging, is itself eroticized, continually forcing its way through the thin veneer of social breeding and expressing itself in terms of violence. The very language of Dugdale's missive is telling: the word "Antiquities" seems to Pelluther to be the "peak of the climax of this summons—the golden word" (89). When he arrives at Dugdale's house, he finds his friend with "cheeks . . . flushed with excitement" (89-90), and in the garden Dugdale, spade in hand, digs feverishly, muttering something about "city dinners, orgies" and looking to Pelluther "like a man in search of his soul." After the expenditure of much

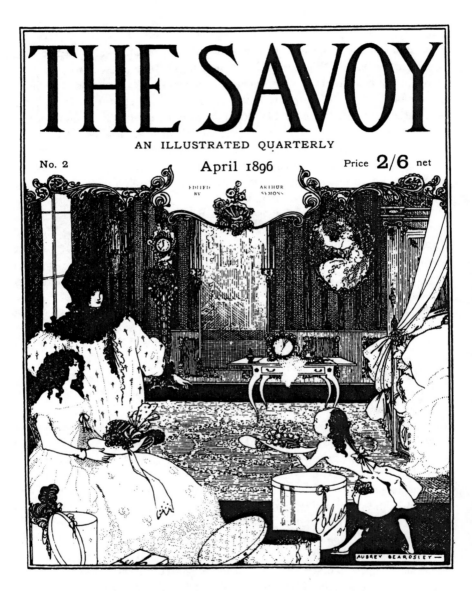

Figure 16. Aubrey Beardsley, cover of *The Savoy*, no. 2 (1896). Courtesy of the Rare Book Collection, The University of North Carolina at Chapel Hill

Figure 17. Aubrey Beardsley, "Lucian's Strange Creatures," intended for *Lucian's True History* (1894) but published separately in *An Issue of Five Drawings Illustrative of Juvenal and Lucian* (1906). Courtesy of Princeton University Library

Figure 18. Aubrey Beardsley, "Dreams," from *Lucian's True History* (1894). Courtesy of Fogg Art Museum, Harvard University Art Museums, Bequest of Scofield Thayer

Figure 19. Aubrey Beardsley, "Incipit Vita Nova" (c. 1893). Courtesy of the Board of Trustees of the Victoria and Albert Museum, London

Figure 20. Aubrey Beardsley, "Enter Herodias," from *Salome* (1894). Courtesy of the Rare Book Collection, The University of North Carolina at Chapel Hill

Figure 21. Aubrey Beardsley, *The Toilet of Salome,* first version (1894). Courtesy of the Rare Book Collection, The University of North Carolina at Chapel Hill

Figure 22. Aubrey Beardsley, design for *St. Paul's* (1894). Courtesy of Sammlung Albertina, Vienna

Figure 23a. Aubrey Beardsley, vignette from *Bon-Mots of Charles Lamb and Douglas Jerrold* (1893). Author's collection

Figure 23b. Aubrey Beardsley, vignette from *Bon-Mots of Sydney Smith and R. Brinsley Sheridan* (1893). Courtesy of the Rare Book Collection, The University of North Carolina at Chapel Hill

Figure 23c. Aubrey Beardsley, vignette from *Bon-Mots of Sydney Smith and R. Brinsley Sheridan* (1893). Courtesy of the Rare Book Collection, The University of North Carolina at Chapel Hill

Figure 23d. Aubrey Beardsley, vignette from *Bon-Mots of Sydney Smith and R. Brinsley Sheridan* (1893). Courtesy of the Rare Book Collection, The University of North Carolina at Chapel Hill

"fanatical energy," we are told, "exquisitely, suddenly, Dugdale's pick struck heavily and hollowly" (92). Although they suspect that it may contain "delicate merchandise," the "two old boys in the plot," as they call themselves, are forced to "pull and push vigorously at the chest," for the hole in which it rests has been made "ragged and unequal" by their violent exertions: "the hole—" urges Dugdale, speaking associatively, cryptically, "it's desecration" (93-94). The box is spirited away to Dugdale's study, where the "desecration" continues in good earnest. "In a cranny at the lid of the chest," Dugdale, the flames of the fire aglitter upon his glasses, "inserted the tool." There is resistance—on "the second jerk," his steel chisel "snapped"—but armed with another, he sets to work once again and this time is able to prise "open the lid at the first effort" (96). A few minutes later, however, confronted by the contents of the chest, their mood changes: Pelluther feels his gorge rise "with the despair of life," while Dugdale sits on the floor, "rocking to and fro with hands clasped over his knees" and complaining that he is "too weak now" (97) to rebury the guilty thing—as though sapped by the rigors of sexual violation and suffering a form of postcoital *tristesse*. At this stage, Dugdale seems less reminiscent of Sir Thomas Browne's antiquarian correspondent than of the infamous purveyor of pornographic and seditious material, William Dugdale, a "kingpin of pornography" whom Ronald Pearsall describes as "the nastiest of all the publishers" of erotica, "a thoroughly disagreeable person, blackmailer and pornographer, adman and publisher," the "slime" of whose "trail" snaked its way through Russell Court, Drury Lane, Wych Street, and Holywell Street, to its final destination in the House of Correction off of Gray's Inn Road, where Dugdale died in 1868.[19]

Much of the language and imagery employed by de la Mare in this parody of an archaeological dig, then, has obvious sexual implications—the excavation as brutal rape—but the dig also reads as a diabolical delivery, Dugdale and Pelluther acting the part of ghoulish surgeons or midwives, ripping from the "belly of the earth" a womb/tomb that incubates the undead. Immediately after he reads Dugdale's note, Pelluther rushes from his house looking like a "doctor, bent on enterprise of life or death" (89). Working by candlelight, and "after great labour," these amateur resurrection men (Dugdale's admission that theirs is "as glum a trade as body-snatching" (93) conjures up the memory of Macfarlane and Fettes, Stevenson's more famous body-snatchers) deliver the leaden box by means of spade, shovel, and pick—the tools usually reserved for burial. The birth imagery becomes overt when they make a "strange and inexplicable discovery": "a thickly rusted iron tube ran out from the top of the chest into the earth, and thence by surmise we traced it to the trunk of the dwarfed yew tree; and, with the light of our candles eventually discovered its termination imbedded in a boss between two gnarled encrusted branches a few feet up. We were unable to drag out the chest without first disinterring the pipe" (93). Like a human fetus, then, this box boasts its own umbilical cord, which Dugdale must saw in half. Thus inverting the plea in the *Pater Noster*, the two fanatical antiquarians deliver themselves not *from* evil but *to* it. Having cleaned away the "mould and rust"—the horrific afterbirth that clings to the chest—they are able to see "three letters, initial to a word . . . which originally ran the whole width of the side, but the greater part of which had been rendered illegible by the action of the soil. 'A-B-O' were the letters" (95).

The "leprous child of the sinner" thus denominated takes its place in a fin de siècle portrait gallery of the emblematic blighted progeny, blasted issue, and decrepit offspring of those who have "sinned" in body or spirit. They lie in a direct line of descent from such ancestors as the crippled (and possibly syphilitic) son of the philandering Viscount Squanderfield in plate 6 of Hogarth's *Marriage à la Mode* (1745), or Hawthorne's Pearl, whom the Salem villagers regard as an "imp of evil, emblem and product of sin," or the "naturally delicate, . . . wan and wistful" Paul Dombey, who, at the age of five, "looked (and talked) like one of those terrible little Beings in the Fairy tales, who, at a hundred and fifty or two hundred years of age, fantastically represent the children for whom they have been substituted."[20] Toward the latter decades of the century, such children are more frequently portrayed as the syphilitic offspring of parents such as Emile Zola's Nana, the courtesan whose son Louis is a "poor little fellow . . . always ill," with "an eczema on the back of his neck, and . . . concretions . . . forming in his ears, which pointed, it was feared, to the decay of the bones of the skull." With his "spoilt blood," "flabby flesh all out in yellow patches," and "poor little face . . . waxen and dumb and white," the child, "never [smiling]" and with "a very old expression," is the repository of all the taints and infections that his strapping mother absorbs and transmits, but only once displays bodily.[21] Sarah Grand, no less severe than Zola, introduces the reader of *The Heavenly Twins* (1893) to the "speckled toad" who is the diseased infant of Edith Beale, a clergyman's daughter who has contracted syphilis from her philandering husband.[22] Yet, although physically similar to these contaminated children (whose disease, although never explicitly named, could not have been rendered with greater clarity of detail),[23] the abortion of de la Mare's story has less in common with them—or with the abject fetus shown crouched amidst the swarming spermatozoa in Edvard Munch's *Madonna* (1894) (fig. 24)—than with a different set of progeny, whose physical appearance does not betray them as nature's "grotesques." Whether literally or symbolically, all of these "beautiful" grotesques— Dorian Gray, the voluptuous creatures of Dracula, the Eloi—have been conceived parthenogenetically, in a process that Margaret Homans (discussing the androcentric conditions under which the monster appears in Mary Shelley's *Frankenstein* [1818]) describes as "an elaborate circumvention of normal heterosexual procreation."[24] Despite the obvious fact that he has "natural" parents, Dorian Gray is more immediately the "creation" of Lord Henry, who imagines that "to project one's soul into some gracious form, and let it tarry there for a moment," or "to convey one's temperament into another as though it were a subtle fluid or a strange perfume" would be "the most satisfying joy left to us in an age so limited and vulgar as our own, an age grossly carnal in its pleasures, and grossly common in its aims." It is perhaps worth noting that the outcome of Lord Henry's efforts proves no less grossly common, his "son's" criminality expressing itself in commonplaces—murder and suicide—while the sublimated carnality that he proposes recalls heterosexual intercourse in every way except for the conspicuous exclusion of the feminine; but the feminine continues to manifest itself in the "feminized" male. Without female involvement, "unmarried," and having "nothing but his own interests to consider," Dr. Moreau creates a brood of "Moreau Horrors," cutting, stitching, and pressing various animals into the semblance of "crippled and distorted men."[25] Dracula's single-mindedness, on the other hand, is as evident in his procreative activities as in everything else that he undertakes. His "creatures," as he calls them—"my jackals when I want to feed"— begin as full-blown daughters and become the means by which he will beget ready-made sons: "Your girls that you all love are mine already," he informs his pursuers, "and through them you and others shall yet be mine."[26] Although a highly sublimated form of lovemaking is common enough among the Eloi—they pelt each other with flowers—differentiation itself (sexual, occupational, behavioral) is lacking because the forces that necessitated it—the struggles, the hardships, the discords of life—have ceased to operate. At a time in which the "[hateful] grindstone of pain and necessity" had been "broken at last"; in a land bereft of stinging bugs, contagious diseases, "processes of putrefaction," "connubial jealousy" and "fierce maternity"; it is unclear how the Eloi come into being at all—it is hard to imagine them emerging from the bloody flux of childbirth.[27] With their "firm lips, children of science" and their eyes "wives of the microscope" (90), de la Mare's characters are so aggressively "masculine" that they betray their own anxieties in an idiom that is undeniably sexualized. In the course of unearthing their creature, for example, they usurp the feminine prerogative of reproduction: "We nursed our excitement," says Pelluther; "we conceived the wildest fantasies, we brought forth litters of surmises" (94); later, meshed in the throes of his ordeal, he finds himself struggling to discipline his thoughts, which carry with them "a pregnant suggestion" (105).

In *Dorian Gray, The Time Machine, The Island of Doctor Moreau,* and "A: B: O.," however, the range of what Elaine Showalter describes as the "living symbols of the devolutionary force of male vice" must be extended to include a deteriorative quality inherent in the species: a quality not necessarily limited to or apparent only in misbegotten heirs—Nana's Louis, for example, or Edith Beale's blighted child.[28] Even Beardsley's homunculi, appropriated for use in his coded language of concupiscence, had as their prototypes the embryos readily available to him in the first chapter of *The Descent of Man* (1871) ("The Evidence of the Descent of Man from Some Lower Form") and in volume 2 (1882) of Wilhelm His's *Anatomie menschlicher Embryonen* (1880-85) (figs. 25 and 26).[29] De la Mare's homunculus also owes its inception to the new biology (and specifically to the organic evolutionary studies of Ernst Heinrich Haeckel, the "fiery apostle of Darwinism in Germany") rather than to what Showalter (noting the preponderance of misshapen offspring in fin de siècle literature) identifies as an evolving discourse revolving around the "conflict between male and female writers over the representation of sexuality," through which "the literary uses and meaning of syphilitic insanity" had been filtered.[30]

Haeckel's theory that ontogeny recapitulates phylogeny—derived from evolutionary theory and introduced in his enormously influential *Generelle Morphologie der Organismen* (1866), which Huxley called "one of the greatest scientific works ever published"—holds that "the history of individual development, or Ontogeny, is a short and quick recapitulation of palaeontological development, or Phylogeny, dependent on the laws of Inheritance and Adaptation."[31] The concept was not entirely original with Haeckel; for—already emergent by the late eighteenth century—the law of recapitulation itself was, as Stephen Jay Gould has noted, "'discovered' many times in the decade following 1859."[32] Darwin, for example, had suggested in *On the Origin of Species* that "the embryo comes to be left as a sort of picture, preserved by nature, of the ancient and less modified condition of each animal"—although this represented a reversal of his earlier opinion on the matter, as expressed, for example, in an 1842 notebook jotting: "It is not true that one passes through the form of a lower group, though no doubt fish more nearly related to foetal state."[33] As early as 1838, however, Darwin had begun to contemplate the possibility that fetal monstrosity might be understood from a recapitulatory perspective, concluding that the "foetus of man undergoes metamorphosis" and that the kind of monstrosity might be determined by the "age of foetus."[34] Whereas at midcentury such speculations had been largely confined to scientific treatises, by the century's close the concept of recapitulation was surfacing in unexpected places, having been appropriated as an explanatory model within widely differing fields. Thus, one encounters Haeckel's premise that "the History of the Germ is an epitome of the History of the Descent . . . of the tribe" redacted in a 1908 essay on ornament and crime by the Austrian architect Adolf Loos, who does away with annoying temporal constraints (Haeckel's "short and quick recapitulation of palaeontological development") and guilelessly blends orders, categories, genera, and disciplines:

> At the moment of birth, human sensations are equal to those of a newborn dog. His childhood passes through all the transformations which correspond to the history of mankind. At the age of two, he sees like a Papuan, at four, like a Teuton, at six like Socrates, at eight like Voltaire. When he is eight years old, he becomes aware of violet, the colour which the eighteenth century had discovered, because before that the violet was blue and the purple snail red. Today the physicist points to colours in the sun's spectrum which already bear a name, whose recognition, however, is reserved for the coming generation.[35]

Figure 24. Edvard Munch, Norwegian, 1863-1944, *Madonna*, lithograph; printed in black and colored by hand, 1895, 59.8 x 44 cm, Print and Drawing Purchase Fund, 1945.229. Photograph © 1996, The Art Institute of Chicago, All Rights Reserved. © 1997 Artists Rights Society (ARS), New York/ADAGP, Paris

It is worth noting—lest we be tempted to attribute Loos's revisionary tendencies to an insouciance bred of the layman's superstitious ignorance and misprision—that the social scientist Herbert Spencer had earlier supported the notion that intellectual and moral development proceed phylogenetically: just "as grammar was made after language," he suggested by way of example, "so ought it to be taught after language: an inference which all who recognise the relationship between the evolution of the race and of the individual, will see to be unavoidable"; and in another context, "a common trait of [geographical models] is, that they carry each child's mind through a process like that which the mind of humanity at large has gone through." In essence, the "education of the child must accord both in mode and arrangement with the education of mankind as considered historically," for "if there be an order in which the human race has mastered its various kinds of knowledge, there will arise in every child an aptitude to acquire these kinds of knowledge in the same order"; thus, "education should be a repetition of civilisation in little."[36] As Gould points out, late-nineteenth-century education reformers (whose interests were pedagogical, linguistic, and anthropological) were also enthusiastic adherents of social recapitulation. He cites the example of several school boards that "prescribed the *Song of Hiawatha* in early grades, reasoning that children, passing through the savage stage of their ancestral past, would identify with it."[37] Convinced that the "mental development of the child corresponds in general to the chief phases in the development of his people or of mankind," Tuiskon Ziller, a nineteenth-century German educational reformer, sought to implement a recapitulatory curriculum in which, as Gould notes, each "of the eight years of primary education" would focus on "the period of cultural and literary history that the child is recapitulating during the given year." Ziller offered the following core texts as part of prototypical recapitulatory curriculum:

1. Stories from epic folklore.
2. Robinson Crusoe (redomiciled in Germany).
3. Biblical patriarchs.
4. Judges of Israel.
5. Kings of Israel.
6. The life of Christ.
7. Apostolic history.
8. The Reformation.[38]

Less interdisciplinary in his application of the concept, perhaps, than Loos or Ziller had been, de la Mare betrays his own working knowledge of what Haeckel had established as a "fundamental biogenetic principle" in his rendering of the A: B: O.—and in his having fixed at all on an abortion in which now lost ancestral morphological detail would be temporarily recovered (although he might also have fixed with impunity on a more fully developed child, since it had

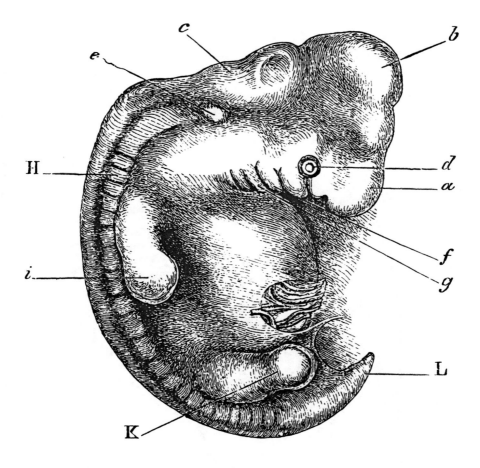

Figure 25. Human embryo, from chapter 1 ("The Evidence of the Descent of Man from Some Lower Form") of the 1871 edition of Charles Darwin's *The Descent of Man*. Courtesy of the Rare Book Collection, The University of North Carolina at Chapel Hill

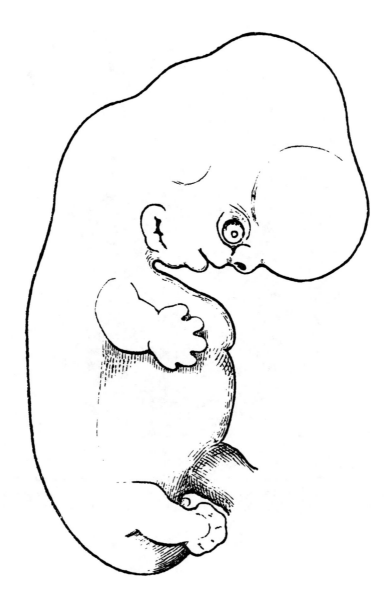

Figure 26. Human embryo of about sixty days, from vol. 2 (1882) of Wilhelm His, *Anatomie menschlicher Embryonen* (1880-85). The primitive ear located in an early stage of development near the chin seems an odd anticipation of the gill-like protuberances of Herodias's attendant in Beardsley's "Enter Herodias" (fig. 20).

also been determined that vestiges of brute ancestry were readily apparent in
human young, who were often styled "little monkey" by their mothers, because,
as Alexander Francis Chamberlain notes in "The Child as Revealer of the Past,"
their "bodily characteristics . . . smack of the monkey").[39] The defining features
of de la Mare's homunculus are its "hideous and ungodly resemblance" to the
human face and its hairiness. "Lanugo" is the term that Darwin assigns in *The
Descent of Man* to the "fine wool-like hair" that first develops on the "eyebrows
and face" of the five-month human fetus. Although it thickly covers the body by
the sixth month, lanugo is largely shed at or shortly following birth, and Darwin
associates this "woolly covering" with "the first permanent coat of hair in those
mammals which are born hairy."[40] Given "the presence of the woolly hair or
lanugo on the human foetus, and of rudimentary hairs scattered over the body
during maturity," Darwin went on to infer that "man is descended from some
animal which was born hairy and remained so during life." With its "coarse
lashes" and "tangled eyebrows," de la Mare's hirsute creature uncannily resembles the early progenitors of man, resurgent only in utero, in children possessing a "rain-thatch," or in those cases in which hairiness in maturity signals
a "partial reversion . . . to a lower animal type"—in "idiots," for example, or in
"certain races" whose hairiness is "the result of reversion, unchecked by any
form of selection."[41] Uncomfortable with the idea that the A: B: O., as aboriginal,
resembles man in his earliest incarnation, a late Victorian reader would have
been shocked to realize that, with its "coarse fawn hair," it *is* a human being,
though one that, arrested in the course of its gestation, has been unable to rid
itself of the outward signs of its inherent bestiality. In this respect "A: B: O."
serves as a gauge registering the magnitude of the impact that Darwin's semi-
nal 1859 publication (and its many influential offspring) had on horror fiction—
an impact, as Barton St. Armand reminds us, as dramatic as that which it had
"on the debate between science and religion, since Darwin's theory of evolution
allowed for the possibility of new fictional monsters," the newest and most promising of the coming beasts being man himself.[42]

In the spring of 1838, Darwin jotted down in Notebook C (the second of his
self-described "Transmutation of Species" notebooks) an entry in which bestiality—if not explicit monstrosity—and humanity are presented as homologous
states of being: "Let man visit Ourang-outang in domestication, hear expressive
whine, see its intelligence when spoken; as if it understood every word said—see
its affection.—to those it knew.—see its passion & rage, sulkiness, & very actions of despair; let him look at savage, roasting his parent, naked, artless, not
improving yet improvable & then let him dare to boast of his proud preeminence." Works such as Darwin's *The Expression of the Emotions in Man and
Animals* were attempts to replicate the encounter he visualized here—an
epiphanic moment that he recognized as being terrifying but necessary since it
would serve to shock "Man——wonderful Man" out of his complacent view of
himself as "a deity."[43] "A: B: O." was born of the traumatic encounter between

traditional beliefs and the staggering ideas put forth in the published writings of which Darwin's impassioned entry served as an embryonic prelude.

The unique originality of de la Mare's hitherto buried conceit is only partially traceable to such an origin, however; after all, monstrous progeny had made and were making their appearance in the physiognomic drawings of the seventeenth-century French painter Charles Le Brun (figs. 27a-27c). They appear as well in works ranging from Mary Shelley's *Frankenstein* (1818) to Stevenson's *The Strange Case of Dr. Jekyll and Mr. Hyde*; Machen's "Novel of the Black Seal" (1895), in which the reader encounters Jervase Cradock, out of whose body emerges a "slimy, wavering tentacle"; and Wells's *Island of Dr. Moreau*, with its curious collection of creatures (descendants, in all likelihood, of Le Brun's heteroclital menagerie) possessing, in addition to "the rough humanity of . . . bodily form, . . . the unmistakable mark of the beast"—and even to Lovecraft's "The Dunwich Horror" (1929), in which Wilbur Whateley is described as "partly human . . . with very manlike hands and head," though his "torso and lower parts of the body were teratologically fabulous."[44] In each of these fictions we experience some measure of the "certain shock" of which, as Huxley knew from his study of the relations of man to the lower animals, even the "least thoughtful of men is conscious" when "brought face to face with these blurred copies of himself." That shock was due, he claimed, "perhaps, not so much to disgust at the aspect of what looks like an insulting caricature, as to the awakening of a sudden and profound mistrust of time-honoured theories and strongly-rooted prejudices regarding his own position in nature, and his relations to the under-world of life; while that which remains a dim suspicion for the unthinking, becomes a vast argument, fraught with the deepest consequences, for all who are acquainted with the recent progress of the anatomical and physiological sciences."[45]

The certain shock delivered by de la Mare's story differs somewhat from that which we encounter in stories or novels in which we stumble across what the disgusted Edward Prendick, viewing Moreau's morbid menagerie, decries as "grotesque caricatures of humanity"—beings in which, that is, essentially human qualities and conditions are aped and parroted, but otherwise preserved from utter subversion.[46] Although some remnant of humanity is vestigially present in such works, the caricature, more often than not, is rendered—again, largely through an obvious contrivance—sufficiently "insulting" to allow for its being banished to a separate plane of existence. Frankenstein's monster, although branding himself an "abortion," is in fact a conglomerated man, patched and remnanted, just as Moreau's mock men are manufactured, man-made.[47] Mr. Hyde makes his "troglodytic" appearance and evinces an "ape-like fury" only through the aid of compounded agents.[48] Cradock's physiognomic peculiarity is inherited—the blood of the "Little People" is mixed with his own—as is that of Whateley, who is similarly miscegenetically situated, since his father was an extraterrestrial. Even Edward Jessup's ontogenetic dematuration to "a small, not very formidable furred creature with the brain capacity of a gorilla" in Paddy

Chayefsky's *Altered States* (1978) (a twentieth-century testimony to the continuing appeal of recapitulation) comes about after he chemically alters his physiological state.[49] The monstrosity of de la Mare's aborted fetus, however, is a
function of its humanity because it displays atavistic horrors always present in
embryo but removed from sight in the fully gestated human body that has had
time to "compose" itself. To be sure, "A: B: O." is not without its share of contriv-
ances. Who so cared for the well-being of an abortion, for example, that he went
to the length of supplying a map that would record its hiding place, a pipe for
fresh air, and a label upon its leaden chest? And how comes it that the abortion
is still living after so many years? But these devices are subordinated to the
central image—a fetus betrayed by its own evolutionary history—which the theory
of recapitulation, unassailable at the time of the story's composition, had rendered thoroughly plausible. One is tempted to ask, with Michel Foucault, "But
what is it impossible to think, and what kind of impossibility are we faced with
here?"[50] In "A: B: O." the kind of impossibility that de la Mare's readers are faced
with is more willed than warranted, the consequence of Huxley's "dim suspicion" resisting "vast argument."

The question of what constitutes the impossible for Foucault arises in relation not to the "strange categories" and "fantastic entities"—full of "wonderment,"
"exotic charm," and "stark impossibility"—presented in a "'certain Chinese
encyclopaedia'" that he stumbled across in his reading of Borges, but rather to
the "narrowness of the distance separating them from" categories to which one
might assign "a precise meaning," "a demonstrable content," and "very real animals" such as "stray dogs": for him impossibility seems to lurk in "the oddity of
unusual juxtapositions" and "the proximity of extremes."[51] In similar fashion,
the "certain shock" that Huxley prophesies for his audience also originates in
the blurring of fixed ideas, the blunting of necessary distinctions, the blasting of
"time-honoured theories." All three theorizers (Foucault, and behind him, Borges,
and behind him, Huxley) are directly concerned with "the order of things."
Huxley's "On the Relations of Man to the Lower Animals" (1863) is an "inquiry
into the nature and the closeness of the ties which connect [man] with those
singular creatures [man-like Apes] whose history" will provide "some knowledge of man's position in the animate world," this knowledge itself being "an
indispensable preliminary to the proper understanding of his relations to the
universe." Huxley founds his argument on scientific "facts" providing "original
answers" to eternal "riddles," although he grants that his "solutions" and "systems" are themselves little better than "a mere approximation to the truth," only
the latest in a succession of "theoretical coverings" and "new habiliments" that
"the human mind, fed by constant accessions of knowledge," regularly moults
as it would any epistemic skin grown too constricting.[52] The passage that occasions Foucault's inquiry into the nature of words and things appears in a Borges
essay devoted to the analytical language of John Wilkins, the seventeeth-cen-
tury English divine whose "happy curiosities" included the way in which human

thought orders, classifies, and arranges the universe and the way in which language orders, classifies, and arranges human thought. Like Huxley, Borges treats
all taxonomies and orders as provisional and arbitrary. Steadied by the faith of
the "forefathers" whose "featherbed of respected and respectable tradition" he
intends to rend to pieces, Huxley trusts in "the existence of [an] orderly progress
and governance of things," although they are not to be arrived at, he argues, if
one only follows "well-worn and comfortable" tracks; to Borges, Wilkins's investigations suggest that "there is no universe in the organic, unifying sense inherent in that ambitious word," and that even if there were, its purpose would be
shrouded, encased in the hieroglyphics of "God's secret dictionary," for which
there is no key.[53] They lead him, in other words, to a very different conclusion
from that at which Wilkins's contemporary, Sir Thomas Browne (to whose
writings the archaelogically minded Borges and Huxley were equally devoted),
had arrived in the faith-driven inquiries that make up so much of his *Religio
Medici* (1642). Admitting that it was impossible to directly comprehend the divine scheme, Browne saw nature as a vast compendium, a "universall and publik
Manuscript" that, although written out in "mysticall letters" and "common
Hieroglyphicks," revealed to the careful observer the "wisedome" of a "Maker"
who "seldome alters or perverts" and who, "like an excellent Artist . . . abhors
deformity," inclining instead toward "the rule of order and beauty."[54] For Huxley,
however, Nature *defined* herself in what earlier generations would have thought
of as grotesque aberrations. Her "insulting caricatures" and "singular creatures"
seemed to him to be the rule, and not, as they had been for Browne, exceptions,
to be interpreted as a willed deviation in the work of "a skilfull Geometrician"
who prefers a "streight and regular line" but who occasionally swerves from an
otherwise "setled and constant course" in order "to acquaint the world with his
prerogative" to do so.[55] Borges would reinstate the supernatural, whose "intervention" in cosmic processes Huxley had "strictly excluded," but like Huxley, he
discerned in any divine impulse toward contrivance that might exist a bias toward those ingeniously wrought "irregular parts" that Browne isolated as the
"sometimes more remarkable" threads interwoven throughout the "principall
Fabrick" containing them.[56] For Huxley, as for Borges, those irregular parts
constituted the foundational warp of the web of existence, and not merely its
decorative weft.

Browne was isolated from nineteenth-century sappers of past histories by
time and faith and by his devotion to the "wisedome" and "general beauty" of
what had promoted the exercise of his doctor's faith. His conviction that "nature
is not at variance with art, nor art with nature," however, aptly describes the
relationship between Huxley's speculations about nature (and those of his intellectual ilk) and the artistry of the fin de siècle fabula to which they may be said to
have given rise (although Huxley himself had elsewhere recognized only an
essential antagonism between the state of art and the state of nature).[57] Many
late Victorian stories depend for their quotient of horror on the often shocking

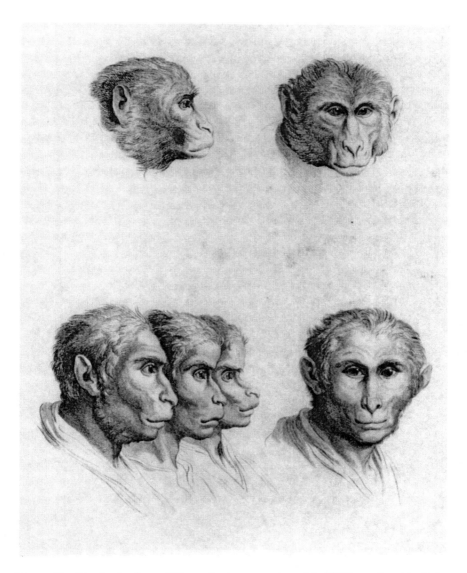

Figure 27a. Charles Le Brun, "Têtes physiognomoniques" (c.1668), reprinted in C. Le Brun, *Dissertation sur un traite de C. le Brun, concernant le rapport de la physionomie humaine avec celle des animaux* (Paris, 1806). Courtesy of the Wellcome Centre Medical Photographic Library, London

Figure 27b. Charles Le Brun, "Têtes physiognomoniques" (c.1668), reprinted in C. Le Brun, *Dissertation sur un traite de C. le Brun, concernant le rapport de la physionomie humaine avec celle des animaux* (Paris, 1806). Courtesy of the Wellcome Centre Medical Photographic Library, London

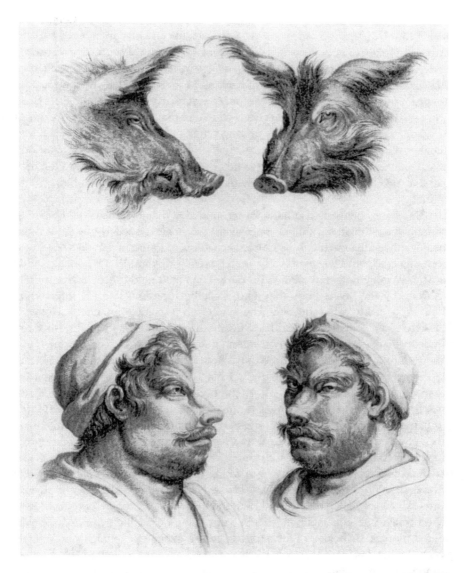

Figure 27c. Charles Le Brun, "Têtes physiognomoniques" (c.1668), reprinted in C. Le Brun, *Dissertation sur un traite de C. le Brun, concernant le rapport de la physionomie humaine avec celle des animaux* (Paris, 1806). Courtesy of the Wellcome Centre Medical Photographic Library, London

recalibration of an accepted system of false weights and mistaken measures, on the confounding of necessary divisions, on the collapsing of protective distances between extremities, and on the destabilizing of established orders. Stevenson's Dr. Jekyll, for example, describes himself as "a mere polity of multifarious, incongruous and independent denizens," all compact of mutually antagonistic good and evil, whereas Wilde's Dorian Gray is the "complex multiform creature" (154) in whom corruption and beauty (among other things) are indistinguishable.[58] Stoker's Count Dracula is the undead, neither living nor dead but an unfathomable *coniunctio* of those opposing states of being; Machen's Helen Vaughan, like the A: B: O. and Wells's infinitely plastic Beast People, is both human and bestial.

The heterogeneous condition foregrounded in these works is not limited to unnatural assimilations taking place within a single disorderly body; it often includes the subversion of boundaries separating autonomous bodies distanced both physically and temporally. Though boxed, for example, the abortion of de la Mare's story does not remain properly contained or repressed. Not merely repulsed by the abject body they find, Pelluther and Dugdale are infected by their exposure to a humunculus whose unclean presence triggers a display of the beast/ancestor that should have been buried deep in the petrified strata of phyletic history, not quiescently awaiting its untimely resurrection in the body. Aware that he is wrestling with "a dim skulking horror of soul and an inhuman depravity," Pelluther realizes that all of his senses have failed him except his hearing, which has grown more keen: he notes that he felt his "ears move and twitch, with the help of some ancient muscle . . . long disused by humanity" (99-100). In *The Descent of Man* Darwin had speculated that, in addition to having been covered with hair, the ears of the "early progenitors of man . . .were probably pointed, and capable of movement."[59] Not content, however, with distinguishing this as merely another in a string of offensive markers—the Ariadne thread running through the dehumanizing history he was determined to narrate—Darwin revealed that this mark of the beast lingered on in humans in "one little peculiarity," consisting in "a little blunt point, projecting from the inwardly folded margin, or helix . . . towards the centre of the ear," which was "visible when the head is viewed from directly in front or behind" (fig. 28a). This galling remnant of "the pointed ear of an ordinary quadruped"—termed the "Darwinian tubercle"—was readily visible "both in men and women" who thus found themselves unexpectedly linked with those "grotesque" deviants—microcephalous idiots and savages and ciminals—who had been lumped together as reincarnated "primitives."[60] The telltale "point," however, constitutes one of those relics—"now become useless"—which, as Darwin noted, had been retained through inheritance, their function recalled only in "the same involuntary and voluntary actions . . . performed by animals nearly related to man"—a recollection parodied, as one might say, in the effort that one of Dr. Moreau's "ungainly" attendants (a conscript in the good doctor's war on Nature) is encouraged to make in order to suppress—*voluntarily*—the innate function of his "pointed ears, covered with a fine brown fur!" (fig. 28b).[61] Pelluther responds equally involuntarily—but only because he responds instinctively, viscerally to this reminder of his own hereditary uncleanliness.

Dugdale's descent into primitivism is more powerfully expressed when, much later, he substitutes himself for the homunculus. Returning to Dugdale's house to help rebury the creature they have unearthed, Pelluther finds his friend sitting hopelessly insane in the chest. By the story's end Dugdale reverts (psychologically, if not bodily) to type. In his regressed state, this cultured man of letters—even to the last, Pelluther insists that he is a "benevolent kindly gentleman . . . fine in intellect . . . eccentric—not mad" (108)—expresses himself in an idiom that lends credence to Lombroso's theory that, since "no evolution is without its involution, no progress without an accompanying retrogression or a succeeding reaction," genius is merely a form of neurotic degeneration, an instance of the recurrence of atavism that, rather than a "continuous rise to immeasurable heights of civilization," represents the future condition of any highly developed culture.[62] The reader has not been altogether unprepared for this eventuality. Acting throughout like senescent parodies of adolescent boys, Pelluther and Dugdale manifest the signs of arrested sexual development that Lombroso took for one of the indices of the regressive atavism "common" to the higher degenerate.[63] Dugdale employs such terms such as "Spellicans" that he has apparently not outgrown since his days as a young scholar at Eton or Rugby or Harrow, and he addresses the elderly Pelluther by his boyhood nickname of "Rattie." One might recall in this context another group of budding gentlemen whose innocent nicknames and adolescent expletives barely mask the brutish bent of their behavior. When Ralph, of *Lord of the Flies* (1954), first realizes that he has become a castaway on a desert island—while he still thinks, that is, that he has been dropped into the middle of the sort of glorious adventure described so often by Defoe, Wyss, and Ballantyne, though the idyll soon transforms itself into nightmare—his irrepressible joy at his unexpected good fortune is expressed in his own boys' language: "Sche-aa-ow!" "Whizzoh!" "Wacco," "Wizard," "Whee-aa-oo!" "Bong!" "Doink!"[64] As William Golding's English schoolboys revert to a primitive state, so Pelluther and Dugdale serve, in word and deed, as de la Mare's sobering reminder that—as Gilbert and Sullian later so glibly put it—"Darwinian Man, though well-behaved, / At best is only a monkey shaved!"[65]

While watching a beggar eat dinner, Pelluther arrives at the same numbing conclusion that has unhinged Dugdale. Unwilling to remain alone in the house once the creature has barricaded itself in an upper chamber, Pelluther invites first his neighbor's caretaker and then the beggar to dine with him. The latter's hunger prevents him from declining an offer that the uneasy caretaker will not accept, and so Pelluther must watch as the "scraggy wretch," as he calls him, guzzles the claret and gnaws "bones and crust like a bony beast"—as he snarls, gobbles, puffs, mouths, and chaws (104). Although he incites him to "eat, drink, and be merry," Pelluther is repelled by "each deplorable action of the rude fellow and sickened at his beastliness" (104) (the slang term "beastliness" here having a wonderfully ironic overtone). And then, just as he concludes that the man's "belly was [his] only truth" (103), Pelluther has an epiphany regarding the creature that is still lurking upstairs: he realizes that it is an "abortion—A-B-O, abortion," raised, as we have noted, from "the belly of the earth" (106). Perhaps Pelluther recognizes in the beggar some vestige of what Havelock Ellis claimed was discernible in the criminal type whose "repulsive, hideous, repugnant" lineaments made an unnamed journalist for *Figaro* (whose experience Ellis recounts) "imagine a sort of abortion."[66] This realization, however, carries with it what Dugdale calls a "pregnant suggestion" (105): the abortion is abominable not merely because it stands as a physical emblem of monstrous (and suppressed) misdeeds, nor because it is so offensive to look at, but because it is, as the insane Dugdale intuits, "neither man nor beast"—and once deciphered, "this vile symbol" hints at the dissolution of the ultimate, and psychologically necessary, boundary that, for the Victorian upper classes, still separated "wonderful man" from the beasts. It is a symbol of a hereditary and inheritable imposition that, before assuming the more material form of the mark of the beast, was taken for original sin.

The notion of the dissolution of necessary boundaries emerges in "A: B: O." in political and cultural as well as in physiological matters. If humanity suffers from indefinition, it follows that the systems it has devised to structure its society and clarify its weltanschauung must partake of this indefinition, offering at best a superficial and ultimately false sense of security and stability. Darwin's theory hastened the demise of an already sorely beset notion—so ubiquitous in English culture and society—of a divinely sanctioned hierarchical system in which class-bound barriers were absolute, permanent, and impenetrable. Having dealt the second of what Freud would come to identify as the "three severe blows" (cosmological, biological, and psychological) by which the "researches of science" had shocked civilization out of its well-worn modes of thinking, Darwin checked the self-glorifying tendency to think that man was somehow "different from animals or superior to them" and that the "acquisitions he [had] subsequently made" had in any way "succeeded in effacing the evidences, both in his physical structure and in his mental dispositions, of his parity with [animals]."[67] As the striker of the third (and, to his mind, the most decisive) blow, Freud himself would frequently return in his own writings to the notion that the same acquisitions—"the whole sum of the achievements and the regulations which distinguish our lives from those of our animal ancestors"—that Darwin had discredited were innately flawed, continually inclining toward the purposelessness, chaos, and barbarity that had necessitated their creation.[68] In "whatever way we may define the concept of civilization," he argued, "it is a certain fact that all the things with which we seek to protect ourselves against the threats that emanate from the sources of suffering are part of that very civilization."[69] Freud's conclusions were not so very different from those of the anthropologists who had preceded him, who were no more hopeful than Chambers had been that "irregular and undue impulses will ever be altogether banished from the system" that (although they thought of it as becoming ever more "just, faithful and benevolent") still had its origins in the "sanguinary, aggressive and deceitful" character of the earlier human society that it had evolved to replace but could never render entirely extinct.[70] Like his precursors, Freud located the source of human discontent—the suffering, the misery, the heightened sense of anxious guilt and the consequent craving for punishment, the conterminous instincts of aggression and self-destruction—in the mysterious depths of a species-wide consciousness (an "original personality . . . still untamed by civilization"), and like them, he thought in terms of a prototypical crime originating in filial disobedience, which, for him, had patricide as its goal.[71]

The first pages of "A: B: O." evoke an atmosphere of guilt and horror along with an anxiety attendant upon a perceived threat to what George Eliot refers to as "the liking to behold society well fenced and adorned with hereditary rank," which she saw as one of the quintessential "English habits of feeling."[72] Just as Pelluther struggles to protect himself from the creature that he has released from its subterranean prison, so he struggles with equal fervor, although far more covertly, to maintain his distance from members of his own society who seem, in his estimation, to be as monstrously predatory as the misshapen creature itself. Pelluther is first lured from his study by a small but feisty boy (a descendant of the old London "Liberty Boys" and a contemporary of Sherlock Holmes's Baker Street Irregulars) who, offended by Pelluther's high-handed and peremptory inquisition, refuses to surrender Dugdale's note. Pelluther does finally obtain the missive, but only after he has been bested in this initial encounter with a slip of a boy (who treats him "like a felon out of stocks" and goes off "lustily . . . whistling the *Marseillaise*"). The introduction of the "Marseillaise" sounds the first note of conflict between Pelluther's innate conservatism and reactionary tendencies and the spirit of social unrest embodied in the French Revolution, which still retained something of its old symbolic significance even in a Victorian Britain in which, as Josephine Guy suggests, historiography was "informed by the Whiggish principle of gradualism which rejected wholesale the ideas of revolutionary change and collective activity [and] which . . . had made the very idea of rupture inconceivable."[73] Initially, Pelluther is eager to route this juvenile disturber of the peace, but later, terrified by the creature that has infiltrated his home, he seeks the companionship of someone from an even lower level of society, enticing the beggar, as we have seen, by mumbling such fragmentary and incoherent phrases (vaguely evocative of Fabian social reforms) as he can muster under the circumstances: "'You shall eat a meal, poor man. How dire is civilization in rags—Evil fortune! Socialism! Millionaires! I'll be bound'" (102). The encounter reveals to the reader, though not to Pelluther, that he and

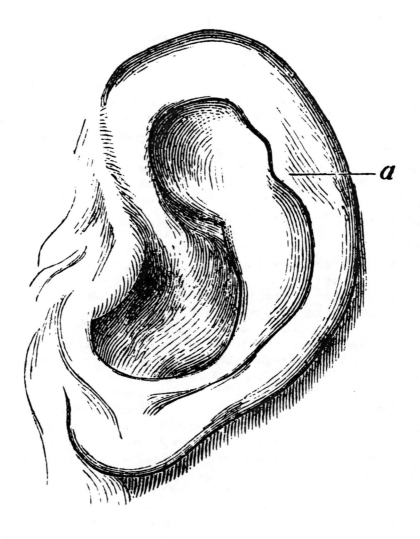

Figure 28a. "Human Ear, . . . a. The projecting point," included as the second figure in the 1871 edition of Charles Darwin's *The Descent of Man*. Courtesy of the Rare Book Collection, The University of North Carolina at Chapel Hill

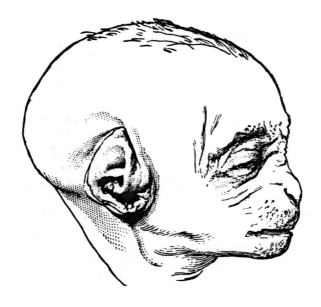

Figure 28b. "Foetus of an Orang. Exact copy of a photograph, shewing the form of the ear at this early age," included as the third figure following that of the human ear in the 1898 edition of Charles Darwin's *The Descent of Man*. Courtesy of the Rare Book Collection, The University of North Carolina at Chapel Hill

his guest are much more similar than he could have thought possible. The beggar attacks his food in much the same spirit with which Pelluther and Dugdale, a little earlier, had undertaken their dig—he guzzling, gnawing, snarling, gobbling, puffing, and chawing like a predatory beast, they digging, tugging, pulling, pushing, hauling, and scraping like two frenzied dogs that, certain of tangible rewards, exert themselves to uncover buried bones. Pelluther sees the beggar as "a bird of prey, a cat, a wild beast, and a man" (103), blind to the fact that he too, poisoned *ab origine,* has been all these things—and to the fact that the taint of the primitive, the contamination to which he has always feared to expose himself, has never been external, but has always lurked within his own being, his own body and soul.

Not merely politically conservative, Pelluther and Dugdale are also *conservators;* as antiquarians they are also preservers of the past and devotees of the dead. Like the boundaries separating the upper from the lower classes, those separating the past from the present dissolve in "A: B: O.," which takes its place among those turn-of-the-century stories poised between a devotion to a past configured as a monument (commemorating the achievements of the descendants of the primitive type whom the monogenistic Morel viewed as "a masterpiece and model of creation") and a distrust of a past conceived of as a charnel house (containing the sordid remnants of bodies hosting diseases sufficiently virulent to wreak a mischievous vengeance on a living present).[74] Like them, too, it asks whether the strength and authority of received traditions and long-standing institutions are legitimately founded on the farsighted wisdom of the giants of old beside whom contemporary men seem sadly diminished, or depend instead on what the anthropologist Sir James Frazer saw as "beliefs which nowadays we should condemn unreservedly as superstitious and absurd."[75] The self-appointed keepers of codes and conventions that conveyed a reassuring but ultimately false sense of order and stability, de la Mare's protagonists are willing victims of the myth of antiquity. Dugdale's letter to Pelluther is meaningless, except for the word "'*Antiquities!*'—'the golden word" (95). The conjunction of the ancestor's map and their own antiquarian lust, however, sets into motion a process of self-discovery—symbolized by the dig—that discloses to the two men that the dead hand of the past can still reach out to destroy them. On the verge of insanity, Dugdale prophesies that "if any suffer, it is you and I who must," his pronouncement recalling Pater's belief that "man's physical organism is played upon not only by the physical conditions about it, but by remote laws of inheritance, the vibration of long-past acts reaching him in the midst of the new order of things in which he lives," itself a post-Darwinian variation on one of Hawthorne's favorite themes—"the wrong-doing of one generation" that "lives into the successive ones, and, divesting itself of every temporary advantage, becomes a pure and uncontrollable mischief."[76]

Pater's conjecture, like Hawthorne's before him and de la Mare's after, has its origin in Exodus, in which a jealous God visits the iniquity of the fathers upon the children "unto the third and fourth generation of them that hate me" (Exod. 20:5).[77] Dugdale and Pelluther are the sons and heirs upon whom the iniquity of the fathers has been visited—which is only appropriate, given that they are fin de siècle versions of the antiquaries (satirized by the elder Samuel Butler) who despise their own parents as "too modern, and no better than Upstarts," preferring to "say to Dust and Worms you are my Father, and to Rottenness thou art my Mother."[78] Antiquarianism can no longer sustain them, however, when, seated in the leaden coffin that once contained the abortion, Dugdale becomes aware of a "deep abstract belief [that] rots into loathing," the belief that what they have uncovered is evidence of "a sin perhaps of yours and of mine." In an apocalyptic world in which the Christian god seemed threatened by a rough beast slouching toward Bethlehem, the unclean sin transmissible from generation to generation is replaced by a beastliness inherent in the doctrine of heredity, which, according to Ellis, had assumed in the latter decades of the century a shape that was "both ancient and modern," given that Plutarch had already expressed it in the following manner: "'That which is engendered is made of the very substance of the generating being, so that he bears in him something which is very justly punished or recompensed for him, for this something is he.' Or again—'There is between the generating being and the generated a sort of hidden identity, capable of justly committing the second to all the consequences of an action committed by the first.'"[79] "Then let parents learn and remember that their prospective children will be the very images of themselves" and their children's "destinies . . . are thus placed completely within [their] control," warned Fowler, the anthropologist's neo-Lamarckian sensibilities betraying themselves in his determined faith in the "NECESSITY" for an individual agency sufficient to countercheck a hereditary predisposition toward degeneracy. The outlook for those who failed to keep this in mind seemed grim, for their sons and heirs were thereby destined to suffer "in consequence of lustful ancestors consigned to the tombs long before their afflicted descendants saw the light."[80]

Eliot might have had individuals like Dugdale and Pelluther in mind when she spoke of those who preferred to see society "well fenced and adorned with hereditary rank." As we have seen, however, their fears about the dissolution of necessary boundaries went well beyond the social to include the sexual, the biological, and the theological. In a deeper sense, "A: B: O." speaks about its protagonists' confrontation with things buried and repressed and occulted, things that come bursting through the tenuous crust of personality (that "thin Earth-rind," as Carlyle called it), importuning interpretation.[81]

For "A: B: O." is also, and perhaps primarily, a story about the act of reading itself—about deciphering hieroglyphic signs and visual symbols, about reconciling what is seen with what is known or thought to be known, about drifting into the liminal space that intervenes between language and the phenomena that it attempts to name—that grey, uncharted area in which interpretation goes forward, in which meaning is loosed from its moorings rather than anchored down, in which every depth of buried signification must be probed. The very title proves an exercise in cryptography and an anticipation, in petto, of the process of discovery and annihilation that the impending engagement with the story will effect. The markings of *A: B: O.* constitute a series of perverse prompters and false starts: having once given us pause to consider what little goes before—and that little being of no very revealing nature where the acronym's (and the story's) meaning is concerned—each colon urges us forward toward a terminating point that aborts the elements of speech and communication themselves. The markings bound material equally esoteric. Although it employs Roman characters, it also retains within itself the remnants of an earlier alphabet, for it begins with the first two letters and ends with the last letter of the Greek, alpha to beta to omega. Encoded within the proleptic device is a portentous coalescence of beginning and ending, of genesis and apocalypse, of the comprehensible and the unspeakable. We are baffled initially by the aborted message that introduces the story, and we begin to make sense of it only when it is too late to exit the tale—only, that is, after we have been caught up in and contaminated by its contents.

In luring us into the attempt to decipher the cryptograph—at once title, creature, and text—and thus to determine the exact correlation between the word and the body, de la Mare establishes an uncomfortable kinship between the story's main characters and the reader who doubles for them. Our own efforts to pull meaning from the belly of the story are echoed in those of the two characters who are continually adjusting ill-fitting spectacles as they struggle to decode missives and maps that will enable them to pull their treasure out of the belly of the earth. The instructions recorded on the fateful "treasure map," conveyed in "divers scrawls in red ink, and crazy figures," baffle but do not dissuade them because they believe that "haste spelt glory" (95-96). Moments before he begins the dig, and equipped with a yard measure, Dugdale commences to read the chart: "Yes tree ten yards N. by seven E. three—semicir—um—square. It's mere A. B. C., 'pon my word." His mutterings, however, make little sense, and the treasure they uncover, of course, proves to be much more than "mere A. B. C."—it is the horrific "A: B: O." Their reading of the various texts is informed by assumptions and expectations not very much more sophisticated than those that other readers once brought to novels by Henty or Marryat, in which haste did spell nothing but glory; or to a primer in which C always does follow B, as B follows A. Thus, "all else" but the provocative reference to antiquities "might be meaningless; as indeed it was," as Pelluther remarks concerning Dugdale's first cryptic message, written in "a fever" and composed of a series of nominals— "*Antiquities!*—the lumber—a mere scrawl"—signaling almost nothing and lacking all coherence outside of the specific context of cultural and historical knowledge necessary for its proper deciphering. Pelluther is not put off by this linguistic underspecification, for he is sufficiently traveled in those realms of knowledge

to suffer little more than a comfortable titillation when confronted by the semantic indeterminacy of the missive. The subsequent transcription of the anomalous map, however, leads not to the anticipated ends and the fixed finalities that
the precursor text promises, but to a grave obscure that complicates the act of
reading itself, here presented as a ritualized convention in which meanings have
been established before any conning need take place; in which knowledge is
secured without the requirement of laborious thinking; in which one asks, as
Pelluther does, "What does it mean?" for mere custom's sake because one does
not expect to learn any more than custom has already taught.

The portrayal of Dugdale's descent into madness proves the more unnerving of the two climaxes following the decoding of the map, for it delivers to the
reader a variation of the "certain shock" consequent, according to Huxley, upon
the caricaturing—"blurring"—of fixed models and types: in this case the literary
conventions, traditional themes, and received structures that de la Mare im-
ports in order that he may violate them, and through them, the complacent
expectations and shopworn assumptions that impede and abort the phenomenon of recognition and revelation that reading is intended to facilitate. Two of
those themes concern buried treasures and antiquarianism—the double-helixed
themes to which we have already referred, both of which are given play in "The
Gold Bug" (1843), Poe's prize-winning tale of ratiocination that employs the
very conventions that the later author would turn to his own purpose. Although
lacking the dry-as-dust pedantry of de la Mare's scholar/adventurers, Poe's
William Legrand is well educated, his misanthropy and familiarity with entomo-
logical lore testifying to his antiquarian sensibilities. Moreover, he is a confident
cryptographer—happily, since a "rare and happy accident" puts him in the way
of a treasure map and, through it, hidden riches. In "The Gold Bug," as in "A: B:
O.," that which is sought is found by midstory, at which point it becomes clear
that the delicate merchandise has its origin in guilt and sin. In both cases the
"climactic" disclosure is subtly deflated, however, for it is not the thematic end
itself, only a means of preparing the way for a subsequent and more sublime
revelation, one which, in both pieces, is predicated upon further deciphering.

When it comes to the nature of what is to be revealed, however, the twinned
texts part company. Poe's Legrand takes possession of a "treasure of incalculable value," a chest containing valuables "heaped . . . promiscuously"—gold ("not
a particle of silver"), diamonds, rubies, and emeralds—and then embarks upon a
lengthy disquisition in which he reveals the necessary conjunction of "common
sense" and "poetical consistency" that had enabled him to decode the instructions that have led him to a "vaster wealth" than even he had anticipated.[82] His
conjectures, as he goes to great lengths to make clear to his audience, have been
correct in almost every detail. A "singular coincidence" (3:829)—a skull discovered on the underside of the fragment of parchment upon which he has drawn a
picture of the "death's head" beetle—baffles him only temporarily, for he becomes certain that "a kind of *connexion*" links these seemingly disparate epi-

sodes and thus begins the process of forging the "great chain" (3:831) that leads him to his fortune. His recognition that the skull is a piratical emblem and that the figure of the goat drawn in the opposite corner of the parchment is the "hieroglyphical signature" (3:833) of Captain Kidd permits him to conclude that "a series of accidents and coincidences . . . *very* extraordinary" (3:833) has put him in possession of a treasure map that once belonged to that notorious pirate. The "whole mystery" is eventually laid bare to him, and he has "little difficulty in solving" (3:831) the other problems that arise. He is sustained by a "deep-seated conviction" that he is not laboring "in vain" (3:843), and he suffers only the bare minimum of setbacks without which his adventure would lack the requisite dramatic leavening—the doubts that threaten but ultimately fail to weaken his certainty that nothing can go amiss because no event, no matter how accidental in seeming, is entirely without significance. Whereas his willfully skeptical friend wanders continually "in the dark" (3:840), early on misconstruing Legrand's insights as a species of "nervous *empressement*" (3:814), a feverish "aberration of mind" (3:817), and "lunacy" (3:819)—and his "bug business" (3:816) as a nonsensical "crochet" (3:813)—Legrand discerns only a gradually evolving web of sense. "[I]rresistibly impressed with a presentiment of some vast good fortune impending" (3:833), armed with a knowledge "amounting to certainty" that ciphers do in fact "convey a meaning," and inspired by the conviction that "it may well be doubted whether human ingenuity can construct an enigma of the kind which human ingenuity may not, by proper application, resolve" (3:834-35), Legrand searches for "the text for my context" (3:833).

As Thomas Dunn English noted long ago, "The Gold Bug" represented Poe's attempt "to carry out his idea of the perfection of the plot," in which, as Poe explained in "The Philosophy of Composition" (1846), "no one point . . . is referrible [*sic*] either to accident or intuition" and the process of literary composition itself proceeds "step by step, to its completion with the precision and rigid consequence of a mathematical problem."[83] Such a perfected plot was, as Poe acknowledged in *Eureka*, "really, or practically, unattainable—but only because it is a finite intelligence that constructs." In other words, the artist's finite intelligence only dimly echoes an infinite one, and the artistic conception reconstructs—modestly, and in miniature—the universe that Poe would come to view as a "plot of God," unflawed because by definition the "plots of God are perfect."[84] Although an incredulous Daniel Kempton dismisses Legrand as a man whose self-fulfilling desire for riches is driven by "the Christian's paranoia, as if temporal reality were a kind of cipher, or encoded message, written for the elect by the hand of God," we might wonder instead whether Legrand, like the narrator of "MS. Found in a Bottle" (1833), is not one of Poe's inspired romantics whose senses have not been sealed to the meaning of the occult hints expressed in an extraordinary series of "accidents" or "coincidences" apparently predetermined by a vast and organizing consciousness whose actions favor Legrand in a way that they did not favor the hapless coadjutors whose bodies are buried with

Kidd's treasure.[85] In any event, Legrand's explication of his methods—"exceedingly clear, and, although ingenious, still simple and explicit" (3:842)—might be said to reproduce stylistically a passage from a leaf of the universal manuscript that contains the plots of God.

Whereas Legrand's intellectual labors are expended in his effort to uncover the text that lends prosaic credence to the context foretold by the telltale clues brought to light with the revelation of the death's-head skull, those of "the two boys in the plot" of de la Mare's story properly begin only *after* an excavation has been "triumphantly" embarked upon. Denied the "confused heap of gold and of jewels" (3:826) with which Legrand's efforts are rewarded, Dugdale begins the process of composing the text called for by the revised context revealed by "the awful terror of the event which has come upon" him. Attempting (in the fashion of Poe's madmen) "to write sanely" and to "discipline" the "mutinous" thoughts that threaten to overmaster him, Dugdale writes a letter in which he admits that his systems and his codes have crumbled and that he is lost: "Science is slunk away shamefaced," he laments; "religion is a withered flower. Oh, my friend, what shall I say! How shall I regain myself?" His most basic expectations as to the underlying nature of things, acquired by rote from the books that now seem to him to be "disconsolate friends offended," have failed him and are now superseded by an oppressive sense that the world is in fact the sort of place that Pater had described, in his imaginary portrait "Duke Carl of Rosenmold" (1887), as being "buried . . . made and re-made of the dead—its entire fabric of politics, of art, of custom, being essentially heraldic 'achievements,' dead men's mementoes."[86]

Dugdale's mad ravings constitute a final text that more accurately renders the proportions of the frightful universe concerning which his prefatory letter offers only broad hints. Huddled in the casket and clutching a Bible to his side, he commences a rambling, disjointed monologue—part funeral sermon, part philosophical disquisition—which begins with the quotation from Job that will serve as his text:

> "'For we are but of yesterday and know nothing because our days upon earth are a shadow.' What is life, Pelluther? A vain longing for death. What is beauty? A question of degree. And sin is in the air,—child of disease and death and springing-up and hatred of life. Fawn hair has beauty and as for bones; surely less for the worms. Worms! through lead? Pelluther, my dear old Pell. Through lead? . . .
>
> "But the sunlight has no meaning to me now. . . . That breeder of corruption, tall here and a monstrous being, walks under my skull strangling all the other beings, puny and sapless. I have one idea, conception, vivid faintness, a fierce red horrid idea—and a phenomenon, too. You see, it is when a deep abstract belief rots into loathing, when hope is eaten away by horrors of sleep and a mad longing for sleep—Mad!

Yet fawn hair is not without beauty; provided, Pelluther, provided—
through lead?" [107-8]

Dugdale's rantings, though enigmatic, are susceptible to reconstruction, in
part because they invoke—as simultaneous points of reference and departure—
the very texts that had until then formed the basis of his experience. Memorable
to him, clutched to his bosom as a type of his own experiences even as his
madness impends, is the story of Job, whose lamentations are echoed throughout Dugdale's *de profundis*. Just as Dugdale rejects the "sunlight" as something
holding "no meaning to me now," so Job curses the day of his birth, saying, "Let
that day be darkness" (Job 3:4), because "it shut not up the doors of my mother's
womb" (3:10), leaving him to be born, live his life, suffer, and be left at length to
wonder why he had not "died . . . from the womb" (3:11). Why, he wonders,
could his not have been "an hidden untimely birth" so that he could have been
one of the "infants which never saw light" (3:16)? Taking the place of the "wretched
abortion" within the chest that he had planned to rebury once the "darkness
comes down to cloak our horrid task from the eyes of the world," Dugdale also
apparently comprehends, at last, that there is some connection between himself and the creature whose hidden untimely rebirth has destroyed his very sanity. And just as, with a "horde of thoughts" pressing upon him, Dugdale contemplates the "awful terror of the event that has come upon" him and Pelluther, so
Job is stunned to think that though bereft of "safety," "rest," and "quiet; yet trouble
came" (3:26): "For the thing which I greatly feared is come upon me, and that
which I was afraid of is come unto me" (3:25).

Job, however, is eventually "comforted," for the "evil that the Lord had
brought upon him" (Job 42:11) passes away, and he is rewarded with "twice as
much as he had before" (42:10) his sufferings, granted answers to his plaintive
questionings, and given a glimpse of "things too wonderful for me, which I knew
not" (42:3): "I have heard of thee by the hearing of the ear: but now mine eye
seeth thee" (42:5). Dugdale, on the other hand, has caught a final glimpse of
things too horrific for him, things of which he knew nothing, and his confused
monologue suggests something of the depths that he has plumbed and the spiritual degeneration that he has suffered as a consequence. Even in the midst of
his despair, Job finds comfort in the thought that the grave will consume the
sinner, that the "womb shall forget him; the worm shall feed sweetly on him; he
shall be no more remembered; and wickedness shall be broken as a tree" (Job
24:20). Dugdale's compulsive reiteration of a single question—"Worms! through
lead? . . . Through lead? . . . —through lead?"—serves as a fragmentary meditation on corruption and on the reality that, because worms cannot penetrate
lead, the "pestilent secret sin" that should have been consumed long ago, and so
remained forever hidden "from the eyes of the sane," has instead lived on, "fes-
tering, weaving snares, befouling the wholesome air," awaiting the day when it
could "[creep] out and [go] stalking midst healthy men" (106). In a world in

which worms cannot eat through lead, in which corpses do not decay, the litany of questions and answers appearing in the burial service of the Church of England's *Boke of Common Prayer*—"How aryse the dead? with what body shal they come? Thou foole, that whiche thou soweste is not quickened, excepte it dye"—lose their power to console the mourner with the assurance that death and decay are necessary precursors to eternal life.[87]

The recipient of a different order of revelation, Dugdale acquires the spiritual insight that transforms him into a raving lunatic and strips him of the abilities that the Victorians valued most highly: the ability to be rational, to maintain one's wits in the face of unfathomable darkness (even as one denied that such darkness existed), and to continue to struggle to make sense of what might in fact prove in the end to be utterly incomprehensible. He is a type of "the sick soul" whose plight William James analyzes in *The Varieties of Religious Experience*, which concerns itself with "the more regenerate sorts of happiness," "the phenomenon of conversion or religious regeneration," and the obverse of this state of "healthy-mindedness": with "a condition of negativity and deadness" and a "consciousness of evil." To the sick soul suddenly overwhelmed not by "the conception or intellectual perception of evil, but [by] the grisly blood-freezing heart-palsying sensation of it close upon" him, the face of nature is transfigured "in the reverse direction" and "the whole expression of reality" transformed: "The world now looks remote, strange, sinister, uncanny. Its color is gone, its breath is cold, there is no speculation in the eyes it glares with. . . . 'I can no longer find myself; I walk, but why? . . . I weep false tears, I have unreal hands: the things I see are not real things.' Such are expressions that naturally rise to the lips of melancholy subjects describing their changed state."[88] Dugdale is one of those melancholy subjects who may be said to have undergone an *inverted* conversion experience, which imparts neither the vision of "wonderful things" that makes Job's latter days happier than his earlier ones nor the "glow-worm-like conception of that truth" that Legrand's adventure brings to "so magnificent a demonstration" (Poe 3:829), but rather "a deep abstract belief that rots into loathing." In the end he is obsessed with one "fierce red horrid idea," which is "a phenomenon, too" and seems to appertain to the "fawn hair" to which his wandering thoughts, otherwise focused on the "monstrous being" that "walks under my skull strangling all the other beings," return as to a riddle in need of solution. If, as Darwin speculated in a notebook jotting of 1838, "nature does nothing in vain"; and if it is also true, as Sir Thomas Browne suggested (in a passage from *Religio Medici* that Darwin had copied into his notebook, just lines before his own comment on the expediency of nature's efforts), that nothing in nature is "ugly" or "mis-shapen," because "Nature is the Art of God"; then only false expectations or flawed conceptions of the nature of God could blind one to the beauty of fawn hair.[89] Trapped in a post-Darwinian world, annihilated by the revelation that "fawn hair has beauty," Dugdale finds in the face that nature has turned upon him evidence that, although perfect of its kind, the plot of the uni-

verse is more sinister than he had been led to expect, and the inevitable conclusion is that the contriver thereof must be a *monstrorum artifex*. Again, we find
ourselves in Poe's universe, in which not "Man" but "the Conqueror Worm" is
the hero of the "tragedy" that bears his name, and in which "much of Madness,
and more of Sin, / And Horror" proves to be "the soul of the plot."

Just as (so Müller tells us) it was "the custom of Nebuchadnezzar to have
his name stamped on every brick that was used during his reign in erecting his
colossal palaces" so that, when they fell into ruins and the ruins "were carried
away for building new cities," other kings might discover "the clear traces of that
royal signature," so the face of the abortion bears the stamp of its creator—and
in the same way, the prose of Dugdale's final speech bears not only the markings of his insanity but also the vestiges of his worldview, his knowledge, his
experience, his most basic assumptions in the realms of theology, biology, aesthetics—structures all suddenly antiquated, all suddenly collapsing into ruin.[90]
The passage containing Dugdale's appositional renaming of the "sin" that satu-
rates "the air" draws its distinctive cadences from a repetition, or parataxis—
"child of diseases and death and springing-up and hatred of life"—that is characteristic of archaic prose styles in which simple or "naive" coordination conveys
faith-driven truths. Pater too had employed a paratactical construction in the
section of his "Conclusion" in which he charts a movement from birth to death
to a kind of resurrection, noting (in a line powerfully reminiscent of Dugdale's)
that the "elements of which we are composed" are "driven in many currents;
and birth and gesture and death and the springing of violets from the grave are
but a few out of ten thousand resultant combinations" (emphasis mine).[91] It is
the same construction that we find in the burial service in *The Boke of Common Prayer*, which tells how, on Judgment Day, "the trumpe shall blowe, and
the dead shall ryse incorruptible, and we shall be chaunged" (205). Both de la
Mare's story and Pater's manifesto appropriate the language and rhythms of
biblical speech in order to imbue their own heretical gospels with an authority
that they would otherwise lack. Exploring the occult means by which "a sharp
and importunate reality" dissolves into "a group of impressions . . . unstable,
flickering, inconsistent," which in turn are reduced to "a single sharp impression," Pater attempts to characterize the "experience" through which one might
achieve "a variegated, dramatic life."[92] In the world according to Pater, the mysterious process whereby one passes swiftly from the external world of concrete
phenomena to the inner world of thought and feeling may be understood only by
an act of faith like that called for in *The Boke of Common Prayer*, which reveals
the "misterie" whereby "thys corruptyble must put on incorrupcion: and this
mortall must put on immortalitie," at which time death will be "swallowed up in
victory" (205). For the older faith that would have discovered "meanings" in the
mysteries expressed in the archaic structures and cadences of such ancestral
texts, "A: B: O." substitutes uncertainty, skepticism, and doubt. At the last,
Dugdale could not answer "why stande we alwaye then in ieopardie" (294); could

no longer believe that "there is one maner of fleshe of men, and other maner of fleshe of beastes" (204); and would have strong reason to doubt that what "is sowen in corrupcion, . . . ryseth agayne in incorrupcion," or that what "is sowen in dishonoure, . . . ryseth agayne in honour," or that what "is sowen a naturall bodye, . . . ryseth agayne a spyrituall bodye" (205). Linguistically and stylistically reversionary, the language of Dugdale's final speech undermines "the comfortable faith in words' reference to things" and displays the "ruptures and discontinuities" that, according to Gayatri Spivak, are uniquely characteristic of the true *decadence* of a literary language.[93]

Inasmuch as he would later remind us "of an important truth; namely, that the first essential purpose in literature is to delight us," we ought not to be surprised that the mature de la Mare would not readily have admitted to having nursed such peccant fancies.[94] We can also begin to appreciate, however, why the young de la Mare—despite the fact that he would soon be designated the poet of childhood—might have been fascinated by the image of a buried, and still living, abortion. In one sense the story served as a boyish prank, the expression of a rebellious youth attempting to cast himself, however surreptitiously, in the role of what one contemporary critic decried as the "latterday literary abortion, the youthful *décadent*."[95] The desire to place oneself beyond the pale of bourgeois respectabilities—or at least to appear to do so—would have been understandable in a young and self-conscious artist looking to make his mark in the realm of English letters at the turn of the century—or, in any event, before Wilde's 1895 trial made flouting conventional wisdom seem a dangerous pastime. Holbrook Jackson reminds us, for example, of Max Beerbohm's belief that many of his own "earlier drawings, which seemed morbid and horrible, were the outcome of a very natural boyish desire to shock conventional folk."[96] "A: B: O." is also, however, one of those texts called for by the irrevocably altered contexts—social, cultural, and intellectual—that Darwin, Huxley, Haeckel, and others had made it impossible to ignore. If nothing else, "A: B: O." remains as one of those "poor relics" that, "simply because they served their temporary purpose, but no other, . . . are saliently characteristic of their day." These are de la Mare's own words, written thirty years after the composition of "A: B: O." in his introduction to *The Eighteen-Eighties*. These poor relics—"the still-born, the dry-as-dust, the dejected inmates of the 2*d*. box," he calls them—"could have come into being only when and where they did."[97] "A: B: O.," and stories like it—such consummate products of their place and time—open for us one more window on the fin de siècle *mentalité*, providing us with important insights into the uneasy period during which the Victorian age was in its death throes even as the coming beast was waiting to be born.

3

Unsealing Sense in Henry James's
The Turn of the Screw

If we look merely into the book of nature, death appears an inscrutible [sic] mystery, a strange and unaccountable anomaly among the arrangements of Providence; but if we look into the book of God's word, we find a satisfactory explanation of the phenomenon.

W.B. Clark, *Asleep in Jesus* (1856)

'Twas like a Maelstrom, with a notch,
That nearer, every Day,
Kept narrowing its boiling Wheel . . .

Emily Dickinson (c. 1862)

AFFORDED PRIDE OF PLACE IN de la Mare's story—which it would be easy though incorrect to characterize as a grotesquely trivial inquest into the fin de siècle culture of decadence—is a character whose experience recalls similarly transmogrifying events in which bodies (physical and narrative) register in their extremity a catastrophic dissolution of ontological security: a literary event common to and saliently indicative of the late-nineteenth-century moment that bore witness to what George Levine describes as "epistemology . . . in crisis," wherein "knowing is dying and killing, as it surprisingly becomes in much nineteenth-century narrative."[1] One thinks in this context of Ludwig Holly's faithful man-servant, Job, whose face—one "only had to look at . . . it"—faithfully transcribes the terror of a man "utterly broken down beneath [the] last dire sight" of the once resplendent Ayesha emerging from the pillar of life a "hideous mockery," "dreadful relic," and "shocking epitome of human beauty and human life." Another unwilling witness of "man unveiled," Stevenson's Hastie Lanyon knows that his life is forfeit—"shaken to its roots"—after, as he says, "I saw what I saw, I heard what I heard" of Jekyll's transformation: "I feel that my days are numbered, and that I must die" (his language here darkly reminiscent of God's stark statement to Moses in Exodus 33:20 that "there shall no man see me, and live").[2] Then there is Wells's Edward Prendick, a "Man Alone" who returns from his sojourn on Dr. Moreau's island less definitively though no less essentially dead to the world; or Basil Hallward, Dorian Gray, and Kurtz, the consequences of whose fateful inquiries into the unknown are too well known to require review; or even, several decades later, Robert Blake, in Lovecraft's "Haunter of the Dark" (1936), in whom body and memoirs (the "blindly scrawled entries" and "frenzied jottings" of a "spasmodically contracted right hand") converge, each made textuary by the markings of convulsive fright.[3] Ancestor to them all is, of course, Poe's nameless author of the manuscript found in a bottle, who has just time enough to record his recognition that his "destruction" will coincide with the attainment of "some exciting knowledge—some never-to-be-imparted secret" to be born of his imminent delivery into "the grasp of the whirlpool" and his "going down!" into the same depths that Emily Dickinson expected to explore once "a Plank in Reason, broke," and, in her imagined postmortem state, she "dropped down, and down— / And hit a World, at every plunge, / And Finished knowing—then—."[4] As tale tellers faced with the dilemma anticipated by Poe's plumber of the depths of the maelstrom (who laments that he will "never be able to tell [his] old companions on shore about the mysteries" he encounters) and desirous, in addition, of setting forth an ingenious way of disclosing some portion of the finalities that are without exception confined to the grave (so the final dash in Dickinson's final line hints), authors sometimes substitute characters who, like Marlow, are permitted to draw back their "hesitating foot" from "the edge" of experience and who are therefore allowed to escape death although limited thereby to a lesser order of knowledge.[5] Before he loses himself a second time, and this time permanently—"as everybody knows now, he has never returned"—

within the epilogue premonitory of a future "black and blank," Wells's Time
Traveller returns from an absence of several hundred thousand years' duration
"greyer" and with "hair disordered." He is seared, that is, with the telltale marker
of near knowing borne by Coleridge's ancient "grey-beard loon"; or Poe's narrator whose hair, once "jetty black, . . . raven-black," has grown white in the space
of the day it takes him to descend into the maelstrom; or Rider Haggard's Leo
Vincey, whose hair, once "of the ruddiest gold," turns "grey" and then "snow
white" in the immediate aftermath of Ayesha's accelerated deteriorative evolution; or Kipling's Peachey Carnehan, who returns from Kafiristan with a "drawn
face, surmounted by a shock of grey hair"; or Stoker's Jonathan Harker, whose
"whitening hair" frames a face grown ashen in response to the narrative that
reveals his wife's defilement.[6]

Rejecting the "old story of the Faustian overreacher" as insufficient to explain or justify "the persisting story of self-abnegation for the sake of truth" that
is ubiquitous in the literature of horror and manifests itself too in the "oppressive fatality" that is so common in Victorian fiction in general, Levine traces the
shared metaphor (common to the epistemological and metaphorical traditions
at work in scientific discourse and literature, respectively) of "'death' or self-
destruction" to an "ideal of objectivity to which science professed allegiance," an
ideal predicated on "the paradoxical assertion of death as a condition of knowing."[7] The senses being suspect because unreliable—so the argument went—
they prevent access to the very knowledge of which, for the Comtean positiv-
ists, they were assumed to be the sole source and conductor. Citing Darwin's
self-effacing assertion that he had attempted to write his own autobiography "as
if I were a dead man in another world looking back at my own life" as an example of the phenomenon whereby "knowledge . . . becomes an odd process of
alienation and possession," Levine goes on to suggest that, in the tradition of
Western positivism, "observation, the first requisite of knowledge, the means
by which it registers in 'experience,' entails both the creation of an 'other' and
possession of it. To observe oneself one must stand outside oneself, divide oneself in two. The act of knowing becomes an act of repossession. So to know is
both to kill and to possess. If you really want to know, you will have to die
(although if you die you can't know), and along the way you will probably have
to kill the thing you want to know."[8]

That Henry James's notorious 1898 exploration of horror (an "excursion
into chaos," as he called it) coils itself about the related issues of discovery,
discernment, death, and possession is perhaps nowhere more temptingly suggested than in the desperately victorious declaration—"*I* have you"—in which the
governess claims as a "supreme surrender . . . and tribute to [her] devotion"
what is surely the most testatory and least soluble "revelation" of the meaning
of the events she describes in the manuscript that she leaves behind: "'Peter
Quint—you devil! . . . *Where?*'"[9] What follows her charge's punctuated cry—part
declarative, part imprecatory, part interrogatory, all parts equally irreducible—is

a series of inversionary statements in which loss is refigured as recovery: "With the stroke of the loss I was so proud of he uttered the cry of a creature hurled over an abyss, and the grasp with which I recovered him might have been that of catching him in his fall"; dispossession as repossession: "I caught him, yes, I held him—it may be imagined with what a passion; but at the end of a minute I began to feel what it truly was that I held"; and irresolution as finality, the concluding word of the story—"stopped"—providing the governess with the occasion for and point d'appui of a narrative in which she struggles to reclaim what the little heart, once "dispossessed" (198), still withholds: access, that is, to its closely guarded store of secrets.

One suspects that any clear statement that Miles might have discovered at the story's close would have seemed as ludicrously inadequate, and as incapable of bearing the weight of emotion that drives the governess's urgent inquiries, as that which Mrs. Grose, "in her simple sharpness," poses as the cause of the boy's dismissal from school—"He stole!" (184). The droll pallor of her hypothesis invites precisely the sort of contempt that James anticipated as his artistic reward had what he owned as "*my* bad things" proven insufficiently bad, shrinking instead "to the compass of some particular brutality, some particular immorality, some particular infamy portrayed" ("Preface," 176).[10] The governess's starkly unanswered questions—"What then did you do?" "But to whom did you say [things]?" "Were they then so many?" "What *were* these things?" "Whom do you mean by 'he'?" (195-97)—seem in themselves disproportionately scant when measured against the critical mass of narrative that comes to contain them. Yet, "the scales of the balance hang with the right evenness" (the phrasing is James's, drawn from his juxtaposing of the familiar and the strange ["Preface," 164]) once they are weighted with the governess's interpretive energies, as she herself acknowledges: "It seems to me indeed," she confesses, "in retrospect, that by the time the morrow's sun was high I had restlessly read into the facts before us almost all the meaning they were to receive from subsequent and more cruel occurrences" (116-17). However blind she may appear in other things, she betrays in this admission a Jamesian sensibility, inclined as she is to appreciate what James identifies in the preface to *The Aspern Papers* (it serves the same critical function for *The Turn of the Screw*) as "that thinness" that allows him space enough in which to insinuate his "artist's interest," deciding "what he shall add to [the bare facts of intimation] and how he shall *turn* them" ("Preface," 170, 163, emphasis mine). Moreover, her qualification—"in retrospect"—establishes her position, temporally, in relation to the precipitating events of her narrative as roughly analogous to that which James seeks to occupy spatially in relation to his own literary sources and shadows: that is, in sight of "a palpable imaginable *visitable* past—in the nearer distances and the clearer mysteries, the marks and signs of a world we may reach over to as by making a long arm we grasp an object at the other end of our own table" ("Preface," 164). One envisions, in retrospective consideration of this aesthetic condition, the table that comes at last to

mark the contested ground (within his conceit, James inverts the space that
figures in his preface as "the common expanse, . . . firm and continuous") between the governess and her opponent ("So we circled about, with terrors and
scruples, like fighters not daring to close" [192]), who is also the object of her
desire: the boy whom, "with a moan of joy," she variously "enfolded," "drew . . .
close," "held" to her breast (193), and finally, with a "veritable leap" (197) across
the space that the table interrupts, presses possessively and conclusively against
herself.

Herself within reach "in the tremor of [her] hands, at arms' length" from her
heart's desire—"the human soul" (193) that waits at the other end of the table at
which she comes at last to sit, in "high state" (187)—the governess eventually
consigns her story to the guardianship of Douglas, who is in turn so fully within
reach of his own narrative's subject ("She was a most charming person. . . . She
was my sister's governess. . . . She was the most agreeable woman I've ever
known in her position. . . . I found her at home on my coming down the second
summer. I was much there that year . . . and we had, in her off-hours, some
strolls and talks in the garden—talks in which she struck me as awfully clever
and nice" [83]) that his subsequent "reading" of her text seems to capture her
with "a fine clearness that was like a rendering to the ear of the beauty of his
author's hand" (88). So persuasive is his conviction that her story "won't tell . . .
in any literal, vulgar way" (84), that the unnamed narrator into whose hands the
manuscript ultimately falls avers in his turn that without "a few words of prologue" a "proper intelligence" (85) of the governess's narrative is impossible
(and behind them all lurks James, still within reach of the "homely pretext" and
the "distinguished host" that put him in possession of "the scantest of fragments,"
"the precious pinch . . . extracted from an old silver snuffbox and held between
finger and thumb," the "germ, gleaming there in the wayside dust of life," deftly
to be "picked up" ["Preface," 169-70]). Still, nothing he can relate concerning
Douglas's prefatory warning that the story is "beyond everything" for "sheer
terror," for "dreadful—dreadfulness," and for "general uncanny ugliness and horror and pain" (82) adequately prepares the reader for the verbal assault leveled
in and through Miles's outraged and outrageous deathbed cry. This is not to say
that what James referred to in his notebook as the "strangely gruesome effect"
of the governess's story does not build steadily from the earliest stages of its
telling: from her receipt of the letter hinting that Miles's may have been a contaminating presence at his boarding school, to her growing certainty that there
are "depths, depths!" (121) that are penetrated by each succeeding turn of the
screw—with the steady accretion, that is, of rumored facts possessed (to her) of
terrible implications.[11] Quint, for example, "did what he wished . . . [with] them
all" (124)—with Miss Jessel and the housemaids, and particularly with Miles,
whom he had sought to "spoil" (115), while Miles "was with the man" and Flora
"with the woman," the arrangement "[suiting] them all" (129). In this sense
James's story is an ironic exemplar of the romance as Hawthorne defined it—its

"high truth . . . never any truer, and seldom any more evident, at the last page
than at the first"; or of Poe's belief that the desideratum of analytical composition is achieved only when the work proceeds "step by step, to its completion
with the precision and rigid consequence of a mathematical problem"; or yet
again, of the "architectural conception of work," a "condition of literary art,"
which, as Pater mapped it, "foresees the end in the beginning and never loses
sight of it, and in every part is conscious of all the rest, till the last sentence does
but, with undiminished vigour, unfold and justify the first"; or still again, of James's
own "sense of the romantic," which, as he defined it (typically vaporously), is
contingent upon the "haunting presences . . . of one's past . . . living on, . . . up to
our own day," the "romance-value" conferred by "long survival" ("Preface," 160-
61).[12] The governess's narrative begins at just the moment when Miles's heart
(and, by extension, her experience at Bly) is "stopped"; and, conversely, the
"depths" of her story are just discernible beneath the pellucid surface of its beginning; yet the fact remains that nothing in the preceding pages sufficiently
braces the careful reader for the shock of horror that Miles's death delivers.

His final cryptic cry may be said to embody what James described in one
letter as "'Terror' *peut bien en être*": "the dear old sacred terror" that the "new
crop or new type" of ghost story, to his mind, failed miserably to convey, so that
the story that contains it, in turn, may be thought of as constituting James's
"lament for a beautiful lost form" ("Preface," 169).[13] True to his manner, however, James subjects to "cold artistic calculation" ("Preface," 172) not only the
literary form ("the literature of horrors," as he calls it in his review of Mary
Elizabeth Braddon's *Aurora Floyd* [1865])[14] whose loss he laments, but also the
cultural traditions and attitudes that facilitated its emergence. In other words, the
Gothic tradition, the Victorian *ars moriendi* (the publicly ritualized and autho-
rized enactment, one might say, of the twin actions of dying and knowing), and
the cult of the child—each a mystery, a mark, a sign of a palpable imaginable
visitable cultural past of which James's reader remains within reach—are invoked, inverted, and reconstituted in the climactic death scene, the final slight
but scandalous turn of the screw that succeeds in transforming James's story
from "a fairy-tale pure and simple" to an "excursion into chaos": a hybridized
"*amusette*" whose charm is reserved for "the jaded, the disillusioned, the fastidi-
ous"—in short, for "the distracted modern mind" ("Preface," 171-72).

Douglas fires his audience's imagination by employing several stock performative
strategies, exercising a "quiet art" that lends the "utmost price" to and assures
the "triumph" of his delivery. He hedges and hunts for words, repeatedly inter-
rupting himself or weighing one word against another, and then rejecting both:

> "It's beyond everything. Nothing at all that I know touches it."
> "For sheer terror?" I remember asking.
> . . . He passed his hand over his eyes, made a little wincing grimace.

"For dreadful—dreadfulness! . . . For general uncanny ugliness and horror and pain."

"Well then," I said, "just sit right down and begin."

He turned round to the fire, gave a kick to a log, watched it an
instant. Then as he faced us again: "I can't begin. I shall have to send to
town." There was a unanimous groan at this. [82]

He continually defers the satisfaction of his listener's curiosity and indeed height-
ens it by avoiding the actual telling of the story of which he has afforded only
tantalizing glimpses:

"Who was it she was in love with?"

"The story will tell," I took upon myself to reply.

"Oh, I can't wait for the story!"

"The story won't tell," said Douglas. . . .

"Won't you tell, Douglas?" somebody else inquired.

He sprang to his feet again. "Yes—to-morrow. Now I must go to
bed. Good night." And, quickly, catching up a candlestick, he left us
slightly bewildered. [84]

The bait that attracts his audience, however, is the actual subject of his story:
that is, a "visitation" that had "fallen on a child" (81). Douglas makes no secret of
the obvious appeal of his subject, openly acknowledging that a "little boy, at so
tender an age, adds a particular touch . . . [and] gives the effect another turn of
the screw" (81), and when he asks what effect *two* children give to a ghost story,
his audience is ready to respond: "two turns!" (81). They need little prompting,
versed as they are in Gothic conventions and in the Victorian celebration of
childhood, both of which provide an aura or penumbra for his question. The
mock Gothic is at work throughout Douglas's story (and, by extension, throughout James's story, which from its outset—"The story had held us, round the fire,
sufficiently breathless" (81)—puts to ironic uses the very Gothic traditions and
modes to which James draws mock-affectionate attention in his preface—in his
allusion, that is, to "the starting-point," itself burrowed within the layered contexts that include "the circle, one winter afternoon, round the hall-fire of a grave
old country-house"; the talk that "turned . . . to apparitions and night-fears"; and
the solicitation "for something seasonable by the promoters of a periodical dealing in the time-honoured Christmas-tide toy" ["Preface," 169-70]). Douglas acts
the part of the necromancer and palingenesist as, "with immense effect" he commences reading to the "hushed little circle on the night" (85) several days after
striking the spark of his audience's imagination with the information that he
possesses a manuscript telling a story "quite too horrible" (82). Their ready
responses—"'Oh, how delicious,' cried one of the women" (82)—bespeak their
recognition that theirs is the role of percipient listener—consumed by "a rage of

curiosity" (85), hungry to decipher and decode elusive hints and partial revelations, but also confident that the story will impart to them what James calls the
"sense, all charming" of "the terrible 'pleasant'" ("Preface," 169-70), the vaguely
erotic but finally nonthreatening feeling that James's disciple M.R. James would
later describe as "pleasantly uncomfortable."[15]

At the time when *The Turn of the Screw* made its first appearance, both
audiences—the fictive and the actual—were equally familiar with the conventions
governing the Victorian cult of childhood. Although it accorded with their larger
belief in the perfectibility of man, the tendency to sentimentalize and idealize
childhood did not, of course, originate with the Victorians, for the influence of
the French philosophes and the German romantics had already begun to shape
cultural attitudes during the preceding century. Rousseau's insistence in *Emile*
(1762) that "childhood has its own ways of seeing, thinking, and feeling" and
that "nothing is more foolish than to try and substitute our ways [for them]"
anticipates what would later become a commonplace: that children represented
a different, and even a higher, order of being and consciousness.[16] Blake associated childhood with divinity, and Arthur Schopenhauer, some years later, associated it with something equally outré: "Every child is, to a certain extent, a
genius," he observed, "and every genius is, to a certain extent, a child."[17] Thomas
Jefferson Hogg reminds us of the afternoon stroll in which Shelley sought to
prove definitively that infants must retain visions of another world, memories
that fall away from us as we grow older. Having caught hold on Magdalen Bridge
of a several-weeks-old infant, he insisted on asking its mother, "Will your baby
tell us anything about pre-existence, Madam?" When she demurred, Shelley
insisted that the baby *could* "speak if he [would], for he is only a few weeks old":
"He may fancy perhaps that he cannot, but it is only a silly whim; he cannot
have forgotten entirely the use of speech in so short a time; the thing is absolutely impossible." The baby failing to relent, the exasperated poet exclaimed,
"How provokingly close are those new-born babes!"[18] By the mid-nineteenth
century, both child and mother had come to be thought of as mediating figures
retaining intuitive and imaginative powers as well as a natural vitality and a
natural (if untutored) piety. As Ruskin saw it, "childhood often holds a truth in its
feeble fingers, which the grasp of manhood cannot retain, and which it is the
pride of utmost age to recover."[19] Wells's characterization of the Eloi may owe
something to the growing conviction that human evolution would reveal itself in
neoteny—in the progressive juvenilization, that is, manifesting itself as an evolutionary phenomenon within a particular species.[20] Seeking biological evidence
for the fact that "the child is really the 'father of the man,' for the modern man is
becoming more and more of a child," Alexander Francis Chamberlain argued in
his turn-of-the-century study of the evolution of man that (within an individual
lifetime, and not within that of the species, which was as a whole, he believed,
entering a neotenous phase) "upward zoological evolution" is most pronounced
in infancy, whereas, with maturation, humankind forfeits "the comparatively

ultra-human character of . . . early childhood": "the 'Fall,' if there be one for the race, is in the descent from the high promise of childhood to the comparative barrenness of senility."[21] To die as a child, then, is to avoid the several "falls" (biological and spiritual) that lie in wait for humankind; and to enter prematurely into that final sleep is to recover early from what A.S. Byatt's nineteenth-century fictitious poet, Christabel LaMotte, conceives of as the regressive "*stumble into the brute sleep of* adult truth."[22] Such, at least, is the message contained in the Victorian comfort books that are the subject of a study by Judith Plotz: "since the loveliness of childhood is obliterated by maturation into adulthood," she writes, "the child who survives into adulthood has, in a sense, died as a child," whereas "the child who dies remains quintessentially childlike—indeed, he is the only lasting child."[23] The dead child, then, was thought twice blessed: granted everlasting life in the memories of those left behind, he or she was deemed far more likely than those who reached adulthood to secure eternal bliss. The Victorians would have remembered, in this regard, the words of Matthew: "Except ye be converted, and become as little children, ye shall not enter into the kingdom of heaven" (Matt. 18:3).

If the living child, then, was understood to be a figure of authority, how much more so the dying child, who, still trailing clouds of glory and imbued with something of the divine afflatus, sinks into the visionary state of grace in which, in the words of one nineteenth-century minister, "hovering as it were midway between earth and heaven, he catches a glimpse of the spiritual world, before he leaves the material."[24] The ardor with which the Victorians celebrated childhood was to be matched only by the fervor with which they celebrated the hour of death, and the intersection of the two—the cult of childhood and the *ars moriendi*—provided for some of the most affective deathbed scenes in Victorian literature. As John Kucich reminds us in his analysis of Little Nell's death in Dickens's *The Old Curiosity Shop* (1841), the Victorians—viewing death as "the most important event of an individual lifetime" and furthermore throwing "themselves into their love of death with a specificity of emotion . . . that signals some greater significance"—"made the etiquette of mourning and burial into an elaborate catechism."[25] Dickens provides us with one version of this ritualized performance in the chapter of *Dombey and Son* (1848) in which Paul Dombey learns "What the Waves Were Always Saying." Lying "tranquilly" in his bed, Paul studies the sunbeams that dance on the walls of his bedroom "like golden water." As he grows weaker, he begins to associate them with "the dark dark river [which rolls] towards the sea in spite of him."[26] Various visitors drift in and out of his flickering consciousness: old Mrs. Pipchin becomes Miss Tox, who becomes Louisa Chick. As his death approaches, he makes various requests: asking, for example, to see his banished nurse, Polly Toodles, and pleading that his father should "remember Walter," for Paul was "fond of Walter!" (224). Locked in the arms of his beloved sister Florence, he can at last hear what the waves are always saying only as he catches sight of eternity: "tell them that the print upon the stairs at school, is not

Divine enough. The light about the head is shining on me as I go!" (225). The scene largely adheres to conventional deathbed rituals: Paul is surrounded by mourning relatives, to whom he makes his final farewells as well as his final requests (which are understood to be sacrosanct), and his spoken behests are followed by less intelligible murmurings that suggest that, for him, the pall of mortality that obscures the afterlife is being lifted. Those ways in which the scene fails to conform to deathbed norms—for example, the fact that his relatives mourn individually rather than communally—are equally significant for what they reveal about the distressed state of Mr. Dombey's domestic affairs. (It is worth noting as well that Mr. Dombey's implacability is evidenced in his subsequent willful failure to honor his dying son's request.)

Such theatrical performances were not limited to Victorian fiction. Margarete Holubetz points out that "the ritual celebration of death . . . was the ideal to which people on their death-beds aspired."[27] Excerpts from memoirs, journals, and letters indicate that most people had absorbed and were prepared to enact the rites of death and dying. Thus, the mother of the American child-poet Frances ["Fannie"] Lavinia Michener records that just as her daughter's "sweet disposition manifested itself in the patience with which she bore her sufferings," her purity and state of grace were evident at the hour of her death.[28] Like Paul Dombey, Fannie bids a tender adieu to her relatives and exacts certain promises from them, telling some "to take care of mother, and her father to meet her in heaven." She then makes her final statement, duly recorded for the benefit of those who survive her, in which she attests to her love for her mother—"best . . . next to Jesus"—and to her belief that her "sins are all washed away in the blood of the Lamb." Her closing comments are followed by a feverish (and, it is implied, an unpremeditated and unedited) recital of her vision of the hereafter:

> Presently she said, "Please turn up the light, for it is growing dark;" and
> a moment later, "The light has gone down." On being told it was still
> burning, she replied, "The light is all right, but it is still dark, and I know
> why; but it is all right. I'm not afraid to die. I'm growing cold." Gazing
> through the darkness, she said, "I can see you all yet," and each name
> for the last time lingered lovingly on her lips,—"Mother—best—of—all
> next to Jesus." Then as if gazing beyond, "It is all light now. Good-by—
> good-by. I'm going home—home—home—forever and forever more."
>   Again her lips moved faintly, but the last word was inaudible, and
> with perhaps the word "Mother" or "Jesus" she had passed through
> the darkness beyond the shadow into the light of the blessed.[29]

Although obviously romanticized in order to fulfill the expectations of Fannie's mourning readers, the report of her death does not differ dramatically in content, form, and ideology from those recorded in private diaries and personal correspondence that would not have enjoyed the same wide circulation as the memoirs of a famous child-poet's mother. In a letter dated August 7, 1784, for example, John Choate of Ipswich, Massachusetts, drew upon what were clearly becoming the several stock accoutrements and attitudes of bereavement as he sought to comfort himself and his brother, in whose care his daughter Hannah had died:

> I received your Letter of June 7 sometime Since, giveing the very Mellancholly and heavy news of the Death of my Dear Daughter Hannah— I should have wrote you before but Want of Opportunity and the discumposure of mind under so Great a Tryall will I hope plead my excuse——although we had no rational Grounds to expect Hannah would continue any considerable lenth of time when my wife left her, yet Death came unexpected, and my wife and Children as well as my Self are greatly Affected with the Loss, and, Oh, Brother I doubt not but you and Sister were sencibly tutch't with the Loss of one who (perhaps not without good reason) you expected much comfort from—but the agreeable Account you give of the Frame and temper of her mind—her calm Composedness, her Resignation to the Divine will, her beautifull expressions to her mourning friends around her; her firm faith in the Blessed Jesus—and her happy prospect of the Heavenly Canaan at the near Approach of Death and wile actually passing thr° the Gloomy Vale and engag,d with the King of Terror, alth° very affecting, yet dos administer unspeakable comfort to her surviving friends—who do not mourn as those who have no hope—but have the fullest evidence to conclude that Our Sweet Child is now in Yonder Glory Celebrating Redeeming Love—I most Heartily Joine you in Adoring the Riches of Gods free Grace in the Wonderfull Plan of Salvation wrought out by our Blessed Jesus, and in perticular for his Communicating his Grace in so wonderfull a manner to my Dear Departed Child—May God have all the Glory—and may we be enabled from the Heart to say Gods will be done. He has our Lives our comforts and our all in his hands,——he give and he takes away and Blessed be his Name—[30]

Aside from the "high degree of cultural shaping," as Michael Wheeler calls it, that is evinced in the shared vocabulary and common structure of such descriptions of deathbed scenes, what links them is the implication that the moment of death is a revelatory one, for both the living and the deceased.[31] The latter struggles (usually with only limited success) to describe some part of his or her divinations, or "communications of grace," as John Choate referred to them. The former, on the other hand, cherish the dying visionary's final statement as a text laden with intimations of immortality: intimations that may, with time and study, generate new texts and provide the impetus for interpreting the prophetic or homiletic inscriptions contained therein. Choate's letter rehearses, in little, this very movement: an expression of his own grief is followed by a description that signals his reception of the message conveyed to and then transmitted by his brother, who witnessed the various stages of his daughter's physical dissolution. Thus, in the text in which he recapitulates her death and deliverance, Choate can speak with confidence of having divined "the Riches of Gods free Grace in the Wonderfull Plan of Salvation wrought out by our Blessed Jesus." His faith is anchored in a culturally sanctioned conception of death as occurring at the authorizing moment when, as Elisabeth Bronfen puts it, "an inherent though invisible truth could apotheotically be fulfilled, where an otherwise incommunicable secret could be made visible."[32] Knowing that the "Eyes glaze once—and that is Death— / Impossible to feign," and trusting moreover that it is impossible to "sham" or "simulate" the convulsions and throes accompanying death—to perform self-consciously, that is, for an admiring audience the coveted acquisition of sublime and eternal truths, and the bodily "narration" thereof—Emily Dickinson confessed to liking "a look of Agony, / Because I know it's true."

In focusing more specifically upon the experience of the dying child, the deathbed scenes featured in Choate's letter or A.E.M.'s memoir recast the child as hero. Debarred because of their youth or frailty from other forms of social or public achievement, such "child heroes" achieve, as Plotz suggests, "a kind of grandeur in their death."[33] Children are memorable figures in death not only (or even primarily) because they show pietistic fortitude in extremis, however, but also because they have not yet fallen into the adulterating world of sophisticated modes and manners, and so retain visions of preexistence (however ineffable, residual, and inarticulable) that only enhance those of eternity that are revealed, and thus intensified, at the hour of death. In his comfort book for bereaved parents, a Reverend W.B. Clark speculated that, poised at such a transformative moment and suspended, "not [in] . . . a state of unconsciousness . . . [but in] a state of vastly increased activity," the "believer" espies "the glories of paradise," which "are partially disclosed to his view" while "the distant tones of its hymns of sweetest melody burst upon his ravished ear."[34] Such beliefs were still widespread in the early twentieth century, although they became less overtly Christian. Wells's "The Door in the Wall" (1911), for example, describes one such vividly portentous experience. The adult Lionel Wallace, Wells's protagonist, admits to a friend that he is haunted by the memory "of a beauty and a happiness that filled his heart with insatiable longings that made all the interests and spectacle of worldly life seem dull and tedious and vain to him."[35] The memory concerns an excursion, undertaken in early childhood, through a green door in a white wall that led to a garden "full of the quality and promise of heart's desire" (10). He recalls that going through the door "was just like coming home" (9), and though fragmentary in nature, his memory consists of "an impression of delightful rightness" (10). That his was an early excursion into an other-, and perhaps an extra-, worldly domain seems clear by the story's end, when, determined not to forgo an opportunity that has several times presented itself to him, but that he has ignored in the course of an ambitious life, he passes through what he takes to be the much-desired door—and falls to his death in a deep excavation. His friend speculates that although by "our daylight standard he walked out of security into darkness, danger and death," viewed from Wallace's own childlike perspective, the door seemed to provide "a secret and peculiar passage of escape into another and altogether more beautiful world" (24).

One of the central tenets of late-nineteenth-century horror literature is that our "reality" is really fantasy, and our visionary (often nightmare) "fantasies," true reality. That perception was exploited by Algernon Blackwood, William Hope Hodgson, Oliver Onions, and others who kept alive the fears and desires that belonged to a pre-Enlightenment, prerationalist worldview. The adult world that Wells reconstructs in "The Door in the Wall" seems grey and dull and common, whereas Wallace's premonitory vision reveals a realm infused with an "indescribable quality of translucent unreality" (13): a reality starkly at odds with that hinted at in the desperate cry to which I alluded earlier: "Peter Quint—you devil! . . . *Where?*" Miles's dying pronouncement proves horrific at least in part because it conveys a truth—if it can be said, that is, to convey *anything* definitive— that seems grossly antithetical to those expressed by the dying innocents so ubiquitous in Victorian literature. In an essay on vulgarity in literature—in which he employs "the sticky overflowings" of Little Nell's death scene as an exemplar—Aldous Huxley claimed that "the suffering and death of children raise the problem of evil in its most unanswerable form."[36] His suggestion is that such a circumstance calls into question the beneficence of the divinity who could sap the vitality of such precious beings and simultaneously beggar those whose best hopes for the future resided in them, forcing a confrontation with what Kucich calls "the abyss of negativity," over the edge of which Pater appears to have peered when, happening upon "a dark space on the brilliant grass—the black mould lying heaped up round it"—an open child's grave—he divined "the physical horror of death, with its wholly selfish recoil from the association of lower forms of life, and the suffocating weight above."[37] The form that Miles's unexpected death takes complicates Kucich's contextualization of such a statement as Huxley's: what happens when, demonically inspired, the child becomes the medium through whom we confront not merely "the abyss of negativity"—contact with which was perceived as facilitating what Kucich terms an "initiation into a kind of transcendental genuineness"—but rather the *abîme* itself, the child in such a context functioning not as an innocent victim but as an active participant in the transmission of evil?[38] What happens, in other words, when the dying child espies not grace and sanctification (the message of the visions figured in the glow of the little match seller's matches) but damnation and demon-madness (what the child of Goethe's "Erlkönig" [c. 1782] encounters in the course of his fatal midnight ride; what the young servant in Braddon's "The Shadow in the Corner" [1879] sees in her room night after night, leading her, in the end, to take her own life)? "What, in the last analysis, had I to give the sense of?" is the question James puts to his reader in the preface to his *amusette*, the question to which he, without delay, answers that the "utmost conceivability" ("Preface," 176)—the "inordinate," the "incalculable," the "tragic, yet . . . exquisite, mystification" ("Preface," 172-73)—of his "sinister romance" ("Preface," 170) depends less on there being a "haunting pair, capable, as the phrase is, of everything" than on the more carefully turned contingency of their exertions expressing themselves "in respect to the children": "the very worst action small victims so conditioned might be conceived as subject to" ("Preface," 176). Douglas's concession that the piquancy ("particular touch" is his phrase) of the tale he has to relate derives from the appearance of an apparition to a child "at so tender an age" is prompted by an allusion to a case in which "a visitation had fallen on a child" (*The Turn of the Screw* 81). The "visitation" that falls upon Miles and Flora (its variant—"visitant"—is the term invoked by the governess to describe Peter Quint and Miss Jessel) is not of the sort that Job experienced, preserving his spirit and delivering "life and favour" (Job 10:12); it is closer in nature to those other biblical visitations that have their genesis in abominations (Jer. 8:12) that deliver desolation and days of recompense (Hos. 9:7) and that reveal the prophet as a fool and the spiritual man's madness (Hos. 9:7).

Miles's cry proves destabilizing in other ways as well. Just as nothing in Douglas's opening comments would have prepared James's late Victorian audience for the shock, so nothing in Victorian deathbed fiction would have prepared them to interpret it. Although hieroglyphic in the sense that the language in which it is expressed reflects the transcendence of the moment, the conventional deathbed utterance was understood to contain a truth that, if carefully scrutinized, could be comprehended, thus serving as a signpost on the path to righteousness for those left behind. The fact that "Gods . . . Wonderfull Plan of Salvation" (bastardized in other contexts by the imperfect and partial terms in which it is limned) comes closest under these circumstances to being phrased in God's own words may help to explain why "texts," "books," and "handwriting" are the tropes most commonly applied to the deathbed utterance. Holubetz reminds us that Margaret Oliphant availed herself of a practice—common "among devout Evangelicals [who recorded] the words of a departing saint, who was expected . . . to utter words of wisdom or prophecies at the moment when the veil of the flesh was thought to become transparent"—in her novel *The Minister's Wife* (1869), in which "the 'prophetess' [Ailie's] . . . 'death-bed ejaculations became the property of the parish, and were repeated far and wide, and finally made into a book.'"[39] Furthermore, the life that draws to a close assumes most strikingly in its concluding hours the quality and texture of a narrative, invested with the significations that a narrative might be expected to convey. In his near-death experience, for example, Wells's Lionel Wallace meets a "sombre dark woman, with a grave, pale face and dreamy eyes, . . . who carried a book . . . in the living pages" of which he sees himself, as well as the "harsh reality" of his life: "it was a story about myself, and in it were all the things that had happened to me since ever I was born . . . " (11-12).[40] At such a supercharged moment, and under such extreme circumstances, the dying speaker is, as Bronfen suggests, "imbued with authority and it is this 'authority,' arising from the aporia of speaking or writing in the shadow of death and against it, that lies at the origin of all narratives. Death is the sanction for all that a storyteller might relate. She or he borrows authority from death."[41] Not merely sanctioning what the storyteller has to tell, death may be said to mimic the narrative that contains it: as Garrett Stewart sees it, death and fiction are "two controlling frameworks within which story and mortality interrogate and exchange with each other."[42]

Miles's final statement, however, constitutes a text from which we cannot extract precise meaning. Because it is so constructed actively to *resist* interpretation, nothing in our training and experience has taught us to *how* to read it. The ultimate solipsistic text, scrutable (perhaps) only to the one whose authority is sanctioned by his imminent death, it creates not meaning but its absence, a vacuum, pulling into itself a series of unanswerable questions: Why does Miles call out "Peter Quint"? Is he admitting to an unwelcome and unholy association? Does he seek Quint's help in his extremity? Has he suspected that the dead man has become the governess's idée fixe, and does he hurl his name at her as a final condemnatory gesture? Who is the "you" referred to in "you devil"? Quint, whose friendship has damned Miles? The governess, whose ministrations have damned him? Like so much in the story whose abrupt ending it enforces, the statement is cryptic and unreadable; we are left only with questions whose answers are locked deep in the heart of the narrative—and of the reader touched by the horrors thus unveiled.

James's readers have been no more successful at reading Miles's final statement than in reading Miles himself. Precursor death scenes had taught the Victorians that the victim's body, inscribed with what George Eliot termed "that terrible handwriting of human destiny, . . . and death," could serve as a signifier of inward as well as past and future states.[43] Thus, as Georges van den Abbeele suggests, the charred corpse of Marquis de Sade's Justine—aptly killed when a lightning bolt enters her mouth and exits her vagina—bears witness to the "(male) inscriptional violence"—the brandings, flagellations, incisions—of which it has been the object throughout *Histoire de Juliette* (1797).[44] One recalls, as well, the mountain of foundering, suppurating flesh—the once relentlessly resplendent "blond Venus" now unveiled and revealed as a charnel house of horrors—with which Zola loads the deathbed scene that closes his *Nana* (1880). Alternatively, in the deathbed scene that dampened spirits and handkerchiefs in both England and America, Little Nell's marmoreal body is encased in a beauty that belies imminent corporeal dissolution and that furthermore testifies to her incorruptibility in life and her sanctity in death. "Peace and perfect happiness were . . . imaged in her tranquil beauty and profound repose."[45] Her face is set in "the same mild lovely look" by which we shall "know the angels in their majesty, after death" (654). In "reading" Little Nell's body, we discover that in its death throes it suffered the seal of salvation and that, consequently, it bears the word. In other words, Dickens establishes a strict correlation between the physical and the metaphysical, for at her grave "all outward things and inward thoughts teem with assurances of immortality" (659). In *The Turn of the Screw*, however, childhood beauty is at best misleading and perhaps a signifier of damnation rather than the state of grace it would seem to embody. Miles and Flora are repeatedly described (by the governess) as being nothing short of seraphic in their beauty. The governess suffers "no uneasiness in a connection with anything so beatific as the radiant image of [her] little girl," who is possessed of an "angelic beauty" (90) and "the deep, sweet serenity . . . of one of Raphael's holy infants" (91). In Miles, as well, the governess espies "on the instant, without and within," a correspondence between outward signs and inward states—that "great glow of freshness" equally discernible "from the first moment" in his sister, whose "same positive fragrance of purity" preludes his own: "Incredibly beautiful," Miles radiates "something divine" that she has "never found to the same degree in any child—his indescribable little air of knowing nothing in the world but love" (98). Because "it would have been impossible to carry a bad name with a greater sweetness of innocence" (98), the governess knows that to so attach such a name to such innocence and to pronounce the loveliness pooled in "the depths of blue of the child's eyes . . . a trick of premature cunning" would be merely to confess a "guilty . . . cynicism" (126) symptomatic of her own innate fallibility or the acquired bad faith of the "fallen" adult.

The children's beauty, however, so far from merely *carrying* a bad name, comes to *name* the very opposite of beatific innocence, and to occasion it: "For what else—when he's so clever and beautiful and perfect" could Miles be indicted, she eventually demands to know, but precisely "for wickedness" (162)? Because she sees in the children "nothing but their beauty and amiability" as readily as she would have assumed the opposite of those qualities had they "been at all visibly blighted or battered," Mrs. Grose rises up before the governess as "a magnificent monument to the blessing of a want of imagination" (140), preferring the correlative, associative hermeneutics that the governess herself has formerly entertained. For her own part, the governess comes at last to list "ugly feeding" as the only crime for which Miles might *not* have been "driven" from his school; whatever else he may be, in table manners he is "irreproachable" (188). Although she has from the start shown both a predilection for inversionary approaches to interpretation and a tendency to judge things according to what they are *not*—as when she earlier constructed the "horror" of Quint's character out of a cluster of negatives and similes (he "isn't a gentleman"; he's "like nobody"; he's "like an actor," as, never having seen one, she supposes an actor to be; "He's—God help me if I know *what* he is!" [110-11])—she finds herself forced to finesse her interpretive procedure, fully everting it in order to accommodate her growing recognition that "their more than earthly beauty, their absolutely unnatural goodness" are in fact "a game, . . . a policy and a fraud!" (145). Herein, then, lies one source of horror for James's late Victorian audience—the possibility that the hypocrisy so familiar to Victorian adulthood might already have infiltrated the carefully guarded nursery and infected those preternaturally precocious children. The beauty and apparently innocent intuition so captivating to the governess seem, in the end, to signal contrivance and to carry with them not the fragrance of purity but an odor of death and corruption powerful enough to penetrate the surrounding environs, so that the term "shrouded" in the passage "the white curtain draping . . . the head of Flora's little bed, shrouded . . . the perfection of childish rest" (133) is a hint that the innocence that had once lain there is (to the governess's engaged imagination) transforming itself into something more ominous.

The shock with which James's late Victorian audience would have witnessed the unceremonious destruction of cherished conventions and stereotypes would have matched the shock it must have sustained in its encounter with *Dracula*, the striking topical and thematic similarities existing between these two fin de siècle Gothics (Stoker's novel had been released the year before James's story made its 1898 appearance in *Colliers*) suggesting that they are intimately related.[46] Where the "prologue" of the one story locates the manuscript in a locked drawer, for example, the epilogic note of the other traces the papers recounting the engagement with and defeat of Dracula back to "a safe," the subjects of both texts being sufficiently contaminatory to require sequestration and containment.[48] In both stories a patrician "Master" conceives of and transmits evil. Like the count, Quint (the surrogate "Master" at Bly) expresses a vampiric hunger for those whom he would victimize (as well as a similarly imperialistic desire to "colonize" the occupants, women and children in particular, of Bly, disclosed in his having been too "free with everyone"—the term "free," as the governess notes, extending not only to the children but also to "the half-dozen maids and men who were still of our small colony" [*Turn of the Screw* 115]). Both exert an infectious influence, the quality of their monstrosity and their powers of contagion being sufficiently salient to affect real bodies. Whereas the count imbues his female victims with an evil of a lesser order (he feeds on the women, they feed on the children), Quint would "spoil" Miles, approaching him with "an infernal message" (151), while Miss Jessel, "pale and ravenous demon as she was" (175), would "get hold" of Flora. Just as Van Helsing is the first to discover the source of as well as the threat posed by the impending evil, so the governess alone perceives that "damnation" is in store for those who are drawn into an intercourse with the "undead" souls of Quint and Miss Jessel. Assuming the role that Mina adopts when, with the "devotion of a martyr," she announces herself prepared to die with the first discernible sign in herself "of harm to any" that she loves (Stoker 373-74), the governess decides to offer herself as an "expiatory victim" and, "by accepting, by inviting, by surmounting it all," to "keep . . . at bay" the evil that threatens "the tranquillity" of her companions: the "children . . . I should thus fence about and absolutely save," she declares (*Turn of the Screw* 114).

Discrete comparatives exist between the works. Just as the Count's powers peak nocturnally, so Bly's human bats tend to show themselves at dusk or in the grey dawn hours (and we might recall here that James characterized his two ghosts as "not 'ghosts' at all, as we now know the ghost, but goblins, elves, imps, demons" who woo "their victims forth to see them dance under the moon" ["Preface" 175]). As the Count enters Lucy's room through a window, so Quint is seen most often peering through windows. And as the Count becomes a hunted predator, his pursuers closing round him in wolf-haunted Transylvania, so Quint (his "white face of damnation" [193] visible beyond the window through which he peers) describes a "slow wheel" rather like "the prowl of a baffled beast" (194) as the governess attempts to recover lost territory. References to "the dead restored" (144), "the return of the dead" (148), and a perception that "sometimes brushed [the governess's] brow like the wing of a bat" (127) further impel one to suspect that James's story sustains an informed dialogue with its predecessor.

In the broadest sense, however, both texts draw for their fund of horror from the overturning of stereotypes and the exploding of certain set expectations—among them the High Victorian conviction that, as Bronfen puts it, "'the good death,' is that of a virtuous and preferably innocent person: of children or virgins."[48] As *The Turn of the Screw* offers an equation in which juvenile beauty may exist in direct proportion to the evil it embodies, so *Dracula* (as many critics have noted) equates the beauty of women—formerly the visible sign of their salvific powers—with predatory allure and mobile sexual desire.[49] The children whom Lucy infects, for example, (the very children whose welfare she would otherwise be charged with preserving in her culturally prescribed capacity as one of those "good women, whose lives and whose truths may make [a] good lesson for the children that are to be" [Stoker 239]), are drawn to her specifically because of her beauty; to their innocent sealed eyes, she is the "bloofer lady" (229).[50] Even as a corpse, Lucy Westenra is "very beautiful" (211), "more radiantly beautiful" after death—"her lips . . . redder, . . . on the cheeks . . . a delicate bloom" (257-58)—than she had been living, so that John Seward, her disappointed suitor, marvels to find that "instead of leaving traces of 'decay's effacing fingers,' [death] had but restored the beauty of life" (213). Over time, however, Seward abandons the discredited rhetoric of the mournful lover: he is no Romeo, discovering "beauty's ensign" in encrimsoned lips and cheeks and finding therein the message that Juliet has not been "conquered" in death. The very fact of her being "so beautiful and calm, . . . so fair to look upon"—like "a creature fresh from the hand of God, and waiting for the breath of life" (Dickens, *Old Curiosity Shop*, 652)—indicates that Dickens's Little Nell has gone to dwell in glory, but Lucy's apparent immunity from corporeal corruption is a sign of her spiritual degradation. Her eyes alone—"Lucy's eyes in form and colour," but "unclean and full of hell-fire" and ablaze "with unholy light" (Stoker 271)—betray her. Under the tutelage of Van Helsing, a seasoned physiognomist and metaphysician, that is, Dr. Seward learns to be suspicious of the bloom of feminine beauty in general and to understand that postmortem pulchritude in particular "means" evil: "If ever a face meant death—," Dr. Seward announces, "if looks could kill—we saw it at that moment" (272).

Just as full-blown feminine beauty comes to be valued as so clear a determinant of uncleanness that Van Helsing rejoices to find the infected Mina Harker looking "thin and pale and weak" (477), so the governess despairs when she considers that little Flora, though rosily resplendent in all her pink-and-golden charm, is "every inch of her, quite old" (179), while her "extraordinary childish grace" (130) and "child's sincerity" (179) are explicable only if read as the dissembling typical of "an old, old woman" (172), versed in the ways of a sophisticated world from which, at Bly, the little girl should have been isolated. Although initially proud of her own capacity for deceit and contrivance—she speaks of "the gentlest arts" (92) by which she wins Flora's trust—the governess increasingly portrays herself as a latter-day Merlin practiced upon by scheming children no less poised for "beguilement" (131) than Nimue herself, so that Miles, for example, with a "charming exhibition of tact, of magnanimity," exercises an influence that leaves her "with a strange sense of having literally slept at my post"; "and yet I hadn't really, in the least, slept: I had only done something much worse—I had forgotten" (168). "What surpassed everything," she marvels, "was that there was a little boy in the world who could have for the inferior age, sex and intelligence so fine a consideration" (132). This consideration she later identifies as the coefficient of "his small strange genius" (190), although what she comprehends by this culturally weighted term is starkly at odds with the conditions that occasion its use. Miles's genius betrays itself in the sort of precocity that, according to Lombroso, "is morbid and atavistic," "common to genius and to insanity," and observable "among all savages."[51] However paradoxically, such precocity was in fact considered to be symptomatic of the arrested stage of human development that, according to Sir James Frazer, was most readily evident in the child who, as Sandra Siegel points out, bore for the Victorian social scientist "the same relation to the savage as the adult does to civilization."[52] Thus, the governess slights the success that Quint and Miss Jessel would seem to have enjoyed in making the children "still cleverer even than nature did," their achievement being diminished, to her mind, by their having had, in the first place, "wondrous material to play on!" (180). Miles's cleverness, his delicacy, his "discrimination" (190) are all attributable, the governess informs us, to "the outbreak in him of the little natural man" (130) ("natural" having its old Calvinist meaning here rather than the romantic one), just as Dracula's cunning is, for all that it seems nearly insuperable, recognizable to Van Helsing as the fledgling expression of "that so great child-brain of his" (390), which, being "predestinate to crime also," renders him in turn "a criminal and of criminal type. Nordau and Lombroso would so classify him, and *qua* criminal he is of imperfectly formed mind" (439).

One of Van Helsing's greatest challenges is to convince his associates that "there are things old and new which must not be contemplate [*sic*] by men's eyes, because they know—or think they know—some things which other men have told them" (246). The brutal discrediting of those false "truths" "which other men have told"—the assumptions about the sanctity of childish innocence, for example, and the faith in the redeeming quality of the "truths" that spill out of the mouths of dying innocents—complicates a text that would have been sufficiently unnerving even had James not produced one last excruciating turn of the screw precisely at the moment of Miles's death. James's treatment of childhood innocence—and in particular of childish insight at the epiphanic moment of death—being less reductive than Stoker's treatment of feminine beauty, we confront in *The Turn of the Screw* something more complex than the mere inversion of the equation plotted by Wilde's Miss Prism ("The good end happily, and the bad unhappily. That is what Fiction means"), or the aesthetic law (mandating that like be happily married to like) that had been written, so Ruskin argued, into the book of nature, so that what was normal and healthy and good would of necessity assume a bright color and a pleasing shape, whereas what was ill-formed—"a venomous wood-fungus, rotting into black dissolution of dripped slime at its edges"—would announce a nature blighted and corrupt (and all this appearing, one might add, in the context of a discussion of the odious Darwin's "ignorance of good art" and the consequent "acutely illogical simplicity" of his explanation in the *Descent of Man* of the "widely founded laws" governing nature's selection and use of color).[53] James's sensibility here is more like what we find, for example, in Flaubert's admission that he cannot look "on a cradle without thinking of a tomb," nor "contemplate a woman" without thinking "of her skeleton."[54] We cannot, after all, say definitively that Miles has not in fact been as thoroughly stainless spiritually as he is physically: moments before she witnesses his death, the governess acknowledges that qualifying her very pity is "the appalling alarm" of Miles's being "perhaps innocent" (196). Discernment, vision, obscurity, what cannot or must not be "contemplate by men's eyes" (which, according to Van Helsing's calculus, becomes the site of sentience): these concerns—at least as pressing in *The Turn of the Screw* as, and in the end conterminous with, the question as to whether or not youthful beauty does indeed figure as an accurate indicator of innocence—are inextricably bound together in a text that might plausibly be thought of as exploring its own hermeneutics. "*Look at him*" (98) is the governess's antiphonal response to Mrs. Grose's "*look at her!*" (95), each pledging a coded allegiance to the High Victorian belief that truth and beauty are interchangeable, cleanly intersecting within a common ground of established equivalencies (and one might recall, in this context, that common past mapped out in James's preface and constituted by a cluster of recognizable cultural markers and signs and artifacts). Both women traffic, as a result, in ocular exchanges. "Prodigious and gratified looks" (91) pass between them, and they "meet" in long looks (111): Mrs. Grose gives "a look" that her confederate remarked "at the moment" (94), and the governess reciprocates, annotating her speech by "[looking] prodigious things" (121). Her looks go everywhere; and they are returned in kind, so that when asked to provide proof of her assertion that Miss Jessel is "a horror of horrors," the governess promptly retorts that she is certain "by the way she looked" (122)—her answer, to her mind, amply definitive and admitting of no ambiguity.

The governess represents specular encounters both as a means of communicating the otherwise incommunicable ("obscure and roundabout allusions" [91] are contained in those prodigious looks that she settles upon Mrs. Grose) and as a more efficacious way of biting into and finally possessing what might otherwise be elusive—and, from the perspective of Bly's ghosts, lost thereby. As the unvarying terminology characterizing her several encounters with him indicates, Quint's appearance fascinates her (as in olden times witches and serpents were said to "fascinate" their victims): his ability "markedly" to fix her "even as he turned away" merely adds "to the spectacle" (103) of his first visitation; she notes her own inability in a subsequent encounter to "quit" his face, although his stare, "deep and hard," quits hers and proceeds instead to "fix successively several other things" (107). The governess is similarly transfixed by the subsequent sight of Miss Jessel's fierce scrutiny of Flora:

> "She gave me never a glance. She only fixed the child."
>
> Mrs. Grose tried to see it. "Fixed her?"
>
> "Ah, with such awful eyes! . . . With a determination—indescribable. With a kind of fury of intention."
>
> I made her turn pale. "Intention?"
>
> "To get hold of her." [122]

Her predecessor's attention, in this regard, is monstrous (in the Jamesian sense) because it places her in the culturally predetermined space in Victorian literature that locates the power to petrify within the typically masculine sphere of active speculation and identifies the consequent condition of petrifaction as an explicitly feminine state of pure being (the same space that T.S. Eliot redefines when he has his lovesick J. Alfred Prufrock imagine himself as being effeminized, "formulated, sprawling on a pin"—immobilized, "pinned and wriggling on the wall," by the "eyes that fix you in a formulated phrase").[55]

Quint's capacity (shared by his ghostly companion) to hold her attention— "to fix me," as she says, "from his position, with just the question, just the scrutiny through the fading light, that his own presence provoked" (102)—commands the respect of the nominally governing governess. In spite of what she represents as the consentaneity of their positions, however—evident, she contends, in their shared (spatial) perspectives and similarly intuited understandings—Quint commands wordlessly, effortlessly, whereas she invariably resorts to brute force as a means of compelling her own attendants' compliance in her fixed meanings, in her determined measures. The dashes that suture her insights to those of Mrs. Grose (forty-four such stitches crosshatch their various conversations) give the impression of seamless effort, the two women thinking with one mind, speaking, though antiphonally, *ad una voce* and arriving, in the process, mutually within sight of a unified field of vision. "You do know, you dear thing," the governess insists in one such exchange,

> "only you haven't my dreadful boldness of mind, and you keep back, out of timidity and modesty and delicacy, even the impression that, in the past, when you had, without my aid, to flounder about in silence, most of all made you miserable. But I shall get it out of you yet! There was something in the boy that suggested to you . . . that he covered and concealed their relation."
>
> "Oh, he couldn't prevent—"
>
> "Your learning the truth? I dare say! But, heavens, . . . what it shows that they must, to that extent, have succeeded in making of him! . . . If Quint—on your remonstrance at the time you speak of—was a base menial, one of the things Miles said to you, I find myself guessing, was that you were another." Again her admission was so adequate that I continued: "And you forgave him that?"
>
> "Wouldn't *you*?"
>
> "Oh yes!" And we exchanged there, in the stillness, a sound of the oddest amusement. Then I went on: "At all events, while he was with the man—"
>
> "Miss Flora was with the woman. It suited them all!"
>
> It suited me too, I felt, only too well; by which I mean that it suited exactly the particular deadly view I was in the very act of forbidding myself to entertain. [128-29]

Although suggesting a discursive cooperation, correspondence, and consonance indicative of "deeper mutual soundings" (184), the dashes that litter these communications are reminiscent of those that creep into the text of Gilman's "The Yellow Wallpaper" (1892), whose narrator can hardly write a sentence without resorting to dashes and parentheses as a desperate means of indicating the ways in which her own attempted statements are imposed upon and hijacked by the instructions from her husband John—all regarding the nature of her problem and state of mind. In the context of the governess's various conversations with Mrs. Grose, the dash-driven statements finally disclose semiotically what the governess indirectly betrays in her tendency in these interviews literally to clutch at her subjects: that is, her fear that her ability to "cross over," command, and unconditionally occupy the other side of experience and signification may be limited to her mere physical capacity to do so, as when, following her second encounter with Quint, she places herself "where he had stood," and applying "her face to the pane . . . looked, as he had looked, into the room" (108). Her appearance to Mrs. Grose—so apparently doubling his that the housekeeper retreats, as the governess notes, "on just *my* lines"—generates not the "shock of a certitude" and "flash of . . . knowledge— . . . knowledge in the midst of dread" (107) that his presence had delivered, but instead a mere "shy heave of . . . surprise," leaving the governess (who is skeptical in any event, because she wonders whether Mrs. Grose's "bloom of" innocence may not be feigned) prosaically to "put out [a] hand to her" and hold "her hard a little, liking to feel her close" (109). Fearful that the meanings (that she, like a detective, so wishes to apprehend) may elude her in the end, lost within the very gaps and apertures upon which, paradoxically, her own Jamesian ability to turn the bare facts of intimation to her purpose depends; and doubtful, moreover, whether she can fulfill the expectations of the audience against whose trust her own faith in her powers of discernment is counterpoised, she takes forcible hold of her subjects. Thus she detains Mrs. Grose, "holding her there with a hand on her arm" (95), then holding her "tighter" (96), dragging her at her heels by the "chain" of her "logic . . . ever too much for her," until, pausing, she "sustains her with a grateful arm" (172-73). She compels her beleaguered companion to comprehend her, if only in an embrace, as she would contain her verbally, making her "a receptacle of lurid things" (141):

> She held me there a moment, then whisked up her apron again with
> her detached hand. "Would you mind, Miss, if I used the freedom—"
> "To kiss me? No!" I took the good creature in my arms and, after
> we had embraced like sisters, felt still more fortified and indignant. [99]

The provisional nature of the governess's linguistic reconstructions (it is she who most often cauterizes the gaping wounds of sentences rent by the typographical gash that punctures speech) becomes more apparent when what substitutes for the momentary silence forced by the dash is the silence that announces the less easily governed spectral exchanges: "the intense hush" in which, for example, moments before her first encounter with Quint, "the sounds of evening dropped" (102), or her sense, later, that "all sounds from [Flora] had previously dropped" (120) in anticipation of Miss Jessel's appearance by the Sea of Azof. She notes that the "stranger sharpness" of Quint's meanings and intentions, like Miss Jessel's, is not in the least diluted or diminished or deflected, and that both the meanings and the impression that they impart are "as definite as a picture in a frame" (102), for all that they are subject to his speechless perspective, which is invariably mediated, seen always "only across, as it were, and beyond—in strange places and on high places, the top of towers, the roof of houses, the outside of windows, the further edge of pools; but there's a deep design, on either side, to shorten the distance and overcome the obstacle; and the success of the tempters is only a question of time" (146). In spite of such spatial exigencies, that is, the haunting pair pull her deeper along the spiraling and tightening vertical axis of fearful intimation, their success in impressing upon her their "deep design" a function not, as she sees it, of distance but of duration only. In a statement equally applicable to her own experience and to the reader's encounter with her text, the governess concedes, "The more I go over it, the more I see in it, and the more I see in it the more I fear," measuring the passage of time over the space of which, as she plumbed "depths, depths," the Jamesian figure in the carpet progressively surfaced, acquiring such clarity and definition that she comes not to know (in her words) "what I *don't* see— what I *don't* fear" (121-22). Although it is more evident to her by her story's close that Quint's "white face of damnation" has been the "hideous author of our woe" (197), the governess arrives, at the end of her speculations, merely at the very point of her embarkation, that being the "awful conception" borne in upon her with a "portentous clearness" of Quint's wanting "to appear to *them*" (114). Having proven no truer by the last page of the story that she scripts than in the earliest, this "deep design"—her ghosts' intention, the site and source of her awful conception—may be said to conform in its essentials to the Paterian condition of literary architecture that, foreseeing the end in the beginning, never loses sight of it. The final purpose, the distinctive sign and design of her experience having merely been fully exposed in the fullness of time, what *has* changed by her story's close is her relationship to the appalling teleology, her awful conception of confronting a "horror of horrors" giving way to a despair lest her "*not* seeing" Miss Jessel will leave her stranded fatally beyond the reach of her ghosts' intentions. Beyond this, she revises an earlier sense that one need "only look, dearest woman, *look*" in order to see what appears "as big as a blazing fire"— namely, the deep design fleshed out in a ghostly presence. "You don't see her exactly as *we* see?—you mean to say you don't now—*now?*" (176), cries the governess, disabused.

The governess had begun by equating mere looking with clear seeing, and clear seeing with absolute knowing, the integrity of her reckoning inscribed in the forward continuity of those statements in which looking and seeing and knowing are recapitulated ("See him, Miss, first. *Then* believe it! . . . *look* at her!" (95), or yet again, "Know [that Miss Jessel is a horror of horrors]? By seeing her! By the way she looked" [122]). She learns that looking and seeing name two essentially different procedures, as well as two distinct states of awareness, and that one is alerted to the existence of "the depths of the sinister" (the phrase is James's, invoked to rename the "portentous evil" ["Preface" 175] with which he would mantle his predatory creatures) and capable, by extension, of descrying the deepest depths of design depending on whether one's eyes are "sealed" to evil, a term that she fixes upon in the latter portion of her narrative as she comes more aggressively to differentiate between the visionary acuities of her companion and her charges and their allied capacity to distill essence from appearance. She fears, for example, that her own "eyes might be sealed just while" those of her charges "were most opened," "a consummation for which it seemed blasphemous not to thank God" (149-50). Although she rues Mrs. Grose's blindness—that good woman's "deep groan of negation, repulsion, compassion" establishing "her exemption" from the sight of Miss Jessel, which in turn stands as proof "that her eyes were hopelessly sealed" (176)—yet she considers it "prodigious" that, through her efforts, Miles's "sense was sealed" (194) to the visitant with whom he would communicate. Even at the last, the boy can catch "with his sealed eyes the direction" of her words only, his confusion recorded in the pocked and punctuated cry that follows his "glaring vainly over the place and missing wholly . . . the wide, overwhelming presence" of Quint (197).

In employing the term as she does, the governess locates the site of insufficiency and incapacity in those baffled recipients of visions and visitations—and transforms, by extension, her "dreadful liability to impressions of the order so vividly exemplified" (113) into the authority that sanctions and seals her own readings of the texts available to her: Quint's appearance (and the design it embodies), Miss Jessel's appearance (and the intention it embodies), Miles's appearance, or look, (and the premature cunning it covers and conceals). James's own invocation of the term suggests a slightly variant designation that highlights its capacity, grammatically and semantically, to occupy several oppositional (and often contradictory) realms of signification and possibility. In his preface, for example, James uses the term to refer to the condition of certain texts (his examples are varied, ranging from literary texts to their "starting-point," their source and the occasion for their transmission), which, in their pre-eminent self-containment, are "absolutely sealed and beyond test or proof" ("Preface" 162). His sense of the word echoes (although it does not duplicate) that conveyed in a passage from Isaiah: "For the Lord . . . hath closed your eyes: the prophets and your rulers, the seers hath he covered. And the vision of all is become unto you as the words of a book that is sealed, which men deliver to one that is learned, saying, Read this, I pray thee: and he saith, I cannot; for it is sealed" (Isa. 29:10-11). Hence the *Oxford English Dictionary* definition of "a sealed book" as a term "used predicatively of something involved in obscurity, or beyond a person's capacity to understand." Because their meanings are so entirely predetermined and discrete (yet simultaneously and paradoxically "outlived and lost and gone" ["Preface" 164], sealed in the silent authority of the past and all its buried sources), such texts grant no license to "fantasticate" ("Preface" 165), as James has it, although one might argue that his alluding at all to the temptation to take such license serves as evidence that, true to form, he is invoking the very definition of the term that the governess draws upon—that which comprehends the capacity (to divine occult possibilities) that in turn allows one either to decipher or to create works such as *The Turn of the Screw* itself; works that bask in an "unattackable ease," will not be "baited by earnest criticism" ("Preface" 169), resist surrendering their meanings, and refuse, like the German book of which Poe writes in "The Man of the Crowd" (1840), to allow themselves to be read ("*er lasst sich nicht lesen*'—it does not permit itself to be read").[56]

In *Heart of Darkness*, the smile of the general manager of the Central Station provides a counterpart to what James here envisions; it suggests as well that, in the context of his own fin de siècle excursion into chaos, Conrad similarly "discovered" in the metaphor of sealed texts an apt expression of the hermeneutical insecurity that betrays itself in an obsession with essential truths and impenetrable surfaces. An "indefinable, faint expression of his lips, something stealthy—a smile—not a smile" conveys what is otherwise occluded in the general manager's body, which seems for the most part to "disclaim the intention" of an attainable meaning: "It was unconscious, this smile was, though just after he had said something it got intensified for an instant. It came at the end of his speeches like a seal applied on the words to make the meaning of the commonest phrase appear absolutely inscrutable. . . . He inspired uneasiness—that was it. Uneasiness. Not a definite mistrust—just uneasiness—nothing more. You have no idea how effective such a . . . a . . . faculty can be." Marlow recalls once more encountering this enigmatic smile in the context of the general manager's characterization of the possession of "insides" as a misfortune: "Once when various tropical diseases had laid low almost every 'agent' in the station he was heard to say, 'Men who come out here should have no entrails.' He sealed the utterance with that smile of his as though it had been a door opening into a darkness he had in his keeping. You fancied you had seen things—but the seal was on." Although indicative of it, the general manager's having come into his position "because he was never ill" and his having retained it because "triumphant health in the general rout of constitutions is a kind of power in itself" are ultimately peripheral to the essential quality of his greatness, which seems to Marlow to be his very unreadability, it being "impossible to tell what could control such a man. He never gave that secret away. Perhaps there was nothing within him."[57] It makes sense, therefore, that of all those whom Marlow encounters on his journey, this man alone, with a gesturing sweep of his "short flipper of an arm," dares to become familiar ("trust to this—I say trust to this") with the forest, which bears on its vast face a mute "high stillness" that is as sealed as his smile, the "immensity" of the forest exactly meeting and measuring the nothingness within him, while the question it poses of most men ("Could we handle that dumb thing, or would it handle us?") precisely balances the secret that the manager never gives away.[58]

The general manager's smile is heir to that of the Gautama Buddha; descended from Monna Lisa's "unfathomable smile, always with a touch of something sinister in it"; and a kin to the smiles on the "expressive and puzzling,

striking and disturbing" heads that face Kurtz's house.[59] Half a century earlier,
Thomas De Quincey recalled seeing the "smile that radiated from the lips" of
Memnon's head, "then recently brought from Egypt," as something "too awful
to clothe itself in adumbrations or memorials of flesh." He fixes on this smile, as
Marlow himself has done, in the context of a larger consideration of the
circumambient natural world, mentioning it in the course of his essay "System
of the Heavens as Revealed by Lord Rosse's Telescopes" (1846). One region of
space, he notes, *the Nebula in Orion,* "hitherto blindly jealous of its secrets, had
rendered them up submissively once William Parsons, the third earl of Rosse,
had developed his "all-conquering telescope," which measured the "frightful
magnitude," "frightful depth," and "dreadful distances" that had made possible
"the unexampled defiance" with which the nebula had "resisted all approaches."
De Quincey compares the "solemn uncovering by astronomy" to "the reversing
of some heavenly doom, like the raising of the seals that had been sealed by the
angel in the Revelation." What is exposed to view and resolved (to use the argot
of the discipline) is, according to De Quincey, "a vision 'to dream of, not to tell'":
although he *does* tell, though not without a few words of prologue, without which,
he claims (in the style of James's Douglas, who is also in possession of a story
too dreadful to tell, and one he claims *won't* tell, though in the end he *does* tell),
"without any fault of mine, my description will be unintelligible." In "order to see
what *I* see, the obedient reader must do what I tell him to do," says De Quincey:
he must take hold, in fact, of the sketch of the great Nebula in Orion as reproduced in John Pringle Nichol's *System of the World* (1846) and "view the wretch
upside down," at which point what will be *"forced to show out"* is

> a head thrown back, and raising its face, (or eyes, if eyes it had,) in the
> very anguish of hatred, to some unknown heavens. What *should* be its
> skull wears what *might* be an Assyrian tiara, only ending behind in a
> floating train. This head rests upon a beautifully developed neck and
> throat. All power being given to the awful enemy, he is beautiful where
> he pleases, in order to point and envenom his ghostly ugliness. . . .
> Brutalities unspeakable sit upon the upper lip, which is confluent with a
> snout; for separate nostrils there are none. . . . But the lower lip, which
> is drawn inwards with the curve of a conch shell,—O, what a convolute
> of cruelty and revenge is *there*! Cruelty!—to whom? Revenge!—for what?
> Ask not, whisper not. Look upwards to other mysteries.[60]

Given what has gone before, it seems unlikely that those "other mysteries"
to which De Quincey would redirect his reader's shocked attention would adum-
brate anything other than more of "the same pomp of malice in the features" of
a universe newly disclosed as "appalling in the exposure"—and, one might add,
only to be seen from his own special perspective, just as it is resolvable only by
Lord Rosse's monstrous telescopic lens. Like De Quincey, who is attempting to

"unseal" the eyes of his "obedient" readers so that they can see a face that, in the final analysis, may not exist outside of his own opium-tinged imaginings. James's governess also insists upon submission to her absolute authority for the proper unsealing of mysteries. And like De Quincey, she may be said figuratively, if not quite literally, to turn the household at Bly upside down as the only means available to her of revealing her perception that the unworldly beauty of Miles's body has become a screen that, according to her calculus, elides, points to, and "envenoms" otherworldly ugliness. In the end, however, she cannot resolve the meaning of Miles's deathbed utterance, which is also like a purloined letter—available to view but finally unseen; or like the letter that, although "sealed and directed" (167), never discloses to the master in Harley Street the mysteries of Bly, because Miles purloins it; or like Quint, whose ghostly presence and intentions the governess calls before her mind's eye as distinctly as she claims to "see the letters" she forms "on this page" (103), although their mystery (that of the "letters," that is, as well as of the presence that they combine to reconstruct) remains sealed in the locked drawer that holds the manuscript containing that page. Ruskin might have argued that the confusion that her narrative fails to resolve—that it indeed transmits—is the unfortunate consequence of a certain human "pride" (we might recall here her own admission of "blasphemous" ingratitude) that, as he maintains in his own brief disquisition on the nature of sealed texts, unreasonably insists upon "perfect intelligibility" as a criterion for "knowledge" that is in turn "ill pursued" and accompanied by a "fall into misery of unbelief" (of the sort that Poe's overweening narrators and their heirs suffer). "I know there are an evil mystery and a deathful dimness," Ruskin conceded, "the dimness of the sealed eye and soul; but do not let us confuse these with the glorious mystery of the things which the angels 'desire to look into,' or with the dimness which, even before the clear eye and open soul, still rests on sealed pages of the eternal volume."[61] Begotten of evil mystery and begetting a deathful dimness, Miles's final enigmatic statement remains for the governess (and by extension, for her readers) a sealed text whose obscurity conveys none of the "nobleness" that Ruskin conceived of as being perceivable in "concealment." Persuaded, as Ruskin was, that "every visible feature of natural things" afforded "glimpses of stable and substantial things," Dickens could comfort those mourning at the death of Little Nell, whose demise he in his capacity as artist was impelled to sanction and oversee by reminding them that "in the Destroyer's steps there spring up bright creations that defy his power, and his dark path becomes a way of light to Heaven" (659).[62] Writing in 1840, nearly half a century before James produced his self-obscuring text, Dickens could still insist upon the existence of an infinitely wise and beneficent author of all things; one defended in the pulpit as "a being of infinite goodness and wisdom, all [of whose] dispensations must be kindly meant, and wisely ordered, however severely they may be felt, and however inscrutable they may appear"; one whose mysteries, as Ruskin had argued, and concealments, even, were "necessary in all great art."[63] Writing six years after Dickens had published *The Old Curiosity Shop,* with "the abysses of the heavenly wilderness" suddenly and appallingly exposed, De Quincey imagines that "the mysterious Architect plays at hide-and-seek with his worlds," letting this world in particular "be tortured into closer compression, again [letting] the screw be put upon it." Although the otherwise conservative De Quincey conceives of his metaphor as a means of celebrating humanity's Sisyphean tendency to "shake off the oppression," yet his faith cannot mask what is revealed in his essay as the eternal temptation of the "great moulding Power" to attempt another turn of the screw, plunging further "into aboriginal darkness" a world "driven back and depressed from one deep to a lower deep."[64] Miming an order of being and limning an order of experience (hermeneutic and teleological) closer to that envisioned by De Quincey than that of Ruskin or Dickens, James offers his late Victorian audience a seraphic child who, following in the Destroyer's steps, is "hurled over an abyss" (198) while he leads his governess "not into clearness, but into a darker obscure" (196).

4

Articulating the Dead

Vernon Lee, Decadence, and "The Doll"

He thought for a long time of how the closed eyes of dead women could still live—how they could open again, in a quiet lamplit room, long after they had looked their last. They had looks that survived— had them as great poets had quoted lines.

Henry James, "The Altar of the Dead" (1895)

THE ABNORMALITY OF THE "hovering prowling blighting presences" he wished to install at Bly, James felt certain, depended upon his departing "altogether from the rules" ("Preface," 175). That he should speak so familiarly of the "rules" governing late-nineteenth-century horror might have come as something of a surprise to his friend Vernon Lee—to whom, nearly twenty years before he had announced in the preface to *The Aspern Papers* that "good ghosts, speaking by book, make poor subjects," he had collegially confided that the "supernatural story, the subject wrought in fantasy, is not the *class* of fiction I myself most cherish (prejudiced as you may have perceived me in favour of a close connotation, or close observation, of the real—or whatever one may call it—the familiar, the inevitable)."[1] The occasion for this perhaps not altogether ingenuous confession was his reception of Lee's first collection of ghost stories, *Hauntings* (1890), which he characterized as "gruesome, graceful, *genialisch*," although his good opinion of "the bold, aggressive speculative fancy" discernible in Lee's work would have been enhanced by her prefatory disclaimer that "no genuine ghosts in the scientific sense" were to be discovered in her "four little tales," which told "of no hauntings such as could be contributed by the Society for Psychical Research, of no spectres that can be caught in definite places and made to dictate to judicial evidence"[2] (an abjuration that James would duplicate in his eventual disavowal of "the mere modern 'psychical' case, washed clean of all queerness as by exposure to a flowing laboratory tap" ["Preface," 169]). One might expect that Lee would have valued the shared perspective of an individual whose work she held in such high regard that she dedicated to him her first and only novel, but in fact such was not the case, and the cooling of their subsequent relations is attributable at least in part to her growing suspicion that James deliberately obscured his indebtedness to her.[3] Could she have known that her own rather prodigious body of work—as well as the influence that it subtly exerted—would until very recently suffer a neglect that Van Wyck Brooks characterized as genteely self-imposed ("her gift has been so gracious that she seems not to have asked for austere consideration"), James's perceived oversight would perhaps have struck her as ironically portentous.[4]

When one suggests that a writer has been relegated to an "undeserved" obscurity, there is often—but not always—an implication that in her own day she *was* noted, or deservedly popular. Yet Vernon Lee (the nom de plume of Violet Paget) was not a "popular" writer in her own lifetime. Born in 1856, dying in 1935, she was admired and feared by her contemporaries, and although she enjoyed something of a vogue during the teens and twenties, she was an unabashedly elitest author who demanded of her readers a peculiar conjunction of culture, taste, leisure, and what Bernard Shaw described as a "cosmopolitan intellectualism" with which few, in the event, were actually equipped; and it is in fact her "distinguished view of life" that Brooks ironically credited as preventing her from acquiring "popularly a clear-cut form."[5] It was Lee whom Shaw cited when he argued that "it is possible to be born in England

and yet have intellect, to train English minds as well as English muscles," conveniently ignoring or overlooking the fact that she was born of English parents then living at Boulogne and that for most of her life she lived as an expatriate in the art centers of western Europe.[6] Designating hers "the most able mind in Florence" (elsewhere, privately, he termed hers "a monstrous cerebration"), James described this belletrist as being "as dangerous and uncanny as she is intelligent which is saying a great deal. Her vigour and sweep are most rare and her talk superior altogether." "Draw it mild with her on the question of friendship," he urged his brother William, underscoring his warning by means of a comparison that transformed Lee into a potentially wild creature to be encountered with circumspection: "But *don't* caress her. . . . She's a tiger-cat!"[7] In his portrait of Lee, her childhood friend John Singer Sargent caught the way her features expressed a lively sardonic intelligence (fig. 29), but to many of her male contemporaries her formidable powers of self-assertion seemed threatening. Perhaps regretting that in his list of experiences that one ought not to miss during one's visit to Florence ("the Pitti, the Uffizi, the Bargello, the Academia!") he had included "Miss Paget to quarrel with," John Addington Symonds attempted to persuade Lee to soften her manner on the principle that it was "possible to be frank without being flippant, rude, or patronising" and "firm without appearing to have posed as an oracle": "there is a certain grave & measured way of expressing difference with accepted wisdom, a certain caution & reserve in asserting our own opinions, . . . wh [sic] I have always been sorry to see you miss."[8] Max Beerbohm made his own feelings plain in a portrait that he (perhaps wisely) reserved for his own private delectation. "The tenacity and volubility with which she expressed her most cherished views," as her biographer Peter Gunn puts it, "exceeded the restrained good taste demanded by so dandiacal a social critic as Max Beerbohm," who tipped into the title page of his copy of *Gospels of Anarchy* (1908) an engraving of "a bonneted middle-aged lady drinking tea," a portrait that he annotated ("to suit the refinement of his malice") accordingly: "Oh dear! Poor dear dreadful little lady! Always having a crow to pick, ever so coyly, with Nietzsche, or a wee lance to break with Mr. Carlyle, or a sweet but sharp little warning to whisper in the ear of Mr. H.G. Wells, or Strindberg or Darwin or D'Annunzio! What a dreadful little bore and busybody! How artfully at this moment she must be button-holing Einstein! And Signor Croce—and Mr. James Joyce!"[9]

A prolific writer, she had produced, by the age of twenty-four, a highly regarded history of eighteenth-century Italy, which was followed by a number of volumes of essays on aesthetic matters (it was, in fact, Lee who introduced the concept of empathy into the vocabulary of Anglo-Saxon aesthetics). The essays contained in her genius loci collections have traditionally been considered to be her most compelling, and her sensitivity to subtle impressions of place prompted Robert Browning to lionize her in a poem entitled "Inapprehensiveness," included in his *Asolando: Fancies and Facts* (1899):

Figure 29. John Singer Sargent, *Vernon Lee* (1881). Courtesy of the Tate Gallery, London

"No, the book
Which noticed how the wall-growths wave," said she
"Was not by Ruskin."
I said, "Vernon Lee?"

The monstrosities of *Miss Brown* (1884)—her shapeless novel—belie her skills as a writer of the supernatural fictions that have received less attention than have her collections of essays, although in recent years they have been rediscovered by critics who have come to recognize in them, as did Edith Wharton, her "most purely imaginative" as well as her most deeply personal work.[10]

Invoking a highly finished, arabesqued, "yellow" style that functioned, in such pieces, as a projection of and correlative to the fevered states of mind that the Decadents sought to cultivate, the majority of her stories, written between 1886 and 1899, conform to the requirements of the sort of literary Decadence that was characteristic of fin de siècle male fantasy fiction, although Beerbohm's caricature of Lee as a bonneted blue-stocking places her in the midst of what Elaine Showalter has called the "threatening daughters of decadence," whose own brand of perversion (as she elsewhere notes) was denigrated as being peculiar to New Women writers, "shriveled prudes whose malign influence enervated a virile male genre."[11] As fully "disputatious, contradictious and perverse" as she was credited with being (the assessment is James's), Lee's explications of her aesthetic suggest that she would have abjured a strict affiliation with literary Decadence while scorning to entertain the secondary implication, although her works are in fact tinged with the same ambivalence that is to be found in the works of writers more readily associated with the Decadent milieu.[12] An "Englishwoman . . . of the English" (Bernard Shaw's designation) who had lived, as Mario Praz reminds us, "all of her life intellectually and aesthetically in a world redolent of the hothouse"; reared in the country that had provided the setting for *The Marble Faun* (1860), a book that Lee confessed to have been "perpetually reading" in Sargent's company, while her own literary productions would come to be imbued, as James thought, "deeply" with "the redolence of the unspeakable Italy"; Lee seems to have waged a lifelong struggle with certain aspects of her own artistry.[13] Although she was a self-proclaimed aesthetician, for example, she became preoccupied, following her first "official" visit to England in the summer of 1881, with what she perceived as a "decadent and erotic strain in aestheticism," and this growing knowledge, as Leonee Ormond reminds us, "disgusted her."[14] Yet her writings reflect precisely this strain, her artistic vision at times running afoul of what James called her "too moral a passion," so that having, at the age of twenty-four, introduced her own *Studies of the Eighteenth Century in Italy* (1880) as the work of "neither a literary historian nor a musical critic, but an aesthetician," she could set about deconstructing aestheticism, attacking the so-called fleshly school in a lumber-

ing multivolumed novel that James saw as "strangely without delicacy or fine-
ness" and deplored as a "mistake—to be repented of."[15] Weighing Lee's "bristling distrust of 'pure' aesthetics and . . . downright distaste for aestheticism and
'art for art's sake'" against her "reverence for art that was nothing short of
religious in its intensity," Vineta Colby speculates that operating always within
her was "a kind of puritanical vigilance far more subtle and refined, thanks to
her European background, than that of the English philistine—but persistent
and persuasive."[16]

The question mark that concludes the subtitle of Ruth Robbins's recent
reconsideration—"Vernon Lee: Decadent Woman?"—registers not only the apparently self-contradictory attitudes embedded in but also the confusion that
marks the history of criticism generated by her work. In his study of Decadent
style, for example, John R. Reed characterizes Lee as "ill-disposed to aesthetes,"
whereas Albert C. Baugh, in his *Literary History of England,* connects Lee's
name with those of Symonds and Pater, the latter of whom whom she designated "master" in her adulatory conclusion to *Renaissance Fancies and Studies* (1895).[17] In his review of her *Juvenalia* (1887), a volume of essays on aesthetic questions intended to supplement those that she had posed in *Belcaro*
(1881), Pater judged that the force of her skill resided both in her prose style ("at
times plethoric and contorted," though also "rich, varied, and expressive") and,
more particularly, in the "picturesque, romantic, and wholly modern sensibility"
that she brings to bear on the subjects of her interest. Pater concludes his review with an allusion to the "ethical tone" that chastens both her style and her
sensibility: "For in truth, together with all those fine qualities, there has been
always traceable in Vernon Lee's work an unaffected sense of great problems,
of the real probation of men and women in life, of a great pity, of the 'sad story
of humanity,' bringing now and again into her exposition of what is sometimes
perhaps decadent art a touch of something like Puritanism."[18] Pater's choice of
gerund phrase ("bringing . . . into") represents Lee as inclusive and multiplicitous
rather than contradictious, recasting her as a "varied" rather than a schizoid
artist. "Various" was the term that she had applied to Sargent's "occasionally
self-conflicting" perspective and "double nature," which she traced back to his
"exuberantly gifted, expressive and *lebenslustige* mother, on the one hand, and
. . . his puritan, reserved and rather sternly dissatisfied father, on the other." In
admonishing Sargent's critics, whom she accuses of having "seen only one side
at a time" of his "many-sidedness and the complexity of his genius," Lee appears covertly to plead for leniency for her "vain self," in whom she claimed
Sargent "secretly expected" to discover his "equal" and "*twin,* in the sister-art of
letters."[19] Like the age to which it responded, Lee's was a complex genius, involving (as she had written of her mother's personality) "a mass of contradictions; but these were all grown into each other, made organic and inevitable by
her passionate and unmistakable individuality which recognized no law but its
own."[20]

Her reproach of Ruskin for his catholicity might be said to serve as an apologia of the contrarities—what she might have preferred to view as the inevitabilities—of her aesthetic sensibility. In "Ruskinism: The Would-be Study of a Conscience," included in *Belcaro*, she takes Ruskin to task for recoiling from the irrefutable fact that "the beautiful to whose study and creation he was so irresistibly drawn, had no moral value; that in the great battle between good and evil, beauty remained neutral, passive, serenely egotistic."[21] Ruskin's failing, in her view, was that it was "necessary for him that beauty should be more than passively innocent: he must make it actively holy."[22] As James had argued that "questions of art are questions (in the widest sense) of execution; questions of morality are quite another affair" (an attitude, perhaps, that explains his restrained response—"'singular'—'most curious'—'nauseating, . . . but how quite inexpressibly significant'"—to the "special vileness" that, as John Buchan notes, the two men encountered when asked to examine some of the skeletons in the Byron family closet); and as Wilde had insisted that "the fact of a man being a poisoner is nothing against his prose," the "domestic virtues" being incapable of serving as the "true basis of art"; so Lee believed that what was beautiful need not conduce to what was morally good any more than that which is ugly—"the putrescent corpse and the murderer's face"—need be reprehensible.[23] She would go further, asserting that a morally delinquent artist was fully capable of rendering beautiful works of art; the materialistic, carnal Renaissance painter Perugino, she points out, produced estimable paintings. "Sin and Pain and Injustice are realities," she concludes in a display of her romantically negative capabilities, "and what is worse, they are necessities": "they are not despite Nature, but through Nature; destructive forces perhaps, but which Nature requires for her endless work of construction. . . . And worse still, evil and good are not opponents . . . . , together they are knit in closest and most twisted bonds of cause and effect; bonds so close, so inextricably crossed and recrossed that severing one of them, tearing and cutting them asunder, it seems as if the whole universe would crash down upon us. . . . Beauty is pure, complete, egotistic: it has no other value than its being beautiful."[24] Lee's insistence that what is beautiful may shape itself by virtue of its proximity to what is ugly and perverse does not override, however, the "touch of puritanism" that colors her observations, prompting her at other points in the essay to "shudder" as, "with reluctance, indeed, and sorrow," she acknowledges their regrettable ("what is worse") truth.[25]

In her expository writings Lee established a clear distinction between what she seems to have hoped aestheticism could entail and what she seems to have feared—equally instinctively—that it would become. In *Renaissance Fancies and Studies*, for example, she argued that "even if beauty is united to perverse fashions, and art (as with Baudelaire and the decadents) employed to adorn the sentiments of maniacs and gaol-birds, the beauty and the art remain," and she urged in *Gospels of Anarchy* (1908)—as Yeats would do in his *Autobiographies*

(1926)—that "art, like science itself, like philosophy, like every great healthy human activity, has a right to live and a duty to fulfil, quite apart from any help it may contribute to the enforcement of a moralist's teachings."[26] Her mouthpiece Baldwin (a character reminiscent of Wilde's Vivian in "The Decay of Lying" or Gilbert in "The Critic as Artist") announces that an artist must be allowed "absolute liberty of selection and treatment of subjects to the exclusion," he hastily adds, "of all abnormal suggestion, of all prurient description, and of all pessimistic misrepresentation."[27] If Lee was unable to resolve these ceaselessly conflicting attitudes, however, she managed, in her fiction and more particularly in her horror stories, to make them more fully "organic and inevitable by her . . . unmistakable individuality which recognized no law but its own."

Although they account for only about one-quarter of the entire body of her work, most of her fictions (and particularly her short prose narratives, for in both the from and the content of her work Lee often gravitated toward the minute) were written before 1905.[28] Here, as in nearly everything she said or wrote or thought, Lee expressed her determined notions both as to what degree of supernaturalism was appropriate and as to the relation of the supernatural to art itself—so that only the orthodox reader of her stories would concur with Horace Gregory's assessment that "ghosts are boldly listed in Vernon Lee's dramatis personae."[29] As her "master" Pater liked to consider that a "finer, more delicately marvellous supernaturalism" existed in contrast to the "crudity" and "coarseness" of the "too palpable intruders from a spiritual world in almost all ghost literature, in Scott and Shakespeare even," so Lee scoffed at the notion that genuine ghosts arise from the experiences "of some Jemima Jackson, who fifty years ago, being nine years of age, saw her maiden aunt appear six months after decease."[30] In the preface to *Hauntings*, she arraigned traditional ghost stories that are "about a nobody," that have "no point or picturesqueness," and that are "generally speaking, flat, stale, and unprofitable."[31] Such things, as she had argued nearly twenty years earlier in *Belcaro*, have less to do with the supernatural and the imagination than with a mistaken attempt to rationalize "phenomena otherwise inexplicable": they represent "abortive attempts to explain phenomena by causes with which they have no connection."[32] What "use has [the supernatural] got," she flatly asked, "if it land us in Islington or Shepherd's Bush?"[33]

The perception of the genuinely ghostly, Lee believed, required an "additional sense" evolving out of "the effect on the imagination of certain external impressions"—impressions, she wrote, that had been "brought to a focus, personified, but personified vaguely, in a fluctuating ever-changing manner; the personification being continually altered, reinforced, blurred out, enlarged, restricted by new series of impressions from without."[34] In other words, the supernatural had something to do with the "lie of the land": with the sensations, the impressions, and the symbols suggested by the spirit of places and the spirit

of things, and, more essentially, with the extent to which such "spurious ghosts
. . . haunted certain brains," engendering in them "things of the imagination,
born there, bred there, sprung from the strange confused heaps, half-rubbish,
half-treasure, which lie in our fancy, heaps of half-faded recollections, of fragmentary vivid impressions, litter of multi-coloured tatters, and faded herbs and
flowers, whence arises that odour (we all know it), musty and damp, but pen-
etratingly sweet and intoxicatingly heady, which hangs in the air when the
ghost has swept through the unopened door, and the flickering flames of candle
and fire start up once more after waning."[35] As this Hawthornean passage
suggests (it recalls, perhaps, the passage in "The Custom House" describing
the genesis of *The Scarlet Letter*), the capacity to be haunted resides in an
individual state of mind and requires some external stimulus—an atmosphere,
an image, the configuration of carefully selected words—to trigger a series of
impressions at once vaguely desirable and unsettling. "Born of the imagination
and its surroundings, the vital, the fluctuating, the potent," Lee's "real supernatural" involves a kind of Paterian exchange of external impression for internal awareness and sensation, and so for Lee could not be apprehended by
means of the traditional Gothic formulas for evoking terror and pity but instead
required indirection, an "unceasing shaping and reshaping" of the creations of
the fancy sponsored from without.[36]

In "The Lie of the Land," an essay included in *Limbo* (1897), Lee expresses
her desire "to talk about something which makes the real, individual landscape—
the landscape one actually sees with the eyes of the body and the eyes of the
spirit—*the landscape you cannot describe*." Convinced of the "extreme one-
sidedness of language" and therefore doubtful of her ability to find a term that
could embody her precise meaning, Lee refers to this landscape as "an unnamed mystery into which various things enter," and these things make her
feel as if she ought to explain herself "by dumb show."[37] Although she portrays
herself as rendered mute by a language insufficiently evolved to accommodate
the rhythms and movements whose existence she intuits, she nevertheless succeeds (if Browning's sense of things in his "Inapprehensiveness" is to be credited) in sketching a landscape invested with a mystery that, so far from unbur-
dening the observer, thrusts "various things" into the field of vision. In his
salutatory poem (a dialogue between two people who lament their inability to
transcend mere sensory perception and to approach direct apprehension),
Browning credits her with having the ability first to notice and then to describe
the peculiar movements of wall-climbing plants: in short, with being able to
discern and communicate not merely the look but the *essence* of things. In a
tribute that he paid to Lee on the occasion of her death, Praz elucidates the
evocative quality of Lee's art: "Vernon Lee had, as few people have, a genius
for unveiling the secret rhythm of the landscape, of an epoch, of a work of art.
She liked to fix in a name, in an emblematic symbol, the uniqueness of her
discoveries."[38] Both Browning and Praz fix on Lee's uncanny ability to capture

the *genius loci et rei*, and their coincident terms of praise suggest that the two men conceived of her as sharing with the impressionists and symbolists what Symons described (in the context of Decadence in art) as a desire to flash "in a new, sudden way so exact an image of what you have just seen, just as you have seen it," that what is simultaneously flashed upon "the 'soul'" is "that which can be apprehended only by the soul—the finer sense of things unseen."[39]

The sort of mystery that Lee sought to evoke, then, required ambiguity and indefinition, and becomes what Praz describes as "a continual speculation in delicate hues."[40] Lee asserts in "Faustus and Helena" that although the two would appear to be closely allied, the supernatural is fundamentally antithetical to art, for the former is "necessarily essentially vague, and art is necessarily essentially distinct: give shape to the vague and it ceases to exist."[41] The image of the ibis on the amulet or the owl on the terra-cotta is more provocative than that of the Venus de Milo "not because the idea of divinity is more compatible with an ugly bird than with a beautiful woman," but because the former, Lee argued, allows the mind to wander off "in the contemplation of the vague."[42] Define too precisely the nature of the uncanny, the horrific, the mysterious, she suggests, and one trivializes them, removing them from the realm of what could be to that which is: "the familiar, the inevitable," as James had chosen to characterize "the real." James shared this view of the supernatural, suggesting that "so long as the events are veiled, the imagination will run riot and depict all sorts of horrors, but as soon as the veil is lifted, all mystery disappears."[43] Necessarily "enwrapped in mystery," the supernatural depends for its full effect—for its very existence—upon symbol and impression, on the "dumb shows" that Lee herself viewed as necessary if she were to be successful in capturing the "lie of the land" as she perceived it. Not surprisingly, then, when a critic had compared "A Phantom Lover" (1886) (an early story that would later reappear in *Hauntings* as "Oke of Okehurst") to Stevenson's *Dr. Jekyll and Mr. Hyde*, she is said to have bristled and pointedly distinguished her own story as "very much better"— although she qualified her judgment by asserting that her own sympathies did not lie with "the prosaic, unpicturesque kind of supernatural."[44]

By what means, then, does Lee manage to avoid the "prosaic" kind of supernatural and conjure up, in her own supernatural stories, what she recalled having once stumbled upon in the House of Pilate church: "*It: It*, a vague terror and sorrow" that was genuinely "terrible to our ancestors and terrible but delicious to ourselves, sceptical posterity"?[45] Taking the stories that she wrote between the years 1890 and 1899 as evidence of her evolving sense of what constituted the "picturesquely" supernatural, we can say that Lee came to rely more heavily upon the florid prose style to which she had been drawn since the earliest years of her career. The style of the Italian poet and novelist Gabriele D'Annunzio, for example—whose writings at one point earned him a reputation as a perverter of public morals—served, in Lee's estimation, to establish the interconnection between syntax, diction, sentence length, and emotion. In

The Handling of Words, Lee suggests that the power of D'Annunzio's prose resides in the suggestive sinuosities of his "long, latinized sentences, where adjectives are rare and verbs vague"—language that in turn delineates rictal horrors, "an impression of something empty, featureless, gaping, but irresistibly emphatic, eerie and tragic, which allows one to read the most revolting or preposterous stories without, as one otherwise would, disbelieving in their possibility outside a madhouse."[46] Although adjectives are hardly a rarity in Lee's own style, during her most prolific period as a writer of supernatural stories she sought to correlate language and content, style and meaning, as she perceived the stylists she admired—Pater and D'Annunzio—to have done. More specifically, she saw that language could be used to evoke and hint at, rather than name and fix, ideas and moods, thus allowing the reader's mind to wander off "in contemplation of the vague." Lee's language—rich and evanescent—stops just short of clarifying exact meanings and instead creates a kind of vacuum that would be filled, so she imagined, with what the ideally sympathetic reader would bring to her work. In her early stories, Lee approximated the picturesque in a prose style that seemed to her critics to be dangerously overwrought: the American novelist and translator Harriet Waters Preston, for example, described it as a "sort of riotous verbiage and eager habit of iteration and reiteration." Van Wyck Brooks, in turn, wrote of Lee's "strange fragments of human experience bearing with them odors and evanescent hues and curious forms," and Burdett Gardner discovered "an unhealthy excess of color and jewelled ornament . . . a style bedecked in ormolu" (his characterization casting him in the role of the "uninstructed reader" who, as Symonds had much earlier warned Lee, "might feel himself in a thick luxuriant wood, *&* long for a little more definiteness").[47]

The conjunction of form and content—which in turn tropes the external and the internal, the spoken and the unspeakable, the physical and the psychic—conducts and condenses the unwholesome weirdness that is a locus of the picturesque in Lee's stories. Thus, the lush descriptions of Venetian gardens are treated as being as likely a source of the vagaries of the young composer of "A Wicked Voice" (1890) as are the offended sensibilities of the ghostly castrato who haunts him. In the material opacity of the story's prose, evident in its descriptions of morbid atmosphere and images of decomposition and decay, place and mind coalesce, the latter shaped by impressions and apprehensions drawn from the surroundings to which it is seamlessly joined. The narrator is haunted not merely by the castrato's voice, but also by the miasmic Venetian landscape, from which he had originally sought inspiration for the composition of his opera *Ogier the Dane,* but which instead contributes to, and is in turn reflected in, his fevered imaginings. He writes that "beneath the dreamy splendour of noontide, Venice seemed to swelter in the midst of the waters, exhaling, like some great lily, mysterious influences, which make the brain swim and the heart faint—a moral malaria, distilled, as I thought, from those languishing melodies,

those cooing vocalisations which I had found in the musty music-books of a
century ago." Later, he blames the failure of his attempts to write his opera on
Venice itself, for it "had merely put all my ideas into hopeless confusion; it was
as if there arose out of its shallow waters a miasma of long-dead melodies,
which sickened but intoxicated my soul. I lay on my sofa watching that pool of
whitish light, which rose higher and higher, little trickles of light meeting it here
and there, wherever the moon's rays struck upon some polished surface; while
huge shadows waved to and fro in the draught of the open balcony."[48]

Shot through with color—one encounters the painted image of "a goddess
in lemon and lilac draperies, foreshortened over a great green peacock" (210);
sound—the narrator is beset by "little, sharp, metallic, detached notes" and "a
voice, very low and sweet" that fills a room with an "exquisite vibrating note,
of a strange, exotic, unique quality" (210); and smell—"a heavy, sweet smell,
reminding [him] of the flavour of a peach" (210) assails the narrator, who in
turn dreams "a very strange dream" in which he is stifled by air laden "with
the scent of all manner of white flowers, faint and heavy in their intolerable
sweetness" (208): the self-conscious materiality of the language of "A Wicked
Voice" blankets the contours of the narrator's psychic landscape, which in its
turn shapes itself referentially in response to external stimuli. The emphasis
on color and form and sound and scent—the *genius rei*—are to Lee's reader
what the opaque atmosphere of Venice—the *genius loci*—is to the narrator of
her story.

"A Wicked Voice" is of particular interest because, as the revision of one of
her earliest ghost stories, "Winthrop's Adventure" (1881), it allows one to trace
Lee's gravitation toward the Decadence of her age, evident (if in nothing else) in
her pastiching of the distinctive features of the late-nineteenth-century Decadent
idiom.[49] Both stories concern the experience of an artist who is haunted by the
ghost of a dead eighteenth-century singer. In the earlier story the narrator tells
us about Julian Winthrop, an "odd," "fantastic," "impressionable" artist devoted
to no particular genre or method of art because he is possessed of "too ungovernable a fancy, and too uncontrollable a love of detail, to fix and complete any
impression in an artistic shape."[50] One afternoon at the villa of his friend Countess S—, Winthrop hears an obscure air that, with its "exquisitely-finished phrases,
its delicate vocal twirls and spirals, its symmetrically ordered ornaments" (146),
agitates him. He explains that some years earlier he had discovered a portrait
of an eighteenth-century Italian singer, Ferdinando Rinaldi, who holds in his
"beautiful plump, white, blue-veined hand" a sheet of music. The title of the
work is "Sei Regina, io pastor sono" (163), and Maestro Fa Diesis, the collector
who owns the portrait, describes it as a typical trunk air. Winthrop's obsession
with the history of the singer with the "yearning, half-pained look" is enhanced
both by his desire to hear the melody (the painted notes are unintelligible, and
the score itself, Fa Diesis claims, is lost) and by his knowledge that the singer
had been murdered after receiving "too great notice from a lady in high favour

at Court" (166). Winthrop eventually winds up at the villa where Rinaldi was assassinated, and, during the evening of his stay in the abandoned building, he hears the elusive tune sung by someone who looks at him with "deep, soft, yearning eyes" (198): as one might expect, it is the spectral Rinaldi.

Although Lee leaves open the possibility that Winthrop's "ungovernable fancy" explains his ghostly vision, the tale is still a fairly straightforward example of the sort of ghost story produced by Lee's precursors—by J. Sheridan Le Fanu or Dickens, for example. The narrator of "A Wicked Voice" is also an artist—an aspiring Wagnerian composer—who, in Poesque fashion, is driven by ungovernable passions. He is haunted, so he believes, by a singer, the castrato Balthasar Cesari, apparently because he (the narrator) has vilified singers as defilers of music who corrupt neoclassical "heroic harmonies" with their romantic "voluptuous phrases and florid cadences" (216). Although the plot, in its broad particulars, is essentially the same in both versions, the revision—chronicling a journey that is at once a confession, an exploration of horror, and a descent into madness—depends for its effects upon narrative and stylistic features that create the sort of uncanniness typical of both fin de siècle Decadence and the traditional tale of horror. Unlike Winthrop, who could not forget the yearning face of his dead singer, the narrator of "A Wicked Voice" is haunted not by the dead singer Cesari (called "Zaffirino" because he possesses "a sapphire engraved with cabalistic signs presented to him one evening by a masked stranger" (199), a detail that reminds us that Lee shared an interest in fin de siècle diabolism with contemporaries such as Aleister Crowley and Arthur Machen) but by his voice and by the melody for which he was famous—the *Aria dei Mariti*. The strains of this "Husband's Air" tyrannize over him, preventing the completion of his own opera, *Ogier the Dane* (the legendary knight who was held in thrall by an enchantress). Scorning not music but the sound of the human voice—because the voice is "but the Beast calling, awakening that other Beast sleeping in the depths of mankind, the Beast which all great art has ever sought to chain up, as the archangel chains up, in old pictures, the demon with his woman's face" (198)—the narrator finds himself desiring the very thing that (consciously, at least) most repulses him. The haunting sound of Zaffirino's voice becomes his "inspiration," and he awaits "its coming as a lover awaits his beloved": "O wicked, wicked voice, violin of flesh and blood made by the Evil One's hand, may I not even execrate thee in peace; but is it necessary that, at the moment when I curse, the longing to hear thee again should parch my soul like hell-thirst? And since I have satiated thy lust for revenge, since thou hast withered my life and withered my genius, is it not time for pity? May I not hear one note, only one note of thine, O singer, O wicked and contemptible wretch?" (237).

The cry of frustrated longing with which "A Wicked Voice" concludes recalls Dorian's troubled response when, casting about for a comparative that will capture the seductive quality of his mentor's discourse, he settles on "music," "sweet as that of viol or of lute," whereas Lord Henry in his turn imagines that the "terribly enthralling" pleasure of talking to Dorian is akin to what would follow from his "playing upon an exquisite violin," the "music of passion" being the answer it would make "to every touch and thrill of the bow."[51] All three passages represent pure melody—pure art—as suborning what is sensuous, erotic, bestial. The motif of music as the veiled expression of sublimated—often homo-erotic—desire recurs in a number of Lee's stories. It is to be found as well in a number of late- nineteenth-century horror stories. We encounter it, for example, in John Meade Falkner's "The Lost Stradivarius" (1895), in which the narrator's brother is destroyed by the music that he draws from a rare Stradivarius that had once belonged to a worshiper of occult mysteries, and in Oliver Onions's "The Beckoning Fair One" (1911), whose protagonist's sanity is forfeited to the music of a harp played by a phantom woman. Abstract and largely antirepresentational, music expresses itself entirely through form; but from "the point of view of form," as Wilde understood, music is "the type of all the arts."[52] Moreover, the cadences, movements, intonations, and harmonies substitute tex-tually for the otherwise unspeakable desire of the body. Lee treats music in "A Wicked Voice" not merely as a prototypical art form, but also as a metaphor for the aestheticism to which she was fiercely devoted but under the spell of which she feared she might fall too completely.

Yet, the fact that Zaffirino's artistry is not merely erotically charged but fatal—his "first song could make any woman turn pale and lower her eyes, the second make her madly in love, while the third song [presumably the *Aria dei Mariti*] could kill her off on the spot, kill her for love, there under his very eyes, if he only felt inclined" (202)—complicates the reading that would interpret the "narrator's anguished peroration to 'A Wicked Voice'" as, to borrow John Clute's characterization, "the mutilating savagery of Lee's own refusal of the haunting licentiousness of art."[53] The sexual aggression that one encounters in "A Wicked Voice" is a curiously recurring thematic motif in Lee's corpus, and although it is not always rendered metaphorically as music, it is almost always feminized, manifested by versions of the despotic femmes fatales and destroying bitch-goddesses beloved of the Decadents. Thus, the duplicitous Medea da Carpi, an infamous figure of sixteenth-century Urbanian history, lures the naive Profes-sor Spiridion Trepka of "Amour Dure" (1890) into a madness reminiscent of that which follows upon the fawning affections of the brutish feminine specter who dogs the misogynistic professor of Robert Hichens's "How Love Came to Professor Guildea" (1900). The title character of Lee's "The Virgin of the Seven Daggers" (1889) is an effigy of a sixteenth-century Spanish Madonna for whom the only sufficient devotional offering or sacrifice is the head of her cavalier worshiper, the debauched Don Juan. With her skirts that "bulge out in melon-shaped folds, all damasked with minute heartsease, and brocaded with silver roses," she is a baroque version of "Parvati, mound-hipped love-goddess of the luscious fancy of the Brahmin," to whom Merimée, the narrator of Shiel's

"Xélucha" (1896), compares the title character, whom he envisions in "the re-
dundance of her *décolleté* development"—"Xélucha, the feminine! Xélucha recalling the splendid harlots of history! . . . expert as Thargelia; cultured as
Aspasia; purple as Semiramis."[54]

The jeweled language—what Bleiler calls the "elaborate word lapidarism"—
of Merimée's experience with Xélucha is paradigmatic of the reader's covertly lecherous experience with the Decadent text, which often features protagonists whose lusts are inflamed and not cooled in the chill of the grave.[55]
This stylistic ormolu also functions as an analog to the demonic Xélucha
herself, who is identified with the abnormal beauty of artifice and hyperre-
finement conducive, however paradoxically, to a corruption that expresses
itself organically: "gamy and marbled with corruption" is the descriptive that
Gautier assigns to the Decadent style.[56] In this respect, Shiel's "Xélucha" exemplifies what critics such as Rémy G. Saisselin and Rae Beth Gordon have
cited as the damning (and otherwise unlikely) identification of femininity with
ornament and the decorative in Western culture, an association characteristic of the writing of late-nineteenth-century decadents and aesthetes (literally
rather than metaphorically expressed in Lord Henry's assertion that women
are "a decorative sex").[57] Lee's otherwise curiously straightforward engagement with the masculine desire to control and contain the perceived threat
embodied in the *ewig weibliche* [the eternal feminine]—an engagement exemplified in the excess of idiom of which she continually avails herself in the
body of her work—is further complicated when one considers her description
of the despotic Zaffirino, who is said to possess an "effeminate, fat face . . .
almost beautiful, with an odd smile, brazen and cruel," the likes of which the
narrator remembers encountering only in "Swinburne and Baudelaire"—whose
works, he says, were characterized by "the faces of wicked, vindictive women"
("A Wicked Voice," 206). The suggested textual politics of Lee's story are
aggravated, not reinforced, however, by the fact that Zaffirino is not a femme
fatale: not the impressionable and melancholic Alice Oke of Okehurst, not
the *femme fée* who is the Snake Lady to whom Prince Alberic betroths himself, not the *femme sorcière* who is Dionea, a young Eastern girl of exotic
beauty whom the narrator takes to be a fatal incarnation of Venus; rather, he
is a castrato, an explicitly feminized man who, in taking his place among the
"feminized male protagonists, who are identified with love of artifice, excess,
and everything unnatural," by extension connects Lee herself with the cadre
of male European avant-garde authors whose writings blurred culturally determined distinctions regarding gender and class. Rita Felski suggests that
the apparently "parodic subversion of gender norms" (typical of this genre),
which is conventionally interpreted as creating "a counterdiscourse of symbolic resistance to the commodification and technical rationality of modern
capitalism," in fact "reinscribes more insistently the divisions that the text ostensibly calls into question, revealing deep-seated anxieties about both gender

and class," although it would appear to be "part of a larger destabilization of conceptions of authenticity" and "a critical response to the presentation of bourgeois values and beliefs as rooted in an organic and unchanging reality."[58]

In assuming such contradictory attitudes and models of expression, Lee positions herself squarely in the midst of the decadence of her age, its apparently conflictive variability providing—just as Lee's did—its only true consistency. Perversity is embedded in and framed by perversity in such stories of hers as "A Wicked Voice" or "The Virgin of the Seven Daggers," both of which serve, as Gardner notes, as prime examples of the sort of writing "which brought the reproach of 'decadence' on the *Yellow Book*"—a publication with which Lee was in any event affiliated, her "Prince Alberic and the Snake Lady" having appeared in the tenth volume in July of 1896.[59] And like *The Yellow Book*, the existence of which was so brief, Lee's excursion into and embattled engagement with Decadence did not long survive the century's close.

By the end of the first decade of the twentieth century, in fact, she had for the most part left off writing "unlikely" stories altogether—perhaps because she felt increasingly that the very writing of them was a self-indulgent as well as a self-incriminating pastime; perhaps because this particular mode of writing had itself become "decadent," the subject of parody or satire. In any case, the change enabled her to focus her considerable energies on the study of literary psychology—and when she returned to her old themes nearly three decades after the turn of the century, Lee turned to something like Henry James's emphasis on a "deeper psychology," abandoning her "ormolu" in favor of a more chastened description of a solitary image, evoked in a title that seems to promise very little. Yet in "The Doll," the fifth of the "Five Unlikely Stories" contained in the collection entitled *For Maurice* (1927), she succeeds in creating her briefest, her most complex, her most uncanny, and perhaps her best story.

Although its chaste simplicity of structure and tone would seem to indicate that Lee was seeking not merely to transcend the consciously artificial style of her Decadent years—a style recalled in the four other unlikely stories of *For Maurice*—but to purge her art of its incriminating aestheticism, "The Doll" represents the culmination of all she had learned in the course of her excursions into Decadence and the supernatural. It therefore takes its otherwise unlikely place in this consideration of fin de siècle horror because it revisits, reconsiders, and in a sense exorcises the unresolved issues that are covertly present in the style and structure of the other tales of the volume (among them, "Winthrop's Adventure"), which had their genesis in an earlier phase of a career that may be said to have prepared her for the writing of "The Doll." Gone are the phantom voices, the crazed narrators, the murky atmospheres, the visions, the tormenting pagan goddesses: those defining markers of fin de siècle horror, the absence of which was apparently sufficient to persuade Bleiler to refrain from commenting on the tale in his *Guide to Supernatural Fiction*, other than to

pronounce it "not supernatural," a judgment with which Jessica Amanda
Salmonson implicitly takes issue in her decision to include it in her anthology
of feminist supernatural fiction, What Did Miss Darrington See?[60] Yet, the
absence of conventional ghosts does not dilute the general uncanniness of
"The Doll." The story begins with a faceless and nameless narrator who
recalls for her auditor (apparently a close female friend) the circumstances
surrounding her discovery in Italy of a life-size manikin. The narrator tells
her confidante that while on one of her "bric-à-brac journeys" in search of
antiquities, she took up residence at a small inn in Foligno, Umbria, where
she met a "delightful curiosity-dealer" whose "Christian" name was Orestes
and who shared her passion for beautiful things and for the past in general.[61]
Three days before the narrator was to depart, Orestes informed her that a
local nobleman wished to sell his collection of Chinese plates. Orestes persuaded her to view them, if only so that they might thereby gain entry to the
late-seventeenth-century palace, "grandiose, but very coarse," in which the
plates were housed. While wandering through the rooms of the palace, she
encountered a beautiful, finely made, and life-size figure of a woman, dressed
in the costume of the 1820s, which had been brought to the housekeeper's
room for its annual dusting and which "is," the housekeeper claimed, the first
wife of the count's grandfather. Sometime later, Orestes cautiously touched
on the subject of the object's strange life, revealing that the old count, after
the death of his beautiful child-bride, had ordered that a doll should be made
in her image. Clothed in her very dress, her silk stockings, her sandal shoes,
her silk mittens, and her own hair (which had been made into a wig that fit
over the cardboard head) the doll had been placed in the dead woman's chamber, where the old count had spent hours with it each day. Gradually, however, his interest waned; his visits grew fewer and eventually ceased altogether, and following his death, the doll was exiled to an obscure corner, from
whence it was finally rescued by the new count's housekeeper, who brought
the doll to her own room, where she dusted and admired it, because it "must
have cost a lot of money" and because its model had been a "real lady" (220).
Although she was eager to leave Foligno, the narrator found herself preoccupied with the story of the doll, whose fate, she came to imagine, rested with
her. She persuaded Orestes to negotiate on her behalf with the new count for
the purchase of the doll and, having secured her, conveyed her in a closed
carriage to Orestes's shop, behind which was a garden that looked out on the
Umbrian mountains. There, they placed the effigy upon a heap of kindling of
myrtle and bay, and lighted the pyre with a burning pine cone. As the small
holocaust subsided, the narrator discovered among the ashes a wedding band
(a precursor, perhaps, of that which the speaker of Sylvia Plath's "Lady
Lazareth" discovers in the midst of the "Ash, ash" that she pokes and stirs,
"Flesh, bone, there is nothing there") and, at the urging of Orestes, kept it,
thus concluding her tenure as a collector. Just as Foligno was the site of St.

Francis of Assisi's renunciation of material possessions, so her experience in the Umbrian village put her "out of conceit with ferreting about among dead people's properties" (209), perhaps because she perceived in herself a version of the "irresistible desire" common, as Nordau insisted, among degenerates who "accumulate useless trifles" and "aimless bric-a-brac, which does not become any more useful or beautiful by being called *bibelots*," or perhaps because she discerned in her rage for collecting a rage of a different order of magnitude.[62]

The doll takes pride of place among the effigies, stone idols, marionettes, and puppets littering the lumber room and enchanted garret of Lee's imagination. References to dolls, effigies, puppets abound in her writings and therefore in the studies or commentaries of her work written by her friends and critics. Lee's friend Maurice Baring—the "Maurice" of *For Maurice*—referred in his memoirs, for example, to the Italian "effigies, dolls, puppets" between whose world and our own Lee acted as a mediatrix.[63] In her first major critical endeavor, Lee herself charted the history of the eighteenth-century Italian *Commedia dell'Arte* tradition, with chapters titled "The Comedy of Masks," "Goldoni and the Realistic Comedy," and "Carlo Gozzi and the Venetian Fairy Comedy," all concerned with such figures as Pantalone, Harlequin, and Cassandrino—characters behind whose masks are live actors whose sole art, Lee stressed, "consisted in having none, in being real."[64] Three years after the publication of her *Studies*, Lee wrote a fairy story, *The Prince of the Hundred Soups*, which was, as its subtitle indicates, a puppet show in narrative.[65] The costumed and bewigged icon of "The Virgin of the Seven Daggers" precedes the dolls and effigies featured in at least four of the seven stories collected in a volume of Lee's work entitled *Pope Jacynth and Other Fantastic Tales* (1904), which includes a protagonist who is transformed into a stone idol in the title story; "Prince Alberic," with its reference to the debauched duke's hairdresser's block; "The Lady and Death," in which two wooden manikins representing St. Theodulus and the devil are locked in combat; "The Featureless Wisdom," in which three finely carved effigies of Athena play a central role; and "St. Eudaemon and His Orange Tree," featuring an unearthed statue of Venus.

Lee's contemporaries shared her obsession with creative automata, which they tended to view as their own creations. "Always make your man before you make your surrounding in spite of the book of Genesis" urged Gordon Craig in *The Mask*, his turn-of-the-century journal of puppetry. Automaton immortality was treated as being less conditional than that even of the immortals: "it is an incontestable and undisputed fact," wrote a contributor to *The Mask*, "that the puppets survived the Gods."[66] Its actions ritualized and contrived, the creative automaton is less susceptible to decay than is the animated nature that it mimics and mocks. Writing in 1897 to his friend Robert Bontine Cunninghame Graham, Conrad announced that marionettes were "beautiful" because their "impassibility in love in crime, in mirth, in sorrow,—is heroic, superhuman, fascinating": "I never listen to the text mouthed somewhere out of sight by invisible men who are here to day and rotten tomorrow," he wrote. "I love the marionettes that are without life, that come so near to being immortal!"[67] Conrad's passing allusion to what is "rotten" renames the instability that characterizes Jean Baudrillard's description of the simulacrum as "a liquidation of all referentials," which are artificially resurrected "in the systems of signs."[68] In the case of the sort of funerary effigy represented in Lee's story, this "liquidation" grows out of the anxious response to the material body's imminent liquefaction, one of the "vicissitudes" that Baudrillard notes the simulacrum "short-circuits" (2). The ideal funerary monument, Lee's doll serves as an incorruptible substitute for the decomposing body of the dead woman. It is the idealized portrait that denies or temporarily effaces the presence of death and thus offsets any anxiety that the living suffer in contemplating their own mortality, made palpably manifest in the body's dissolution following death.

In subjecting the human form to what Symons described as the "over-subtilizing refinement upon refinement" characteristic of literary Decadence, the funerary effigy transforms the destabilized body whose volatile corporeality and imminent dissolution it occludes into an ideal of death in life and life in death, gathering it instead into Yeats's "artifice of eternity."[69] It serves simultaneously, however, as a memento mori, a "reminder" of death and a variant of the classical "skeleton at the feast" tradition (to which we have already referred), according to which invited guests at a banquet pass from hand to hand a corpse-image—called, among other names, a "cadaverino." With their "jointed heads, arms and legs . . . especially designed to represent a lifeless body," these "gloomy convivial marionettes" served as a commentator for *The Mask* notes, either as "a poor jest of the worst kind" or else as "an incentive to the practical propaganda of epicurianism."[70] Some odd blend of jest and egotism, for example, very probably informed Jeremy Bentham's decision to have his own body, upon his death, filled out with straw, dressed in his clothes, and transformed into an entity that was, according to the terms of his will, to be brought out each year to preside over a meeting held on Founder's Day at University College in London, where it still sits—enclosed in a glass case—during the remainder of the year. (Bentham was also the author of a curious work entitled *Auto-Icon, or Farther Uses of the Dead to the Living* [1842?], but his attempt to transform himself into his own memorial statue—the process involved embalming and the use of caoutchouc and shellac—was not altogether successful, for his head decayed and was eventually replaced with one made of wax, and the original was placed between his "feet.") That his preserved self should—through his own head's unruliness—thus betray itself as a mixture of dissimilar parts is not surprising, but serves rather as a piquantly perverse (and, what is better, unvarnished) expression of the essentially conflictive quality of all simulacra, each of which is by nature, as well as by art, an interfusion of unlike parts (it is perhaps worth reminding ourselves that "The Doll" appears in a collection subtitled "Five Unlikely Stories").

In its own way as monstrous as the homunculus in de la Mare's "A: B: O.," the heterogeneous simulacrum often interacts perniciously with those that come into contact with its unruly body, which is the embodiment of the abject, the paradoxically fixed yet irreferable locus at which borders are dissolved and oppositions and contrarieties fused. Maurice Rollinat's admission in *Le Maniaque*, "I always shudder at the strange look of some boot or some shoe . . . and suddenly, on thinking of the foot they cover, I ask myself: 'Is it mechanical, or living?'" suggests that for him not the body itself, but merely one of its displaced appurtenances was required if he were to experience a version of the frisson that E.T.A. Hoffmann had taught his followers (or those, at least, who frequented "waxwork museums") to recognize as "the oppressive sense of being in the presence of something unnatural and gruesome"—a sense itself originating in the instinctive knowledge that the puppet that looks alive might in fact *be* alive (and clustered among these interlocutory texts is the single black-heeled pump, accessorized with lace and an artificial rose, featured in the tenth of the eighteen photographs in which the artist Hans Bellmer documented the life of his sculptured doll, descendant of Hoffmann's Olimpia) (fig. 30).[71] "Das unheimliche" is the now overtaxed term that Freud assigned to that oppressive sense of anxiety and to the "doubts" generated by the unlikely question of whether an apparently animate being—"waxwork figures, ingeniously constructed dolls and automata"—might be "really alive; or conversely, whether a lifeless object might not be in fact animate."[72] The doubts that Lee's narrator sustains in relation to the doll originate not in the uncanny likeness it bears to its predecessor but in its treatment as a living being, for none of the story's characters differentiate between the countess and her effigy. Elaborating on Sally Humphreys's observation that "while the living body is associated with individuality, 'death threatens to put an end to differentiation,'" Bronfen argues that "the corpse is a figure without any distinguishing facial traits of its own, [and] one could say that semiotically it serves as an arbitrary, empty, interchangeable sign, an interminable surface for projections."[73] Lee's story, however, resists what both critics identify as the semiosis of the cultural representations of the dead woman, for the countess is represented as having enjoyed no greater degree of individuation in life than her memorialized body does in death. In filling so integrally the gap left by the death of the lady, Lee's doll suggests that, in life, the living countess was perceived as though she were an *it*, a dead object worthy of being loved just as a doll is—an *it* that is treated as though it were a *she*, her associates as blind to the essential differences between the living and the dead as the artist represented in Jean Wéber's *The Puppets* (1900), beside whom lies sprawled the naked body of a woman as passively immobile as the dolls upon which the artist's attention is fixed (fig. 31).

It is the doll's ability to efface the distinction between literal and figural—to assume, as Freud would have it, the culturally legitimized functions and meanings of the object it embalms and pacifies—that so profoundly disturbs the narrator of Lee's story. Yet although the narrator recognizes an essential disjuncture between form and essence, like the lady's earlier associations, for whom her face and form bear in death precisely the same contours that they assumed when animate, she of necessity reads her own meanings into the idealized portrait that presents itself to her view. The fact that she does so emphasizes cultural assumptions about a woman's inability to exercise any semblance of control over the meanings assigned to her, particularly in her aestheticized condition as art object, the various incarnations of which include, as Susan Gubar notes, "the ivory carving or mud replica, an icon or doll."[74] The degree to which nearly all of the story's characters—including the sympathetic narrator—control and articulate the terms of the lady's humanity is made manifest in a scene in which the housekeeper manipulates the doll and "positions" her, bending "the articulated arms, and [crossing] one leg over the other beneath the white satin skirt." While begging the "old witch" to desist, the narrator watches fascinated as "one of the poor feet" continues "dangling and wagging dreadfully" (216). This is the first of the only two instances in which Lee invokes the word "articulate" in relation to the doll. The second passage describes her condition in life as an "inarticulate" one, the consequence of her having been married, "straight out of the convent," to a man who "never . . . showed any curiosity as to whether his idol might have a mind or a character of her own" (217-18). His behavior is, presumably, determined by his expectations, among which "quietness" would figure as one of the preeminent "merits of women . . . while the opposite demerit of a tongue too loud, too ready, or too importunate in its exertions," as Sarah Stickney Ellis taught her readers to recognize, was objectionable—"universally condemned"—by members of a "nobler sex" who were contented to find in woman what Edward Carpenter would many years later attempt to teach the readers of his *Love's Coming-of-Age* (1896) to recognize as "an emblem of possession—a mere doll, an empty idol, a brag of man's exclusive right in the sex."[75]

Quietness, or "silence," and "obedience" are, not surprisingly, the two distinguishing virtues out of which springs what Gordon Craig designated as "chief" among the marionette's virtues: namely, the "humility" that, if it "is only an assumption in men," is particularly so in the "living actor," who, Arthur Symons alleged, "even when he condescends to subordinate himself to the requirements of pantomime, has always what he is proud to call his temperament; in other words, . . . this intrusive little personality of his."[76] Thus, the actress Eleonora Duse insisted that, because they poison the air of the theater and make its drama impossible, "actors and actresses must all die of the plague," whereas Gordon Craig suggested, somewhat less apocalyptically, that the theater might be saved merely by installing in place of flesh-and-blood actors whose bodies are "*by nature* utterly useless as a material for an art" the "über-marionette," a life-sized puppet that constituted the ideal actor, the "actor plus fire, minus egoism" (the latter a liability of the theater to which Craig, as the son of the legendary actress Ellen Terry and the architect William Godwin, would have had a good deal of exposure).[77]

Its traits allow the marionette to "respond to an indication without reserve or revolt," to "be trained to perfection," and to content himself with waiting "anywhere for any length of time, . . . hidden in a box, . . . in a cellar . . . or even in a century. But he will wait . . . and when he is brought forward and made to feel at home he will still wait . . . then he waits upon you and all of us like a true servant."[78] Impressed with the "passive, remote, impersonal and automatonlike nature of the marionette as it fruitlessly confronted the forces of destiny," Maurice Maeterlinck wrote his three dramas for puppets, *Alladine et Palomides, Intérieur,* and *La Mort de Tintagiles* (1894). Recognizing that "it is not nature that one looks for on the stage" but "what is illusive in the illusion . . . [of] this kind of spectacle," Symons lauded the marionettes for whom/which the playwright had conceived of his plays, discerning in these inspired pieces of "painted wood" the "perfect medium between the meaning of a piece, as the author conceived it, and that other meaning which it derives from" an audience's reception of it. Max Beerbohm in his turn speculated that puppets are better suited to convey "the artfulness . . . of nature," one hardly believing that "anyone but a marionette ever lived" in the midst of stylized settings.[79]

The salient differences in their respective situations might otherwise undermine the likelihood that a dead countess could meaningfully be compared to the marionettes, whose lives are so suitably framed by a proscenium arch. Even memorialized, as she is in death—indeed, *because* she has been memorialized in death—the countess is the perfect household icon, the ultimate art object and object of desire, sufficiently untraveled in the darker passages of the demimonde but still possessing something of the erotic attraction of the elegant courtesan of haute prostitution, as though she were the most expensive of bibelots. Isolated from the world of business—"the 'real world' in which real men . . . are . . . at war with each other"—and thus protected from "the battle of the streets," which, according to Saisselin, "exemplifies the male principle" (what Mrs. Ellis called "the potent [I had almost said the *omnipotent*] consideration of worldly aggrandizement"), enshrined within a sanctified realm, and therefore fully hidden from view, the marionette would appear to be able to acclimate itself to any situation, since the defining features of its existence are exposure—both through arrangement (the limp body of the doll invites intimate engagement) and through performance (the falsely animated body of the doll is wholly available to public view)—and contrivance, the latter characteristic at odds with the organicist, "natural" principle that throughout the nineteenth century was associated with the feminine principle.[80] Both art and women, as Felski points out, were "divorced from the work ethic and the real-

Figure 30. Hans Bellmer, plate 10 of *Die Puppe* (1934). © 1997 Artists Rights Society (ARS), New York/ADAGP, Paris

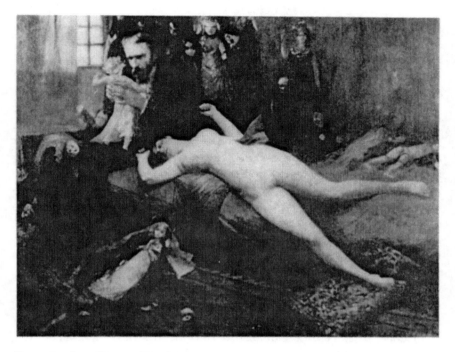

Figure 31. Jean Wéber, *The Puppets* (1900). Courtesy Phaidon Press Ltd, London, from Philippe Jullian, *The Symbolists* (1973)

ity principle," and both came increasingly to be "seen as decorative, function-
less, linked to the world of appearance and illusion"—particularly if one considers the association between the decorative feminine and interior decorating (an
appropriate avocation, as Saisselin notes, for the middle-class woman otherwise excluded from the spheres in which "true culture" was carried forward and
"great art" produced). The memorialized body of the woman perfects the room
she adorns, serving as the ultimate example of the "movable ornaments" that
the nineteenth-century American romantic Harriet Prescott Spofford, in her
discussion of bric-à-brac, saw as engrafting "a life and vivacity upon what would
frequently be but a dead dulness without them."[81] Moreover, the woman memorialized in death may be said to provide the occasion for and even, as in the case
of the marionette, the means by which a performance is carried forward. The
count in Lee's story spends "hours every day weeping and moaning before"
(219) the dead image of his wife, his expressions of grief (which counterbalance
his earlier effusions of love) requiring for their full effect an admiring audience,
which would ideally consist of the object of the devotions in whose eyes one
might read the mute gratitude that prostration so scrupulously performed would
surely merit.

Henry James's George Stransom deconstructs the motivations underlying
the similarly obsequious devotions that he performs at the altar of his dead and
suspects that, although he had initially indulged himself in the belief that he was
ministering to the needs of his departed friends, "it was essentially in his own
soul" that "the revival" of the dead had taken place, and it was "his presence . .
. that had made the indispensable medium." The dead, as he comes to understand, were witnesses to his "secret rites" in a way that the living could never
duplicate—the strange life of the object being such that it cannot conceive, as Lee
would elsewhere note, that it likes or dislikes anything done to it or said about it,
its existence being entirely subject to the satisfaction and (often casually cruel)
pleasure of another.[82] Thus, Maggie Tulliver keeps in the attic of the mill a large
wooden doll whose head records "a long career of vicarious suffering," the three
nails that it sports commemorating "as many crises in Maggie's nine years of
earthly struggle."[83] The tortuous affections that Eliot's heroine lavishes upon
her "Fetish" are an early, less intentionally murderous (if such is possible) version of those that the fourteen-year-old Gisèle Prassinos would many years
later imagine meting out to the life-size doll that became the photographed subject of Hans Bellmer's Die Puppe (1934): "When I press her full cheeks with my
hands," the real-life girl fantasized, "a whitish liquid will run out of her mouth.
There will be pink bubbles issuing from her nose. Then I will hug her very hard
to the point of killing her blue eyes, to the point of giving them a life of my own."
Her own desires, as she so well recognized, merely intersected those of the
doll's maker ("He wanted a big dead doll, to hold in his arms and stifle," she
precociously announced), who had expressed his own desire to adjust the
joints and arrange his doll in "childlike poses" so that once everything had

been made "pretty" he might proceed "ruthlessly" to "spill the salt of deformation."[84]

Prassinos's desire to read in the blue eyes of her idol "a life of my own" is
not fundamentally different—although the sadistic intent that informs it is more
artlessly divulged—than that of her contemporaries: of Bellmer himself, for example, who remembers having described the body of his doll "like a sentence
that invites us to rearrange it, so that its real meaning becomes clear through a
series of endless anagrams"; and before him, of Symons, who begrudged the
living actor his "little intrusive personality"; of the fictitious Stransom, who at
length understands that it is his own life that blazes in the candles of his altar,
and it is his own desire that he has read in the "looks that survived" long after
"the closed eyes of dead women . . . had looked their last"; and before these, of
Browning's Duke, the dizzying proliferation of the "I's" and "my's" of his monologue unveiling the true motivation behind his attempt to paint his duchess's
portrait in words.[85] Unnervingly—"contradictiously"—among them all is Lee
herself. In her admission, entered into her diary, that in the death of her friend
Anne Meyer, she "lost nothing or but little in the possible loss of the real Mme
Meyer—"for does there not remain, unchanged and unchangeable, the imagined one?"—she assures herself that "one cannot lose" the creature "born of
one's fancy and one's desires, the unreal," and the desires that she voices are
inseparable from those she felt "for artificial ideal beings, . . . who can never
shift the moral light in which we see them, who can never turn round in their
frames and say 'see, we are not what you imagined.'"[86] Thus "framed," such an
idealized being can never be other than a *divo amico desideratissimus,* a composite of the wishes and interests of another (and in this context it is perhaps
worth recalling Lee's coy admission that the symbolically named "Pier
Desiderio," whose surname expresses a desire for what is lost, was the one
who dictated her story to her). What is in fact exhibited more or less explicitly
in such devotionals is the power that supersedes the desire to possess, arrange,
and articulate: a power that, in much nineteenth-century writing, tended to to
define itself in textual terms in relation to the feminine, which, according to Mrs.
Ellis, required the faculty of "instrumentality" (a cross-purposed term signaling
an agency at once proactive and passively inclined, embodied in the "ability" to
"be used" and to serve), without which women could aspire only to the condition
of "dead letters in the volume of human life, filling what would otherwise be a
blank space, but doing nothing more."[87]

However sensitized she may be to the fact that the idealized portrait is no
less the object of a proprietary gaze, and made no less textuary a subject than
its antecedent had been, Lee's narrator, in the process of recovering the doll's
story, becomes a detached spectator as well—a role for which, as it turns out,
she is well fitted by nature as well as by necessity. For a brief while she con-
founds both the woman and her effigy in her indiscriminate use of the pronoun
"she," and elsewhere she admits that she initially allowed "no distinction be-

tween the portrait and the original" (217); even in retrospect she scarcely knows whether she ought "to call it a thing" (209). Only later in her narrative does she make an effort to correct herself, as when she claims to have known (in her words) "all about the Doll when she was alive—I mean about the lady" (218), a provocative presumption of knowledge given that the doll is a cipher—silent, motionless—and figures in this respect as a type of the daughter of England who (according to Mrs. Ellis) would ideally comport herself as one "who has nothing, and is nothing, of herself; whose experience, if unparticipated, is a total blank; . . . who, in her inexhaustible sympathies, can live only in the existence of another."[88] Mrs. Ellis's construction of the feminine curiously resonates with what Adolf Furst, in his "Note on Marionettes," later defined as the quintessence of the inanimate, proposing that "it is this doing nothing, this saying nothing, this meaning nothing which raises [the puppet] to an altitude that is limitless."[89] Richly abundant (nothingness is, for Mrs. Ellis, inexhaustible) and full of potential (nothingness possesses, for Furst, limitless possibility), what is "nothing" (the feminine, the inanimate) is so wholly accommodating and so expansive in terms of what it can be made to contain that it eventually does away with itself in favor of what seeks to occupy its place. Such, as Baudrillard would come to represent it, is "the vital function of the model in a system of death." In subsuming so completely the functions of the real, the model—or simula-crum—not only renders the real in which it originates redundant, but casts doubt on the plausibility of its ever having existed in the first place: "Never again," Baudrillard assures his reader, "will the real have the chance to produce itself" (2)—and we see here that in such a system of signs, one set of "vital" functions may substitute for another, less stable set. In this way, according to Baudrillard, the simulacrum—or hyperreal—threatens, assaults, and in the end destroys the "charm of abstraction," which rests in the "sovereign difference" (2) between "the true" and "the false," between "the real" and "the imaginary" (3). Such, he concludes, is the "murderous power of images" (5), and his phraseology hints at—although it avoids explicitly naming—yet another paradox and unlikelihood: the simulacrum must commit murder in order to efface death.

Although "irresistibly impelled" (217), as she says, to reconstruct the original story of the articulated woman, whatever "life" Lee's narrator in "The Doll" describes will not be peculiarly her subject's, for that is irrecoverable. She is likened both to an Ingres Madonna and to a Canova goddess, the comparative at once establishing generically and effacing the unique features of her face. Just as the divinities (whose mythologized lives are understood to have influenced the shape her own life has assumed) have themselves been purged, as Lee explained, of the "vitality of the myths of paganism," the doll has been drained in a process endlessly recuperated, but slightly diminished with each successive arrogation.[90] In this respect "The Doll" articulates in fictional terms an analysis that Lee had undertaken in those of her essays devoted to the cult of the Virgin, or Mariolatry (and it is perhaps worth noting in this context that the term *marionettes*, meaning "little Maries," refers to the diminutive versions sold by Venetian toy venders of the "Marioles" or "Marie di legno" [wooden Marie] or "Marione" [big Maries], pious images associated with the annual festival of the Maries, in which mechanical figures eventually came to substitute for the girls who, in the earliest years of the festival, were selected to represent twelve Venetian maidens who had been abducted by Barbary pirates, rescued, and then married—the puppets reenacting, that is, the narrative in which the virgin is threatened with dishonor and then reclaimed, her sexuality ceded to the state of marriage). Although willing to concede that their descendants could stand as plausible substitutes for the antique gods and goddesses—for "is [Our Lady] not the divine Mother of Gods as well as God, Demeter or Mary, in whom the sad and ugly things of our bodily origin and nourishment are transfigured into the grace of the immortal spirit?"—Lee more regularly inveighed against the Christian doctrines that had facilitated a "puritanic deprecation of whatever, throughout ages of greater faith, had survived of the antique gods and their jovial rites." Just as, for Lee, what was truly supernatural could not be regularized, defined, or explained, so the insufficiencies of the Christian supernatural system were due "not to overwrought fancy, but to overtaxed reason": "Christianity, born in an age of speculation and eclecticism, removed its divinities, its mystic figures, out of the cosmic surroundings of paganism; it forbade the imagination to touch or alter them, it regularised, defined, explained, placed the Saviour, the Virgin, the saints and angels, into a kind of supersensuous world of logic, logic adapted to Heaven, and different therefore from the logic of earth, but logic none the less."[91] She charged the "congress of men of science" who regulated the official Christianity with having banished "any vagaries of the imagination which might show themselves in their mystico-logic system" and thereby having extinguished the genuinely supernatural as well.[92] The supernatural is part of a larger engendering process, and to Lee it seemed that the myths of paganism derived their vitality from the "unceasing shaping and reshaping of [the fancy's] creations," for the real supernatural is "born of the imagination and its surroundings, the vital, the fluctuating, the potent."[93]

She argued, too, that Christianity, and particularly its feminine ideal, had grown increasingly asexual. Although Mary evolved out of a Hellenic culture and although she might perform many roles—mother, queen, bride, courtly lady—she does so always as a virgin, as *the* Virgin, her *in partu* and perpetual virginity what Michael P. Carroll points to as the defining feature of the Catholic Mary cult.[94] The ideal Victorian woman, having been created in the image of Mary (now "an effective instrument of asceticism and female subjection," Marina Warner notes), acquired not only her humility and submissiveness, but also a sexuality that perversely defines her as perfectly chaste matron and mother.[95] Hence the popularity of the archetypal *femme-enfant* portrayed in Abbott Handerson Thayer's *Virgin Enthroned* (1891) (fig. 32), or Thomas

Gotch's *The Child Enthroned* (1894) or *Holy Motherhood* (c. 1902); in the subject of each work, perfect juvenile chastity blends by degrees into serene maternal devotion. Lee suggests, however, that in having denied the Virgin (and by
extension, the woman in whose image she was remade) the sexual powers
that she had inherited from her pagan precursors, modernity had in fact deprived itself of genuine mythmaking powers. As her commentary to her story
featuring the impaled Madonna makes clear, a bloodless, intellectualized sensibility requires an equally etiolated divinity as the object of its devotions: a
virgin dressed in a "vast farthingale," her body "cased like a knife in its sheath"
in a network of seed pearl, her face "made of wax, white with black glass eyes
and a tiny coral mouth," and in the little clearing "made among the brocade
and the seed pearl" at her bosom, "seven gold-hilted knives."[96] This "knife-
riddled Spanish Madonna" of the Counter-Reformation receives the devotions
of a "super-rake and super-ruffian," both united "by common ancestry in the
wickedness of man's imagination."[97] Threatening, savorless, enervating—truly
decadent—she is akin to what Lee had elsewhere described as the "fair dame
in the velvet embroidered gown, with the long, hanging hair"; the sister of "that
slily sentimental coquette, the Monna Lisa of Leonardo"; the counterpart of
what Henry Adams, writing in 1900 in America, characterized as "the monthly-
magazine-made American female" who had "not a feature that would have
been recognized by Adam": all of them simulacra (of one sort or another),
their artificial bodies—the wax figure, the painted image, the illustration fixed
on a page of a magazine—retaining only the most superficial features, or shell,
of the female body in whose very tissues, organismically speaking, they may
be said to have been parthenogenetically conceived.[98]

　　Not even so much as what is left to the Virgin of Venus's sexual power—
although even in its diminished state, Adams considered it a force to be reckoned with, referring to it in "The Dynamo and the Virgin" (1900) as "the greatest and most mysterious of all energies"—remains to the central character of
Lee's story, as rigidly encased in her culturally determined role as the daggered
Virgin is in her farthingale.[99] Unable to mediate between the living and the dead,
unequal to the task of negating the void it was created to fill, the doll can no
more reciprocate the count's love than could its unlessoned precursor, "a mere
shy, proud, inexperienced child" who, until she lay dying in childbirth, at which
point she escaped the thrall of the "stupid, inconceivable incapacity for expressing
her feelings," could not know what answer to make her husband's "overflow-
ing, garrulous, demonstrative affection," although "in a deep, inarticulate way
she had really cared for him more than he cared for her" (217-18): an ominous
prospect for the woman who attempts to deliver herself of her desire. Even the
belief that as a household idol the doll possesses an icon's immortality proves
illusory, for when the narrator encounters it, the satin white frock it wears has
"turned grey with engrained dirt," its black fringed kerchief is "almost red," its
"poor white silk mittens and white silk stockings" are "almost black," and even

its wig is "dusty, unkempt" (215), standing as brutal testimony that nothing survives the grave, not even artifice.

In her final apocalyptic act, as I have noted, the narrator ritualistically burns
the doll on a pyre of myrtle and bay (both symbolic of immortality). The narrator's
devotions might be read as a ritualized purification—a purging of failed vision,
failed interaction, and the artistry that must in its turn fail within a disintegrat-
ing society that encases women in roles that efface the reality of their lives and
require them instead to occupy a fixed space in which, as Theresa de Lauretis
notes in *Technologies of Gender*, they serve merely as "a marker of boundary,
. . . inanimate even when anthropomorphized." "Female is what is not susceptible to transformation, to life or death," de Lauretis writes, her supposition
ironically implicated in the history of Gustave Courbet's unfinished *Toilet of the
Dead Woman* (c. 1850), in which a mirror (judiciously placed if awkwardly introduced by a later painter-bowdlerizer) is all that was apparently required to transform the limp corpse of the dead woman being prepared for her burial (considered too morbid a topic to assure a good price for the painting) into the happy
subject of what came to be known as *Toilet of the Bride* (fig. 33).[100] Such a
reading of "The Doll," however, is insufficient to explain why a woman whom
the critic Cyril Connolly had designated as one of the "mighty-mouthed international geysers" of the nineteenth century should conclude her tenure as a writer
of short fiction—should in essence go silent—with a story in which she abandoned her standard heroines of choice—the lamias, the Venus Verticordias, the
Medeas, and the "knife-riddled" Madonnas of the Counter-Reformation ("all pomp
and whalebone and sorrow and tears wept into Mechlin lace")—in favor of one
who does nothing and says nothing.[101] History records other immolations, the
blazing fires of which as fully consumed the beloved possessions of their
votaresses as that which consumed Lee's doll and, by extension, Lee's life as a
fabulist. A description of one such ceremony comments indirectly on Lee's final
unlikely story, revealing it as less a defeatist gesture than an encoded rite of
passage, accessible only to the initiated, who could share sympathetically in its
essence.

In his *Reminiscences* Thomas Carlyle recalls the "shame" that followed his
wife's first encounter with Virgil and the grief occasioned by her attempt to rid
herself of her shame. "She made great progress in Latin," Carlyle begins, "and
was in Virgil when nine years old": "She always loved her doll; but when she got
into Virgil she thought it shame to care for a doll. On her tenth birthday she
built a funeral pile of lead pencils and sticks of cinnamon, and poured some
sort of perfume over all, to represent a funeral pile. She then recited the speech
of Dido, stabbed her doll and let out all the sawdust; after which she consumed
her to ashes, and then burst into a passion of tears."[102] Carlyle represents his
wife's immolation of her doll as a requisite, if painful, rite of passage, necessitated by her being "in" Virgil: that is, by her awakening into adulthood and the

world of loss and death from out of the untroubled innocence of youth, the author of her fate in this matter being the same poet who ushered Dante through hell and purgatory. Jane Carlyle's choice of eulogy, however—that which serves as the dirge for her doll and the renunciation of her girlhood fancies—is the speech of the queen of Carthage, who, prior to throwing herself on the sword of Dardania, assembles a huge pyre of oak and pine on which she burns the belongings of Aeneas and his men. Her husband's desertion—the act that she interprets as betrayal—determines her in her suicidal course, although the egoism of her claims—to have "built a renowned city," to have seen her "ramparts rise," and by her brother's punishment to have avenged her husband "of his enemy"—transforms the apparently self-negating character of her action into something powerfully self-affirming: it is, after all, his body that she would have "riven . . . in sunder and strewn . . . on the waves," so that she might have "blotted out father and son and race together," but, denied this chance for revenge, she undertakes her own death, which, unavenged, will "be the omen he carries on his way."[103]

Lee's doll is incapable of such willed self-destruction, requiring instead a narrator sufficiently sensitized to her plight to act for her. And no such angry denunciation as Dido's appears in Lee's narrative, which is instead holed with silences that demand interpretation, much as the drama of the marionette's meanings is folded in silence: "In the olden days," writes Furst, "a marionette performance was called a 'Motion,' and this 'Motion, [sic] took place in silence."[104] The countess's reticence in life, compounded by the definitive silence that succeeds it with her death, is absorbed into another silence, yet more resolute, that emerges in the body of the narrative. Discerning some indication of restless incredulity on the part of her confidante, a hint that reminds her of "what people are" and of "how impossible it is ever *really* to make others feel in the same way as ourselves" (218), the narrator grows jealous of the story that she has embarked upon and announces, almost petulantly, "I knew all about the Doll when she was alive—I mean about the lady—and I got to know, in the same way, all about her after she was dead. Only I don't think I'll tell you. *Basta*" (218-19). "Basta," of course, is the Italian for "enough," and as an expletive it mandates silence, as in "No more! Enough said; enough heard; Silence!" The narrator does not literally go silent—she concludes her story with the brief description of the auto-da-fé over which she presides—but of the doll's hidden life she has nothing more to say. Her silence at just that moment would appear to figure the doll's life as the blank page that invites the inscription from without that Mrs. Ellis claimed would vivify it, preserving it from dead-letter status and sanctioning its inclusion in the volume of human life. Spivak later reconceived of this page as the hymenal folded space that invites the pen to disseminate its words, or, as she has it, writes its dissemination; her conceit is not entirely strained, judging from Bellmer's disclosure of the "real meaning" he expected to discover in the body of his doll, "sentenced" to successive rearrangement: "I

wanted to reveal what is usually kept hidden—it was no game—."[105] His need
to obsessively pull her apart and reconstruct her, however, betrays his fear
that what was kept hidden would remain hidden and in the end elude him,
leaving him perpetually submerged in the depths he had set about to plumb:
perhaps not recognizing meaning when he finds it; suspecting that the meaning he fixes upon might be other than what it presents itself as being; never
entirely certain either way. Such is the oppressively suspenseful state that
Hoffmann claimed would result from one's contact with what is *unheimliche*—
the nothingness of woman, the indeterminacy of the automaton, the whiteness of the sheet, the silence that interrupts speech—the term, as Freud pointed
out, shading by degrees into its opposite, *heimlich*, which itself signifies both
"what is familiar and agreeable" and "what is concealed and kept out of sight."[106]
Thus, Lee's contemporary, George Egerton, could survey the same domain
that Bellmer later attempted to map out and respond by feeling not threatened by what did not readily present itself to view, but released, as from an
immobilizing thralldom: "I realised that in literature, everything had been better done by man than woman could hope to emulate. There was only one
small plot left for her to tell: the *terra incognita* of herself, as she knew herself
to be, not as man liked to imagine her—in a word to give herself away, as man
had given himself in his writings."[107] In anatomizing the feminine in this way,
she reconfigures those characterizing patches—the plot, the sheet, the silence,
the nothingness, the absence—about which Gubar writes most persuasively
about in describing nineteenth- and twentieth-century women's writing as "a
mysterious but potent act of resistance."[108]

The narrator of Lee's story undertakes a potent act of resistance when
she assumes her secondary role as "daduchos" [torchbearer] and ritualistically burns the funeral pyre, which she ignites with the flaming pine cone
sacred to Dionysus, who shared a mystic connection with Demeter, the central divinity of the Eleusinian mysteries, the preeminent rituals of ancient Athens (rituals that survived for at least two thousand years). If anthropologists
are to be relied upon—Frazer notes in *The Golden Bough*, for example, that "a
sect in Orissa . . . worshipped the late Queen Victoria in her lifetime as their
chief divinity"—then it would appear that versions of these feminine mysteries
involving the worship of the Magna Mater survived well into the nineteenth
century.[109] We might recall, for example, Sarah Orne Jewett's conflation of
Victoria and Demeter in "The Queen's Twin" (1899) and Charlotte Perkins
Gilman's self-imagined role as the more exotic Ashtaroth. In enfolding the
doll's secret in silence, however, the narrator discloses her primary role as
hierophant, the highest of the Eleusinian officials; the one whose name means
"displayer of holy things." Her censure—"*Basta*"—and the burden of silence it
imposes upon the text give a false sense, however, of her ultimate power either to convey or to withhold any information about the doll, whose story the
initiated will know without the intervention of an intermediary, just as the

Figure 32. Abbott Handerson Thayer, *Virgin Enthroned* (1891). Courtesy of the National Museum of American Art, Smithsonian Institution, gift of John Gellatly

narrator herself entered into what she understood to be "a sudden friendship with a woman whose secret I had surprised, as sometimes happens, by mere accident" (216). In a fragment from a lost dialogue called *On Prayer*, Aristotle reveals that the Eleusinian mysteries could not be taught, but only intuited. The philosopher notes that those undergoing initiation "are not to learn anything but to experience something and be put into a certain condition."[110] Thus, the central Eleusinian mystery is that transformative moment when, as Lewis R. Farnell notes in his study of the cults of the Greek states, having been placed "in a peculiarly close and privileged relation with the divinity or deified spirit," the initiate, or "mystes," is assimilated into and comprehended within the mystery that she seeks to comprehend.[111]

The narrator's own guide cannot enlighten her "in the least," because, as she indicates, "I somehow knew everything about [the doll], and the . . . information which I gained from Orestes . . . merely confirmed what I was aware of" (216-17). She knows all about the doll's life, that is, because she has lived that life, her narrative performing linguistically the service that the "old witch" performs physically when she secretly delivers the doll from the obscurity to which she had briefly been consigned—an obscurity from which the housekeeper herself, by virtue of her status as a bastard daughter, cannot hope to be rescued, the recognition of which presumably allows her to enter into a sympathetic engagement with "a *real* Lady" (220), whose life would otherwise bear little relationship to her own. Just as the inapt descriptions of outrageous angles, unheard-of contradictions, and suicidal plunges betray the authorial confusion buried in the lines and patternings of the noxious yellow wallpaper whose aesthetic principle Gilman's tormented narrator has set out to disclose, so the defining features of Lee's eponymous doll suggest that several intersecting narratives are embedded in the "life" of the doll, the occasion for its recovery itself camouflaged, represented as having occurred in the course of the narrator's suitably feminine procuration of bric-à-brac. In this way her story, like that of the "old witch" housekeeper—and behind hers, that of the doll, and enfolding them all that of Lee herself—conforms to the code of secrecy imposed by the Eleusinians upon their mysteries, feminine mysteries of transformation that, like the "feminine desire" that Luce Irigaray writes about, "may be recovered only in secret, in hiding, with anxiety and guilt."[112]

The Eleusinian mysteries came, of course, to be supplanted by one of the central practices of the early Christian church, the Disciplina Arcani, in its turn as occult and jealously guarded as the feminine mysteries it sought to subvert. The Disciplina Arcani is "the practice of concealing from heathen and catechumens the more sacred and mysterious doctrines and rites of the church, either by not mentioning them at all or by mentioning them only in enigmatical language. The motive for this," as the historian A. Dwight Culler reminds us, "was partly to prepare the candidate gradually for the reception of sacred truths and partly to preserve the mysteries from violation and sacrilege."[113] The evocative

Figure 33. Gustave Courbet, *Toilet of the Dead Woman* (c. 1850). Courtesy of the Smith College Museum of Art, Northampton, Massachusettes; purchased, Drayton Hillyer Fund, 1929

similarity between the two sets of arcane mysteries—those adopted by the church fathers, and those held by the heathen (which some historians take as the source of the Christian sacraments)—reminds us that one set of mysteries is as "sophisticated" as the other, one language as enigmatical as the other; and this the early doctors of the church surely recognized, else they would not have written against Eleusis with such self-incriminating hostility.

Harriet Waters Preston found in the example of the twenty-five-year-old Lee evidence of "how far the emancipated, encouraged, and enlightened women of the now rising literary generation [were] beginning to find places among this excellent stock company of writers" publishing in such respected journals as the *Westminster Review, Blackwood's Magazine,* and the *Fortnightly.* In her own sober claim that "no one reads a woman's writing on art, history, or aesthetics with anything but mitigated [*sic*] contempt," the subject of Preston's effusions expressed both her doubts about the sincerity of the "encouragement" an aspiring woman author could expect to receive—although she could not have known of James's allusion in a letter to his brother William to "a great second-rate element in her first-rateness," she appears to have discerned sufficient disdain on his part to persuade her that hope of encouragement from that quarter would be ill-founded—and her doubt that the excellent stock company of writers would welcome into their midst a "Violet Paget" as readily as they would a "Vernon Lee."[114] The history of the critical reception of her writings would seem to have borne out the accuracy of her estimation, obscured as they were by the withering glare of the enormous condescension of posterity—a condescension more fully disclosed than masked by the courteous language in which Brooks expresses his opinion that by its very nature Lee's oeuvre begged off austere consideration. James's consideration of the dubiety of Lee's "first-rateness"; Brooks's characterization of her gift as "gracious": such assessments suggest that her work would be perceived, at least by some, as merely a more cultured version of the "enigmatical language" of women's writing that Virginia Woolf had prophesied would come in our own day to be misinterpreted by the uninitiated as expressing "not merely a difference of view, but a view that is weak, or trivial, or sentimental."[115]

In the years that followed the writing of "The Doll," Lee focused her energies on exposition, as though she became fully reconciled to a theory she had posed years earlier in *Belcaro:* specifically, that when art is mature—no longer the product of "fever-stricken, starved visionaries" but of conscientious artists who cease to strain after the impossible and instead set about trying to capture and embody their ever-shifting fancies in definite forms that grow more contrived and decadent—the supernatural ceases to truly exist.[116] Lee's tenure as a writer of supernatural stories culminated with the writing of her final "Unlikely" story, in the apocalyptic ending of which she acknowledges the difficulty of trying to reconcile fancies that might be with facts that are.

The woman is perfected.
Her dead

Body wears the smile of accomplishment.
The illusion of Greek necessity

Flows in the scrolls of her toga . . .

Sylvia Plath, "The Edge" (1963)

Part 2

What the Frenchman did for SPECIES—between England & France
I will do with *forms*.

Charles Darwin

For him, the *form* was the work itself. As in living creatures, the blood,
nourishing the body, determines its very contour and external aspect,
just so, to his mind, the *matter*, the basis, in a work of art, imposed,
necessarily, the unique, the just expression, the measure, the rhythm—
the *form* in all its characteristics.

Walter Pater

5

The Word Made Flesh

Protoplasmic Predications in Arthur Machen's "The Great God Pan"

Nature, if we believed all that is said of her, would be the most extraordinary being. She has horrors (*horror vacui*), she indulges in freaks (*lusus naturae*), she commits blunders (*errores naturae, monstra*). She is sometimes at war with herself, for, as Giraldus told us, "Nature produced barnacles against Nature"; and of late years we have heard much of her power of selection.

Nature is sometimes used as meaning simply matter, or everything that exists apart from spirit. Yet more frequently Nature is supposed to be itself endowed with independent life, to be working after eternal and invariable laws. Again, we sometimes hear Nature used so as to include the spiritual life and the intellectual activity of man. We speak of the spiritual nature of man, of the natural laws of thought, of natural religion. . . .

But while *nature* seems thus applicable promiscuously to things material and spiritual, human and divine, language certainly, on the other hand, helps us to distinguish between the works of nature and the works of man, the former supplying materials for the physical, the latter for the historical sciences; and it likewise countenances the distinction between the works both of nature and of man on one side, and the Divine agencies on the other: the former being called natural and human, the latter supernatural and superhuman.

F. Max Müller, *The Science of Language* (1864-66)

No student of the science of language can be anything but an evolutionist, for, wherever he looks, he sees nothing but evolution going on all around him.

F. Max Müller, *The Science of Thought* (1887)

FOR ALL THAT SHE HAD MADE the requisite conciliatory gestures—having written, at midcareer, her own version of a "visionary" novel in which her readers were granted a fleeting glimpse behind *The Lifted Veil* (1859), and having distinguished, at career's close, between works of "visionary excitement" (embodying a "passionate vision of possibilities" and "the sensibility of the artist [seizing] combinations which science explains and justifies") and works by "strictest reasoners" (who generated "an illusory world in the shape of axioms, definitions, and propositions, with a final exclusion of fact signed Q. E. D.")—George Eliot had failed to convince some of her more aesthetic readers that she was anything but the charwoman of choice for the Pentonville transit authority, lavishing attention on a world of tangible "verities" that they derogated as little more than a variegated shadow veiling what Arthur Machen viewed as "un monde de grands mystères, de choses insoupçonnées et tout à fait stupéfiantes!"[1] To Machen the "poor, dreary, draggle-tailed George Eliot" seemed hardly capable of lifting veils, since she was one of the pitiable ones fettered by an unshakable but mistaken faith in the importance of the detrital minutiae that constituted "these 'chases in Arras, dreams in a career,'" the stuff of "dreams and shadows . . . that hide the real world from our eyes."[2] Believing that the true "Realists"—Keats, for example, and especially Poe, whom Machen dubbed "The Supreme Realist"—understood that "the whole earth, down to the very pebbles," was merely a frustratingly impenetrable barrier veiling "a quickening and adorable secret," Machen sought an idiom capable of unmasking the delitescent world: an occult style in which, as Symons suggested, "the visible world is no longer a reality, and the unseen world no longer a dream."[3] Machen's "The Novel of the White Powder" (1895), a story of the midnineties, fleshes out the contours and image patterns of his chosen idiom.

One of several apparently disparate but ultimately related narratives that, taken together, enable his protagonists to identify the individuals referred to by the title of *The Three Impostors* (1895), "The Novel of the White Powder" (Machen's variation on Poe's "Facts in the Case of M. Valdemar" [1845]) tells the story of Francis Leicester, a London law student whose too-ambitious course of study undermines both his health and his spirits. His elderly family physician, Dr. Haberden, proposes to remedy this "mischief in the nervous system" with a prescription that "ought to do great things," and an aged apothecary provides him in turn with "an innocent-looking white powder."[4] His character is so transmuted that, within a few days, the formerly relentless student becomes "a lover of pleasure, a careless and merry idler of western pavements, a hunter out of snug restaurants, and a fine critic of fantastic dancing" (164). As the story progresses, he becomes more and more dissipated, his tame epicureanism giving way to an ominous indulgence in secret lusts that eventually betray themselves on his body. While Dorian Gray's epicurean appetites act as a reminder that what serves the senses may slay the spirit, Leicester's prove that what initially seems to minister to the body may in fact hasten its corruption. The former

reads his portrait for external signs of his spiritual malaise—"the visible emblem," as he puts it, "of conscience"—whereas the latter actually becomes the
embodiment of physical corruption.[5] What begins as "a small patch about the
size of a sixpence, and somewhat of the colour of a bad bruise" (165), eventually
consumes his whole body, for when, at the story's climax, his sister and Haberden
force their way into the bedroom in which he has barricaded himself, they discover upon the floor only "a dark and putrid mass, seething with corruption and
hideous rottenness, neither liquid nor solid, but melting and changing . . . and
bubbling with unctuous oily bubbles like boiling pitch." All that remains of the
once eminently presentable young man are "two burning points like eyes, and . .
. a writhing and stirring as of limbs, and something . . . that might have been an
arm" (177). These extraordinary events, as we discover in a postscript written
by a Dr. Chambers (to whom the apothecary's originally innocuous white powder had been given for analysis), have their origin in a peculiar accident: over the
course of many years the powder had been subjected to "certain recurring variations of temperature . . . with varying degrees of intensity and duration" (182)
and was in consequence transmuted into the Vinum Sabbati, the sacramental
wine of the Black Mass. Chambers is not surprised to learn of Leicester's fate,
for in his own earlier days as a confirmed skeptic and materialist, he had himself
discovered that, during the Black Mass, those who consume the Vinum Sabbati
experience both a temporary physical regression to a primal state and a spiritual revelation, Machen's version of the Freudian primal scene: "the house of life
was riven asunder and the human trinity dissolved, and the worm which never
dies, that which lies sleeping within us all, was made tangible and an external
thing, and clothed with a garment of flesh. And then, in the hour of midnight, the
primal fall was repeated and re-presented, and the awful thing veiled in the mythos
of the Tree in the Garden was done anew" (183-84). To Chambers, a world in
which such things are possible seems "as strange and awful . . . as the endless
waves of the ocean seen for the first time, shining, from a peak in Darien" (180).

Among other things, then, "The Novel of the White Powder" provides
Machen with an opportunity to paraphrase and update Keats, who, in "On First
Looking into Chapman's Homer" (1816), had compared himself to "stout Cortez"
(though he meant Vasco Núñez de Balboa), the explorer who, in the company of
his awestruck men, had "star'd at the Pacific . . . / Silent, upon a peak in Darien."
In his guise as adventurer/explorer, Keats identifies Homer's world—which is
really *his* own world stripped of what Machen described as "veils of apparent
monotony and meanness" (*The Three Impostors*, 128)—as being one of those
"realms of gold" and "goodly states" into which he longed to escape. Machen's
Dr. Chambers is similarly awed and humbled by the revelation of the existence
of a world that, like the one that Keats had discovered, is not readily accessible to
the senses, although it is "clothed with a garment of flesh" (184). In "Chapman's
Homer," however, Keats breathes "pure serene" when at length he penetrates to
Homer's demesne, whereas Machen's characters are destroyed by their unan-

ticipated glimpse of an appalling reality that lies behind all that they have hitherto known.

Although crediting them with being the first to recognize that the "spectacle
of external nature" implied "much more than mere pleasantness or sensuous
beauty," since it could impart "a revelation of things hidden in things which are
open to all"—things "more splendid and more awful than we used to dream"
(*The Three Impostors*, 181)—Machen maintained that the romantics were necessarily limited in the extent to which they could transcribe the secret language
that nature itself had revealed to them: "Coleridge and his fellows," he argued,
"were but the forerunners of a new doctrine which was not fully revealed to
them."[6] The runic characters of this secret language were embedded within the
material forms of a world more prosaically present, although—for Machen—no
less sacrosanct for having been probed, its occulted mysteries raised to the surface and scrutinized by the scientists whose exploratory motives Tyndall had
lauded. The world at whose existence Machen hints in such stories as "The
White Powder" and "The Great God Pan" is (as we shall see) nothing less than
a "tremendous sacrament; a mystic, ineffable force and energy, veiled by an
outward form of matter" (*The Three Impostors*, 181); but it is a sacrament that
most of us, surfeited on the "lethargy of custom," are capable of apprehending
only "in a dim and broken and imperfect manner." It is a Catholic lexicon that we
recognize when we find the universe described, even in his horror stories, as a
"great sacrament," and it is a Catholic sensibility that informs Machen's sense of
sin as "an effort to gain the ecstacy and the knowledge that pertain alone to
angels, [so that] in making this effort man becomes a Demon." Death or madness await those doomed characters who, either by accident or in a misguided
attempt to obtain "something which was never" theirs, repeat a "Fall" into damning knowledge.[7]

It required, not another Champollion to decipher the symbolic striae expressive of inward movements and hidden motions, but someone sufficiently skilled
to create a literary style capable of translating nature's circumambient, if esoteric, style. In his appropriately entitled *Hieroglyphics* (1902), Machen announced
that style was "the outword [*sic*] sign of the burning grace within"—the linguistic
equivalent of a sacrament, defined in the *Book of Common Prayer* as "an outward and visible sign of an inward and spiritual grace."[8] By extension, then,
style became the linguistic analog of a sacramental world that it anatomized.
Recalling Wilde's credo that "nothing can cure the soul but the senses, just as
nothing can cure the senses but the soul," Machen noted that "the way to the
spiritual things is by the gate of the sensible things," insisting that, by "its capacity when exquisitely arranged of suggesting wonderful and indefinable impressions," literature causes the "delicious sensations" that make one viscerally re-
sponsive to occult mysteries and the mysterious letters that express them.[9]

The telltale trope by which Machen distinguished his own body of work is
appropriately outward, visible, incarnate—and drawn, moreover, from the physi-

cal sciences that had helped to darken the glass through which he surveyed, as if for the first time, a world grown manifestly strange and awful. Moreover, he found his significator in the arguments of someone who, like his Dr. Chambers, was a confirmed skeptic and materialist; someone appreciative of but not likely to have been put off by Machen's veiled warnings of the dangers to which one seeking greater insight into first principles might be exposed; someone for whom the material world provided an end in itself, all other considerations appearing chimerical. Machen, for his part, fixed on a protoplasmic metaphor that suited his aims too well and captured—perhaps too fully—the hidden labors, evolutions, and devolutions of a language fleshed out in the outward vestiture of matter.

"We live in a world which is full of misery and ignorance, and the plain duty of each and all of us is to try to make the little corner he can influence somewhat less miserable and somewhat less ignorant than it was before he entered it."[10] This was the end toward which Huxley was working—as part of a lifelong task— in his essay "On the Physical Basis of Life," in which he sought to establish definitively that a semifluid, semitransparent, colorless substance called "proto- plasm" must be "the physical basis of life" and that this viscid compound was common to all the diversities of vital existence—common to the microscopic fungus, the body of the living fly, the great finner whale, and "the flower which a girl wears in her hair and the blood which courses through her youthful veins" (129-30). Huxley's essay was published in the February 1, 1869, issue of The Fortnightly Review, three months after he had delivered his lecture on the sub- ject at a public forum in Edinburgh. Both the talk and the essay that followed were extravagantly successful. The number of The Fortnightly featuring Huxley's essay ran into seven reprintings, and John Morley, then editor of the Fortnightly, claimed that "no article that has appeared in any periodical for a generation back (unless it be Deutsch's article on the Talmud in the Quarterly of 1867) excited so profound a sensation as Huxley's memorable paper On the Physical Basis of Life (1869)." "The stir," he went on to say, "was like the stir that in a political epoch was made by Swift's Conduct of the Allies, or Burke's French Revolution."[11] Even the American popular press took note of what the New York World described as Huxley's "Remarkable Discourse" on a "New Theory of Life." It is worth noting that hypotheses about a basic living substance had been put forth years before Huxley delivered his lecture.[12] He merely did for protoplasm what he had done for Darwinian biology: he "bulldogged" it, intro- ducing into a public forum what had previously been consigned to scientific jour- nals. As historian Gerald L. Geison has it, Huxley "made protoplasm quite liter- ally a household word."[13]

Putting protoplasm into the mouths of his readers, however, was not neces- sarily the sole or even the primary reason he had taken up this topic of discus- sion. A subheadline from The World's transcription of the essay indirectly touches on Huxley's ulterior motive: "Matter the Basis of Vitality." Huxley was in fact out to kill vitalism. Vitalists argued that the distinction between living things and inanimate matter lay in the fact that the former were infused with and operated upon by certain unique and mysterious processes that could not always be iden-tified or explained and might even involve the supernatural, or what Lionel Smith Beale, the most eloquent of the vitalists, cautiously described as the intervention of some "wonderful power or agency."[14] Huxley, however, would have no part of the occulting of matter—of the conception of life, that is, "as a something which works through matter, but is independent of it" (129). He believed that knowl-edge, cognition, and feeling ("which we rightly name the higher faculties") were all firmly grounded in matter, originating, in some instances, in "transitory changes in the relative positions of parts of the body" (131). "It may seem a small thing," he reasoned,

> to admit that the dull vital actions of a fungus, or a foraminifer, are the properties of their protoplasm, and are the direct results of the nature of the matter of which they are composed. But if, as I have endeavoured to prove to you, their protoplasm is essentially identical with, and most readily converted into, that of any animal, I can discover no logical halt-ing-place between the admission that such is the case, and the further concession that all vital action may, with equal propriety, be said to be the result of the molecular forces of the protoplasm which displays it. And if so, it must be true, in the same sense and to the same extent, that the thoughts to which I am now giving utterance, and your thoughts regarding them, are the expression of molecular changes in that matter of life which is the source of our other vital phenomena. [140]

In other words, he suggested, since "the realm of matter . . . is co-extensive with knowledge, with feeling, and with action[,] . . . thought may be regarded as a property of matter" (143, 145). Knowing this to be the case, the right-thinking materialist and skeptic could then dispense with what Huxley terms "lunar poli-tics" involving questions "about matters of which, however important they may be, we do know nothing, and can know nothing" (144-45). As a skeptic, then, Huxley stands with Hume, whom he quotes in his own defense: "'If we take in hand any volume of Divinity, or school metaphysics, for instance, let us ask, *Does it contain any abstract reasoning concerning quantity or number?* No. *Does it contain any experimental reasoning concerning matter of fact and exist-ence?* No. Commit it then to the flames; for it can contain nothing but sophistry and illusion'" (144).

Pater may be thought of as having taken Hume's advice to heart when he committed not his school metaphysics but himself to the flames—or at least to the oft-invoked "hard, gem-like flame" that would allow him to engage in some uniquely human way with (and at the same time to protect himself from) the flux of a world that was impressing itself too materially upon him.[15] He was not, however, responding directly to the terms of the argument as set forth in Huxley's essay, for his equally notorious "Conclusion" had made its first unassuming appearance as an unsigned review titled "Poems by William Morris" in *The Westminster Review* of October 1868, a month before Huxley addressed his audience in Edinburgh. The materialism driving Huxley's argument—reflecting what a commentator in an 1869 issue of *Macmillan's Magazine* called "the secular habit of mind" that "has for some time had the predominance" at Oxford— became increasingly pervasive in nineteenth-century scientific and philosophical discourse.[16] One need not venture very far afield for evidence of the growing fear that a critical mass of quantifiable physical research—what a disturbed Stevenson would characterize as "this mountain mass of the revolting and the inconceivable"—threatened to render immaterial the immaterial.[17] The grammar of materialism holds temporary sway in Pater's essay, which begins, quite self-consciously, "with that which is without—our physical life" (217). The first half of the "Conclusion" is freighted with references to "phosphorus and lime and delicate fibres," to "the passage of the blood, the waste, and repairing of the lenses of the eye," to the "tissues of the brain," to "currents" and "pulses," and to the microscopes that make these things known to us (217, 219). Amidst this perpetual flux we recognize that the "clear . . . outline of face and limb" is "but an image of ours"—"a design in a web" (217-18) fashioned by individuals patterning themselves after the mythical shipwrecked sailor who, feeling similarly oppressed by cosmic inscrutabilities, spent twenty-eight years in erecting fences, drafting charts, laying in supplies of comestibles, and renaming people. In the enormously influential and what is by now the almost too-well-known conclusion to the "Conclusion," Pater declares that art alone generates the "wisdom, the poetic passion, the desire of beauty" that can trigger the "quickened, multiplied consciousness" that is the only compensation available to one allotted a "counted number of pulses only . . . of a variegated, dramatic life" (219-20). For Pater, art and artifice maintain an inviolable presence in an organic world held hostage by "natural elements" and "elementary forces" (217). Although emerging within and perhaps compounded of the material agents of an organic world, art constitutes what Pater—three years earlier, in his essay on Coleridge—had determined to be "a new presence in the world." He could not therefore countenance the romantic's having "likened" art to "a living organism," because such a comparative, although it expresses "the sense of a self-delighting, independent life which the finished work of art gives us[,] . . . hardly figures the process by which such work was produced," since it reduces the artist to a mere "mechanical agent" and the artwork itself to "some blindly organic process of assimilation"; it substitutes a "blind ferment of lifeless elements" for the "exquisite analysis," the "calculating," "the most intuitive, the power of the understanding in them, their logical process of construction, the spectacle of a supreme intellectual dexterity which [works of imagination] afford."[18]

Like philosophers and creators of fiction, individual members of the demonized scientific community were haunted by what Huxley referred to as "this great truth" of materialism that "weighs like a nightmare . . . upon many of the best minds of these days" (143). Like Pater, some sought refuge in the notion that certain artifacts were essentially immune to what Stevenson would call "the disease of agglutinated dust" that smites the "monstrous spectre" man.[19] The German philologist F. Max Müller, for example, advanced what might be viewed as a vitalistic argument for language. Granting the validity of Darwin's otherwise chastening theory of the descent of man—a theory "inevitable, but hardly welcome"—he balked at the notion that language is materially based: that it had evolved, that is, out of imitative shrieks and gestures common both to man and to beast.[20] "However much the frontiers of the animal kingdom have been pushed forward, so that at one time the line of demarcation between animal and man seemed to depend on a mere fold in the brain," he argued, "there is *one* barrier which no one has yet ventured to touch—the barrier of language": "*as yet* no race of animals has produced a language" (1:13). The "fold" being real (ponderable, palpable) but insignificant, the intangible barrier of language—"the one great barrier" (1:489), as he would later qualify it—was vast enough, in Müller's estimation, to forestall any possibility of an adulterating crossover. Of one truth Müller had no doubt: "Language," he announced triumphantly, is *"our Rubicon which no brute will dare to cross"*(1:xxxv, 490). This conceit—treated as both anxious hypothesis and reassuring axiom—underlies many of the assumptions in his lengthy two-volume study of the science of language: assumptions that in turn underlie his anchored belief that comparative philology should properly be classified as a "historical" rather than, as the clergyman-philologist Frederic William Farrar would insist, a "*natural*" science, since its primary object of inquiry was something possessing a material existence—language, which had "a real natural life."[21] As Pater had fixed on artifice, so Müller fixed on language as the *differencia specifica* that would preserve humanity from the progressive desacralization of an encroaching positivism. Huxley challenged Pater's mandate by arguing that "Protoplasm . . . is the clay of the potter: which, bake it and paint it as he will, remains clay, separated by artifice, and not by nature, from the commonest brick or sun-dried clod" (135). The evolutionist and physiologist George Romanes, Müller's materialist opponent, leveled a similar challenge, warning that since "it is to Language that my opponents appeal: to Language shall they go"—where, he implies, they will be humbled in the agglutinated dust and "hopelessly condemned."[22]

Müller, denouncing the arguments that had been put forth by Darwin and Romanes in support of the notion that the origins of language were strictly imitative—the "Bow-wow" and the "Pooh-pooh" theories, as he deprecatingly called them—suggested that a more-than-human agency had been at work in the inception and evolution of language. What Beale had suggested of germinal matter, Müller echoed in hinting that language too was a divine gift—had its place in the general "beauty and harmony of nature," in the midst of which the "eye of man" might discern "the eye of God beaming out from the midst of all His works"

(1:16). He resisted the empiricist orthodoxies of such brethren as Schleicher, who qualified what is very nearly a metaphysical speculation—"our ancestors were not what we could call 'man' from the beginning, but became human only when language appeared"—by insisting upon a "systema naturae of languages." "Development of language," Schleicher urged, "means the same for me as development of the brain and speech organs."[23] Whether or not it bore materially the sign of an inseminating *logos*, however, language nevertheless figured for Müller as a *natura naturans*, a natural effect embodying an abstract principle. "If . . . we ourselves are right," he reasoned, "in pointing to language as the one palpable distinction between [man and brutes], it would seem to follow that language is the outward sign and realisation of that inward faculty which is called the faculty of abstraction, but which is better known to us by the homely name of Reason" (1:492). Language—seen both as the sign system out of which innumerable texts might be constructed and as an encompassing text within which one might read "the primeval and never-ending autobiography of our race"—approached for Müller a sacramental condition, serving as the embodiment ("the outward sign") of an ideality ("that inward faculty").[24] "The word is the thought incarnate" (1:527)—the thought made flesh—and it was not to be expected that we could "understand the real nature of the human Self" until we understood "the real nature of language": "those who want to read the true history of the development of the soul of man," he announced, "must learn to read it in language."[25]

Having incrementally and almost incidentally moved in the direction of corporealizing the language he had undertaken to spiritualize, Müller went further, availing himself of the organicist metaphors common to the arguments of his colleagues—and thereby, as Romanes was quick to note, inadvertently laying the groundwork for his own defeat. Wary of the language-as-geneaological-tree metaphor advanced by Frederick Schlegel and others, Müller fancied instead a paleontological comparison in which "the mass of human speech" served as a fossil record of the history of language, "whether in the petrified strata of ancient literature or in the countless variety of living languages and dialects" (1:25).[26] More, however, than just a desiccated manuscript lying exposed to common view—a vast literary monument built up out of "the ruins of the ancient languages"—language seemed "the living and speaking witness of the whole history of our race," and since in its essential features it recalled all that had gone before, it also served as a witness that might yet connect us, "through an unbroken chain of speech, with the very ancestors of our race" and might be thought of as "still [drawing] its life from the first utterances of the human mind" (1:386, 27). Falling just short, in this passage, of an explicit endorsement of its recapitulatory capacity, Müller eventually grants that language enacts what Haeckel had described as the ontogenous repetition of phylogenetic modifications, for one can infer the former existence of now extinct parts of speech by "the changes . . . wrought in the body of the word" (1:470-71). Moreover, Müller was willing to conceive of language as an organic body subject not merely to the laws of inheritance and adaptation, but to the diseases and disorders assailing the mutable bodies—both physical and linguistic—out of which it had emerged. Curiously, whereas Huxley had cast speech as a devitalizing activity—"Every word uttered by a speaker costs him some physical loss" (137), he wrote—Müller supposed that phonetic changes might easily follow from the ongoing physiological changes occurring within the body of the host: "For a long time the usual phrase in linguistic works was, *k* becomes *g, t* becomes *d, s* becomes *r;* but how one letter could become another letter was never so much as asked. . . . I believe I was the first to suggest the prosaic reason that all phonetic change was due to laziness, to an economy of muscular effort required in pronouncing vowels and consonants" (1:xvii). Linguistic decay was not limited to or necessarily contingent upon special or individual "laziness" or decrepitude, however, for language itself was prone to its own variety of decay—"the virulence of this phonetic change, that . . . will sometimes eat away the whole body of a word, and leave nothing behind but decayed fragments" (1:53). Such a statement would constitute hardly an eddy within the general drift of the writings of someone like the comparative linguist Franz Bopp, who had urged that languages be regarded "as organic bodies, . . . bearing within themselves an internal principle of life" and thus prone to "develop and . . . gradually die out" and to "discard, mutilate, or misuse" once significant components or forms that have become "superficial appendages."[27] It was, however, an extraordinary admission coming from one intent on refuting the notion of a merely mechanical agency of language and bent instead on establishing its origins as something more esoteric than "a fold of the brain or an angle of the skull" (1:490)—"the faculty of abstraction . . . better known . . . by the homely name of Reason" (1:492)—human reasoning itself being only a faint echo of that engaged in by the Divinity.

Such organic comparatives—so popular with philologists such as Wilhelm Bleek, Bopp, Farrar, Schlegel, Schleicher, and even Müller himself, whose ambivalence betrays itself in his tendency to return to them after having drawn attention to their inexactitude—paved the way for literary and fictional treatments of language as subject both to sickness and to what Huysmans termed "a slow and partial decay" that eventually gives way to a purulent deliquescence.[28] Language might be viewed as one type of Paterian artifice, a means by which humanity might stave off impermanency and decline, but it was also entirely possible to conclude (as the Decadents, who thought of themselves as Paterian disciples, were fully aware) that because language was a human construct, it might also bear what Machen refers to as the "brand" of human imperfection. Terms such as "lassitude," "neurosity," "depravity," and "madness," for example, emerge in the various definitions of Decadent language and style put forward by Max Beerbohm, Gautier, and Baudelaire. Their literary creations were afflicted by what Symons termed the "*maladie fin de siècle*": as already noted, he had determined that Decadent literature sought to emphasize and even flaunted its own debilities.[29] Nordau came to roughly the same conclusion when he charac-

terized both art objects and literary creations as "psycho-physiologically accurate": capable, that is, of assuming the psychological and physiological stigmata
of their makers.[30] Huysmans's Des Esseintes—a littérateur of no mean stature
and a connoisseur of corrupted styles—takes pleasure in reflecting upon the
decline of the classical "Latin tongue" from a sound condition to a state in which
it possesses a "special gamy flavour" to one in which it is "dropping to pieces . .
. rotten through and through and hung like a decaying carcase, losing its limbs,
oozing pus, barely keeping, in the general corruption of its body, a few sound
parts, which the Christians removed in order to preserve them in the pickling
brine of their new idiom."[31]

This passage from A rebours—which Nordau condemned as a "debauch in
pathological and nauseous ideas of a deranged mind with gustatory perversion"[32]—provides us with one example of the way in which scientific paradigms
are troped in the literary artifacts of the culture from which they have emerged.
Machen's "The Great God Pan" does more than merely redact key concepts or
repeat terminology already made popular by the Huxleys and the Müllers: it is
but one of many examples of the late Gothic that structure themselves around
the body-as-text/text-as-body analogy that had become central to the arguments
of biologists and philologists, and as such it exposes as well the anxieties of
those familiar with those arguments—or at least with the popularized distortions
of them. When "The Great God Pan" appeared in the second volume of The
Whirlwind in 1890, it was largely ignored by both readers and critics. In 1894 it
resurfaced as the fifth book of John Lane's Keynote Series, with a frontispiece
by Beardsley depicting a faun (which one reviewer mistook for a "nymph" whose
"admirably-realised repulsiveness" seemed well suited to the story).[33] In the company of such notorious pieces as Grant Allen's The Woman Who Did, Shiel's
Prince Zaleski, and Fiona Macleod's The Mountain Lovers—all of which had
earned their place in the Keynote series specifically because of their stylistic
modishness or "daring" content—it attracted the attention that it had failed to
receive four years earlier. Whereas the editors of the Westminster Gazette dis-
paraged Machen's "nightmares of corruption" as examples of the type of story
that was "most truly decadent," Oscar Wilde was delighted to be able to declare
"The Great God Pan" "Un succès fou! Un succès fou!" (even as he rejoiced in the
discovery that Machen was the "author of our sacraments of evil, just as there is
that of the sacraments of goodness").[34]

Machen's macabre tale tells of a rash of suicides inspired by the actions of a
creature, half human and half pagan god, whose birth is the result of an ill-
conceived experiment in which Dr. Raymond, a typical Faustian overreacher,
tampers with certain nerve cells in a woman's brain, thereby breaching the solid
wall of sense that hides the real world from his patient's sight. This lifting of the
veil, Raymond explains, was what the ancients meant when they spoke of "seeing the god Pan." Something terrible happens to the woman: she experiences a
brief moment of ecstasy, but she is immediately overwhelmed by a panic dread

that leaves her hopelessly insane. The remaining seven sections of the story detail the efforts of three men who set out, many years later, to uncover the identity of a beautiful and mysterious young woman who seems to have been intimately associated with certain men who have committed suicide or who met premature death under peculiar circumstances. Eventually, the men learn that the young woman's name is Helen Vaughan, that she is the daughter of Raymond's sacrificial patient and the god Pan, and that she has been amusing herself by introducing her male friends to her father.

There are many things worth talking about in what is arguably the most celebrated story in the corpus of a writer whose "powerful horror-material of the nineties and earlier nineteen-hundreds" Lovecraft saw as standing "alone in its class" and marking "a distinct epoch in the history of" the tale of supernatural horror.[35] Of particular interest here, however, is an eye-witness's account of the manner of Helen's demise:

> "Though horror and revolting nausea rose up within me, and an odour of corruption choked my breath, I remained firm. I was then privileged or accursed, I dare not say which, to see that which was on the bed, lying there black like ink, transformed before my eyes. The skin, and the flesh, and the muscles, and the bones, and the firm structure of the human body that I had thought to be unchangeable, and permanent as adamant, began to melt and dissolve.
>
> "I knew that the body may be separated into its elements by external agencies, but I should have refused to believe what I saw. For here there was some internal force, of which I knew nothing, that caused dissolution and change.
>
> "Here too was all the work by which man has been made repeated before my eyes. I saw the form waver from sex to sex, dividing itself from itself, and then again reunited. Then I saw the body descend to the beasts whence it ascended, and that which was on the heights go down to the depths, even to the abyss of all being. The principle of life, which makes organism, always remained, while the outward form changed.
>
> "The light within the room had turned to blackness, not the darkness of night, in which objects are seen dimly, for I could see clearly and without difficulty. But it was the negation of light; objects were presented to my eyes, if I may say so, without any medium, in such a manner that if there had been a prism in the room I should have seen no colours represented in it.
>
> "I watched, and at last I saw nothing but a substance as jelly. Then the ladder was ascended again . . . *[here the MS. is illegible]* . . . for one instant I saw a Form, shaped in dimness before me, which I will not farther describe. But the symbol of this form may be seen in ancient sculptures, and in paintings which survived beneath the lava, too foul to

be spoken of . . . as a horrible and unspeakable shape, neither man nor beast, was changed into human form, there came finally death.

"I who saw all this, not without great horror and loathing of soul, here write my name, declaring all that I have set on this paper to be true."

Robert Matheson, Med. Dr.[36]

This passage reveals, among other things, that Machen had not always subscribed to the dicta that he would later castigate Poe for having failed to uphold in some of his stories: that it is possible to overstep the point at which "tragedy becomes melodrama" and that "decay and dissolution are far from being the supreme subject for the artist."[37] For dissolution defines this passage. Helen's death throes embody a reverse ontogeny: an accelerated retrogression to what Lovecraft described as "the most primal manifestations of the life-principle," what Machen himself would later call "Protoplasmic Reversion" (*The Three Impostors*, 124).[38] Unlike Rider Haggard's Ayesha, whose spiraling descent is arrested once her outward form resolves itself into the simian shape of her more recent ancestors—her "gracious form" degenerating into that of a "hideous little monkey frame, covered with crinkled yellow parchment," her "shapeless face" sealed with "the stamp of unutterable age"—Helen's body wantonly sheds the exuviae of the ages, descending at length "even to the abyss of all being."[39] The protoplasm into which Helen's outward form eventually melts is *the* sublimely abject substance—indefinite, unstable, amorphous—and thus betrays its origins, for Helen's father is described as a similarly abject creature: "neither man nor beast, neither the living nor the dead, but all things mingled, the form of all things but devoid of all form" (176). Enacting a terrific version of the Paterian "weaving and unweaving" of the self, Helen's body becomes the quintessential site of Gothic horrors, and her death would certainly have piqued the fears of an audience recalling with regret the days when it *could* complain of the encroaching frontier of a *brute* kingdom. For with the discovery of protoplasm had come the suggestion that humanity dwelt in what Huxley termed "an intermediate kingdom, a sort of biological No Man's Land" in which "it is admittedly impossible to draw any distinct boundary line" between "the vegetable world" and "the animal," it being "a mere matter of convention," as Huxley saw it, "whether we call a given organism an animal or a plant" (134-35).

But what, then, are we to think of language, the "Rubicon" that no brute, much less a plant, dare cross? "The Great God Pan," with its emphasis on the "illegible" and the "unspeakable," treats language as "an organism without organs" (the phrase is Romanes's); one that seemed in danger, that is, of reverting to the primitive condition of structure characteristic of aboriginal languages that have not yet undergone a "differentiation into parts of speech."[40] Linguistically exhausted, structurally degenerative, the story itself suffers from an abjection that reveals its atavistic character. The integrity of the narrative structure dissolves before the reader's eyes: though it falls into eight sections, the various episodes appear to be randomly ordered, and after having encountered them all, the reader must struggle to discern the reticulated network of associations that bind them into a coherent whole. Displaying a polyphony precisely analogous to the polymorphousness of the material bodies whose actions and reactions they recount, the various narrative voices behave, not cacophonously, as do the dissociated voices in Eliot's "The Waste Land" (1922), but rather as independent but interpenetrating fragments, each providing points and counterpoints within the larger movement that contains (even as it is defined by) them. One voice blends almost imperceptibly into another; one interrupts or is absorbed into another; sometimes several clump together or merge.[41] Thus, Mr. Clarke's memoirs, contained in "three or four pages densely covered with Clarke's round, set penmanship," are straightaway represented as being the "Singular Narrative told me by my Friend, Dr. Phillips" (181).

More unsettling than the erratic manner in which the story progresses or the loosely fugal principles it enunciates, however, are the lacunae that pock the narrative, for "The Great God Pan" is rife with omissions, gaps, and silences. The various episodes are truncated, their conclusions inconclusive; manuscripts are sealed at just the moment when it would appear that long-sought revelations are imminent. Just as we are about to learn what it is that the anonymous "Rachel M.," half dressed and weeping distractedly upon her bed, saw during her walk in the woods with Helen Vaughan, her childhood playmate, Mr. Clarke (Dr. Raymond's accomplice) snaps shut the book in which the "wild story" is recorded, punctuating his gesture with an outburst that, in essence, opens the book once again to further but unverifiable speculation: "'My God! . . . think, think what you are saying. It is too incredible, too monstrous; such things can never be in this quiet world'" (187). After a glance at only the first page of a manuscript produced by one of Helen Vaughan's victims, another character hurls the text from him, crying that "the dread and horror of death itself . . . are as nothing compared to this" (231). We also never learn by precisely what means "Mrs. Beaumont" (one of the several aliases by which the multifarious woman is known in London) induces her gentlemanly suitors to subject themselves to slow and torturous forms of suicide. Appropriately, the textual record of Helen Vaughan's death is the most corrupt and gnomic of all, taking the form of "pencil jottings" in Latin (Huysmans's suppurating language) contained in a chapter entitled "Fragments." The transcription of her demise is followed by an epilogue that enacts a kind of narrative recapitulation: by returning to the house in Caermaen where Helen had lived as a girl, Mr. Clarke rounds off a story that began when he witnessed the ill-fated experiment during which she was conceived. While in Caermaen, he finds a small pillar of white stone that had originally stood in a woods penetrated by a Roman road. Some of the letters are illegible, but Mr. Clarke transcribes the inscription as follows:

DEVOMNODENT*i*
FLA*vi*VSSENILISPOSSV*it*
PROPTERNVP*tias*
*qua*SVIDITSVBVMB*ra*

The "local antiquaries were much puzzled," we are told, "not by the inscription, or by any difficulty in translating it, but as to the circumstance or rite to which allusion is made" (241).[42] The full implication of the Latin words is being ineluctably lost as the letters fall away from the bodies of the words, leaving behind fragments that admit of translation, but resist interpretation or contextualization. Any kind of significance is recuperable only by the literal burying of the decayed linguistic residue in the body of a language not yet decomposed and thus able to contain the skeletal remains if not to help them resume their former shape and essential quality and power of definition.

Romanes had elsewhere termed this degenerative condition of language "the undifferentiated protoplasm of predication" and had suggested that it was most readily to be observed in the language of "the child which is just beginning to speak."[43] In alluding to the language of the child, Romanes not only provides a practical example of a phenomenon otherwise difficult to observe, but indirectly characterizes it for an audience who would have interpreted one term (language) in the light of the other (childhood) and understood both to imply recidivist, primitive, undeveloped conditions.[44] Moreover, his focus on the speech patterns of children qualifies him as a recapitulationist—one, that is, who has appropriated Haeckel's theory that in the course of their development to adulthood individuals reenact the evolutionary history of their species and evince, sequentially, characteristics of the adult ancestral forms. The "Evolution of the Tribe," as he wrote in *The Evolution of Man* (1874), "which is dependent on the laws of Heredity and Adaptation, effects all the events which take place in the course of the Evolution of the Germ or Embryo."[45] Thus, the child might truly be termed the father of the man, since children were by definition passing through a more primitive stage in the developmental history of their species. To study the child of "dominant" cultures—or, alternatively, the adults of "inferior" classes or races, whose "childlike" status and capacities drew marked attention among recapitulationists—was, in essence, to resuscitate primitive man and make him, his modes of behavior, and his capabilities available for examination. By extension, to study the language patterns of the child—or of a more "primitive" race— was to hear the faint suspirations of what had been for their progenitors a newly congealed and only barely differentiated language. The idea had not originated with Romanes; as early as 1842, in his *Vestiges of the Natural History of Creation*, Robert Chambers pitied the otherwise advanced Chinese for their language, which "resembles that of children, or deaf and dumb people": the "sentence of short, simple, unconnected words, in which an infant amongst us attempts to express some of its wants and its ideas—the equally broken and difficult terms which the deaf and dumb express by signs, . . . these are like the discourse of the refined people of the so-called Celestial Empire."[46] In *The Time Machine*, a nightmare of devolution, the Eloi, at once adult and child, provide a fictional illustration of this evolutionary phenomenon. Bodily, these neotenous people, with their Dresden-china prettiness, pink hands, hairless faces, and "girlish rotundity of limb," represent the heights that the species has scaled, their bodily juvenilization expressive of an evolutionary advance over rudimentary progenitors. Linguistically, however, they have undergone recapitulation, for "their language was excessively simple—almost exclusively composed of concrete substantives and verbs," with sentences "usually simple and of two words." Bereft of "abstract terms," of "figurative language,"[47] their verbal system is sufficient to meet the needs of a people "on the intellectual level of one of our five-year-old children," for like children, they need express only "the simplest propositions."[48] Here Wells is appropriating the findings of contemporary philologists who, in their investigations into the "mysterious first principles of language," had already determined, with Romanes, that "languages become simpler in their structure the further they are traced backwards, until we arrive at their so-called 'roots,'" so that one finds in "the primitive condition of language-structure" that "'every noun and every verb was originally by itself a complete sentence,' consisting of a subject and predicate fused into one—. . . not yet differentiated into the *two*, much less into the *three* parts which now go to constitute the fully evolved structure of a proposition."[49] Romanes's was a theory with which Machen must have been familiar at the time of his writing "The Great God Pan," for in "The Novel of the Black Seal" (1895)—a later story similarly inclined to the protoplasmic—a character recalls being "struck by the phrase 'articulate-speaking men' in Homer," taking this as evidence of the fact that "the writer knew or had heard of men whose speech was so rude that it could hardly be termed articulate"; had known or heard, that is, of folk equipped with "a jargon but little removed from the inarticulate noises of brute beasts" (and exemplifying, apparently, Darwin's bow-wow theory).[50]

The narrative hesitations as well as the stylistic disruptions of "The Great God Pan" thus serve as signposts of linguistic and structural degeneration that we might think of as being analogous to biological and cultural dissolution. Bourget, for example, treated textual decomposition both as a correlative of organismal degeneration and as a symptom of cultural breakdown and decay: in his view a Decadent style emerges when an advanced society is poised at the threshold of—or already embarked upon—its decline. Such a society, he argued in his *Essais de psychologie contemporaine* (1883), is like "an organism" in that "it may be resolved into a federation of smaller organisms, which may themselves be resolved into a federation of cells": "If the energy of the cells becomes independent, the lesser organisms will likewise cease to subordinate their energy to the total energy and the anarchy which is established constitutes the decadence of the whole." Given that the law governing "the development and decadence" of the social organism also governs "that other organism which we call language" (the latter, by necessity, an appendage of the former), a Decadent style will betray itself—he argues—in a textual and linguistic atomization made manifest when "the unity of the book is decomposed to give place to the independence of the page," when that of "the page is decomposed to give place to the independence of the phrase," and when that of "the phrase [gives] place to the independence of the word."[51] As cultures and societies decay, language may also decay, and in the stories discussed here, we see the effects when a society is exposed to and reinfected by the noxious or destructive influences bred by the poisonous texts—the "yellow" books of the Decadents—that it has itself engendered.[52] Thus, fearing contagion, the narrator of Chambers's "The Yellow Sign" refuses to come into contact with the fatal play "The King in Yellow":

> I had long ago decided that I should never open that book, and nothing on earth could have persuaded me to buy it. Fearful lest curiosity might tempt me to open it, I had never even looked at it in book-stores. If I ever had had any curiosity to read it, the awful tragedy of young Castaigne, whom I knew, prevented me from exploring its wicked pages. I had always refused to listen to any description of it, and indeed, nobody ever ventured to discuss the second part aloud, so I had absolutely no knowledge of what those leaves might reveal. I stared at the poisonous yellow mottled binding as I would at a snake.[53]

In *Nana*, Zola resorts to the same protoplasmic vocabulary that drives Machen's dark conceit, both as a means of fleshing out the portrait of "Venus . . . rotting" featured at the novel's end and as a means of animating his representation of a social organism corrupted by that which it had itself perverted. Our final glimpse of Nana—the woman who, no matter how dissolute her life, has looked always "clean, and solid, and as brand-new as if she had never seen service"—is of a being dissolving in a "heap of matter and blood, a shovelful of corrupted flesh," her face a "formless pulp" in which one eye "had completely foundered among bubbling purulence" while the other "remained half open," looking "like a deep black ruinous hole," the nose was "suppurating," and the mouth was invaded by quite "a large reddish crust . . . peeling from one of the cheeks."[54] Lest his readers might somehow manage to overlook what he has been at pains to articulate—namely, Nana's "rage for debasing things," for destroying and soiling them, and for "leaving abominable traces" upon whatever her delicate hands had broken—Zola makes explicit at his novel's close the connection between the moral and the physical bases of her life: "It seemed as though the poison she had assimilated in the gutters, and on the carrion tolerated by the roadside, the leaven with which she had poisoned a whole people, had but now remounted to her face and turned it to corruption."[55]

Zola's sociological analysis recalls the monogenistic view that Morel had developed in his extended study of heredity and the degeneration of the human species, in which he speaks of the various human races as so many morbid deviations from "a primitive type . . . from the original type" that he thought of as having been uncorrupted until social and cultural evils had acted upon it.[56] Machen's description of protoplasmic horrors, on the other hand, with its own not-very-covert sexual subtext, emphasizes the devolutionary quality of degeneracy: the tendency of organic entities—of human bodies, for example, and bodies of writing—to retrogress from a complex and specialized state to one "undifferentiated," primitive, and (as Nordau would have it) even brutish.[57] Both Zola and Machen, however, emphasize the essentially corruptive—and by extension the transgressive—power of the decadent bodies with which they are obsessed. Nana crosses class boundaries, drawing her victims from both the highest and the lowest levels of the society that has corrupted her. Even more unruly than that of the uncontrollable Nana, the body of Machen's Helen Vaughan defies physical and intellectual limitations, just as the gelatinous plasmas sealed within her body ooze out from beneath the skin stretched over them, eventually consuming the organism that they formerly fed. Her morbid dissolution triggers a correspondingly physiological response in the doctor who, witnessing Helen Vaughan's demise, "melts" and "dissolves" accordingly: "horror and revolting nausea rose up within me, and an odour of corruption choked my breath" (236). Her bodily exudations are vaguely mirrored in his response (gagging and wretching being one means by which the body voids insalubrious matter or responds to noxious influences); in this sense her body may be said to exist in two places at once, both within itself and within the body that registers its infectious presence physically.

If contemporary responses to Machen's conceit may be taken as a gauge, then her bodily revolt is more radically transgressive still, violating not integumentary and spatial encasements only, but fictional borders as well. Only too ready to dismiss it as so much "baby-Satanic-tommy rot," its "burried nastiness" fit reading only for those "who are morbid and unhealthy in mind," many of Machen's reviewers fixed—however sardonically—upon the story's distinctly physiological and pathological qualities, treating it as though it were a diseased body in need of quarantining. W.L. Courtney of the *Daily Telegraph,* for example, assumed the role of a "Physician" and diagnosed the text as suffering from "'the Yellow Book . . . disease . . . a very virulent form of jaundice, due to an imperfect digestion and a morbid condition of liver.'"[58] Metaphors involving digestion—or, more accurately, indigestion and accompanying nausea—abound in the various commentaries on Machen's work. A reviewer from the *Dundee Advertiser* concluded that the sorts of visions one encounters in the protoplasmically predisposed *The Three Impostors* "have before been given to little boys who complained of headache and divers other pains," but whose sufferings are ultimately traced by the family doctor back to "'mince pies and pickles.'" Another, speaking for the *Athenaeum,* pointed out that this same story "produces on the normal waking mind much the same effect as a hearty supper of pork chops on the dream fancies of a person of delicate digestion: 'velut aegri somnia, vanae finguntur species.'"[59] Although their original intent was satirical, these reviews also remind us that as Aidan Reynolds and William Charlton have put it, such stories treat of horror "elevated to the intellectual plane without losing its nauseousness": horror, that is, which is capable of overleaping the boundaries of the text that contains it and of conflating divergent orders of being and awareness, exerting a physical as well as an intellectual influence upon the reader.[60]

As has already been suggested, "The Great God Pan" was designed to produce in the reader the symptoms of confusion, indeterminacy, and destabilization that are integral both to many of the theories that had emerged in the biological sciences and to similar horror stories that had also adopted materialist principles, phylogenetics, degeneration, and recapitulation as their subject matter—and also as their source of horror, which in this case may be equated with the sort of "abjection" defined by Julia Kristeva as "what disturbs identity, system, order. What does not respect borders, positions, rules. The in-between, the ambiguous, the composite."[61] In their unveiling not merely of a decompositive body occupying an otherwise unthinkable plane of existence, but also of those other bodies that are degraded by what is itself degraded, many works of fin de siècle horror explore precisely this form of abjection, which seeks to elicit a physical response in the reader—a visceral shudder or a sense of physical aversion brought on by the propinquity of something lacking "cleanliness or health," something degenerative, "radically separate, loathsome," often something unnameable.[62] The propriety of such a response is never in doubt because in all such stories the hero or narrator reacts in precisely the same fashion—setting an example, as it were, for the reader to follow. Thus, in the presence of atavistic behavior rather than actual physical degeneration, the narrator of John Buchan's "The Grove of Ashtaroth" (1912) feels "an overpowering repugnance," growing "sick with disgust—not terror, but honest physical loathing."[63] Stevenson's Mr. Utterson seeks urgently for a term with which to describe the peculiar quality— "There must be something else. . . . There *is* something more, if I could find a name for it"—that inspires "the hitherto unknown disgust, loathing, and fear," the "nausea and distaste of life" that he and others feel in the presence of the "pale" and "dwarfish" Mr. Hyde.[64] Made desperate by his own exposure to the A: B: O. and thus prompted to cross a social boundary that he would never otherwise have transgressed, Pelluther seeks the company of a caretaker who, as he approaches Pelluther's contaminated house, speaks of a physical revulsion made worse by his inability to determine its cause: "'Say, Master, what is moving in the house? . . . Why is my 'ead all damp, and my 'ands a shiverin'. I tell you there's a thing gone wrong in the place.'" In Stoker's *Dracula* Jonathan Harker records in his diary that he "could not repress a shudder" when the Count was in close proximity: "It may have been that his breath was rank, but a horrible feel-

ing of nausea came over me, which, do what I would, I could not conceal."[65]
When he encounters Dr. Moreau's Beast People, but before he is aware that he
is in the company of hybrid monstrosities, Wells's Edward Prendick responds to
a "something in their faces"—he knows "not what"—that triggers in him "a queer
spasm of disgust," "a shuddering recoil," and "a nasty little sensation, a tightening of [his] muscles," whereas what begins for his Time Traveller as a "peculiar
shrinking" from the pallid bodies of beings who are "filthily cold to the touch" in
turn leads to an irreferable feeling of "deadly nausea" in response to "something":
"the sickening quality of the Morlocks—something inhuman and malign. Instinctively I loathed them."[66] Each of these stories in its own way recalls the archetypal story of nausea, Poe's "The Facts in the Case of M. Valdemar" (1845), in
which "no person present even affected to deny, or attempted to repress, the
unutterable, shuddering horror" that the few audible words uttered by the living
corpse "were so well calculated to convey."[67] The reactions of those in attendance vary in degree (a medical student swoons; the nurses flee the death chamber and refuse to return), but all become nauseous and are barely able to repress
the "hysterical vomiting" that Freud identified in his study of the etiology of hysteria as symptomatic of the conjunction of "great fright" and an experience "jus-
tifiably" productive of "a *high amount of disgust*": for example, the "ghastly and
revolting sight" of "a decomposing dead body."[68]

The physiology of fear that Lovecraft fixes on is, he claims, constructed out
of "the exact . . . lines and proportions that connect up with the latent instincts or
hereditary memories of fright" and that "stir the dormant sense of strangeness."[69]
Although indicative of a related physiology, the "sickening quality" that discon-
certs Utterson and the Time Traveller is located for the reader not in the "lines"
but in the intervening spaces: in the pauses, the linguistic lapses, the qualifying
auxiliaries—"it may have been"—and the elliptical nouns that seem to name something—"something else," "something more," "something inhuman"—but "mean"
almost nothing. The decomposing or otherwise unstable body elicits an analogous regression in the observer, who lacks a vocabulary sufficient to describe
the encounter: "My own impressions," laments the witness to Valdemar's mesmeric rapport, "I would not pretend to render intelligible to the reader." The living
corpse produces sounds that have never before "jarred upon the ear of humanity"—"such as it would be madness in me to attempt describing": "There are,
indeed, two or three epithets which might be considered as applicable to it in
part; I might say, for example, that the sound was harsh, and broken and hollow;
but the hideous whole is indescribable" ("M. Valdemar" 3:1240). The shuddering, spasming, and swooning of those who witness such horrors amount to a
visceral expression of an emotion analogous to the "sympathy" that Darwin
saw as permitting us, when confronted by a frightened person, to put ourselves
"in the position of the sufferer, and feel something akin to his fear." Under such
circumstances, the muscular system contracts in much the same way that
Darwin's facial "muscle of fear" contracts in the presence of another's fright,

thus allowing the body to express in its own appropriately primitive "language" its awareness of the proximity of the *unheimlich* and, through it, the immanence of things buried, occulted, and repressed.[70] Those who must find a way to express the nauseating quality of their experience often turn to the realm where the corporeal and the conceptual overlap, so that Poe's narrator, fearing "that it will be impossible to make [himself] comprehended," notes that the dying Valdemar's voice "impressed" him synesthetically—"as gelatinous or glutinous matters impress the sense of touch" (3:1240). Poe's story articulates a mordant pun: Valdemar, continuing to report on his own decay, becomes a memorable example of what may be comprehended in the phrase "*in articulo mortis*" (3:1233).

Trapped in their pre-Freudian nightmare worlds, such tongue-tied characters (Valdemar's tongue is swollen and blackened, exposed to view with the falling away of his lower jaw) seek to express an irreferable something that triggers an unnameable response—a condition that may best be described as the uncanny, the *unheimlich*. Their encounter with the *unheimlich* coincides with a momentary surcease of expressiveness, in a stifling of speech signaling an abrupt reversion to hereditary memories, latent instincts, perhaps instinctive loathing.[71] Freud (a confirmed recapitulationist) associated the uncanny with absences and lapses, with what is "concealed, kept from sight, so that others do not get to know of or about it, withheld from others. . . . *something hidden and dangerous*" (the "meaning" of *heimliche* usually ascribed to what ought to be its opposite, the ambiguous *unheimliche*).[72] Moreover, what is hidden, not revealed, kept from sight is also "in reality nothing new or alien," he continues, "but something which is familiar and old-established in the mind and which has become alienated from it only through the process of repression. This reference to the factor of repression enables us, furthermore, to understand Schelling's definition . . . of the uncanny as something which ought to have remained hidden but has come to light."[73] The *unheimlich* provides us with another way of reading, and naming, the shuddering silences that emerge in response to encounters with bodies that have regressed or are in the process of devolving to former states of being, infecting what is around them. That uncanny moment is expressed textually by the silence in which the narrative decomposes—literally unwrites itself—as verbal and linguistic systems become infected (and inflected) by what ails them. Although the witness to Helen's death attempts to remain firm, his disgust is so intense that it precludes him from writing legibly, and thus he creates a corrupt record of a corrupt death, "much abbreviated" (235), illegible at those points at which his horror and nausea and loathing of soul—symptomatic of his own imminent dissolution—render him speechless. As "the virulence of phonetic change," to return to Müller's biolinguistic hypothesis, "will sometimes eat away the whole body of a word, and leave nothing behind but decayed fragments" (Müller 1:53), so the virulence associated with devolutionary change will sometimes eat away not only the body itself (leaving behind only decayed fragments or unctuous patches) but other bodies in close proximity, and even, if the "decadent" author has his way, the verbal structures—the sentences, the pages, the texts—in which they are contained, crossing in this way over yet another border, disturbing yet another order.

The lacunae of Machen's story dissolve one final barrier—that which, according to Tzvetan Todorov, naturally arises out of our inability to forget, when we read, that "it is only 'literature' and not 'life.'"[74] By knowing (or pretending to know) more than it reveals, the text forces us, against our better judgment and even against our will, to reveal more about our inner selves than we wish to know; forcing us to speculate and, in speculating, to confront what is otherwise occulted and concealed. When the text falters, we falter as well and are drawn into its decline. Forced to fill in the gaps and omissions with material drawn from private reserves of guilt and anxiety, we discover or invent in the white and decomposing spaces that which proves as infectious as the "odour of corruption" emanating from the various degradations to which the story's characters are exposed: the regressive, instinctual feelings that combine to make up what Lovecraft termed the "hereditary impulse"— and what Freud, Lovecraft's contemporary, would recast (in psychoanalytical terms) as "what is known of old and long familiar."[75] The brothers de Goncourt reveal the potentially corrupting role of the elliptical silence when, in a journal entry, they recall the "commissioner of police who . . . had played with the idea of prosecuting" the unnamed author "of a line of asterisks which appeared in a number of *Le Paris* and which had seemed obscene to this same M. Latour-Dumoulin."[76] In his defense of his notorious novel of the 1890s, Wilde makes explicit what is only hinted at in the de Goncourt journal entry: the revelatory nature of the unspoken and suppressed. "Each man," Wilde writes, "sees his own sin in Dorian Gray. What Dorian Gray's sins are no one knows. He who finds them has brought them." And again, he announces that the work of art that is "rich and vital and complete . . . will fill the cowardly with terror, and the unclean will see in it their own shame. It will be to each man what he is himself."[77] Required to play their own role in the collaborative effort to resuscitate meaning, readers are invited to imagine a private confrontation with "The Great God Pan"; encouraged to ask themselves what secret horror Helen Vaughan's victims—conscripted visionaries—could have looked upon that made them long for death.

Few other horror writers of the period—Conrad excepted—were in the end so readily associated as Machen was with an elliptical style in which, as one critic complained, "much is intimated and little is told."[78] Although an appreciative Lovecraft might credit the "gradual hints and revelations" with "the cumulative suspense and ultimate horror with which every paragraph [of "The Great God Pan"] abounds," William Rose Benét, another contemporary, angrily condemned Machen as an "ellipsist" who, though he was "not at all sure of" the incidents he described, tended to transcribe them "in his own particular hieroglyphic."[79] Most emphatically, then, Benét did not share Lovecraft's opinion that "the charm" of Machen's stories lay "in the telling."[80] Perhaps the richest tribute—or, alternatively, the most creative insult—paid to Machen on this score was the parody "A Yellow Creeper" (1895), dedicated by its author, Arthur Rickett, to "the Author of 'The Great God Pan, and the Inmost Light.'" In this brief jeu d'esprit, a doctor—"the Doctor"—mixes "a green fluid" with a "red fluid," which, when he adds to it "something black," becomes "a clear, limpid, crystal-like fluid": a chemical compound in which "R_2OT_3 reacts on its agent $P_4IFF_5LE_6$." When a small quantity of this agent is dropped upon an unsuspecting fly, "the bluebottle paused stupefied; then it lubricated its legs together with violence, gave a fearful buzz of despair, and turned into an old blowfly. Only for a second. It rapidly became a red-bottle ('Best Scotch'), then an alligator, a scarecrow, a Beardsley poster, and finally dissolved into nothing."[81] Of interest in this spoof—as in the precursor text to which it playfully responds—is the concluding section, the written statement of a witness to the experiment.

> I, Doctor Bunkum, have been asked to recount what I saw. My knowledge of the English language is but slight, owing to the excessive attention given in early manhood to the classical subjects in the Little-Go. But I will do my best. When I was called in, the temperature of the room was 212° Fahr., and a green twilight suffused everything. I am a stolid man, but my pulse beat 599 to the minute; yet I retained my self-control.
>
> The thing was buzzing fiercely after a dissipated course of fly-papers. I felt its pulse, and gave it a bottle of influenza mixture. It rapidly grew worse; it resembled a saneless, painless, brainless lump of blue jelly. Neither male nor female, animal, vegetable or mineral. Then it began to dissolve. I have been at the Dissolution of Parliament, but never have I—!! yet words fail!! I crept under a copy of the *Westminster Gazette*, and waited for the finale. No, excuse me, I did not wait, I hurried out, wrote down my impressions for the Public, and then made my will. When these pages are being read, I shall probably be either dead or living.[82]

With its sardonic linking of viscosity and silence, Rickett's parody succeeds because it recreates, intensifies, and exaggerates the defining characteristics not only of Machen's style (the "spontaneous" reticences rendered typographically by means of dashes, exclamation points, and semicolons, as in "I have been at the Dissolution of Parliament, but never have I—!! yet words fail!!"), but also of his fictional universe (the bluebottle degenerating into "a saneless, painless, brainless lump of blue jelly").

There were those among Machen's contemporaries who showed a more sober appreciation of the expressiveness of textual silences. Mallarmé, for example, believed (as Wilde did) in the potency of interstitial blanks, claiming that the "intellectual armature of the poem must be hidden; it is contained—it *lives*—in the very spaces which isolate the stanzas, and all through the whiteness of the paper: meaningful silence which gives no less pleasure in its composition than the verses themselves."[83] Symons proposed that Pater's prose style "found a large part of mastery in reticence, in knowing what to omit."[84] In the essay entitled "Silence" that introduces his book of meditations, *Le Trésor des Humbles* (1896), Maurice Maeterlinck confesses his reverential attitude toward those writers who "cultivate silence" and whose works "commune in divine silence." Echoing Carlyle's insistence that silence "is the element in which great things fashion themselves together, that at length they may emerge, full-formed and majestic, into the daylight of Life, which they are henceforth to rule," Maeterlinck goes on to note in turn that "as gold and silver are weighed in pure water, so does the soul test its weight in silence, and the words that we let fall have no meaning apart from the silence that wraps them round."[85] For such writers, silence is a shaping force, helping to construct not merely the overall design of a work of art but also the reader's attitude toward and response to the artifact. Like the "holes" in Hugo's blottesques—those burnt-out passages that silently comment upon the lacy figurations that contain them—stylistic absences and omissions call attention to themselves, complementing the elaborately worked prose sections they abut. When strategically placed, they can be more expressive in their reticence than words would otherwise be in their self-aware (and often doomed) attempts to fix meaning.

The omissions and ellipses of Machen's story disclose an essentially decompositive strategy, betraying language's constitutional vulnerability to the entropic forces that surround and beset it as they simultaneously induce the emotional and intellectual short-circuits in which reason gives way to elemental human emotions—to fear, anxiety, and shame. Though we suffer an emblematic death in those spaces, however, we are productive in them as well, for we must become the cocreators of an evolving horror that, in blasting speech, renders speechlessness expressive. At such moments and in such spaces, a decompositional urge sits astride the procreative urge. Jorgis Baltruvaitis put it another way: the deformation that "radically decomposes a body" is also a "formation."[86] Pater anticipated such a view when, in reminding his readers that an "undefinable taint of death" awakened in Rousseau "the literary sense," he acknowledged that visionary gestures are often born of mortal disease (220). In this passage from the "Conclusion," vitalist and materialist perspectives converge, for Huxley had also argued that we not only live in the midst of death, but batten upon it: "Under whatever disguise it takes refuge, whether fungus or oak, worm or man, the living protoplasm not only ultimately dies and is resolved into its mineral and lifeless constituents, but is always dying, and, strange as the paradox may sound, could not live unless it died" (136). His imminent recourse to mutton, Huxley informed his readers, would prove a necessary, a creative, and even an occult act, for in eating he would "transubstantiate sheep into man" and thereby "raise the complex substance of dead protoplasm to the higher power . . . of living protoplasm" (137-38). Such physiological certainties would later be raised to the higher power of a living truth of the sort extolled by the twentieth-century Dutch writer Multatuli, whose aesthetic, he claimed, was fed by the notion that "he who dreads putrefaction is an enemy of life."[87]

6

The Anatomy of Failure

Joseph Conrad's *Heart of Darkness*

There was no sign on the face of nature of this amazing tale that was not so much told as suggested to me in desolate exclamations, completed by shrugs, in interrupted phrases, in hints ending in deep sighs.

Joseph Conrad, *Heart of Darkness* (1899)

LIKE THE THORNY BRUSH of the well-known fairy tale, literary commonplaces and critical clichés have grown up around Conrad's *Heart of Darkness*, so much so that it has now been inadvertently cast in the role to which Marlow, recalling the extravagant dangers that beset the rescue team dispatched to retrieve the wayward agent, assigns Kurtz: that of "an enchanted princess sleeping in a fabulous castle."[1] Central among these assumptions is the belief—uncontested here—that, as Garrett Stewart puts it, "*Heart of Darkness* harkens back to origins."[2] By "origins," however, this essayist understands not the thematic devolution to which Stewart alludes but the literary and cultural influences, trends, and attitudes that prevailed in the *decennium mirabile* of the 1890s, in which, as Ian Fletcher reminds us, Conrad had his "beginnings."[3] The influence of choice among critics who have proceeded along these lines has been the tradition of imperial discourse that came into its own in the years just preceding Victoria's 1876 coronation as crown empress of India and endured long after. Such a choice—both reasonable and apt, given the story's repeated allusions to the actions of the "sordid buccaneers" whose motives are akin to those of "burglars breaking into a safe" (31)—nevertheless overlooks or ignores several of Conrad's disclaimers concerning the sociopolitical themes that *Heart of Darkness* introduces in its earliest pages. In the same letter (to his publisher, William Blackwood) in which he described his subject as being "of our time distinctly," for example, Conrad also emphasized that the story itself had not been "topically treated"—if only because he believed that "fiction is nearer truth" than history, which is "based on documents, and the reading of print and handwriting—on secondhand impression" (*NLL* 17).[4] Furthermore, in a letter to R.B. Cunninghame Graham, who had apparently written a warm appreciation after the publication of the first installment of *Heart of Darkness*, Conrad warned that his new friend might curse him "by and bye for the very same thing," for, in the two installments that were to follow, "the idea is so wrapped up in secondary notions that You—even You!—may miss it." Conrad may have been thinking that his anticolonialist friend favored themes that he would de-emphasize in the later installments, for he makes it clear that he does not start "with an abstract notion"—a critique of imperialism, for example—but "with definite images," which, because their rendering is "true," produce some "little effect" (*JCL* 116).

In general, Conrad's "aesthetic" (the informal principles of which, never gathered together and refined into a coherent statement of art, are scattered throughout his prefaces and numerous letters) is elusive at best, and thus one hesitates to place undue emphasis on any two statements such as those made to Blackwood and Cunninghame Graham. Both letters make clear, however, that two truths, interrelated but distinct, coexist within his story: as Marlow sees it, there is the "surface-truth" consisting of "things to save a wiser man," but also "the overwhelming realities of this strange world of plants, and water, and silence"—the "essentials of this affair," which he claims "lay deep under the surface, beyond [his] reach, and beyond [his] power of meddling" (36-40). The dichotomy that each letter isolates can be seen as one expression of yet another conviction expressed more or less consistently throughout the corpus of Conrad's writings: the belief that "realism in art will never approach reality" (*JCLL* 1:303).[5]

The frustration and even despair that characterize Conrad's letters detailing his own artistic labors attest to the earnestness with which he tried, as he put it (in terms drawn from the argot of the spiritualism of the day), "to get through the veil of details at the essence of life" (*JCLL* 1:200). This statement, and others of its kind, establish Conrad's kinship with certain writers, some of whom are rarely if ever mentioned in discussions of Conrad's work in spite of the fact that, their years of productivity coinciding, they published in the same journals and moved in roughly the same circles. Recognizing that "everything visible was the veil of an invisible secret," Machen, for example, understood that "things which are most clear may yet be most closely hidden, and hidden for long ages," so that "we . . . gaze at great wonders, both of the body and the spirit, without discerning the marvels that are all around us."[6] He found those closely hidden marvels in the works of Poe, who, being a "true realist, . . . the true interpreter of man to man," mirrored "in forms beautiful and terrible the secret and innermost core of man's being."[7] Discerning in the statements of his literary precursors a fear that a finer sense would impart to the visionary only a consciousness of evil—what William James (quoting Leo Tolstoy) described as a grinding sense of "the meaningless absurdity of life— . . . the only incontestable knowledge accessible to man"—Lovecraft (himself an admirer of Conrad's ability to portray "dark secrets" and "lonely and maniacally resolute men") would later refine their definitions accordingly, characterizing the realist as one who "coldly and sardonically reflected some stable, mechanistic, and well-established horror-world which he saw fully, brilliantly, squarely, and unfalteringly."[8] We can look to science for an analog to—perhaps the source for—the obsession with this "essence of life," or what Symons understood to be the "essence of the truth . . . of the visible world . . . and the truth of spiritual things": "a perfect truth to one's impression, to one's intuition—."[9] In the last decade of the nineteenth century, the German physicist Wilhelm Röntgen, in a series of experiments using the cathode-ray tube, produced radiation that could pass through solid substances. No longer merely a metaphysical conceit or a fantastic hypothesis posed by members of the Society for Psychical Research, the idea that a different reality coexisted with our own seemed grounded in scientific fact. "The secret of the universe"—"*the* secret of the universe"—"is in the existence of horizontal waves whose varied vibrations are at the bottom of all states of consciousness," wrote an enthusiastic Joseph Conrad to Edward Garnett following his visit with the pioneer radiologist Dr. John McIntyre. Having learned about the phonograph and X rays, and having talked about the secret of the universe and the nonexistence of matter, Conrad explained:

If the waves were vertical the universe would be different. This is a truism. But, don't you see, there is nothing in the world to prevent the simultaneous existence of vertical waves, of waves at any angles; in fact there are mathematical reasons for believing that such waves do exist. Therefore it follows that two universes may exist in the same place and in the same time—and not only two universes but an infinity of different universes—if by universe we mean a set of states of consciousness; and note, *all* (the universes) composed of the same matter, *all matter* being only that thing of inconceivable tenuity through which the various vibrations of waves (electricity, heat, sound, light, etc.) are propagated, thus giving birth to our sensations—then emotions—then thought."[10]

Those writers who speculated about this transcendent reality were, as Conrad himself had been, quick to realize that these simultaneous universes were just as likely to be governed by laws and systems wholly antithetical, and even hostile, to those (often comfortably anthropocentric ones) that humanity had devised for itself.

In seeking to render verbally what he saw as "the mystic nature of material things," and in hinting elsewhere that this *vérité vraie* might just as easily prove damning as liberating, a "haunting terror" as well as a "visible wonder" (*PR* 130, 92), Conrad allied himself (however covertly or unconsciously) with writers whom we have come to associate with certain dominant literary movements of the period, two of which are of especial interest to me in this chapter: Decadence and the late Gothic. His indebtedness to the Decadent movement and its cousins-german (aestheticism, impressionism, symbolism, their influence already obvious in the purple prose of his earliest works and his allusion in the preface to *The Nigger of Narcissus* [1897] to "the supreme cry of Art for Art, . . . a cry . . . heard only as a whisper, often incomprehensible, but at times and faintly encouraging" [*CP* 53]) has been explored nearly (but not quite) as thoroughly as has his adoption of anti-imperialist themes and rhetoric.[11] Because Conrad publicly distanced himself from the tradition of supernatural literature, however, or because his story depends for its final horrific effect upon stylistic and textual decomposition rather than upon the final disclosure of conventional frights, scholars have not been prepared to recognize it as pursuing one of the "many different types of association with the supernatural" that (as Bleiler has argued) the late Gothic had established by the century's close.[12] Yet, Marlow affirms that his journey has taught him to know, among other things, the "sheer blank fright, pure abstract terror" that is "unconnected with any distinct shape of physical danger" (63). More essentially, the keynote of *Heart of Darkness* is "the horror."

I hesitate, nevertheless, to reclassify *Heart of Darkness* strictly as a "late horror story," if only because it has already been defined in so many ways—as, for example, late adventure story, Gothic romance, anti-imperialist invective—all of which are limiting and none of which is wholly accurate. As William Scheick rightly notes, "Influences are present, but not systematically or with uniform intensity in any given work by Conrad, and not in such a way that they will yield some monolithic measure of all of his writings; nor is any given work simply the sum of the influences it evidences."[13] The same may be said of Decadence and the fin de siècle literature of horror, certain formal characteristics of which are to be found in Conrad's central work of the 1890s. The two genres exist in a peculiar (and heretofore unexplored) conjunction with each other: it seems likely that each influenced the other and that both evolved strikingly similar narrative features in response to the attritive sense of dislocation, futility, and alienation that dominates the literature of the 1890s. Of greater interest and relevance, perhaps, is the simple fact that the narrative technique with which Conrad experiments in *Heart of Darkness* bears a considerable—almost an uncanny— resemblance to that which characterizes both fin de siècle literature of horror and the Decadent style of literature. Viewing each, therefore, as a tributary stream of sorts, which, while charting a serpentine path to the same river, retains its own distinctive characteristics, I would like to look first at a specific instance of Conrad's indebtedness to the Gothic romance and to proceed from there to a discussion of the convictions that he held in common with both the Decadents and writers of late-nineteenth- and early-twentieth-century horror literature. Preeminent among these was the belief that, living in a world in which, as Conrad wrote, one loses "all sense of reality in a kind of nightmare effect produced by existence" (*JCL* 114), one must seek for a new style of writing capable of conveying Gautier's "subtle confidences of neurosity," "confessions of aging lust turning into depravity," and "odd hallucinations of fixed ideas passing into madness."[14] I shall conclude the study by anatomizing the narrative technique that *Heart of Darkness* shares in common with both genres. It is a technique that, in depending for its final effect primarily upon stylistic and linguistic disruption, hesitancy, and instability rather than the disclosure of conventional frights or aberrant behavior, bears the mark of the cultural moment in which it was engendered.

Patrick Brantlinger suggests that *Heart of Darkness* suffers when it is read in isolation from the conventions of Gothic romance, which it in fact appropriates and remakes into "high art."[15] One early Gothic romance to which it would appear to owe a very great debt, for example, is Poe's "The Fall of the House of Usher" (1839), itself an important precursor of the late Gothic.[16] Deliberate echoes of Poe's story, in fact, suggest that Conrad may very well have used it as a model for his own treatment of internal anxiety, degeneration, and guilt. Both stories stress the subjective nature of perception and cognition through their emphasis on the surreal and the ephemeral and through their invocation of dream-like atmospheres. The "miasmata" of Poe's story—the "pestilent and mystic vapor, dull, sluggish, faintly discernible, and leaden-hued" that clings to and surrounds everything and that furthermore contributes to Usher's belief in the "sentience of all vegetable things"—may be compared to Marlow's numerous descriptions of the fierce sun that makes the "land . . . glisten and drip with steam" (16), of "silvery sandbanks" (35), of "white fog . . . more blinding than the night (41).[17] Outlines lose their integrity and borders are dissolved in such an atmosphere, and thus both narrators very often find they cannot see to see. To Poe's narrator it seems that trees, wall, tarn, the house and its occupants are all interrelated, just as Marlow, some months and many thousand miles after encountering the director of the company (who conveys "an impression of pale plumpness in a frock-coat" [14]), nearly stumbles over the "great" man's unnumbered victims, "black shapes . . . clinging to the earth, half coming out, half effaced within the dim light" (20). The concluding climactic scenes of both works, too, take place in similarly darkened, shadowy chambers entirely suited to the wraiths and phantasmagoric beings who haunt them. When, after many years' absence, Poe's narrator first enters his friend's house, he notes that "the eye . . . struggled in vain to reach the remoter angles of the chamber, or the recesses of the vaulted and fretted ceiling," in spite of the fact that the "very large and lofty" room in which he finds himself is outfitted with "windows . . . long, narrow, and pointed," though "at so vast a distance from the black oaken floor as to be altogether inaccessible from within" (401). Marlow feels similarly dwarfed—or, more accurately, entombed—in the "lofty drawing-room" of the house of the Intended, which is ill-illuminated by the "three long windows from floor to ceiling that were like three luminous and bedraped columns" (72). Aside from a piano that (in the alembic of Marlow's morbid imagination) assumes the shape of a "sombre and polished sarcophagus" (and in this way establishes the house of the Intended as one of the story's many sepulchral echoes of Brussels itself), the enclosed furnishings are distinguishable merely as "indistinct curves" (72). Just as Poe's narrator attributes to an "excited and highly distempered ideality" the "sulphurous lustre" (2:405) with which the House of Usher is imbued, so Marlow's impression of his final destination is washed in the evanescence of the illness that has come to him at his journey's end and that (to his fevered mind) has expressed itself "in an impalpable greyness, with nothing underfoot, with nothing around, . . . in a sickly atmosphere of tepid scepticism" (69), recalled as "a vision of greyness without form filled with physical pain" (69).

Feeling similarly imprisoned in the narrator's own dream of a world, seeing only what he sees and knowing only what he perceives or imagines, the reader begins to doubt, at times, the integrity of a story in which various characters (and effects) are as undifferentiated as the environs in which they materialize. Just as Madeline is the feminine embodiment of her brother, in whom the features of the ancestral house are reincarnated, so doubles abound in Conrad's story. Thus, Fresleven, through whose ribs the grass has grown "tall enough to hide his bones" (13), correlates with Brussels itself, in the streets of which Marlow finds "grass sprouting between the stones" (13). Marlow's allusion to the brick maker as a "papier-mâché Mephistopheles" whom one could "poke [a] forefin-

ger through" and find little else but "loose dirt" (29) immediately follows his description of the general manager—one of the gang of entrail-less men best adapted
to cultural displacement and barbarous intentions—as one in whom "there was
nothing" (25). Critics have pointed as well to the relationship that exists between
the Intended, her arms stretched out "as if after a retreating figure," and the
African woman; or between the Intended and the sepulchral city, whose external fairness harbors internal corruption.[18]

Most striking among the doublings, or pairings, however, are those that
exist between the engimatic Kurtz and nearly all of the other characters, and
more especially between Kurtz and the narrator himself. In both works the focus of each narrator's attention is a Decadent, the overbred product of an overly
refined civilization. As if surfeited on sensory stimuli, Roderick Usher suffers
from "a morbid acuteness of the senses" (2:403); a hyperconscious aesthete, he
improvises dirges, paints pictures whose subjects are "pure abstractions" (2:405),
and creates verses imbued with mystic currents of meaning. Like Usher, Kurtz
is a Decadent who, in spite of his "weirdly voracious aspect," bears an expression of "composed languor," looking to Marlow as though he were "satiated and
calm," a "shadow" that "for the moment had had its fill of all the emotions" (59).
An accomplished musician, painter, and orator whose compositions focus on
abstractions and idealities, Kurtz has a good deal in common with a type known
as the "highly-gifted degenerate," the salient features of whose character were
so carefully delineated in Nordau's *Degeneration*, a work Conrad very probably
mined as he constructed the psychological profiles of a number of his characters.[19] Yet despite the fact that both are described in considerable detail, Usher
and Kurtz are finally elusive and impalpable—and these dark luminaries impart
these qualities, too, to those who attach themselves to them. Of the Harlequin,
for example—Kurtz's attendant and disciple—Marlow wonders whether he had
"ever really seen him—whether it was possible to meet such a phenomenon!"—a
speculation that comes to him in "the darkness of an impenetrable night" (62-
63). Though careful to point out that he lacked the sort of destructive heroism
that allowed his friend to search the *abîme*, Marlow seems at times to play a
greater role in his own story than that traditionally assigned him by those critics
who, as Stewart suggests, dismiss him as merely "an eavesdropper on tragedy,
our mediator between visionary depths and the everyday."[20] Just as it is Poe's
narrator who is twice designated the "Madman," though Usher himself never is,
so it is Marlow who is first described as "no more . . . than a voice" (30), whereas
Kurtz begins as "just a word" for Marlow (29) and only much later ascends to
the rank of "voice." Just as another unnamed narrator's intimate knowledge of
her subject's thoughts and needs is otherwise inexplicable unless she is understood to *be* the woman trapped behind the yellow wallpaper of Gilman's 1892
horror story, so Marlow's intimate knowledge of Kurtz's struggles, of the "shadowy images" that haunted Kurtz's weary brain (67), of Kurtz's "extremity"—his
own extremity he dismisses as something amorphous and intangible—implies

that the "nightmare" that Marlow is forced "to dream . . . out to the end" (69) may be his own. The impression conveyed by these curious details is that each of the highly impressionable narrators functions both as the subject and as the object of his own narrative.[21] In short, the repeated (almost obsessive) references to the "nightmare" effects, the "dream-like" state in which actions are not so much undertaken as enacted, and the phantasmagoric quality of the experience tempt the reader to interpret the novel as a number of critics have interpreted Poe's tale: to wit, as the purgative brainchild of a tormented dreamer in which each of the attendant characters acts as a fragment, a projection of one discrete, albeit shattered, consciousness.[22] As Stewart suggests, the "psychic scheme" of *Heart of Darkness* encourages the reader to view "all things external" as radiating from "Marlow as percipient center."[23]

Apocalyptic in their proportions, the endings of both stories are weighted with and shaped by the accumulated horrors, as yet unpurged, of each narrator's inescapable nightmare vision. At the conclusion of *Heart of Darkness*, Marlow returns to the sepulchral city to deliver to the Intended a packet of letters belonging to Kurtz, now dead. All who knew him or knew of him agree that Kurtz was a remarkable man. Those who knew him only by his reputation, and those who were acquainted with him before he departed to make his fortune in Africa, conceived of him as a type of the Nietzschean übermensch: a "'prodigy,'" an "'emissary of pity, and science, and progress, and devil knows what else,'" a "'universal genius'" (28, 30). Those who encountered him in Africa, however, found him to be remarkable first for his ability to procure vast quantities of ivory, and second for the depths of degradation that he had plumbed. To Marlow he seems at first to be "just simply a fine fellow who stuck to his work for its own sake" (34); only later does he become "a gifted creature" possessed of the "gift of expression" (48). Eventually, Marlow finds himself standing before the "high and ponderous doors" of the imposing home of the Intended, and there he is haunted by a vision in which Kurtz appears to him as a "shadow insatiable . . . of frightful realities; a shadow darker than the shadow of night" (72). Accompanied, so he imagines, by the phantom vision that has entered into the house where the Intended has been placed, as it were, "living in the tomb," having promised to preserve Kurtz's illusory "reputation," and finding himself unwilling to desecrate the Intended's cherished memory of Kurtz's supposedly altruistic efforts in Africa, Marlow confirms her hope that her lover's final act was to speak her name. After doing so he expects "that the house would collapse before [he] could escape, that the heavens would fall upon [his] head" (76), not because he has lied but because the implacable vision of Kurtz, with "his abject pleading, his abject threats, the colossal scale of his vile desires, the meanness, the torment, the tempestuous anguish of his soul" (72), hovers about him as he speaks to the Intended. Marlow's vision at length resolves itself into an echo of the words that Kurtz did in fact whisper before his death—words that even then Marlow hears ringing throughout the room, throughout the house, throughout the city; words that nearly drive him to cry at the Intended "'Don't you hear them?'": "The dusk was repeating them in a persistent whisper all around us, in a whisper that seemed to swell menacingly like the first whisper of a rising wind. 'The horror! the horror!'" (75).

Marlow's lie, however, is not sufficiently horrendous to topple the Intended's house. He knows that the "heavens do not fall for such a trifle," though he wonders, ironically, whether they might not, in fact, have done so after all had he found it in himself to reveal that at the last Kurtz had been consumed not with longing for his Intended, but with his own sense of what (as Marlow himself imagines it) the Romans must have felt when they found themselves immured in England's impenetrable darkness: "the growing regrets, the longing to escape, the powerless disgust, the surrender, the hate" (10). Had he "rendered Kurtz that justice which was his due" (76) by disclosing that this remarkable man had succumbed extravagantly to the "fascination of the abomination" (10), he might have anticipated that the rising wind born of that threatening whisper would have purged the "whited sepulchre" that Brussels seemed to him to be. In writing the passage, Conrad was perhaps recalling the wrathful storm that consumes another repository of rottenness and corruption. Moments before the tenuously fitted walls of the ancestral House of Usher rush asunder amid the "fierce whirlwind" that had begun as "the breath of a rising tempest" (2:411), a "harsh, protracted, and most unusual screaming or grating sound" (2:414) echoed throughout the edifice, provoking Roderick Usher to make a damning and horrified confession: "'Not hear it?—yes, I hear it, and *have* heard it. Long—long—long—many minutes, many hours, many days, have I heard it—yet I dared not—oh, pity me, miserable wretch that I am!—I dared not—I *dared* not speak! *We have put her living in the tomb!*'" (2:416).

With its almost biblical hint of an impending doom that is also the intimation of a purging of internal disease, the final scene of *Heart of Darkness* echoes the apocalyptic ending of Poe's story but does not duplicate it. Had Conrad loaded his stage with the shocking evidence of accumulated sins and evils rather than invoking the dark and apocalyptic tone characteristic of other horror stories also indebted to Poe's tales—Machen's "The Great God Pan," for example, or Shiel's "Vaila" (1896), or Buchan's "The Grove of Ashtaroth"—he would very probably have elicited merely a conditioned response from an audience that had by the latter decades of the century become accustomed to the internal rhythms and dynamic (the "formula") of the Gothic romance. *Heart of Darkness* is not, of course, entirely bereft of certain well-chosen "Gothic" effects likely to challenge the assumptions of a late Victorian audience that would have encountered it for the first time in 1899 in the thousandth issue of the eminently respectable *Blackwood's Magazine*.[24] One confronts, for example, a disheveled white man "in an unbuttoned uniform . . . very hospitable and festive—not to say drunk" who is supervising the "upkeep" of a road in the middle of which lies a "middle-aged negro, with a bullet-hole in the forehead" (23); hears "on some quiet night the tremor of far-off drums, sinking, swelling, a tremor vast, faint; a sound weird, appealing, suggestive, and wild—and perhaps with as profound a meaning as the sound of bells in a Christian country" (23); observes Kurtz, the best that Western civilization could breed, participating in "certain dances ending with unspeakable rites" (50), "getting himself adored" (56), "crawling on all-fours" toward a midnight gathering of his adorers who are bedecked in "horns—antelope horns" (64); meets Kurtz's African mistress at whom the wilderness, "the colossal body of the fecund and mysterious life," looked "as though it had been looking at the image of its own tenebrous and passionate soul" (60). Each of these images stands as a warning against the allure of a particular devil—Marlow identifies both the "strong, lusty, red-eyed devils" of "violence, . . . greed, and . . . hot desire," and also "a flabby, pretending, weak-eyed devil of a rapacious and pitiless folly" (20)—to which the white man must inevitably succumb once he ventures beyond his cultural context, in which his conduct is monitored by the mere fact that he lives in "holy terror of scandal and gallows and lunatic asylums" (49).

Such images, however, function as little more than deliberate distractions, for despite the degree to which they may shock an audience that values stability, order, restraint, and efficiency, they ultimately have little to do with the creation of that which is genuinely disturbing in his story. We can, after all, visualize such potentially destructive scenes and, having once fixed them, begin the process of defusing them by subjecting them to the various processes—rationalization, explanation, categorization—by which we neutralize and regain some control over threatening material.[25] The horror engendered by the text transcends that which a mere catalog of government-sponsored cruelties or individual acts of degradation and barbarism could convey, just as the craftsmanship it displays surpasses that required merely to outrage bourgeois sensibilities.[26] Traditional literary phantoms fail to elicit the sort of intense existential anxiety that one experiences when, as Conrad wrote, one discovers that "it is impossible to know anything" (*JCL* 45)—neither "what forgiveness is, nor what is love, nor where God is" (*JCL* 65). In common with other writers of the fin de siècle, Conrad resorts to textual disruption, hesitancy, and instability as literary devices that embody, rather than merely emphasize, themes of madness, alienation, and decay and that permit the portrayal of what Lovecraft, many years later, described as "the actual anatomy of the terrible or the physiology of fear."[27] The reader is netted by the same frustration and fear with which the narrator, thwarted in his attempts either to establish narrative stability or to salvage any meaning from his fleeting (and possibly deceiving) impressions, (apparently unconsciously) invests his narrative. Afflicted by an anxiety bred of the nearly Herculean effort required to determine what, if anything, is "real" and credible within the narrative, the reader struggles to find meaning, to complete ellipses, to understand the dynamic that prevails within a cluster of unrelated and even seemingly irrelevant images, and, finally, to complete a story that, because its meaning is only par-

tially disclosed, is, like the Harlequin, "improbable, inexplicable, and altogether
bewildering. . . . an insoluble problem" (54). Whatever there is of the mysterious,
the marvelous, or the horrific in Conrad's central and most complex work of the
1890s derives in part from the narrator's subjective portrayal of himself and his
experience and in part from the reader's own individual response to that portrait; it is not imposed from without, through the author's "mechanical" introduction of consciously supernatural or occult effects. In short, the very sentences of
the story are imbued with and embody the author's fear that "Life knows us not
and we do not know life—we don't know even our own thoughts" (*JCL* 65). When
life holds no meaning, language as we understand it must inevitably fail to convey fixed and substantive meanings, for, as Conrad confessed to Cunninghame
Graham, "Half the words we use have no meaning whatever and of the other
half each man understands each word after the fashion of his own folly and
conceit": "thoughts vanish; words, once pronounced, die" (*JCL* 65).

Such a fear would seem at first to be at odds with what Conrad described
elsewhere as the "creative art of a writer," a type of "rescue work" by which the
artist snatched "vanishing phases of turbulence . . . out of the native obscurity
into a light where the struggling forms may be seen, seized upon, endowed with
the only possible form of permanence in this world of relative values—the permanence of memory" (*NLL* 13).[28] His reasons being "not moral but artistic," he
maintained that the artist's world, which he creates for himself and makes "in
his own image," is "fated to remain individual and a little mysterious" (*CP* 90;
NLL 6). The peculiar nature of Conrad's comments establishes his close affinities with the Decadents who were also determined to create worlds in their own
image: worlds that, in privileging artifice over nature, would not be fated, in
Conrad's words, to "end in cold, darkness and silence" (*JCL* 65).[29] Underlying
this apparently heroic perspective, however, was a fear common to Conrad and
the Decadents: namely, that the artist, having turned within himself to find the
terms of his appeal and the character of his self-expression, would discover that
he was empty, that he contained a moral, intellectual, and emotional void. The
Decadent artist who undertakes what John R. Reed describes in *Decadent Style*
as the "Nietzschean . . . effort at self-creation" recognizes "a nothingness at the
center of existence and dreads the emptiness within himself." Ultimately, his art,
says Reed, although it may initially search the natural world for the sources of
its design, "does not lead back to the organic world but to the nothingness that
man has discovered within himself and hence in nature."[30] We find Conrad too
suffering from what he described in a letter to Edmund Gosse as "a sense of
unreality, from intellectual doubt of the ground" he stood upon, anxieties to which
he was particularly prone during "periods of difficult production" (*JCLL* 2:14).
This sense of unreality is recognizable as a manifestation of what Baudelaire
called "*les stérilités des écrivains nerveux*" (*JCLL* 2:14). In a letter to Edward
Lancelot Sanderson, Conrad considered the implications of his artistic struggles
that, as he feared, pointed to some internal emptiness: "It is strange. The unreal-

ity of [writing fiction] seems to enter one's real life, penetrate into the bones, make the very heartbeats pulsate illusions through the arteries. One's will becomes the slave of hallucinations, responds only to shadowy impulses, waits on imagination alone. A strange state, a trying experience, a kind of fiery trial of untruthfulness. And one goes through it with an exaltation as false as all the rest of it. One goes through it,—and there's nothing to show at the end. Nothing! Nothing! Nothing!" (*JCLL* 1:283).

Conrad's fear is that he might be unequal to the task of performing his "rescue work," and he confronts the grim possibility that there is nothing either outside or (even worse) within himself that can be fashioned into an artifact capable of resisting the onslaughts of time—but more hateful still is the suspicion that "the menace and danger or weakness are in me, in myself alone." Of this possibility, he writes, "I fear! I fear!" (*JCLL* 1:282). It follows that the "danger," "menace," or "weakness" that is inherent in man will necessarily be found in his various progeny: in his culture, in his artificial creations, and particularly in his literature, his secularized scripture. An organism in its own right—capable of being "diagnosed" and susceptible to influences inimical to essential textual stability and integrity—it is inscribed with the anxiety of its creator. Such is the case with *Heart of Darkness*, in which, as Vincent Pecora points out, "Conrad makes of his central character a *text*" that is inscribed with "the 'metaphysical need' of his time."[31] Marlow's anxiety of creation (and, by extension, Conrad's) as well as his covert fear that "[his] speech or [his] silence, indeed any action of [his], would be a mere futility" (40) is symptomatic of the loss of the High Victorian faith in semantic and linguistic stability and in the belief, tidily expressed by the nineteenth-century philologist and essayist George Washington Moon, that "the English language is destined to be that in which shall arise, as in one universal temple, the utterance of the worship of all hearts."[32] Charles Eric Reeves points out that Conrad's early fiction dramatizes "precisely a loss of such faith": "Whatever bleakness of outlook we might see in Dickens or Hardy, whatever the difficulties or obscurities of moral exploration in George Eliot and the earlier James, there is nowhere a fundamental loss of faith in language, in its symmetry with a world that it can at least partially illuminate or explicate." The horror of *Heart of Darkness* consists not in Conrad's oblique references to unnameable rites nor in the thinly veiled suggestions of midnight orgies, human sacrifices, and cannibalism, but rather in our confrontation with a text that, in its linguistic, stylistic, and thematic corruption, levels an assault on the reader possessed of what Reeves designates as a "European moral and linguistic complacency."[33]

The origins of this corruption are complex. As Linda Dowling points out in her *Language and Decadence in the Victorian Fin de Siècle* (1986), Coleridge's insistence on an "identification of national spirit and written language" insured that later generations—and the late romantics in particular—would find evidence of their "cultural decline" manifested in "linguistic demoralization." She explains that the "same displacement of cultural ideals and cultural anxiety onto language explains why we also glimpse in the background of Victorian Decadence no lurid tales of sin and sensation and forbidden experience but a range of stylistic effects, of quiet disruptions and insistent subversions."[34] *Heart of Darkness* is a similarly Decadent text, which, because it masquerades as a story of sin and forbidden experience, distracts its reader's attention from the real source of his discomfort, which lies in the "quiet disruptions," the "insistent subversions," the deliberate exclusions, and the subtle cadences of the prose—in short, in the *physiognomy* of the text, whose story is (like that of the jungle through which Marlow struggles) "not so much told as suggested . . . in desolate exclamations, completed by shrugs, in interrupted phrases, in hints ending in deep sighs" (56). These stylistic effects are evidence of a failed endeavor to fix and convey meaning—and, by extension, to define or describe "the horror," but they nevertheless succeed in creating horror. For although Marlow's thwarted attempts to express "the inner truth" (which "is hidden—luckily, luckily" [36]) obscure rather than disclose meaning, a good deal is discernible, as Edward Said reminds us, in "the sheer telling of the tale, for what the tale usually reveals is the exact contours of this obscurity."[35] In this sense Marlow's medium *becomes* rather than reveals his message.

Heart of Darkness explores not merely the subjective (and elusive) nature of cognition and (through cognition) experience, but also, from the opening pages of the first section, the relationship between language and meaning, form and content, phrases and ideas—thereby playing out, as critics have come increasingly to understand, "a *drama* of narratability."[36] In particular, however, *Heart of Darkness* stresses the paradoxically corrupted, and corrupting, nature of highly refined, carefully wrought language. Conrad juxtaposes the various forms of communication—both verbal and nonverbal—of the indigens with the more grammatically complex (although not necessarily more sophisticated) exchanges that take place between the white men. Just as they are about to weigh anchor and cover the last mile leading to Kurtz's remote jungle outpost, for example, the crew and passengers aboard Marlow's steamboat are greeted with "a cry, a very loud cry, as of infinite desolation" that is followed by a "tumultuous and mournful uproar" (41). It is all the more disquieting because it seems to issue from the mist (premonitory of darkness). Marlow believes that he can read the cry, receiving "an irresistible impression of sorrow" and "unrestrained grief" (44). Convinced that his interpretation of the cry is correct, he ventures to guess that the hidden natives who are greeting them in this fashion will not attack.

When, moments later, they are ambushed, the native helmsman of Marlow's steamboat takes a spear just below the ribs. With his hands clutching the shaft, the man looks at Marlow "anxiously, . . . with an air of being afraid [Marlow] would try to take it away from him" (47). As he lies dying, he settles upon Marlow an "inquiring glance," as though to put to him "some question in an understandable language." At the very last moment, as though in response to an unseen sign or an unheard whisper, "he frowned heavily, and that frown gave to his black death-mask an inconceivably sombre, brooding, and menacing expression" (47). Having repulsed the attack, won through to the jungle trading post, installed in one of the boat's cabins the emaciated Kurtz (who had, in fact, ordered the ambush of his "rescuers"), and prepared to depart, Marlow's crew is approached by "a wild and gorgeous apparition of a woman" (60). No apparition, the woman, with her "tragic and fierce aspect of wild sorrow and of dumb pain," comes abreast of the steamer and, opening her bare arms, throws them "up rigid above her head, as though in an uncontrollable desire to touch the sky" (60). A short time later, as they pull away from the shore, the woman begins to shout something that Kurtz's "followers" take up. When asked if he understands the meaning of this "articulated, rapid, breathless utterance," which is utterly incomprehensible to anyone else on board the ship, Kurtz answers simply, "'Do I not?'" (66). The very meanings that Kurtz cannot avoid in the messages of the natives are not easily or readily apparent to Marlow, as his insistent comparatives and similes indicate. In nearly all of these instances (and there are others), the gesture, the look, or the cry is followed by an "appalling and excessive silence" (41)—the empty silence in which Marlow has an opportunity either to discover or to impose a meaning that frequently eludes him.

He reaches only partial truths in his attempt to decipher the cryptic messages of the natives, but he is utterly misled and deceived in his exchanges with the white men, whose habitual (often intentional) misuse of language is particularly marked when it occurs outside its cultural context—in a foreign land where their imperialistic aims are most "pronounced" and therefore most in need of the protection that only European, nonnative language, with its innate capacity for innuendo and insinuation, can provide. There are the "criminals," chained black men whose every rib is visible and the joints of whose limbs are "like knots in a rope" (19). These are superseded by "enemies" (19), "black shapes . . . clinging to the earth, half coming out, half effaced within the dim light" (20) (themselves premonitory of the "rebels," whose "rebellious heads looked very subdued . . . on their sticks" [58]). Although these shadows and dismembered beings might once have been "workers," "criminals," "rebels," or "enemies," in the grove of death or "drying on the stakes under Mr. Kurtz's windows" (58) they are no longer any of these things, but merely "nothing earthly now"; destroyed by the alien language "that had come to them . . . from the sea," they have moved beyond the pale of its influence. If the English language is, like the "outraged law" that it embodies, an "insoluble mystery" (19) to the natives, presumably it would be more accessible to the white men whose means of communication it is, but this is not the case. Between the white men, little of what is said is intended to convey entirely accurate information—if it is in fact intended to convey any meaning at all. Thus, the brickmaker of the Central Station (who does not, and never will, make any bricks) assures Marlow that he does not "want to be misunderstood, and especially by [Marlow,] who will see Mr. Kurtz long before [he] can have that pleasure" (29), when in fact he wants specifically to be misunderstood, particularly by Marlow, who will soon see Kurtz, whom the brickmaker hates bitterly.

It is not surprising, then, to find that Marlow eventually invests his impending meeting with Kurtz with a special, if not a saving, significance. In the midst of the greed, the duplicity, and the hypocrisy, he has heard Kurtz described, even by his detractors, as being one of the "gang of virtue," someone who wants "for the guidance of the cause intrusted to us by Europe, so to speak, higher intelligence, wide sympathies, a singleness of purpose" (28). All of Europe having "contributed to the making" (50) of this cultured and well-educated man, Kurtz would appear to be the person to clarify the nature of Marlow's experience, able fully to expose meanings that have been revealed to Marlow only in a partial and erratic fashion. So far from being the person to enlighten him, however, Kurtz is the most dangerous person of all those whom Marlow will encounter—not, paradoxically, because, in organizing the natives to serve as his personal army, he had amassed tremendous power, but rather because, as the most "civilized" man in the territory, he is also the most corrupt, and because his language, which is an extension of his inner self and of which he is a superbly capable manipulator, is similarly debased.[37] Marlow recognizes, for example, that the manager of the Central Station is a confidence man and that the brick maker is opportunistic and hypocritical: although he cannot always gather the full import of their words, he knows better than to trust their assurances. More fully in control of his language, Kurtz hides "the barren darkness of his heart" in the "magnificent folds of eloquence" (67) and is therefore more threatening than are the other men, whose greed and ambition are poorly disguised. Kurtz's report to the International Society for the Suppression of Savage Customs, with its "unbounded power of eloquence . . . of burning noble words" (50), fits the description of the Decadent style given by Gautier, who argued that this "ingenious, complex, learned style, full of shades and refinements of meaning," embodies "the subtle confidences of neurosity, . . . the confessions of aging lust turning into depravity, and . . . the odd hallucinations of fixed ideas passing into madness."[38] Treated in this fashion, language becomes what Wilde described as "the parent, and not the child, of thought."[39] Mesmerized by the "magic" of form, by the cadences and textures of language, Kurtz's audience is lulled into an apathy that it cannot shake, even after it sees that such stylistic beauty may mask vile, "savage," and "uncivilized" ideas.[40] Only the report's hastily appended postscriptum—"a kind of note at the foot of the last page, scrawled evidently much later in an unsteady hand . . . 'Exterminate all the brutes!'" (51)—signals its collapse into utter abjection. As Stewart points out, "Rhetorical sonority in a moral vacuum boils down to a curt, criminal injunction."[41]

Marlow's narrative is shaped, as Kurtz's creations are, by his experience and his worldview, and its various substructures reflect nothing more profoundly than the violence with which Marlow is stripped of his saving illusions concerning Kurtz's "gift of expression." Describing the ambush to his small audience seated aboard the *Nellie,* Marlow is distracted for a moment by the memory of the lonely desolation and the attendant sense of sudden dislocation that he felt when he realized that Kurtz had probably been killed in the attack and that he [Marlow] had lost the opportunity to meet someone who was not so much a man as "a voice." The point, as he assures his listeners, lay not in Kurtz's having "swindled, or stolen more ivory than all the other agents together," but in his "being a gifted creature": "of all his gifts the one that stood out pre-eminently, that carried with it a sense of real presence, was his ability to talk, his words— the gift of expression, the bewildering, the illuminating, the most exalted and the most contemptible, the pulsating stream of light or the deceitful flow from the heart of an impenetrable darkness" (48). As so many of the individual sentences or discrete images in *Heart of Darkness* do, this single sentence echoes, in petto, Marlow's exchange of ignorance for knowledge, for the sentence itself moves from positive values—words seen as being illuminating and exalted—to negative ones; and from the false comparison of Kurtz's gift of expression to a "pulsating stream of light" to a more darkly realistic one. The thought itself flows, or is absorbed, into an impenetrable darkness—both the metaphorical one, which sits waiting at the end of the sentence, and the literal one, which envelops Marlow as he tells his story.

It is interesting to note that the development of the sentence is duplicated within the larger scheme of the passage. Shortly after he makes this observation, Marlow is interrupted by one of his listeners, who sighs, apparently offended by his melodramatic admission that losing the opportunity to hear Kurtz speak would have been like being "robbed of a belief" or missing his "destiny in life" (48). He answers the charge that such a reaction is "Absurd" by assuring his critic that he showed commendable fortitude given the fact that he had been "cut to the quick at the idea of having lost the inestimable privilege of listening to the gifted Kurtz" (48). No sooner does he praise Kurtz in these terms than he admits that he was wrong in his assumption, that the "privilege" of hearing Kurtz speak was waiting for him: "Oh yes, I heard more than enough. And I was right, too. A voice. He was very little more than a voice. And I heard—him—it—this voice—other voices—all of them were so little more than voices—and the memory of that time itself lingers around me, impalpable, like a dying vibration of one immense jabber, silly, atrocious, sordid, savage, or simply mean without any kind of sense. Voices, voices—" (48-49). Violently, vengefully, he deflates the idea of a voice and merges that of Kurtz—once unique and inviolable—with those of the others, whose talk was silly, sordid, or senseless. He approximates the barrenness of their speech through a language that is itself degenerate, devoid of "any kind of sense": "I heard—him—it—this voice—other voices." His allusion to the "dying vibration of one immense jabber" foreshadows, and serves as the cultural counterpart to, the "roaring chorus of articulated, rapid, breathless utterance" with which the natives curse the "fierce river-demon" that is robbing them of their god. Although the chorus seems to Marlow to consist of "the responses of some satanic litany," it is in fact the "jabber" of his colleagues, the most pre-eminent among them being Kurtz, that is the more diabolical. Like the "voice of the surf," which Marlow views as "something natural," possessed of "its reason, ... a meaning" (17), the former, although (and perhaps *because*) it resembles "no sounds of human language," is nonetheless organic, coordinated, and unadulter-ated, whereas the latter is too fully a product of its Western civilization: discor-dant, cacophonous, morally bankrupt, it anticipates the fragmented and sordid lamentations of those "hooded hordes swarming / Over endless plains, stum-bling in cracked earth / Ringed by the flat horizon only"—the urban equivalent of the jungle, the heart of darkness—of "The Waste Land."[42]

Pecora suggests that, like "the events of the story, the words spoken by Marlow and Kurtz at the time are inevitably changed, are socially and morally transformed by Marlow's re-presentation of them to the community on board," and are thus rendered "morally significant—or insignificant—in ways that con-tradict their original content."[43] I would argue, however, that Marlow's narrative does in fact mirror his experience fairly closely in part because, although it is an experienced Marlow who speaks, nevertheless he fails to fully comprehend the nature of what has happened to him. In the preface to *An Outcast of the Islands* (1896), a novel written three years before *Heart of Darkness,* Conrad, suggest-ing that the "discovery of new values in life is a very chaotic experience," in-forms the reader that when he finds himself in such a situation, he lets his "spirit float supine over that chaos" (*CP* 41) (just as the Harlequin remains "thought-lessly alive" in the midst of chaos and imminent doom). Marlow has also discov-ered new values in life that have deeply impressed him. These values derive not from his having witnessed the savage behavior of the company agents, but from his realization that his assumptions concerning the acquisition and transmis-sion of meaning through language and ideas are false. (According to Pecora, an instance of this "hermeneutical dilemma" occurs when Marlow overhears Kurtz's "last words" and "is faced (as are we) with words that could mean any number of things, but are *supposed to mean* something fairly important and, in the end, justifying, reassuring, *edifying*"—in precisely the ways, we might add, in which Hannah Choate's father, or Gannie Michenor's mother, or Little Nell's and the prophetess Ailie's "audiences," fictive and real, expected to be reassured and edified.[44]) Casting himself in the role of the traditional hero of myth, he empha-sizes the mythic quality of his own adventure when he portrays himself as being in pursuit of some elusive "It" (which may be Kurtz, or the Inner Station, or the penetration of one of the blank spaces on the map of the world, or his confronta-tion with the subconscious, submerged other) that represents, as he says, "the farthest point of navigation and the culminating point of my experience" (11). Whereas traditional heroes such as Aeneas or Ulysses gain power both by pre-vailing over external forces and by reaching certain definite conclusions about the nature of their experiences and themselves, however, Marlow struggles even after the fact to attach some meaning to Kurtz's haunting refrain, "The horror! the horror!" The meaning for which he gropes will, he suspects, give meaning to his own enigmatic experiences. Sitting cross-legged before his audience, with his "sunken cheeks, a yellow complexion, a straight back, an ascetic aspect, and, with his arms dropped, the palms of hands outwards" (7), Marlow becomes a desiccated Buddha, an idol combining the image of the Western knight-errant with that of the Eastern epitome of enlightenment. He has acquired neither the divine insight nor the faith reserved for successful questers, however, in part because he has lost faith in the power of words, having become convinced that language must fail in its appointed task of conveying meaning. He voices his doubt continually throughout the course of his narrative: "I've been telling you what we said—repeating the phrases we pronounced—but what's the good? They were common everyday words—the familiar vague sounds exchanged on every waking day of life. But what of that? They had behind them, to my mind, the terrific suggestiveness of words heard in dreams, of phrases spoken in nightmares" (65). His acquired language, the form of which is at odds with its meaning, fails him in his attempt to articulate these alien experiences and therefore leaves him with no means of transforming them (and in this he speaks, perhaps, for Conrad, who, Said speculates, "discovered . . . that the chasm between words saying and words meaning was *widened*, not lessened, by his talent for words written [116]). Like Coleridge wakened from his visionary trance by the man from Porlock, or more significantly, Wells's Time Traveller, who, addressing a group of nameless associates—like Marlow's friends, identified by profession only—gathered round him to hear his tale, questions the very existence of the Time Machine and wonders whether his adventures have been "all only a dream . . . a precious poor dream at times—," Marlow is forced repeatedly to acknowledge his defeat: "Do you see him? Do you see the story? Do you see anything? It seems to me I am trying to tell you a dream—" (30).[45] He abandons the attempt to consciously order his ideas and instead allows his memory and imagination as well as his doubts and insecurities to determine not only the form that his story will take but also which organizing metaphors will surface within the narrative. In short, the best he can do is to efface himself and allow his own "spirit to float supine" over the memory of the chaos that dominated his African experience. Devoid of a carefully constructed "plot" indicative of reasoned, ordered thought, his story thus records in a particularly powerful fashion the nature and degree of Marlow's intellectual, perceptual, and emotional struggles.

The feature of Conrad's artistry that has drawn the most critical attention is, of course, what Wells first described (in relation to *An Outcast of the Islands*) as the "river-mist" that is his "style" ("a great grey bank of printed matter, page on page, creeping round the reader, swallowing him up"), and what F.R. Leavis later denounced as the "adjectival insistence upon inexpressible and incomprehensible mystery," "the monstrous hothouse efflorescences" of *Heart of Darkness*—evidence, he claimed, of "something simply and obviously deplorable—

something that presents itself . . . as, bluntly, a disconcerting weakness or vice."
The problem, for Leavis, lay in Conrad's insistent desire "to impose on his readers and on himself, for thrilled response, a 'significance' that is merely an emotional insistence on the presence of what he can't produce."[46] Seeing in Conrad a
writer whose "practical and even theoretical competence" was, according to Said,
"far in advance of *what* he was saying," recent critics tend to resist suggesting, as
Marvin Mudrick once had, that Conrad's dependence on the "oracular-rumina-
tive" proves merely that his "great and somber theme" was "beyond his own
very considerable powers" to convey.[47] Yet, they often make essentially the same
claim (however inadvertently) when they speak of the reader's struggle to fix
"meaning and intelligibility in a language dense and problematically referential."[48]
In a letter to Edward Garnett in which he described his abortive attempts to
capture the "evading shape" of *The Rescue*, then a work in progress that he
could not "get hold of" although it was "all there—to bursting," Conrad expressed
his familiar fear that he had "lost all *sense* of style" even as he was "haunted,
mercilessly haunted, by the *necessity* of style" (*JCLL* 1:232). However, he does
not appear to have been so utterly victimized by the effort required to compose
his *Heart of Darkness* (which he abandoned *The Rescue* in order to write); he
told Richard Curle that "its 40,000 words occupied only about a month in writing" (*LE* 234). Furthermore, he insisted upon what he described to Symons as
his "inalienable right to the use of all [his] epithets" (*JCLL* 1:73). Many years and
several works later, he continued to feel harassed and victimized, for he complained to Curle that a "strange fate" had dictated that everything he had, "of set
artistic purpose, laboured to leave indefinite, suggestive, in the penumbra of initial inspiration, should have that light turned on to it and its insignificance (as
compared with, I might say without megalomania, the ampleness of my conceptions) exposed for any fool to comment upon or even for average minds to be
disappointed with."[49] In *Heart of Darkness*, it is Marlow's hesitancy and doubt
that produce ambiguity, and his incoherence is a source of meaning, as well as a
source of darkness.

Conrad's adjectival insistence is in fact one manifestation of what Dowling
identifies as a central trope in Decadent literature: "the unutterability *topos*, the
familiar convention that asserts the total inadequacy of language to express
what is meant."[50] It is not, however, the only means by which Conrad generates
ambiguity within the text and fosters a sense of dis-ease and dislocation within
his reader. As we have seen, Conrad indicated that it was through the "true"
rendering of "definite images" that he hoped to produce some "little effect" in his
story. *Heart of Darkness* (as the title alone suggests) is dominated by images
(as well as a range of treatments of those images) that—because they are im-
pressionistic in nature—emphasize Marlow's determination to avoid rationaliz-
ing his experience and ordering his ideas (or, conversely, his inability to rationalize or order either one). A dynamic exists within the works between "oracular"
adjectives and intensely visualized images. Early in the story, for example, Marlow

indulges in the first of many abstractions, alluding to the "unselfish belief" in the "idea at the back" of the conquest of the earth: the only redeeming feature of such a belief, he suggests, is that it provides one with "something [one] can set up, and bow down before, and offer a sacrifice to" (10). Although he breaks off at this point, unable, as he so often is, to complete his thought or carry it to any sort of logical conclusion, an image of flames gliding in the river—"small green flames, red flames, white flames, pursuing, overtaking, joining, crossing each other—then separating slowly or hastily" (11)—overtakes his silence, setting his thought against a backdrop of phosphorescent if not infernal gloom. Writing to Curle, Conrad characterized his art as "fluid," dependent for its overall effect upon "grouping (sequence) which shifts, and on the changing lights giving varied effects of perspective" (*JCLL* 2:317). Moods, nuances of meaning, and atmosphere also evolve out of the dynamic that exists within and between clusters of images that arise within the work; as Said reminds us, "one remembers *objects* in Conrad's fiction, not merely words."[51] In some instances, images are concentrated within a single paragraph, and their combined effect constitutes an assault upon the reader—as, for example, when Marlow describes a stretch of the river that he navigated early in his voyage: "A rocky cliff appeared, mounds of turned-up earth by the shore, houses on a hill, others with iron roofs amongst a waste of excavations hanging to the declivity. A continuous noise of the rapids above hovered over this scene of inhabited devastation. A lot of people, mostly black and naked, moved about like ants. A jetty projected into the river. A blinding sunlight drowned all this at times in a sudden recrudescence of glare" (18-19). The syntactical parallelism, the staccato rhythm of the sentences, the heaping of visual detail—a cliff, mounds, houses, the noise of the rapids, the undifferentiated bodies, a jetty, sunlight—and the vaguely synesthetic effect produced by the onslaught of sensory impressions do not so much *describe* anarchy and confusion as *reproduce* them textually.

Conrad explores the thematic and stylistic possibilities of other combinations of images as well. We have the cumulative effect of certain memorable scenes: a French steamer lands "custom-house clerks to levy toll in what looked like a God-forsaken wilderness, with a tin shed and a flag-pole lost in it" (16); amid the empty immensity of earth, sky, and water, a French man-of-war, her ensign "limp like a rag," fires tiny projectiles into a continent (17); a well-dressed, well-starched accountant exhibits gentle annoyance at the groans of a dying man, a distraction that leads to "clerical errors" (22); a foreman on Marlow's ship, required to crawl in the mud under the bottom of the steamboat, ties up his waist-length beard "in a kind of white serviette he brought for the purpose," with "loops to go over his ears" (31-32); a Russian dressed in motley (and "wonderfully neat withal," for one can see "how beautifully all this patching had been done" [53]) is ready to kiss Marlow merely for the return of his book, *An Inquiry into Some Points of Seamanship*, because the loss of a book, like the loss of one's life, is one of the many accidents that can "happen to a man going about

alone, you know" (54). Then there are Marlow's similes: the river that, penetrat-
ing one of the enticing blank spaces on a map, resembles "an immense snake
uncoiled, with its head in the sea, its body at rest curving afar over a vast country, and its tail lost in the depths of the land" (12); a beastlike boiler "wallowing in
the grass" (19); the leader of the "Eldorado Expedition," who recalls "a butcher
in a poor neighbourhood" (33). The very proliferation of such images and
comparatives—which often, as Reeves points out, "interpenetrate and blur with
one another"—induces (as mere authorial commentary could not) the hallucinatory, insane, utterly *unreal* quality of Marlow's experience.[52] The text becomes,
then, a simulacrum of the reality it seeks to describe; and the anxiety that the
reader experiences in the midst of this textual chaos is analogous to that which
Marlow experiences while in the depths of the jungle.[53]

Not merely the dynamic interaction of various images (which in turn creates a kind of resonance within and beyond the text), but also the form taken by
the story itself—which may be said to be *in-formed* by, or *in-scribed* with, its
hidden ideas and meanings—proves illuminative.[54] The peculiar ordering of
Marlow's thoughts within uncharacteristically lengthy paragraphs indicates the
sea-drift of those thoughts and establishes the indirect manner in which he arrives at various conclusions concerning his journey. Shortly after he has been
rebuked for making disparaging comments about the daily routines of his
confreres, for example, Marlow moves, in the space of one paragraph, through
a sequence of topics or descriptive details that, although broadly related, follow
the idiosyncratic and discontinuous logic of his innermost consciousness. He
alludes first to the considerable fear that he felt during the early days of his
journey when he strove to keep his steamer from scraping the river bottom; to
the cannibals with their rotten hippo meat; to the isolated stations, the empty
reaches and "Trees, trees, millions of trees" that he and his crew passed in the
course of their journey; to the roll of the native drums that shattered the silence
of their nights; to a chiaroscuro scene of whirling limbs and rolling eyes, half
glimpsed amid the droop of motionless foliage; to his final observation that he
and his crew felt "cut off from the comprehension of [their] surroundings" past
which they glided like phantoms, "wondering and secretly appalled" (37). Marlow
works his way through his material hesitantly, tentatively, with many false starts
attending the fresh departures that he makes within his story. His shifting consciousness not only underscores the disjointed manner in which he receives
information, but also bewilders the reader, who, prepared to trust to narrative
authority and textual integrity, instead finds himself lost in a wilderness of unresolved impressions and half-glimpsed truths—the flux of a sorely tried mind.

The same anxiety of creation that determines the shape both of the narrative itself and of the paragraphs that constitute that narrative also informs the
structure of individual sentences, investing them with what Symons identified
as the "physiological quality" of Conrad's prose.[55] The tentative and uneasy
manner in which Marlow reaches any determination about himself or his un-

canny venture finds expression within the grammatical subtleties and syntactical complexities of Conrad's prose. In alluding, for example, to the complicated
"network of paths" etched upon a section of the wilderness that he had traversed
by foot, Marlow (apparently unconsciously) conveys his idea by means of a sentence that winds its way through its message and, through the alliteration and
choppy rhythms of its syntax, duplicates the features that characterized those
paths and the journey itself: "Paths, paths, everywhere; a stamped-in network of
paths spreading over the empty land, through long grass, through burnt grass,
through thickets, down and up chilly ravines, up and down stony hills ablaze
with heat; and a solitude, a solitude, nobody, not a hut" (23). Somewhat later he
employs two sentences to describe the riotous vegetation of the jungle and the
silence that pervades it: the first is itself ready to collapse under the weight of its
own luxuriant verbiage, and the second is, as its subject is, fixed and motionless:
"The great wall of vegetation, an exuberant and entangled mass of trunks,
branches, leaves, boughs, festoons motionless in the moonlight, was like a rioting invasion of soundless life, a rolling wave of plants, piled up, crested, ready to
topple over the creek, to sweep every little man of us out of his little existence.
And it moved not" (32).

Meaning resides, then, in what might at first seem to be the most inconse-
quential of passages. To Conrad, however, the "apparently irrelevant is often
the illuminative"; he advised an aspiring writer never to be "afraid of remote
connections: you must let your mind range widely about your subject" (*JCLL*
2:116). It is through such "remote connections" existing between multifarious
images, between formal, stylistic, and thematic concerns, that Conrad establishes a symbiotic relationship between the text and its descriptive matter. Thus,
Marlow's allusion to the "blank space of delightful mystery—a white patch for a
boy to dream gloriously over. . . . a place of darkness" (12) applies not merely to
unexplored territory depicted on an early-nineteenth-century map but to the story
itself, which, with its innumerable blank spaces and gaps, holds the same fascination for its reader as the map does for Marlow: both invite endless speculation and musings. In another sense Marlow's narrative impresses its reader in
much the same fashion that the Central Station manager's smile does Marlow
himself. He remembers it, but cannot explain it: "It was unconscious, this smile
was, though just after he had said something it got intensified for an instant. It
came at the end of his speeches like a seal applied on the words to make the
meaning of the commonest phrase appear absolutely inscrutable" (24). Similarly, the gaps and silences within Marlow's narrative (both his innumerable
references to "silence" and his actual hesitations) serve not only to highlight
what goes before and what follows them, but also to invest even the most casual
observations with an appearance "absolutely inscrutable."

As his own youthful conscience had been "fashioned" (or so Conrad states
in *A Personal Record)* as much by the "silences and abstentions surrounding
one's childhood" as by "the words, the looks, the acts" (*PR* 94), so *Heart of*

Darkness conveys its tension as much by what it avoids—by its very gaps and silences—as by the complicated rhythms of its prose. In particular, ellipses and dashes—evidence of a man struggling with a language that he fears will fail him and with ideas that he fears will elude him—dominate Marlow's narrative, documenting his hesitations and his confused search for appropriate modes of expression. (In a sense, these idiosyncracies of punctuation are of a piece with the "adjectival insistence" so offensive to Leavis.) He searches for the terms with which to express to Kurtz the nature of his pilgrimage, which, he says, "was sombre enough too—and pitiful—not extraordinary in any way—not very clear either" (11) while of other destinations to which he has journeyed he has even less to say: "I have been in some of them, and . . . well, we won't talk about that" (11). To a certain extent, this punctual hesitation offers Conrad the means by which he can avoid the explicitness that, he assured Curle, "is fatal to the glamour of all artistic work, robbing it of all suggestiveness, destroying all illusion."[56] It also allows him to achieve what he once identified as the aim of his literary efforts: to establish "the intimacy of a personal communication" within a text that is nonetheless "perfectly devoid of familiarity as between author and reader" (*JCLL* 2:317). This textual intimacy is reminiscent of the sort of telepathic communication that Mallarmé hoped to perfect in his verse and even in his epistolary writings: in a letter to Eugène Lefébure, for example, he acknowledged that there "can be only one language between the two of us, a language of half-words exchanged amid silences, allowing each of us to see what point the other has reached."[57] In other words, the author provides a modicum of information beyond which the reader, resorting to his own imagination, must become a collaborator in the creation of the text. Thus, Conrad valued having so percipient a reader as Symons, for such a reader "puts so much of his own high quality into a work he is reading, directly the writer has been lucky enough to awaken his sympathy!" (*JCLL* 2:83).

In this sense *Heart of Darkness* provides us with an important example of what Dowling identifies as the fatal book, which, in blurring the line that demarcates fiction and fact, fantasy and reality, encourages its readers to respond to it as though they were confronted with an actual experience.[58] With its stylistic disruptions, it mounts upon its reader a cerebral assault (of the sort produced by Kurtz's mesmeric eloquence) and demands of that reader a degree of complicity in the completion of the text and in the unveiling of the story. The text will not readily yield the underlying significance of Marlow's experience in part because, although he has arrived at the "farthest point of navigation and "the culminating point" of that experience (11), he has *not* been able fully to articulate any meaningful finalities concerning his singular journey. He does not ultimately understand what Kurtz means by "the horror," although he knows that so far as he himself is concerned it represents "an affirmation, a moral victory paid for by innumerable defeats, by abominable terrors, by abominable satisfactions" (70). Invested primarily with Marlow's anxiety (which is generated in part by his conviction that when presented, as Kurtz had been, with "the last opportunity for pronouncement . . . probably [he] would have nothing to say" [69]), *Heart of Darkness* is another of those fin de siècle texts that display what Dowling identifies as the Decadent tendency to indulge in "the most extreme form of stylistic solecism—a language so perfected in its private symbolism that it will no longer yield its meaning even to the select few, but only to the unique reader," who is usually the narrator of the text itself.[59] Thus, just as the marginalia in *An Inquiry into Some Points of Seamanship* is in cipher and therefore meaningful only to the man who found something worth noting in the volume (all three—scrawl, book, and man—being inscrutable to Marlow), so many of the perceptions and impressions that Marlow draws from out of the heart of his dark journey are reserved for him alone; and so, too, much of the meaning that the reader gleans from the depths of the story is that which he brings to it himself when he encounters the story not as a narrative, but as a discrete experience.

To see that *Heart of Darkness* functions as both subject and object of its own story is to arrive at a somewhat clearer understanding of one of the central images of the story, which is introduced in an early passage wherein the anonymous narrator describes the peculiarly resonant character of Marlow's narratives. As Marlow is about to embark upon his story, the primary narrator, familiar with Marlow's narrative technique, compares the anticipated tale to those of other seamen. The traditional maritime yarn has a "direct simplicity," its whole meaning residing "within the shell of a cracked nut," but Marlow's stories reflect his own narrative tendencies to the extent that, to him, "the meaning of an episode was not inside like a kernel but outside, enveloping the tale which brought it out only as a glow brings out a haze, in the likeness of one of these misty halos that sometimes are made visible by the spectral illumination of moonshine" (9). Scholars, predictably intrigued by such an obviously significant observation, have expended a good deal of critical energy upon this particular leitmotiv. Some, for example, trace the source of the image back to both the literary and the visual impressionism to which, it would appear, Conrad had been exposed shortly before the composition of his story.[60] It is, perhaps, more illuminating to see the image both as a metaphor for and a deliberate effect of a prose style and structure that is meant to embody the ineffability of the reality that exists at the heart of experience—a reality that may be, in essence, alien, hostile, horrific. *Heart of Darkness* succeeds because it meets Conrad's stipulation, enunciated in his preface to *The Nigger of the 'Narcissus'* (1897) (perhaps the most important work that he wrote before *Heart of Darkness*), that a "work that aspires, however humbly, to the condition of art should carry its justification in every line. . . . bringing to light the truth, manifold and one, underlying its every aspect" (*CP* 49). This in itself is a fairly traditional way of looking at the function of literature. Reviewing Hawthorne's *Twice-Told Tales* (1837), for example, Poe commented that the "skilful literary artist" who has settled upon the "certain and unique single *effect*" that he wishes to produce within his story will nevertheless fail in his self-appointed task if "his very initial sentence tend not to the outbringing of this effect."[61] In his preface to *The House of the Seven Gables* (1851), Hawthorne (as we have already noted in the discussion of James's *The Turn of the Screw*) voiced a similar conviction (one perhaps familiar to Conrad, given the striking similarity between the two statements and the authors' mutual interest in the genre of romance) insisting that when "romances do really teach anything, or produce any effective operation, it is usually through a far more subtle process than the ostensible one": "A high truth," he argues, "fairly, finely, and skilfully wrought out, brightening at every step, and crowning the final developement of a work of fiction, may add an artistic glory, but is never any truer, and seldom any more evident, at the last page than at the first."[62] For all three writers, then, the "truth" with which the artist seeks to encode his creation will be no less true nor less self-evident in the concluding sentence of the work than it is in the first; viewed in these traditional terms, the "haze" that characterizes and enshrouds both Marlow's and Conrad's tales functions both as an emblem and as an ultimate effect of writing itself.

For Marlow, as for Conrad, truth and meaning, as well as the attendant sense of horror and revulsion that they contain, neither reveal themselves nor grow more persuasive as the work progresses; instead, they remain circumambient, moving outside of the boundaries of the text to incorporate the reader's realm of experience. As Marlow encounters Kurtz's inscrutable phrase "The horror! the horror!" at the farthest point of navigation—poised, as it were, at the edge of the world—so we expect to arrive at the secret meaning of the story at the culminating point of our experience within the text, as conventional works of romance or horror literature have taught us that we will do. In anticipation of that epiphanic moment, we sit poised, like the primary narrator who "listened, listened" to Marlow's tale, "on the watch for the sentence, for the word that [will] give [us] the clue to the faint uneasiness inspired by this narrative that [seems] to shape itself without human lips" (30). Through what he once described as his "unswerving devotion to the perfect blending of form and substance," Conrad sought to create a stylistic and textual dis-ease whose cumulative effects, although more intensely felt at the end of *Heart of Darkness*, have nevertheless been present from the very outset (*CP* 51). The reader confronts this textual anxiety and, unwittingly, labors from the first to fix fleeting impressions and to fill in the yawning gaps of meaning, thus acting from the earliest moments of the story as a coconspirator in the creation of an evolving horror. Conrad implicitly hints at such a strategy in his first letter to Cunninghame Graham, in which, declaring himself "very sincerely [sic] delighted to learn" that this as yet new acquaintance can "stand" his prose, he hastens to add that although it is "good news" to realize that one has any readers, he also recognizes that "one writes only half the book; the other half is with the reader" (*JCL* 46). Depending upon omissions and silences and the subtly disturbing cadences of a carefully crafted prose, *Heart of Darkness* draws its reader into a complicity that requires that he complete that obscurely-hinted-at "other" half of the fatal book in which horrors take shape and dark secrets are revealed.

Conclusion

The truth is—my dear Miss LaMotte—that we live in an *old* world—a tired world—a world that has gone on piling up speculation and observations until truths that might have been graspable in the bright Dayspring of human morning—by the young Plotinus or the ecstatic John on Patmos—are now obscured by palimpsest on palimpsest, by thick horny growths over that clear vision—as moulting serpents, before they burst forth with their new flexible-brilliant skins, are blinded by the crusts of their old one—or, we might say, as the lovely lines of *faith* that sprung up in the aspiring towers of the ancient ministers and abbeys are both worn away by time and grime, softly shrouded by the smutty accretions of our industrial cities, our wealth, our discoveries themselves, our Progress.

Randolph Henry Ash to Christabel LaMotte, c. 1859

"THERE ARE PARTS OF ONE'S PAST," Henry James reflects as he relives his redis-covery of the old Venice of his "Aspern Papers," "that bask consentingly and serenely enough in the light of other days—which is but the intensity of thought; and there are other parts that take it as with agitation and pain, a troubled consciousness that heaves as with the disorder of drinking it deeply in"; the latter engagement, he implies, if approached from "too thick and rich a retro-spect" may prove as confounding as it is revelatory ("Preface," 160-61). Such, perhaps, may be the final effect of *The Shape of Fear*, from the pages of which I have had, inevitably, to omit discussions of works by many authors whose literary experiments place them squarely at the center of the intersecting realms of thought and imagination—Decadence and late-nineteenth-century horror, and the prophecies of degeneration that may be said to have shaped the fears em-bodied in each—that are the subjects of this study. History, trends in critical thought, and popular tastes have all proven reasonably kind to some of these authors, such as Bram Stoker, M.R. James, John Meade Falkner, and Algernon Blackwood, while others—Ralph Adams Cram, R. Murray Gilchrist, Robert Hichens, William Hope Hodgson, Oliver Onions, Vincent O'Sullivan, and H.B. Marriott Watson come readily to mind—have fared less well. What emerges from the works considered here is a portrait of a past assembled out of constitu-tive and unlikely parts that, although perhaps approached at times from too thick and plethoric a retrospect, are intended to interact and cohere in much the same way that the subjects (simulacra, they are sometimes called) featured in the paintings of the sixteenth-century artist Giuseppe Arcimboldo are composed of a multitude of objects that remain recognizably themselves—fruit, flowers, fish—and yet, taken as a whole, are immediately recognizable as a bold, gro-tesque human face. Deliberately gnomic, hermetic, esoteric, continually risking or actually courting the alienation of a mass audience, the stories with which *The Shape of Fear* has concerned itself (as well as those that have after all been excluded from its pages) remain to us as cultural artifacts, the "relics" that we have already had occasion to hear de la Mare judge to be "saliently characteris-tic of their day . . . simply because they served their temporary purpose, but no other."[1]

A review of the works that are treated in this study suggests that "their purpose"—which in many cases, as we shall see, has proved to be less transient, less circumscribed, less tied to a cultural presence, now past, than de la Mare's assessment might have seemed to allow—was to provide fin de siècle writers with a means of silencing the nagging suspicion that they had a good deal more to fear than the mere fear of cultural decadence itself. The ostensible obsession with the imminent prospect of decay—biological, psychological, cultural, and even linguistic—is inseparable from a more fundamental preoccupation with the past, for to define decadence as the falling down and away from a better or a higher or a more vital state of existence is to assign to it a predicate of a temporal nature. Such a preoccupation with the past would explain in part why antiquaries, pedants, professors, collectors—seekers after the buried artifacts and the hidden secrets of the past—have been the protagonists most favored by horror writers, and why their quests have involved a search for origins, sources, provenances, and first principles: the disclosure of what Lovecraft referred to as "man's very hereditary essence."[2] More often than not, they discover that what Lovecraft termed the "hereditary impulse" shapes itself in response to an "innermost biological heritage," as the Poesque narrator of his "Rats in the Walls" (1923) discovers, for example, when he journeys ever deeper into the past, retreating to his family's ancestral manor in England, where he restores the family name, Delapore, to its original spelling, "de la Poer"—the first harmless anticipation of his regression.[3] In the course of restoring Exham Priory, he uncovers a series of hidden subterranean cellars, and as he explores each in succession, he is brought ever nearer to a confrontation with the dark and repressed truths that explain the barbarous behavior of his ancestors and his own latent atavistic tendencies—tendencies that find their full expression at last as he crouches, insane, over the bloody corpse of the man whom he has just devoured. In enacting a dialectic descent into its primitive origins, however, the language of his ravings provides an accurate account of his vertiginous recursion to his ancestral past (precipitated by his desire to investigate the contents of his family's "hereditary envelope"): "Why shouldn't rats eat a de la Poer as a de la Poer eats forbidden things? . . . The war ate my boy, damn them all . . . and the Yanks ate Carfax with flames and burnt Grandsire Delapore and the secret . . . No, no, I tell you, I am *not* that daemon swineherd in the twilit grotto! . . . Who says I am a de la Poer? He lived, but my boy died! . . . Shall a Norrys hold the lands of a de la Poer? . . . It's voodoo, I tell you . . . that spotted snake . . . Curse you, Thornton, I'll teach you to faint at what my family do! . . . 'Sblood, thou stinkard, I'll learn ye how to gust . . . wolde ye swynke me thilke wys? . . . *Magna Mater! Magna Mater! . . . Atys . . . Dia ad aghaidh's ad aodaun . . . agus bas dunach ort! Dhonas's dholas ort, agus leat-sa! . . . Ungl . . . ungl . . . rrlh . . . chchch . . .*"[4]

Lovecraft's primeval past is related to, and may in fact be viewed as a direct descendant of, those addressed in fin de siècle horror stories—a tangled accrescence of pasts represented in various ways: as having been embedded in the petrified strata of a paleontological record, or in phonetic or grammatical relics lingering vestigially in the morphologies of living languages, or in the stylistic excrescences of the literary and artistic productions of those men of genius whose physical bodies often suppressed the figurations of a cosmic process—figurations more readily apprehended in the body of the criminal. Like the bodies of knowledge they delineate, these competing yet correlative records were often teratologically inclined: characterized by missing parts (producing *monstres par défaut*, to borrow a classification established by nineteenth-century French medical anatomists), or extra parts (*monstres par excès*) whose function was not immediately discoverable, or misplaced normal parts.[5] One might begin, as Pater had hoped, "with that which is without—our physical life," but one quickly discovered that the history recorded in the host of texts available for scrutiny was fragmented, often indecipherable, and—like de la Poer's elliptical and cryptic statement—where decipherable, horrific.[6] Any reengagement with the past, then, was of necessity fraught with agitation, and pain, and a troubled consciousness that heaved with disorder, particularly when such an exploration led, as it often did for Lovecraft's literary ancestors, back to a time that was older, more threatening, more distinguished even than that which James associates with his "old Venice." Whether conceived of as continuously present but eroded by the passage of time or buried beneath the accumulated speculation of the ages (such are the twin fates assigned to the past by A.S. Byatt's fictional Victorian poet and naturalist, Randolph Henry Ash), or whether imagined, as it seemed to Pater, as a series of autonomous engagements "with a sharp and importunate reality," in duration and character exactly that of the carriage wheel that (as described in the fifth-century Buddhist tract the *Visuddhimagga*) "touches the ground in only one place when it turns": either way, the past seemed largely irrecoverable; and where recoverable, hateful since it disclosed a material reality that tended to express itself atavistically and retrogressively in the form of the Darwinian ancestor, whose coat of fawn hair or faintly fluttering gills betrays its inherent bestiality.[7] This recognition, Conrad stressed, accounted for the cry of the artist of his day—"'Take me out of myself!'"—a cry heralding a recoil from "perishable activity into the light of imperishable consciousness" where "struggling forms" are endowed with "the only possible form of permanence in this world of relative values—the permanence of memory."[8] The cry, at least as Conrad reports it, is inherently self-contradictory, because the movement that it urges leads not away from solipsism toward a wider field of vision, but merely further inward to that "narrow chamber of the individual mind" in which, as Pater had earlier argued, the "flood of external objects" would lose their power to distract; in which organic imperatives surrender their claims; in which the corrosive memories contained within the corrupted palimpsests tossed up by the tide of history find no purchase upon a diminishing shore of faith; and in which language would be protected from what Jacques Derrida, in his discussion of the pressing presence of the present (and the "being" it harbors), would later identify as the threats to ideality: "empirical existence, factuality, contingency, worldliness."[9]

Others had heard the cry (or a version of it) that spurred Conrad to recreate in his fictions the *esse* of the material world as *percipi*. G.K. Chesterton, for example, speculated that the mannered ennui of the Decadents was really a "yawn" intended to "conceal . . . a silent yell" of anguish.[10] Their creative efforts (to which they assigned no such redemptive value as Conrad implies in his reference to the artist's labors as "rescue work") were devoted to the crafting of what Edmond de Goncourt, speaking of and for Pater's disciples, characterized as "une langue personnelle, une langue portant notre signature."[11] Their language was officially à *rebours*—"against nature," and against, by extension, the

culture that had, according to Max Beerbohm, betrayed its heirs and successors
by sacrificing everything "to Nature."[12] For Decadence in literature (to repeat
what has elsewhere been too extensively pursued to warrant more than a passing acknowledgment here) was officially "against" (or, conversely, "for" what
Jerome Buckley calls the "unnatural perversion" of) a cluster of constrictive
codes, conventions, and assumptions—invested with the authority of Cartesian
certainties—concerning the nature of reality, of art, and of progress.[13] The Decadent style shaped itself in opposition to what Symons characterized as the "ready-
made impressions and conclusions" derived from a "ready-made . . . language."[14]
It made no secret of—indeed, it flaunted—its desire "neither to be read nor to be
understood by the bourgeois intelligence" that sought for no meaning beyond
what was comprehended by "the trembling lips, the flashing eyes, the determined curve of the chin, the nervous trick of biting the moustache": what
Beerbohm had enumerated as the "old properties" of the realists, of "the ordinary novel" of his day—and what we in turn might view as the literary equivalent
of Duchenne de Boulogne's network of facial muscles that produced a language
requiring no more than instinct to be understood.[15] Beerbohm longed for the
day (it was, he believed, close at hand) when "the masking of the face" by means
of cosmetics would baffle the shrewdest of physiognomists, whose science degraded the visage "from its rank as a thing of beauty to a mere vulgar index of
character or emotion." The day that would accomplish the "secernment of soul
and surface" would also be that which would bring to its conclusion a "very
reign of terror" during which "all things were sacrificed to the fetish Nature."[16]
      Beerbohm was on the watch for the "signs" and "portents" that would an-
nounce that "the day of sancta simplicitas is quite ended" and the "new epoch of
artifice" begun, although he conceded that "of the curiosities of history not the
least strange is the manner in which two social movements may be seen to
overlap, long after the second has, in truth, given its deathblow to the first."[17]
With this casual and otherwise innocuous observation, Beerbohm unmasks
contradictions within a movement that his defense of cosmetics appears to glam-
orize, and he proposes as well motivations that Osbert Burdett may not have
anticipated when he questioned whether "the children of any age so recoiled
from their parents as those of the Victorian have done?"[18] An engagement with
Decadence (of whatever degree of intensity) has often been regarded as a gesture of defiance hurled in the direction of Wells's "mild and massive Sphinx of
British life"—though it is perhaps worth recalling that this impassive idol would
reemerge as the winged Sphinx that Wells would transport to the future in his
Time Machine: an idol with "sightless eyes" and "the faint shadow of a smile on
the lips" featured upon a "white, shining, leprous" face otherwise unreadable but
for the sense that it conveys to the baffled Time Traveller of forbidding his passage into the future while prohibiting his return to a familiar past that, whatever
its ills and disparities, had not, at least, the semblance of the future, "black and
blank— . . . a vast ignorance."[19] As the distant future settles upon the narrator of

The Time Machine a featureless wisdom, so the (more imminent) new century presented to its assigns a prospect stimulating but also terrifying, indicative of a future unfolding in a universe that Lovecraft envisioned as "an automatic, meaningless chaos devoid of ultimate values or distinctions of right and wrong."[20] The fin de siècle writers discussed here were, by and large, young people who were struggling under related burdens: the overt desire to throw off the yoke of the past and thereby begin the process of cultural self-determination, and the simultaneous (although far more covert) desire to recruit into the new century—of which they were to be the cultural arbiters—the comforting attitudes and beliefs of that same past. It was in recognition of the fact that his late-Victorian precursors suffered acutely from a fear that they were being disinherited from their immediate past and cultural heritage that Lovecraft, in a passage to which we have already had occasion to refer, envisioned the "most terrible conception of the human brain" as "a malign and particular suspension or defeat of those fixed laws of Nature" that had as their analog the fixed laws that govern and control human behavior.[21]

Since blasphemy is possessed of relevance only in a context in which faith is also relevant, the Decadent texts treated in this study prove inherently self-contradictory, revealing a desire (which is both latent and reactionary) to resurrect a faith in the secular standards of Victorianism: its codes, its organizing principles of belief, and its stabilizing systems, all of which testified to a sober acquiescence in the prospect of continued progress and improvement. Their authors implicitly mourn the loss not merely of the traditions themselves, but of a peculiarly Victorian worldview and the attendant confidence born of a saving ignorance of propositions and principles that the prevailing scientific trends of the time seemed to represent as inevitabilities. Byatt's Randolph Henry Ash pictures this faith as having been shrouded by palimpsest on palimpsest of speculation and observations, but the texts considered herein suggest that such a faith was chimerical. After all, long before Wilde's Lady Bracknell evaluates Cecily Cardew's personal appearance—considers, that is, how both her hair (which is regrettably "almost as Nature might have left it") and her style of chin might be altered by the arts of a "thoroughly experienced French maid"—Dickens's "Cleopatra," herself constructed almost entirely of cosmetics, had concluded that Florence Dombey's "heart," so "extremely natural," might be improved upon had she a new mother to assist "in the formation of her mind."[22] And if he did not have this particular literary pairing in mind, other precursors, as easily recalled, would have permitted Beerbohm to wonder how the prejudice in favor of "a more complicated life, [and] the love for cosmetics . . . ever came into being": would allow him to suspect, that is, that the "day of sancta simplicitas" may itself have been illusory. It might just as easily be asked of an apparently "artless" mask as of the more conventionally enameled mask of paint and powder: "Of what treacherous mysteries may it not be the screen?"[23]

What was said of William Faulkner's Emily Grierson (living out her own

late-nineteenth-century horror story in refusing to surrender the corpse of her
dead father) might well be said of the Decadents: they clung to that which had
robbed them. Though they arrayed themselves against nature and against the
culture that had betrayed them, the Decadents also—however perversely and
characteristically self-contradictiously—took up arms against themselves. In
emphasizing form—the rhythms and contours derived from diction and syntax—
over function, and thereby establishing what Lovecraft described as the "actual
physiological fixation of the old instincts in our nervous tissue," the Decadent
style facilitated the creation of a text that, rather than addressing the idea of
cultural decadence, actually encoded the degenerative tendencies peculiar to
the consciousness that had conceived of the works themselves.[24] As Conrad's
"rescue work" returns the self to the self, a style that is predicated upon and
wraps itself around notions of aberration and corruption, entropy and degeneration—however much it is represented as an abomination to those who up-
held the standards of High Victorian culture, thought, and patterns of behavior—is by its very nature tied to the fetish Nature to which, during the so-called
reign of terror that prevailed in Victoria's England, all things were perceived as
having been sacrificed. Perhaps because they perceived it as self-infecting or, at
the very least, given its covertly organicist inclination, destined to experience a
natural death; or perhaps because they regarded it as a revolutionary style possessed of a reactive potential (evident in its ability to inspire its readers with an
antipathy for the sordid truths and realities that it purports to celebrate); many
of the writers treated in these pages (particularly those whose experiments with
Decadence were more tentative and troubled—such preeminently conservative
authors as Vernon Lee, John Buchan, and even Joseph Conrad, after all, appropriated the Decadent style) availed themselves of the opportunity to purge themselves and their select group of readers of their "fascination of the abomination." In short, they nurtured the silent (and, as they recognized, the futile) hope
that Decadence had evolved as its own antidote, impeding the encroachment of
an existential terror, suspiciously modern in nature, that had evolved out of an
earlier and pervasive sense of cultural decline.

     Linguistically fragmented and psychophysiologically accurate, Decadent
horror stories convey the sense of cultural crisis that preyed upon the minds of
their makers, variously described as a "modern melancholy," "the 'hysteria' of
modern development on human consciousness," and, in our own society, "future shock."[25] If, according to Matei Calinescu, it did not provide "*the* solution to
the painful uncertainties and contradictions of modern life," the Decadent style
of literature, particularly as it manifested itself in late-nineteenth-century horror
stories, prompted twentieth-century writers to reconsider ways in which the artistic text could generate a sense of disease within the reader by functioning
both as medium and as message; and in so doing it encouraged many of those
later writers to *recreate* their precursors—or to reconsider, at least, their Decadent past.[26] In other words, the tendencies discernible in the fin de siècle litera-

ture of horror did not disappear with the movement itself. In some twentieth-century works, the debt is quite direct. For example, the idea behind "Room 101" in *Nineteen Eighty-Four* (1949) clearly derives from the treatments of horror and evil that Orwell encountered in the works of his precursors of the fin de siècle, all of whom recognized, as we have seen, that explicitness is fatal to the portrayal of that which is genuinely terrifying. In a meditation upon his treatment of "portentous evil" in *The Turn of the Screw*, James asked, "How was I to save that, as an intention on the part of my demon-spirits, from the drop, the comparative vulgarity, inevitably attending, throughout the whole range of possible brief illustration, the offered example, the imputed vice, the cited act, the limited deplorable presentable instance?"

> What, in the last analysis, had I to give the sense of? . . . What would *be* then, on reflection, this utmost conceivability?—a question to which the answer all admirably came. There is for such a case no eligible *absolute* of the wrong; it remains relative to fifty other elements, a matter of appreciation, speculation, imagination—these things moreover quite exactly in the light of the spectator's, the critic's, the reader's experience. Only make the reader's general vision of evil intense enough, I said to myself—and that already is a charming job—and his own experience, his own imagination, his own sympathy . . . and horror . . . will supply him quite sufficiently with all the particulars. Make him *think* the evil, make him think it for himself, and you are released from weak specifications. ["Preface," 176]

Orwell's "Room 101" is, of course, a specific place, just as the mode of torture with which Winston Smith is threatened is a particular infamy to which different readers (depending upon the degree of their aversion to rats) will assign different degrees of brutality. The informing idea behind Room 101—an idea that has remained tied in readers' imaginations to the scene and site of Smith's abject surrender, though it has an older provenance than Orwell's *Nineteen Eighty-Four*—is that somewhere there exists a room or, as we have seen, a "fatal text" in which the reader will confront his or her own deepest and most abject fears. It is this that Smith's tormentor describes as "the worst thing in the world" because "for everyone there is something unendurable—something that cannot be contemplated"; this that Shiel referred to as "those 'faint manifestations of the Unknowable'" that lurk "in our hearts and in our pantings."[27]

The "pantings" to which Shiel alludes, those physiological expressions of an unknown and finally unknowable horror, assume monstrous proportions in Stanislaw Lem's *The Futurological Congress* (1974), a contemporary work that paradoxically attests to the modernity of the fin de siècle mentality. In Lem's nightmarish jeu d'esprit, the cosmonaut Ijon Tichy imagines himself in a future—the year is 2039—in which people are perpetually winded. When he is exposed to a dehallucinogen that counters (though only temporarily and only to a limited degree) the effects of the vast number of "psychotropes" that this future society employs to regulate—or rather create—its populace's perception of a ghastly reality, De Quincean or Piranesian in its fearful proportions, Tichy finally comprehends the "reason for all the heavy breathing" ("So that's how it is," he marvels, "What a world!"): "Holding their hands out chest-high and gripping the air like children pretending to be drivers, businessmen were trotting single file down the middle of the street. Now and then between the close columns and rows of these gallopers, who were furiously pumping their legs and leaning back from the waist up, as if reclining in deep seats, a solitary car would appear, puffing and chugging along."[28] In this world, Tichy discovers, existence without the mitigating effects of psycho-chemicals such as argumunchies (for those feeling disputatious), or rhapsodine (for the poet suffering from writer's block), or placatol (which brings peace to warring families) or, for those seeking a violently hallucinatory resolution to an Oedipal frustration, patricidol popsicles, or "throttle-pops," has become intolerable. More than a means of (apparently) achieving the impossible—after ingesting metamorphine, for example, one might "have an affair with a goat, thinking it's Venus de Milo herself" (130)—psycho-chemicals have become a requisite for survival in an overpopulated world, even one in which "there must exist some biological minimum—the bare necessities of life—which no fiction can ever replace." "One has to live *somewhere*, after all, eat *something*, breathe *something*" (130), and since it is irrevocably the case that "this is the way we must live, eat, exist," reasons Professor Trottelreiner, Tichy's friend and fellow futurologist, "at least let us have it in fancy wrappings" (119).

In recommending the "fancy wrappings" that "experiential engineering" (113) has synthesized, Professor Trottelreiner offers his own futuristic defense of cosmetics, for the most powerful drugs available in his "age of pharmacocracy" (97) are the "mascons" that trace a morphological descent from terms such as "mask, masquerade, mascara" (114), which in turn had their own inception in the earlier epoch of artifice when pessimists (as Chesterton writes of the Decadents), rather than "swallow the world . . . like an unpleasant pill," resorted in their extremity to paints and powders compounded from more primitive substances: "from stimmis, psimythium and fuligo to bismuth and arsenic," according to Beerbohm.[29] The function of mascons—which is, like that of their linguistic antecedents, to "*falsify* the world" (113)—has evolved in response to the same imperatives that influenced Beerbohm to urge the use of "brush and pigment . . . to make fair the ugly and overtop fairness": "If but for a single instant you could see this world of ours the way it *really* is—undoctored, unadulterated, uncensored—" Professor Trottelreiner assures an incredulous Tichy, "you would drop in your tracks!" (114).[30] Like so many reconstructed Dorian Grays, the devotees of experiential reality persuade themselves that, having begun with the body, which is "merely the means to an end," they move beyond its corporeal importunings, and in the final analysis "are dealing not with the body, but with the soul" (102). Even they are forced to concede, however, that biological imperatives can only be masked and not surmounted, and that the very drugs by which the material world is remade into an apparential world "take their toll on the organism," so that "every second inhabitant of New York is spotted, has greenish bristles growing down his back, thorns on his ears, flat feet, and emphysema with an enlarged heart from constantly galloping about." "All this must be concealed," confides Professor Trottelreiner to Tichy, by means of the very "supermascons" (130-31) that triggered the physiological eccentricities in the first place. But it is not concealed—not, at least, from a suspicious Tichy, who, subjected to a dose of an even more powerful antipsychem agent, catches a glimpse of the foulness lurking within what he perceives as an "elegant, courteous façade" (104), a "monumental masquerade" and "tinseled cheat" that lies "sprawled across the horizon" (120). The rictal horrors disclosed shock even the professor, who, in his role as one of his society's "soothseers," is permitted and even encouraged "to take vigilanimides—for the purpose of determining how things are *in reality*" (132). Though aware, for example, that when he seems to feast upon "steaming pheasant" he is in fact swallowing "the most unappetizing gray-brown gruel," while the "silver dish" upon which it is served is likely to be "a chipped earthenware plate" and the "sculptured pot" beside his table a reeking "slop bucket" (115), he has not, apparently, penetrated to the core of reality— else he would have known that not much is left of the face that he dines with; that his sunken cheeks are covered with "the rotting shreds of a bandage that hadn't been changed in ages"; that the vocoder that had been inserted in his trachea bobs up and down as he talks; that in his chest is "a gaping hold lidded with a cloudy plastic window" through which can be seen "a heart, held together with clamps and staples" and beating "in blue-black spasms"; and that the hand that holds the pen that records his thoughts (about what exists *in reality*) is "fashioned out of brass and green with verdigris" (138).

Tichy's experience recalls in theme and substance other keynote scenes of disclosure in fin de siècle horror, scenes in which the mask slips and the evil background, "really there to be thought of," as William James insisted, allows itself to be apprehended.[31] The scarlet-and-gold beauty of Dorian's youth enamels not a passionate purity but the leprosies of sin, just as the darkened chamber to which Shiel's Xélucha lures her companion, though appearing to be possessed of a "gorgeousness not less than Assyrian"—an "ivory couch at the far end [of the chamber] was made sun-like by a head-piece of chalcedony forming a sea for the sport of emerald ichthyosauri"; copper "hangings, panelled with mirrors in iasperated crystal, corresponded with a dome of flame and copper"— in the end betrays a "clayey ponderance," its luxuries, "thinned to air," not extending beyond "one little candlestick of common tin containing an old soiled curve of tallow" on a table "of common deal." Sickened yet enthralled at her horror of interest—the courtesan savors the recollection that, as they "fall, one

by one, from the lipless mouths" and "roll to the floor of stone," the teeth of
those seated in Norse passage graves make a dripping sound that provides the
seated dead with "a dialect largely dental" in contrast to that of the premonitory
ape, which was "wholly guttural"—and attracted by her scent of spice and or-
ange-flowers while repelled by an "abhorrent faint odour of mortality over-ready
for the tomb," Merimée rushes to embrace the numinous object of his fevered
desire, only to fall back in horror as the dead Xélucha disappears in "a belch of
pestilent corruption" that puffs "poisonous upon the putrid air."[32] The clayey
ponderance of the word lapidarism of Shiel's story, and its organic properties,
anticipate stylistically a truth that, many years later, Borges discovered in the
course of his speculation on the nature of time: the "world, alas, is real."[33]

Stylistically, then, late Victorians shared with their modernist heirs a sense
of the appropriateness or even the inevitablity of the narrative technique that
blended *esse* and *percipi* and that would as a result facilitate the emergence of
the fabulations of an Orwell or a Borges or a Lem, or the stream-of-conscious-
ness explorations of a Joyce or a Woolf, or the fractured versifications of a T.S.
Eliot. In their own ways, the Wildes and the Machens, the Shiels and the Conrads
dismantled prevailing narrative structures in an effort to transcribe textually the
unstable and even disjointed nature of human cognition and perception as it
exists in a world bereft of empirical absolutes, of a priori truths, of a finality
beside the grave. Thus, while it guided writers and artists in their endeavors to
develop literary and artistic vessels substantial enough to contain the corrosive
anxieties with which they were filled, Decadent literature performed the equally
important task of exposing its readership not merely to corrupting influences,
but to radically new ways of "reading" and thinking about texts. In this way it
prepared its readers for their confrontation with what is perhaps the most complex restatement of "the horror!" produced in the twentieth century.[34] Like fin de
siècle literature, "The Waste Land" presents itself as the artistic creation of a
civilization "grown over-luxurious, over-inquiring, too languid for the relief of
action, too uncertain for any emphasis in opinion or in conduct."[35] Where the
Decadent refashions what Yeats calls "this marred and clumsy world" into his
own solipsistic dreamworld, the voices in Eliot's poem are unable and even
unwilling to escape the Baudelairean "Unreal City," a sordid place that no longer
functions as a mode through which one could realize one's conception of the
beautiful, as it had still done for Dorian Gray. Clinging to that which has robbed
them of their humanity, Eliot's voices have grown accustomed to the perpetual
murmur of "maternal lamentation." They lament an irretrievable cultural past
(so slighted and so regretted by the Decadent) that has withered away, its myths
diminished, its defining works of literature misunderstood or dismissed as no
longer relevant, its remote values bastardized or merely forgotten in an age of
historical decline. They lament a present consisting of a disjointed series of
isolated and grotesque impressions, connected only by the paranoia of various
narrators whose most casual statements—"HURRY UP PLEASE ITS TIME"—

are fraught with intimations of a final spiritual annihilation, a collapse into utter chaos and a nihilism of apocalyptic proportions. They lament the ushering in of the Darwinian beast that, after crouching for a generation within the interstices of the late-Victorian horror story, has at last arrived, fulfilling Wells's prophecy that the "Coming Beast must certainly be reckoned in any anticipatory calculations regarding the Coming Man."[36] The Coming Beast *is* the Coming Man, however; his destination is not Bethlehem but the Waste Land. Disordered, cacophonous, anarchic, "The Waste Land" is "a handful of dust"—the decomposed, atomized remnants of a once organic whole—each grain a little sermon on the ubiquitous and ignoble horror of a deplored modernity. The movement of which Eliot's poem is the center, then, is itself the culmination of earlier literary and artistic movements such as Decadence (and even, in its less visible way, the fin de siècle preoccupation with horror), which were themselves inspired by the first faint stirrings of the awful consciousness of the modern existential fear, dread, and loathing that are brought to fruition in the aborted lines, the terminated rhythms, and the "heap of broken images" that punctuate this twentieth-century dirge. The forces and traditions to which "The Waste Land" (if only indirectly) owes its horrible inception, then, might be said to represent the "awful daring of a moment's surrender / Which an age of prudence can never retract."

Notes

Introduction

1. Bleiler, *Victorian Ghost Stories*, 5.
2. W. James, *Varieties of Religious Experience*, 120; T.H. Huxley, "Prolegomena," in *Evolution and Ethics*, 103.
3. H.G. Wells, cited in Jackson, *The Eighteen Nineties*, 228.
4. Knoll, "The Science of Language," 19 n. 15.
5. Myers, "Nineteenth-Century Popularizations," 335, 313.
6. Lombroso, *The Man of Genius*, 7.
7. Darwin to L. Horner, Aug. 29, 1844, letter 480, *More Letters of Charles Darwin*, 2:117.
8. August Schleicher, "Darwinism Tested by the Science of Language," in Koerner, *Linguistics and Evolutionary Theory*, 45. Critics have noted that, although nineteenth-century linguistic theory was influenced early in its development by the methods and paradigms of biology, paleontology, and zoology, the borrowings were not always direct, nor were they always based on an exact understanding of the principles underlying those disciplines and the models they generated. Brigitte Nerlich points out that although "Schleicher used Darwin to defend main-stream linguistic ideas about languages that grow and decay . . . [his] organismic view of language remained essentially pre-Darwinian, that is static." His application of the term *evolution*, she argues, is typical of that of most other nineteenth-century linguists, who "continued to use it in a pre-Darwinian way" although its meaning in the biological sciences had evolved, "being now connected with the terms 'variation' and 'selection'" (Nerlich, "Linguistic Evolution," 104, 101).
9. Foucault, *The Order of Things*, 162, xxi.
10. Darwin, *Expression of the Emotions*, 195.
11. Romanes, *Mental Evolution in Man*, 238.
12. Darwin, *Expression of the Emotions*, 12.
13. Pater, preface to *The Renaissance: Studies in Art and Poetry*, in Pater, *Three Major Texts*, 74-75.
14. Altick, *Presence of the Present*, 4.
15. E.P. Thompson, *The Making of the English Working Class*, 12.
16. Peattie, *Shape of Fear*, 8.
17. Müller, *The Science of Language*, 1:xxxv; Romanes, *Mental Evolution in Man*, 421.

1. Rictus Invictus

1. Pierre Georgel, who has written extensively on the substantial body of drawings that Hugo produced over the course of his lifetime, reminds us that although Hugo's collagraphs could not strictly be termed "innovative"—Alexander Cozens, J.M.W. Turner, and John Constable had already contributed works to an evolving blottesque tradition, whereas James Gillray and Thomas Bewick had experimented with assemblages—their popularity facilitated the discovery or recovery of techniques and movements that would prove revolutionary, among them automatism and surrealism. See Georgel, *Drawings by Victor Hugo* and *Dessins de Victor Hugo*.
2. Hugo to Charles Baudelaire, April 29, 1860, in *Oeuvres complètes*, 12:1098.

3. Gautier, "Venté du mobilier de M. Victor Hugo."

4. The source of my information concerning Hugo's reliance upon a single shred of lace is Georgel, who writes that since Hugo "always used the same piece of lace, a prolonged utilization is hardly likely. The drawings in question would therefore span a relatively brief period" (Georgel, *Dessins de Victor Hugo*, 130).

5. Hugo, "Preface to *Cromwell*," 350.

6. Ibid., 385. In the context of his discussion of an "estimable insane taste" in art, Walter Bagehot similarly deduces that beauty and ugliness are necessarily proximate, the one constitutive of the other: "An exceptional monstrosity of horrid ugliness cannot be made pleasing," he insists, "except it be made to suggest—to recall—the perfection, the beauty, from which it is a deviation" (Bagehot, "Wordsworth, Tennyson, and Browning; or, Pure, Ornate, and Grotesque Art in English Poetry," in *Literary Studies*, 2:374).

7. M.R. James, "Mr. Humphreys and His Inheritance," in *More Ghost Stories*, 269-70.

8. W. James, *Varieties of Religious Experience*, 119, 118.

9. Verhaeren, "Les dessins de Victor Hugo," 181.

10. Vacquerie, "Les dessins de Victor H.," in *Demi-Teintes*, 96; Constant, "Les dessins de Victor Hugo"; Mallarmé to Théodore Aubanel, Oct. 16, 1865, letter 35, *Selected Letters*, 55.

11. Gautier, "Texte," 7-8; Huysmans, "Les dessins de Victor Hugo," 136. These individuals were also the arbiters of French and English Decadence, and early in their careers they adopted Hugo as "un compositeur de décadence" (the phrase is the young Charles Baudelaire's) (Baudelaire, cited in Calinescu, *Five Faces of Modernity*, 337 n. 22). Hugo's corresponding experiments with language—with the rhythms and cadences of lines, with the sounds and evocative qualities of words—were the subject, for example, of a study by Algernon Charles Swinburne, who lauded the "poet's unequalled and unapproached variety in mastery of metre and majesty of colour and splendid simplicity of style, no less exact than sublime, and no less accurate than passionate" (Swinburne, *Victor Hugo*, 131). Hugo's works, both literary and visual, also served as one important source for Baudelaire's theory of mystical correspondences, which asserts that the imagination alone imposes order upon and arrives at meaning within the world by establishing correlations between various sensory perceptions, which in turn provide us with intimations of the universal language.

12. Wilde, *The Picture of Dorian Gray*, in *Oscar Wilde*, 56 (hereinafter cited in the text).

13. Gautier, "Texte," 16.

14. Hawthorne, *American Notebooks*, 510.

15. Hardy, *Tess of the d'Urbervilles*, 384, 177.

16. Conrad, *Heart of Darkness*, 56-57.

17. Ollinger-Zinque, *Ensor by Himself*, 49.

18. Petronius Arbiter, *Satyricon*, in *Works*, 70. For a history of this image, see Cody, "Hawthorne's 'Christmas Banquet.'"

19. Symons, "Decadent Movement," 859.

20. Darwin, entries 114, 115e, "Notebook E," in *Charles Darwin's Notebooks, 1836-1844*, 429.

21. Darwin, entry 252, "Notebook B," in *Charles Darwin's Notebooks, 1836-1844*, 233.

22. Darwin, entry 40, "Notebook M," in *Charles Darwin's Notebooks, 1836-1844*, 529.

23. Wordsworth, preface to 2d ed. of *Lyrical Ballads* (1800), in *Selected Poems and Prefaces*, 456.

24. Ruskin, "The Storm-Cloud of the Nineteenth Century," lecture 2, *Works of John Ruskin*, 34:72; Ruskin to Henry Acland, M.D., May 24, 1851, *Letters of John Ruskin*, in *Works of John Ruskin*, 36:115. Unless otherwise indicated, all subsequent references to Ruskin's works are to this edition, and are cited by volume and page number.

25. Ruskin, "The Storm-Cloud of the Nineteenth Century," 34:72-73.

26. Wordsworth, preface, 456.

27. Müller, *The Science of Language*, 1:xx.

28. Tyndall, *Heat a Mode of Motion*, viii.

29. T.H. Huxley to Charles Kingsley, Sept. 23, 1860, in *Life and Letters*, 1:235. Absent from Huxley's representation of the nineteenth-century scientist as questing explorer are the claims of high adventure, of culminating discovery and proud conquest of territories that Sir Thomas Browne had long since optimistically claimed for the metaphysical explorer when he wrote "wee carry with us the wonders, wee seeke without us: There is all *Africa*, and her prodigies in us; we are that bold and adventurous piece of nature, which he that studies wisely learnes in a *compendium*, what others labour at in a divided piece and endlesse volume" (*Religio Medici*, 24). The Livingstons and Mungo Parks had explored the physical Africa; but by the 1890s, Huxley was comparing "the present Flora of the Sussex Downs . . . [with] that of Central Africa" ("Prolegomena," in *Evolution and Ethics*, 61) as evidence of the variability of the earth's surface, while Conrad was beginning to explore in his fiction an Africa that was at once "a blank space of delightful mystery—a white patch for a boy to dream gloriously over" and "a place of darkness" (*Heart of Darkness*, 12) within the human psyche. Conrad subjects his fictional character to a version of the "three severe blows" (cosmological, biological, and psychological) that Freud would later describe as having been dealt (by the very researches of science that troubled Huxley, even as he promoted them) to "the universal narcissism of men, their self-love": blows that had shattered man's earlier and "naïvely" aggrandizing perception of himself as existing "in the centre of a circle that enclosed the external world" (Freud, "A Difficulty in the Path of Psycho-Analysis" [1917], in *Standard Edition*, 17:139-40).

30. G. Eliot, *Mill on the Floss*, 29.

31. Ruskin, "The Best Hundred Books," letter 1 to the editor of the *Pall Mall Gazette*, Jan. 13, 1886, *Arrows of the Chace*, 34:582.

32. Ruskin, letter 2 to the editor of the *Pall Mall Gazette*, Feb. 1886, in *Arrows of the Chace*, 34:586.

33. Ruskin, "Darwinism," letter to the editor of the *Pall Mall Gazette*, May 24, 1886, in *Arrows of the Chace*, 34:596.

34. Nordau, *Degeneration*, 105 (hereinafter cited in the text).

35. Darwin to J.D. Hooker, Feb. 9, 1865, letter 185, *More Letters of Charles Darwin*, 1:260-61.

36. T.H. Huxley, "Prolegomena," in *Evolution and Ethics*, 59-60.

37. Hardy, *Tess of the d'Urbervilles*, 19-20.

38. T.H. Huxley, "Prolegomena," in *Evolution and Ethics*, 61.

39. In *The Time Machine* (1895) H.G. Wells, a student of Huxley's, takes up this very idea but considers it from a technological and cultural, as well as a biological, perspective. Struggling to understand the "Quiet" that surrounds him in the year Eight Hundred and Two Thousand odd, the Time Traveller realizes that what had been mere dreams in his own day had become "projects deliberately put in hand and carried forward. And the harvest was what I saw!" (*The Definitive Time Machine*, 50). These projects, however, themselves the result of an "abundant vitality," "strength," "physical courage," and "strength of constitution," merely create conditions that facilitate the emergence of what may *seem* to be diametrically opposed qualities—"weakness," "languor," "decay," and "a contented inactivity"—but which are in fact complementary, ingrained, and (appropriately) incipient states of being.

40. T.H. Huxley, "Prolegomena," in *Evolution and Ethics*, 69.

41. Cesare Lombroso, *L'homme criminel* (1887), cited in Gould, *The Mismeasure of Man*, 124.

42. Jean Esquirol, cited in Maudsley, *Physiology and Pathology of the Mind*, 300; H. Ellis, *The Criminal*, 85. The phrase "born criminal" turns on one of the many contradictory definitions at work in the competing treatments of *dégénérescence*, a term that "served to anchor meaning," although, as Daniel Pick points out, "paradoxically its own could never be fully stabilised, indeed was in doubt more than all the others; it explained everything and nothing as it moved back and forth between the clinic, the novel, the newspaper and the government investigation" (*Faces of Degeneration*, 8). To Lombroso and others, the "born criminal" seemed a *lusus naturae*, freakish in the sense that a devolutionary urge over which he had no control manifested itself anatomically in atavistic, generally simian, traits distin-

guishing him as a throwback to a primitive evolutionary type. This seems to have been Darwin's interpretation of degeneracy as well, for he refers, in a notebook entry of September 7, 1838, to the "Law of monstrosity · as being "not prospective, but retrospective" (entry 66 in "Notebook D," *Charles Darwin's Notebooks, 1836-1844,* 355). Crime itself was, for Lombroso, what Pick calls a "bio-historical anachronism": "the ontogenic development of the criminal" having been arrested, this "anomalous individual thus languished behind phylogeny" (Pick, *Faces of Degeneration,* 126). Others, such as Bénédictin Augustin Morel and the natural historian Robert Chambers took degeneration to mean a deviation from a proto- or ur-type ("which the human mind takes delight in conceiving to be a masterpiece and the model of creation"), and thus a return to such an "original type," according to Morel, could only "erroneously" be termed "degeneration" ("Treatise on the Degenerations," Mar. 25, 1857, 10:136-37). For Maudsley, as for Morel, it was the unceasing forward momentum of progress—expressed in what the former described as the "feverish activity of life, the eager interests, the numerous passions, and the great strain of mental work incident to the multiplied industries and eager competition of an active civilization"—that conduced to a degeneration evident in "an increase of insanity," the "penalty which an increase of our present civilization necessarily pays" (*Physiology and Pathology of the Mind,* 200-201). Nordau, on the other hand, availed himself (whether consciously or not is unclear) of both definitions, asserting early in his *Degeneration* that the "clearest notion we can form of degeneracy is to regard it as a *morbid deviation from an original type*" (16). Like Morel and Maudsley, he identified this deviation as a "direct consequence of certain influences of modern civilization" (41). Somewhat later, however, he substitutes the Lombrosian for the Morelian school of thought, arguing that mysticism is a function of "debilitated brain-activity"—that the brain "relinquishes the advantages of the differentiated perceptions of phenomena" so that the person thus afflicted sees things in a hazy sort of way that is itself a sign of "a retrogression to the very beginning of organic development" (142). Elsewhere, he defines literary impressionism as "an example of that atavism"—"the most distinctive feature in the mental life of degenerates"—that "carries back the human mind to its brute-beginnings" (485), while degeneracy in all its incarnations represented "not the future, but an immeasurable remote past" (556).

43. Morel, "Treatise on the Degenerations," 10:267. Wing's abridged version, published in piecemeal fashion in two consecutive volumes of *The Medical Circular* of 1857, represents the only English translation currently available of Morel's tomic work. The citation for this serialized translation is as follows: *Medical Circular* 10 (Mar. 18, 1857): 122-23; (Mar. 25): 136-37; (April 1) 150-51; (April 8): 161; (April 15): 173; (April 22): 187; (May 6): 207-8; (May 13): 219-21; (May 20): 232-33; (June 3): 254-55; (June 10): 267-68; and 11 (July 8): 14; (July 22): 37; (July 29): 49-50; (Aug. 5): 61-62; (Aug. 12): 73-74; (Sept. 2): 109; (Sept. 16): 133-34; (Sept. 23): 146; (Oct. 14): 182; (Oct. 21): 193; (Oct. 28): 205; (Nov. 4): 218; (Nov. 11): 229-30; (Nov. 18): 241; (Dec. 9): 277-78; (Dec. 23): 302-3. Morel's allusion to "the engraver" charged with "giving a very exact idea of the different types of degenerated beings" touches in an interesting way upon the idea of the nature of the representation of deviancy, deformity, and illness. The body served as a text, and it was also textualized in the various representations upon which interpretations of and theories about deviancy were based. For an extended discussion of "the various forms of artistic reproduction" upon which "[eighteenth-] and early nineteenth-century students of the physiognomy of the insane relied," see chapter 8, "The Science of Visualizing the Insane," in Sander L. Gilman's *Disease and Representation,* 127-39.

44. Nordau speaks here with uncharacteristic compassion of the plight of those upon whm he elsewhere confers picturesque titles indicative of the depth of his scorn. Thus, Ruskin, one of "the most turbid and fallacious minds," is "a Torquemada of aesthetics" (77); Dante Gabriel Rossetti is to "be counted among Sollier's [Dr. Alice Sollier of the Bicêtre in Paris] imbeciles" (94), who engage in a "parasitic battening on the body of Dante" (87); Walt Whitman "a vagabond, a reprobate rake" given to poetic outbursts of "erotomania" (231); Maurice Maeterlinck a "pitiable mental cripple" (239); and Richard Wagner "the last mushroom on the dunghill of romanticism" (194). More to the point, his allusion to "fault" and "punishment" establishes the obvious, if unstated, correlation between the bodily stigmata of degeneration

and the Christian concepts of original sin and the fall—a comparative whose accuracy Nordau here questions but that others (Morel and Orson S. Fowler among them) employed both literally and figuratively in their expositions of degeneracy.

45. To the extent that it centered on internal difference, the positivistic theorization of degeneration possessed a certain occult quality. Those undertaking to gloss the bodies of recidivists were not merely drawing out indwelling, invisible agencies, but also reading past events and prophesying future ones. Criminals and "savages" (in general, nineteenth-century anthropologists made little distinction between the two) bore what seemed to Robert Chambers to be "the outward marks of a low and barbarous condition," marks characteristic of an earlier phylogenetic stage (*Natural History of Creation*, 195). Secrets obscured in the fossil record were thought to have been made manifest in the black skin of the Africans, the red skin of American Indians, or the "flat features" of the Chinese. With the primitivisms of an ancient past rendered vestigially present in the body, *"the various races of mankind"* were thus disclosed as *"representations of particular stages in the development of the highest or Caucasion type"* (213-14). Though officially uninterested in "stigmatizing," Darwin devoted an entire book to a "brief consideration of the outward signs of some of the stronger sensations and emotions" in man and animals, seeking evidence of what fossil remains and mollusks alone would not prove definitively: that the "community of certain expressions in distinct though allied species"—as, for example, "in the movements of the same facial muscles during laughter by man and by various monkeys"—is rendered "intelligible" only if those species are understood to have been descended "from a common progenitor" (*Expression of the Emotions*, 69, 12). Darwin shared with the medical psychiatrist Jean-Martin Charcot (a contemporary who also sought for outward manifestations of subliminal disease and degeneration) the belief that the "anatomy of the exterior forms of the human body [does] not speak only to artists; it is of even greater utility to doctors," for "exterior forms . . . manifest, through their relations with interior ones, . . . what is hidden in the depths of the body through what is visible on the surface" (Charcot and Richer, "Note sur l'anatomie," 13-14). To the extent that it gave voice not merely to past criminal episodes, but to future sins or crimes of which the subject as yet knew nothing, the language of the body was seen as possessing a prophetic, as well as an occult, quality. Thus, the woman possessed of excess facial down or anal hair was likely to attempt infanticide. As they had been for the medieval physiologist, so "uncommonly long," "voluminous," or "projecting" ears, continued in the nineteenth century to be regarded as signifiers of a "morbid character," so that "the longest ear . . . ever seen in man or woman" by Luigi Frigerio (the authority who devoted an entire study, *L'oreille externe; étude d'anthropologie criminelle* [Lyon, 1888] to the ears of the criminally insane) "was in a woman convicted of complicity in the murder of her husband: the left ear was 78 mm., the right 81 mm. (the normal being 50-60 mm.) in length. Her father, two sisters, and three cousins all possessed excessively large ears, and were all convicts" (H. Ellis, *The Criminal*, 65-69). Those with mobile features, dextrous hands, eyes "small and restless," eyebrows "thick and close," forehead "narrow and receding," and complexion "pale or yellowish, and incapable of blushing" were thieves, or potential thieves, whereas a "peculiar delicacy of the skin, an infantile aspect, and abundance of hair" betrayed the potential incendiary (83).

46. Duchenne de Boulogne, *Human Facial Expression*, 19; H. Ellis, *The Criminal*, 85.

47. Fowler, *Hereditary Descent*, 128; H. Ellis, *The Criminal*, 85.

48. Nancy Stepan, "Biological Degeneration: Races and Proper Places," in Chamberlin and Gilman, *Degeneration*, 113.

49. Georges Louis Leclerc, Comte de Buffon, cited in Morel, "Treatise on the Degenerations," 10:268. As there is a rich corpus of nineteenth-century treatises addressing the "science" of anatomizing degeneration, so there is a growing body of secondary work devoted to the topic of the semiology of degeneration. Some useful studies—both primary and secondary—include Boime, "Portraying Monomaniacs"; Chamberlin and Gilman, *Degeneration*; Chambers, *Natural History of Creation*; H. Ellis, *The Criminal*; S. L. Gilman, *Disease and Representation*; Ferri, *Criminal Sociology*; Gould, *The Mismeasure of Man*; Haley, *Healthy Body and Victorian Culture*; Leps, *Apprehending the Criminal*; Lombroso, *The Man of Ge-*

nius: Lombroso-Ferrero, *Criminal Man;* Maudsley, *Physiology and Pathology of the Mind;* Morison, *Physiognomy of Mental Diseases;* Nisbet, *Insanity of Genius;* Nordau, *Degeneration;* Pick, *Faces of Degeneration;* Sandra Siegel, "Literature and Degeneration: The Representation of 'Decadence,'" in Chamberlin and Gilman, *Degeneration,* 199-219; Stepan, "Biological Degeneration"; Talbot, *Degeneracy.*

50. The idea that "CHARACTER IS AS SHAPE," as Fowler suggested, was hardly new to the nineteenth century (*Hereditary Descent,* 127). Graeme Tytler reminds us that Aristotle paid homage in his *Physiognomonica* to those who preceded him in the study of physiognomy. Tytler's *Physiognomy in the European Novel* provides an informative history of physiognomy up to the eighteenth century, as well as a careful discussion of the subject identified in his title. Not merely the study of physiognomy, but also the tendency to establish a one-to-one correlation between physical beauty and virtue on the one hand and coarseness and villainy on the other, dates back to classical times as well. Perhaps one important difference between nineteenth-century physiognomists—who tended by and large to be anthropologists—and earlier authorities such as the eighteenth-century physiognomist Johann Caspar Lavater was that whereas the latter wrote his enormously influential *Physiognomische Fragmente* (1775-78) to remind his readers that, having been made in the image of God, man was worthy of being studied and understood and above all loved (Tytler, *Physiognomy in the European Novel,* 65), the Lombrosos and Nordaus sought to identify, isolate, and eliminate undesirable, "inferior" groups who, possessing the earmarked simian features of anthropoid ancestors well adapted to the world they occupied, represented a contaminating presence in a civilized world already caught up in what Nordau termed "a twilight mood" (43).

51. Actually, Lombroso had also described an intermediary character, one, as Stephen J. Gould reminds us, that allowed him to protect his theories against potential falsification by suggesting that "a man with stigmata performs [criminal acts] by innate nature, a man without stigmata by force of circumstances"; thus, "murder might be a deed of the lowest ape in a human body or of the most upright cuckold overcome by justified rage" (Gould, *The Mismeasure of Man,* 132).

52. Lombroso, "Atvism and Evolution," 42.

53. Lombroso, *The Man of Genius,* 4 (hereinafter cited in the text).

54. *Dictionary of Philosophy and Psychology,* s.v. "genius," 1:410.

55. Melville, *Pierre,* 1406-7; Nisbet, *Insanity of Genius,* 56; Darwin, entry 226e, "Notebook C," in *Charles Darwin's Notebooks, 1836-1844,* 311.

56. Maudsley, *Physiology and Pathology of the Mind,* 200-201.

57. Ibid., 251.

58. H. Ellis, *The Criminal,* 190.

59. Doyle, "The Final Problem," in *The Complete Sherlock Holmes,* 470-72.

60. Rolfe, *Chronicles of the House of Borgia,* 143. Rolfe's guise as anthropologist attests to the influence exercised by such works as Lombroso's *The Man of Genius* and Nordau's *Degeneration,* the latter of which ran through seven impressions before the end of 1895, the year in which it was translated into English, having first made its appearance on the Continent in 1893 with the title *Entartüng.* Although Rolfe's language retains vestiges of phrenological discourse, his familiarity with the appropriate terminology—exemplified in his reference to "the physiognomy of the mattoid"—illustrates the way in which "scientific" discourse was absorbed into a popular culture, appropriated by those who might not, in fact, have had a firsthand knowledge of or even a clear understanding of the ideas they were remaking into "art." The piquant irony of his adopting such an idiom was perhaps not lost on Rolfe, who, with his florid literary style and homosexual inclinations, must surely have guessed that Nordau would have found in him a perfect example of the degenerate.

61. Morel, "Treatise on the Degenerations," 10:232.

62. August Schleicher, "On the Significance of Language for the Natural History of Man" (1865), reprinted in Koerner, *Linguistics and Evolutionary Theory,* 79.

63. The statement that the "word is the thought incarnate" is taken from Müller, *The Science of Language,* 1:527; Müller, "Darwin's Philosophy of Language," 529.

64. Scott, "On the Supernatural in Fictitious Composition," 81, 74, 78, 81, 97.

65. Ainsworth, review of *Moby-Dick*. To the author himself, interestingly enough, Ainsworth attributed (long before Stevenson, of course) a Jekyllean schizophrenia, describing him as a man capable, when "he pleases," of writing in a "lucid, straightforward, hearty, and unaffected" style, yet unaccountably producing an offensive "rhodomontade." Surely Herman Melville "is two single gentlemen rolled into one," he announced; "the one sensible, sagacious, observant, graphic, and producing admirable matter—the other maundering, drivelling, subject to paroxysms, cramps, and total collapse." An anonymous reviewer for *The Southern Quarterly Review* had a similar reaction, suggesting that Melville's "ravings" might be justification for "a writ *de lunatico* against all the parties" involved in the publication of the book. "Melville's *Moby Dick*."

66. Macaulay, "Horace Walpole," in *Critical and Historical Essays*, 2:98-99; Arthur Symons, *Confessions*, 2. It is worth noting that *Confessions* is an autobiographical reminiscence charting Symons's own descent into madness and is thus his attempt "to trace, to retrace" in language the lineaments of his pathology as a means of "[defining and divining] the way in which one's madness begins" (1).

67. Pater, "Style," in *Three Major Texts*, 412.

68. Ibid., 396, 408.

69. Barbara Spackman develops something of the same analogy in her discussion of the critical gestures embedded in nineteenth-century medicolegal/anthropological studies. "Something speaks through the subject," she writes of the text that serves not as "a work of sign production" but as "a set of sympoms": "but in the pre-Freudian texts that are the most ambitious proponents of [the rhetoric of sickness], it is not language, not yet the unconscious. Behind the disturbed syntax, the disturbing contents of decadent texts, there hides a diseased, degenerate body." *Decadent Genealogies*, 1.

70. Hollywood gave us a very vivid example of the "Gothicizing" of medical discourse—or, conversely, of the "authenticating" of the Gothic—in James Whale's 1931 version of *Frankenstein* starring Boris Karloff. At one point in the film, "Henry" Frankenstein's former professor of anatomy is lecturing on the human brain. On the table before him are two preserved specimens, one a "normal" brain, the other abnormal. The abnormal brain, he tells his students, distinguishes itself by a "scarcity of convolutions and a degeneration of the frontal lobe" (material derived, however indirectly, from nineteenth-century sociomedical texts). He then tells his students that the person to whom the brain belonged had been a very brutal criminal. (Mary Shelley's novel, we might note, offers a discussion neither of the shape of criminal brains nor of the provenance of the monster's brain.) The abnormal brain finds its way into the monster's head, and the audience is thus alerted to the fact that the constructed man's monstrousness is criminal. Like Lombroso's criminal who was "born" to his destiny, the monster's unwilled but gross deformity constitutes at least some part of his crime. Given his fatal heritage, he engages in very violent behavior, even when he is trying to show affection, as when he playfully tosses the little girl Marie to her death in the lake. Of particular interest here, however, is the correlation—in the movie, at least—between the monster's monstrosity and that of the doctor. Even allowing for individual taste, the doctor, played by Colin Clive, is far better looking (in a pale, emaciated sort of way) than is his misbegotten son. We are first introduced to the doctor not in person, but through a glossy photo (showing only his head) perched on a desk: he is striking a studio pose, head pertly angled, hair slicked back, features set, calm and authoritative. When the anatomist confronts him in his laboratory, however, and charges that he is "crazy," Frankenstein answers that he will show his mentor "just how crazy" he is, and he points to the reconstructed man. What he intends to prove, of course, is that he is not crazy at all but brilliant; and his creation *does* provide overwhelming evidence of his unquestioned genius, which in this case just happens to be synonymous with criminal insanity. He is just as criminal as the monster he creates—in fact, more so, but we would never know it by looking at his picture.

71. Nordau's application of Lombroso's "scientific" semiology to the realm of aesthetics, and to Decadent style in particular, might at first seem misgauged. The Decadent style is

factice, referring, in Gayatri Spivak's words, "not to a world of nature but always to a world already made into artifice" ("Decadent Style," 229). The traits Nordau ascribes to Decadent poetry—"richness" of rhyme and a "brilliant" style, for example—attest to a reflexivity and conscious craftsmanship denied the criminal born of a nature that, according to H.G. Wells's Urthred, in *Men Like Gods* (1923), had "made [all her children] by accident . . . without rhyme or reason" (in *The Works of H.G. Wells*, 28:107). Accident and nonconsciousness are precisely what are occluded in the baroque embellishments that constitute Decadent style. There would seem to be a disjuncture between the body of the ornate work of art whose central idea is vested in what Bagehot saw as "the richest and most involved clothing that it will admit" and the organic body inscribed not by the criminal imprisoned therein but by a natural process taking no heed of any measure of excellence ("Wordsworth, Tennyson, and Browning," in *Literary Studies*, 2:351). Yet the born criminal was not always barred from representing his own degeneracy. In what were consideed to be "the more severe and incurable cases of mental degeneration" (H. Ellis, *The Criminal*, 107), some criminals were given to tattooing (surely an act of pure genius on the part of those instinctively mimicking nature in recreating the body—quite literally—as a multilayered text, the self writing the body representing the self). Seeing the *"evolution of culture"* as being *"synonymous with the removal of ornament from objects of daily use,"* the Austrian architect Adolf Loos wrote in 1908 that the "modern man who tattoos himself is a criminal or a degenerate." Thus, if "a tattooed person dies at liberty, it is only that he died a few years before he committed a murder" ("Ornament and Crime," 100). Conversely, even when consciously undertaken, stylistic embellishment and ornamentation, involving either the painting of the body or what Bagehot called the rouging of literature ("the rouge of ornate literature" that "excites" the eye ["Wordsworth, Tennyson, and Browning," in *Literary Studies*, 2:355]), were taken to represent what Loos insisted be understood as a "backwardness or even a degenerative tendency" ("Ornament and Crime," 101), although Lombroso had earlier drawn a connection between artifice, cosmetics, and degeneracy when he noted that Baudelaire's insanity manifested itself in the simile that the poet assigned to his discovery of the sublime in the artificial: "'like the rouge which enhances the beauty of a handsome woman'" (325). Criminality and corruption are highlighted in the French art critic Félix Fénéon's description of the sentence that Huysmans "discovered" in *A rebours* (1884): "a virulent sentence, threatening and without underside, tattooed with savage metaphors, apt to give birth to nauseating, dense and tumultuous things" (Fénéon, *Petit bottin des lettres et des arts*, in *Oeuvres plus que complètes*, 2:543).

72. Bagehot, "Wordsworth, Tennyson, and Browning," in *Literary Studies*, 2:380.

73. Bourget, *Essais de psychologie contemporaine*, 1:12.

74. Nietzsche, *The Will to Power*, 25, 27.

75. Théophile Gautier, "Une Notice," 17.

76. Ibid.

77. Poe, preface to *Tales of the Grotesque and Arabesque*, in *Collected Works*, 2:474; Charles Baudelaire, "Edgar Allan Poe, His Life and His Works," *Revue de Paris*, Mar.-April 1852, cited in *Fatal Destinies*, 15. Lombroso's point is that in insisting upon his own rationality, Poe was in fact betraying his insanity, and yet Poe had anticipated Lombroso many years earlier in "The Tell-Tale Heart" (1843), in which the narrator's constant allusions to his own sanity provide the clearest indication of his insanity: "You fancy me mad. Madmen know nothing. But you should have seen me. You should have seen how wisely I proceeded—with what caution—with what foresight—with what dissimulation I went to work! I was never kinder to the old man than during the whole week before I killed him" (*Collected Works*, 3:792). Both men, in turn, provide us with the historical and cultural backdrop against which to judge Henry James's post-Freudian suggestion that the "artist is present in every page of every book from which he sought so assiduously to eliminate himself" (cited in Edel, *Writing Lives*, 140).

78. R.B. Gordon, *Ornament, Fantasy, and Desire*, 4.

79. Spackman, *Decadent Genealogies*, 12. George Bernard Shaw reached this very

conclusion in his defense of the sanity of art, a characteristically vigorous response to Nordau's attack on Oscar Wilde and the Decadents in general, in which, even granting that he could "prove Nordau to be an elephant on more evidence than he has brought to prove that our greatest men are degenerate lunatics," Shaw credited the "splenetic pamphleteer" with being "a vigorous and capable journalist, . . . a stronger clearer-headed man than ninety-nine out of a hundred of his critics, . . . a born theorist, reasoner, and busybody; therefore able, without insight, or even any very remarkable industry . . . to produce a book which has made a very considerable impression on the artistic ignorance of Europe and America" (*The Sanity of Art*, 92, 100, 64). Judged by his own criteria, Nordau's own obsessive analysis of the Decadent genius, as well as his own rhetorical excess, is symptomatic of the very degeneracy he seeks to isolate.

80. Charles Baudelaire, cited in "A Note on Paul Bourget," in H. Ellis, *Views and Reviews*, 53; Saltus, "An Answer," in *Honey and Gall*, 205-6.

81. Gautier, "Une Notice," 17.

82. T.S. Eliot, "Baudelaire," in *Selected Essays*, 375.

83. Symons, "Decadent Movement," 859.

84. Vicaire, "'Vie d'Adoré Floupette,' par Marius Tapora, Pharmacien de 2ᵉ classe," in *Les déliquescences*, 39.

85. Kingcaid, *Neurosis and Narrative*, 13.

86. Lévy, *Le roman "gothique" anglais*, 602.

87. Ramsay MacDonald, cited in Stone, *Europe Transformed 1878-1919*, 15; Huxley, "Prolegomena," in *Evolution and Ethics*, 66-67.

88. Huxley, "Prolegomena," in *Evolution and Ethics*, 102.

89. Huxley, *Evolution and Ethics*, 143.

90. Lovecraft, *Supernatural Horror in Literature*, 15. A neoclassical precursor to—and an indirect source for—Lovecraft's conception of the "suspension of . . . those fixed laws of Nature" is book 4 of Alexander Pope's *The Dunciad*, which contains a meditation on poetic and intellectual Decadence in neoclassical society. The final lines of "The Triumph of Dulness" describe the flight of "*Wit*," "*Art*," "*Truth*," "*Philosophy*," "*Mathematics*," "*Religion*," and "*Morality*," at the "felt approach" of "*Night* Primaeval" and "*Chaos* old!" The apocalyptic ending of Pope's poem, in which "CHAOS! is restor'd" and "Universal Darkness buries All" (book 4, lines 630-56, in *Poetry and Prose of Alexander Pope* [Boston: Houghton Mifflin, 1969], 377-78), anticipates the similarly somber conclusion of Poe's "The Conqueror Worm" (1843), which closes with the descent of a curtain—"a funeral pall"—upon a tragedy entitled "Man," the hero of which is the eponymous Conqueror Worm. Poe's poem in turn contains the germ of what would eventually become Lovecraft's Cthulhu Mythos. Technologically advanced but malevolent entities who inhabited earth before man, the "Old Ones," or ancient gods, of the Cthulhu Mythos seek to reclaim the earth, from which they have been banished. We can trace a direct line of descent through these various works that address the related ideas of cultural decadence, the impending destruction of civilized society, and the imminent extinction of humanity. The difference, perhaps, between the later pieces and their precursors rests in the degree to which scientific discourse centering on degeneration theory, uniformitarianism, and the dissipation of energy, for example, lent an "authority" to ideas otherwise chimerical.

91. Hodgson, *The Night Land*, 44-45.

92. Müller, "Darwin's Philosophy of Language," 525.

93. Edgar Allan Poe, preface to *Tales of the Grotesque and Arabesque*, in *Collected Works*, 2:473; Gautier, "Une Notice," 17.

94. Lovecraft, "Pickman's Model," in *Best of H.P. Lovecraft*, 43.

95. Hogarth, *The Analysis of Beauty*, 26. We can see both men fixing on the associative quality of lines, a notion that the French aesthetician M. Charles Blanc further pursued, speculating that "straight or curved, horizontal or vertical, parallel or diverging, all lines have a secret rapport with feeling *[le sentiment]*. In the spectacles of the world as in the human figure, in painting as in architecture, the right lines respond to a sentiment *[un sentiment]* of

austerity and of force, and can give to a composition where they are repeated an aspect grave, imposing, rigid" (*Grammaire des arts du dessin*, 536).

96. Darwin, *Expression of the Emotions*, 8-9, 304. Ellis commented on a related occurrence of "an unfavorable impression" that may be triggered by one's proximity to a criminal; worse still is the "revealing glance" that unmasks the criminality of one "already familiar." One's response, according to Ellis, is part "of the organized experiences of the race," which, when subject to "intellectual control," may serve as "legitimate guides to conduct" (H. Ellis, *The Criminal*, 78-79).

97. Duchenne de Boulogne, *Human Facial Expression*, 89-92; the term "muscle of fright" is also cited in Darwin, *Expression of the Emotions*, 298.

98. Darwin, *Expression of the Emotions*, 78. Significantly, Darwin puts with his own portrayal of maternal grief another description of feminine grief that he draws from a novel (*Miss Marjoribanks* [1866]) by Margaret Oliphant, in his estimation an "excellent observer"— and one, no doubt, entirely uninterested in sentimentalizing for her audience the grief of "a girl at the sudden death of her father" (80).

99. Stevenson, "On Some Technical Elements of Style in Literature," in *Works*, 15:269.

100. Wilde, "The Decay of Lying," in *Intentions*, in *The Complete Works*, 5:18.

101. Pater, "Style," in *Three Major Texts*, 411, 397.

102. Pater, "Leonardo da Vinci," in *Three Major Texts*, 144-45.

103. Huysmans, "Le Monstre," in *L'art moderne/certains*, 388.

104. In his behavior, if not in his description of himself as a "Realist," Wilde's character serves as a spokesperson for the author himself, who insisted that his story be seen as "an essay on decorative art" that "re-acts against the crude brutality of plain realism," its perfection standing as its excuse for its alleged "poisonousness" (reply to the editor of the *Daily Chronicle*, July 2, 1890, reprinted in Mason, *Oscar Wilde*, 52, 61).

105. Tennyson, "Merlin and Vivien," in *Idylls of the King*, 316; H. James, *Turn of the Screw*, 11:83-84; Stevenson, *The Strange Case of Dr. Jekyll and Mr. Hyde*, in *Works*, 6:44.

106. G. Eliot to John Blackwood, Nov. 5, 1873, in *The George Eliot Letters*, 5:455; John Wordsworth to Walter Pater, Mar. 17, 1873, in Watson, *Life of Bishop John Wordsworth*, 90.

107. Wilde to Leonard Smithers, Nov. 19, 1896, in *Letters of Oscar Wilde*, 676; Ellmann, *Oscar Wilde*, 509-10.

108. Chambers, "The Yellow Sign," in *The King in Yellow*, 18.

109. Buckler, *"Picture of Dorian Gray,"* 158.

110. In this respect, Wilde's portrait might fruitfully be compared with Hugo's *Dentelles*. Both are psychically accurate texts in which patterns of thought—neither re-produced, nor re-created, nor re-visioned—are captured at the moment of their inception and may be said, in fact, to have been conceived or recognized at precisely the moment in which they appear upon the paper. By their very nature, Hugo's imprints forestall the urge to preconceptualize ideas; they encourage instead a freely associative engagement with an artifact that comes into existence before its creator attempts to discover meaning in its emerging shapes and structures.

111. Everprone to self-plagiarization, Wilde wrote in reply to the *Scots Observer*'s harsh review (July 5, 1890) that those endowed with "artistic instincts will see [his novel's] beauty," whereas "the unclean will see in it their own shame": "It will be to each man what he is himself. It is the spectator, and not life, that art really mirrors" (Wilde, reply to editor, in Mason, *Oscar Wilde*, 70).

112. One might compare Dorian's desire to "see the change taking place before his very eyes" to that of the doctor in Conrad's *Heart of Darkness* who knows that it would be "'interesting for science to watch the mental changes of individuals on the spot'" but who, recognizing the unlikelihood of his ever having such an experience, contents himself with measuring the crania of the agents who go to the Congo as a means of approximating the changes that "'take place inside'" (15).

113. *Aut Diabolus aut Nihil*, 46, 54, 56-57. "Aut Diabolus aut Nihil" was originally published in *Blackwood's Magazine* 144 (Oct. 1888): 475-99 and later appeared in *Littell's Living*

Age 64 (Nov. 3, 1888): 270-86 and in *Eclectic Magazine* 48 (Dec. 1888): 721-39. Its author, X.L. (the nom de plume of author Julian Osgood Field), felt the need to defend himself against the charge of having produced a roman à clef, offering in the preface (written in 1894 when the story appeared in book form) "an emphatic and unqualified denial to the rumour that the characters in this little drama are portraits" of his intimate friends, although the work concludes with a quite striking representation of "the Prince of Evil"—"the only real portrait which it contains" (vii, ix).

114. Barbey D'Aurevilly, *The She-Devils (Les Diaboliques)*, xvii-xviii.

115. Huysmans, "Instrumentum Diaboli," 27, 28, 37.

116. Wilde, "Pen, Pencil, and Poison," in *Intentions*, in *The Complete Works*, 5:72.

117. Wilde to Ralph Payne, Feb. 12, 1894, in *Letters of Oscar Wilde*, 352; Sybil Montgomery Douglas, Lady Queensberry, to Alfred Douglas, quoted in Ellmann, *Oscar Wilde*, 414. In "The Critic as Artist as Wilde" (in *Golden Codgers*), Richard Ellmann discusses, with his signal elegance and erudition, Wilde's treatment of the artist/critic as criminal.

118. Joyce to Stanislaus Joyce, Aug. 19, 1906, in *Selected Letters*, 96. Not finding it "very difficult to read between the lines," Joyce could imagine "the capital which Wilde's prosecuting counsel made out of certain parts of" the novel.

119. Justice Charles, reprinted in Mason, *Oscar Wilde*, 136; "On 'Dorian Gray,'" *Daily Chronicle*, June 30, 1890, reprinted in Mason, *Oscar Wilde*, 55.

120. Wilde, "The Critic as Artist," in *Intentions*, in *The Complete Works*, 5:186.

121. Wilde, "The Decay of Lying," in ibid., 5:13; Wilde, "The Critic as Artist," in ibid., 5:194; Wilde, "Pen, Pencil, and Poison," in ibid., 5:100; Wilde, "The Soul of Man under Socialism," in *The Complete Works*, 10:29-30.

122. Wilde to the Home Secretary, July 2, 1896, in *Letters of Oscar Wilde*, 402.

123. Herford, *An Alphabet of Celebrities*; Sidney Colvin to D.S. MacColl, July 27, 1914, cited in Ellmann, *Oscar Wilde*, 177.

124. "A Study in Puppydom," reprinted in Mason, *Oscar Wilde*, 21; the *Daily Chronicle* on "Dorian Gray," reprinted in ibid., 55; Haley, *Healthy Body and Victorian Culture*, 66.

125. Ruskin, "Traffic," in *Works of John Ruskin*, 18:434, 443.

126. Wilde, reprinted in Mason, *Oscar Wilde*, 31; Pater, review of *Dorian Gray*, reprinted in ibid., 121. Nizida, the author of "'The Picture of Dorian Gray': A Spiritualistic Review," similarly urged eaders that the "lesson taught by Mr. Oscar Wilde's powerful story" be "not *believed* merely, but accepted as a literal fact, a mysterious verity in the life of a human being" (reprinted in ibid., 95).

127. Wells, *Story of a Great Schoolmaster*, in *The Works of H.G. Wells*, 24:320.

128. Wilde to Mrs. Allhusen, [early 1890], in *Letters of Oscar Wilde*, 255.

129. Pater remarked that *Dorian Gray* "turns on that very old theme; old because based on some inherent experience or fancy of the human brain, of a double life: of Döppelgänger—" (review of *Dorian Gray*, reprinted in Mason, *Oscar Wilde*, 123).

130. Borges, "About Oscar Wilde," in *Other Inquisitions, 1937-1962*, 79.

131. Dorian Gray describes the style of the yellow book that Lord Henry gives him as a "curious jewelled style, vivid and obscure at once, full of *argot* and of archaisms, of technical expressions and of elaborate paraphrases, that characterizes the work of some of the finest artists of the French school of *Symbolistes*. There were in it metaphors as monstrous as orchids, and as subtle in colour. . . . The heavy odour of incense seemed to cling about its pages and to trouble the brain. The mere cadence of the sentences, the subtle monotony of their music, so full as it was of complex refrains and movements elaborately repeated, produced in the mind of the lad . . . a form of reverie, a malady of dreaming" (141).

132. Huysmans, *Against Nature*, 199.

133. Chambers, "The Yellow Sign," in *The King in Yellow*, 18; Müller, *The Science of Language*, 2:648.

134. Pater, "Leonardo da Vinci," in *Three Major Texts*, 150.

2. Walter de la Mare's "A: B: O."

1. De la Mare, "A Revenant," in *The Wind Blows Over*, 177.
2. De la Mare, "Edgar Allan Poe," in *Private View*, 194-95.
3. Charles Baudelaire, cited in H. Ellis, *Views and Reviews*, 52-53.
4. Charles Baudelaire, preface to *Histoires Extraordinaires*, cited in *Fatal Destinies*, 45, 60. Baudelaire, the first to produce serious critical studies of Poe's work, began "Notes Nouvelles sur Edgar Poe," his prefatory essay to his second translation of Poe's stories, *Nouvelles Histoires Extraordinaires* (1857), with a section entitled "Littérature de décadence," thus combining two of his favorite topics. Henry James intended to slight both parties when he suggested that Baudelaire had appointed Poe as his "metaphysician" ("Charles Baudelaire," in Miller, *Theory of Fiction*, 306), whereas Nordau claimed that Baudelaire so admired Poe because, as a "degenerate subject," he necessarily "felt himself attracted in the characteristic fashion by other degenerate minds, mad or depraved, and appreciated, . . . above all authors, the gifted but mentally-deranged Edgar Poe" (286).
5. Walter de la Mare, introduction to *They Walk Again*, 9.
6. Charles Baudelaire, preface to *Histoires Extraordinaires*, cited in *Fatal Destinies*, 49; John Ruskin, "The Mountain Gloom," in *Works of John Ruskin*, 6:396.
7. De la Mare buried his "A: B: O." well, and the story's publication history remains something of a mystery. De la Mare was at first unreceptive to Wagenknecht's proposal that he consider reprinting the *Cornhill Magazine* stories with which "his career as fictionist may be said properly to have begun." In the introduction to *Eight Tales*, Wagenknecht recalls that his friend's initial reaction to the suggestion "was that he could not possibly sanction such ghoulish proceedings under any circumstances" (Wagenknecht, introduction to de la Mare, *Eight Tales*, ix). Wagenknecht cites there the *Cornhill Magazine* as the source of the story but does not give a date of publication, as he does for the seven other tales included in the collection (xiii). "A: B: O." was not in fact published in the *Cornhill Magazine*, however, nor is it to be found in any of the periodicals that were de la Mare's favorite repositories for his early stories. During a 1989 telephone conversation with Wagenknecht, I learned that de la Mare had provided his long-time friend and correspondent either with information concerning the location of the story or else with the manuscript itself. Wagenknecht could no longer remember many of the details, and the manuscript itself, if in fact he had it, seems to have been lost or destroyed. The story has since been republished in Jack Sullivan's 1977 anthology of English ghost stories, *Lost Souls*.
8. John Buchan, "Prefatory," in *Scholar Gipsies*.
9. Walter de la Mare, "A: B: O.," in *Eight Tales*, 97 (hereinafter cited in the text).
10. Long a friend and correspondent of Sir Thomas Browne, Dugdale drew upon Browne's "vast reading" as a resource for his *History of Imbanking and Drayning* (1662) and occasionally sent Browne such curiosities as he thought might prove of interest, as, for example, "one of the Bones of that fish, wch [sic] was taken up by Sr Robert Cotton, in digging a pond at the skirt of Conington downe" (Dugdale to Dr. Browne, Nov. 17, 1658, letter 194, in Browne, *Letters*, 337).
11. Hawthorne, *American Notebooks*, 242-43.
12. Wells, "Story of the Stone Age," in *Famous Short Stories*, 644.
13. The chances that de la Mare found his phrase "wretched abortion" buried in the pages of a radical newspaper seem remote, but it is not entirely impossible that he read the pamphlet *Newspaper Warfare! The Grand Ink Battle between Figaro and Reynold's Newspaper* (1872), recounting a radical newspaper's having thus described the dead infant son of the princess of Wales; in any event, the story itself is too compellingly coincidental to pass over entirely. The funeral services held to commemorate the death of the son born to the princess of Wales in April of 1871 condemned as a "miserable mockery" the "interring with royal funeral ceremony a piece of skin and bone, grandiloquently called 'Prince,' not twenty-four hours old"—and "to augment the folly of the entire proceedings the Court goes into mourning for the loss of the wretched abortion" (cited in Jarrett, *The Sleep of Reason*, 88).

14. "The Peach in Brandy" is still a difficult tale to swallow, as it was even for Walpole's less squeamish contemporaries. "You had reported to me . . . that you wrote a great deal, and that you thought only in writing, and I see that it is in writing that you don't think": this the complaint of Madame du Deffand, one of the few people—all intimate friends—whom Walpole had acquainted with the themes that he was introducing into his *Hieroglyphic Tales*. Claiming "to prefer entirely" Walpole's letters, du Deffand considered the three tales that he had described to her to be the products "des délires ou des rêves" [of deliriu or of dreams]—a response that seems appropriate when one further considers that Walpole decided that the first person to read his story ought to be his friend John Fitzpatrick, second earl of Upper Ossory, whose wife Anne had miscarried of twins shortly before "The Peach in Brandy" was written (du Deffand to Horace Walpole, April 3, 1772, in *Horace Walpole's Correspondence*, 5:215). Walpole may have known his audience, however: although to our own rather more scrupulous sensibilities the story may lack in taste and refinement, it may not, as Kenneth W. Gross points out, have been seen by its eighteenth-century audience as being in quite such questionable taste since "metaphors of sexual perversion, mutilation, and miscegenation [were] part of the inherited language of satire and not necessarily evidence of an aberrant imagination" (introduction to *Hieroglyphic Tales*, nos. 212-13, x).

15. Beardsley to Leonard Smithers, Mar. 7, 1896, letter 17, in Beardsley, *Letters*.

16. Pater, "Leonard da Vinci" in *Three Major Texts*, 138. The cryptic reference to the "procured . . . abortion," with its several possible meanings, is contained in a postscript to a letter from Beardsley to his sometime publisher Leonard Smithers ("'the most learned erotomaniac in Europe'" whose name, according to Pearsall, Beardsley "made" [*The Worm in the Bud*, 390]): "All right about the canary. I have procured an abortion. Good old Collins managed it for me" (to Leonard Smithers, Nov. 19, 1896, letter 84, in *Letters*).

17. Kuryluk, *Salome and Judas*, 147. Kuryluk reminds us that in the printed, "harmless" version of Beardsley's *Toilet of Salomé*, the more explicitly sexualized detail of what was in fact the first version of the drawing (misleadingly titled *The Toilet of Salomé II* [fig. 21]), the androgynous attendants and the statuette of an embryon seated before a selection of books— of which only two titles, *Les fleurs du mal* and *La terre*, are discernible—has been replaced by books carefully foregrounded, their titles legibly printed. In other words, what is coded in the titles of the expurgated version of the drawing is more explicitly represented in the original version, in which the embryon serves as the correlative to and the consequence of the activities that are the subject of the writings of the Marquis de Sade as well as such works as Emile Zola's *Nana*, Paul Verlaine's *Fêtes galantes*, Abbé Prévost's *Manon Lescaut*, and Apuleius's *The Golden Ass*.

18. Beardsley, *Under the Hill*, 37-39.

19. Pearsall, *The Worm in the Bud*, 52, 372, 389. See also Ashbee, *Forbidden Books*, which is a compendium of the three lengthy bibliographies of erotica—*Index librorum prohibitorum* (1877), *Centuria librorum absconditorum* (1879), and *Catena librorum tacendorum* (1885)—assembled by the noted Victorian erotologist and nineteenth-century bibliophile, Henry Spencer Ashbee. Of the roughly sixty-seven miscellaneous entries included in this volume and randomly culled from Ashbee's bibliographies, nearly one-third represent reprints published by "W. Dugdale"—a suggestive (if unscientific) indication of Dugdale's preeminence among purveyors of pornography, and an indication as well that his name would not have been entirely unknown among the literati of the day—or among those like the young de la Mare who aspired to be thought of as such.

20. Hawthorne, *The Scarlet Letter*, 93; Dickens, *Dombey and Son*, 91, 93.

21. Zola, *Nana*, 2:126, 156, 159.

22. Grand, *The Heavenly Twins*, 301.

23. Few contemporary readers would have failed to recognize the "'small, wizened, atrophied, puny, weakly, sickly creature,' with a senile and decrepit appearance" as a syphilitic infant—the sort of being who seemed, to the author of a 1906 study of syphilology and venereal disease, to resemble nothing so much as a "monkey or a little old man" with "skin . . . flabby, wrinkled, and bistre-coloured" (Marshall, *Syphilology and Venereal Disease*, 328).

24. Homans, *Bearing the Word*, 101.

25. Wilde, *The Picture of Dorian Gray*, in *Oscar Wilde*, 74-75; Wells, *The Island of Doctor Moreau*, 89-90.

26. Stoker, *Dracula*, 394-95.

27. Wells, *The Definitive Time Machine*, 50-52.

28. Showalter, "Syphilis, Sexuality, and the Fiction of the Fin de Siècle," 95.

29. The library of Beardsley's grandfather, an army surgeon, would undoubtedly have contained Darwin's *Descent*, and, as Malcolm Easton speculates, very possibly His's embryological study, published in three volumes between 1880 and 1885 (Easton, *Aubrey and the Dying Lady*, 178-81). Beardsley may have found the prototypes for his own embryos in the second volume (1882) of His, *Anatomie menschlicher Embryonen*, which features two-month embryos approximating, in shape and development, those scattered throughout Beardsley's illustrations.

30. Müller, "Darwin's Philosophy of Language," 661; Showalter, "Syphilis, Sexuality, and the Fiction of the Fin de Siècle," 108, 98.

31. T.H. Huxley, cited in Gould, *Ontogeny and Phylogeny*, 76; Haeckel, *The History of Creation*, 1:10-11; 2:33. In a subsequent study, *The Evolution of Man*, Haeckel offers a more descriptive explanation of the concept: "the series of forms through which the Individual Organism passes during its progress from the egg cell to its fully developed state, is a brief, compressed reproduction of the long series of forms through which the animal ancestors of that organism (or the ancestral forms of its species) have passed from the earliest periods of so-called organic creation down to the present time" (1:6-7).

32. Gould, *Ontogeny and Phylogeny*, 148, 76.

33. Darwin, *Origin of Species*, 338; Darwin, *Foundations*, 42.

34. Darwin, entry 57 in "Notebook B," in *Charles Darwin's Notebooks, 1836-1844*, 351.

35. Haeckel, *The Evolution of Man*, 1:6-7; Loos, "Ornament and Crime," 100.

36. Spencer, *Education*, 106-8, 122-23.

37. Gould, *The Mismeasure of Man*, 114.

38. Tuiskon Ziller, cited in Gould, *Ontogeny and Phylogeny*, 150.

39. Chamberlain, *The Child*, 226. Havelock Ellis also devotes a section of his study of the criminal to the relationship between atavism, the arrest of development, and precocious criminality, since "there is a certain form of criminality almost peculiar to children, a form to which the term 'moral insanity' may very fairly be ascribed": "The child is naturally, by his organisation, nearer to the animal, to the savage, to the criminal, than the adult" (*The Criminal*, 211-12). With their swinish totems, talismanic shells, rhythmic, pulsing chants, wooden spears, and body paint, the boy/beasts of Golding's *Lord of the Flies* serve as a reminder that recapitulation remained a compelling metaphor even after it had been challenged and, by the midtwenties, set aside as a universal principle.

40. Darwin, *The Descent of Man*, 21:23.

41. Darwin, *The Descent of Man*, 22:624-26. Darwin noted that, in primitive man, the direction and thickness of hair on the forearms and back would serve to throw off rain (21:156-57). Chamberlain gives the name "rain-thatch" to the "growth of hair on a child's head from crown to forehead" as well as the "direction of hairs on arms," both examples of simian traits in children (Chamberlain, *The Child*, 227-28).

42. St. Armand, *The Fiction of H.P. Lovecraft*, vi.

43. Darwin, entries 78 and 79 in "Notebook C," in *Charles Darwin's Notebooks, 1836-1844*, 263-64. One might almost imagine Rudyard Kipling's having had this notebook entry before him as he composed "Bertran nd Bimi" (1891), a lesser-known story featuring an orangutan, "Bimi," which is "child und brother und opera comique all round" to the naturalist who adopts "him" (*The Phantom 'Rickshaw*, 154). The orangutan's antics are uncannily reminiscent of the human: it sleeps in a bed with sheets, smokes a cigar, eats at a table, comprehends speech, levels threats in dumb show, and has love enough for the man with whom it walks "hand in hand" to feel a murderous jealousy for the bride whom it annihilates, leaving behind "nothing that might be a woman" (154, 158).

44. Machen, "Novel of the Black Seal," in *The House of Souls*, 393; Wells, *Island of Doctor Moreau*, 99; Lovecraft, "The Dunwich Horror," in *Best of H. P. Lovecraft*, 114.

45. T.H. Huxley, "On the Relation of Man to the Lower Animals," in *Man's Place in Nature*, 80-81.

46. Wells, *The Island of Doctor Moreau*, 119.

47. Shelley, *Frankenstein*, 169.

48. Stevenson, *The Strange Case of Dr. Jekyll and Mr. Hyde*, in *Works*, 6:23, 30.

49. Chayefsky, *Altered States*, 121.

50. Foucault, *The Order of Things*, xv.

51. Ibid., xv-xvi.

52. T.H. Huxley, "On the Relation of Man to the Lower Animals," in *Man's Place in Nature*, 78-81.

53. Ibid., 78; Borges, "The Analytical Language of John Wilkins," in *Other Inquisitions, 1937-1952*, 104.

54. T.H. Huxley, "On the Relation of Man to the Lower Animals," in *Man's Place in Nature*, 54; Browne, *Religio Medici*, 24-26.

55. Browne, *Religio Medici*, 25.

56. T.H. Huxley, "Prolegomena," in *Evolution and Ethics*, 64; Browne, *Religio Medici*, 26.

57. T.H. Huxley's "Prolegomena" might be said to focus almost entirely on the various incarnations of the "constant struggle to maintain and improve, in opposition to the State of Nature, the State of Art of an organized polity," the latter being an ephemeral state enjoying at best a temporary and illusory prerogative until "the State of Nature prevails over the surface of our planet" (in *Evolution and Ethics*, 102-3).

58. Stevenson, *The Strange Case of Dr. Jekyll and Mr. Hyde*, in *Works*, 6:72.

59. Darwin, *Descent of Man*, 21:166. The tone and content of a brief but telling footnote in Havelock Ellis's *The Criminal* provides some indication of just how troubling many found Darwin's insistence upon the ubiquity (among races and types) of the presence of the cleft notch or folded-over apex discernible along the upper rim or helix of the ear. In the section of the third chapter ("Criminal Anthropology [Physical]") devoted to facial characteristics, Ellis discusses the "most common (so-called) atavistic abnormalities of the ear—*i.e.*, those most frequently and prominently seen among the anthropoid and other apes—," one of which he identifies as "the Darwinian tubercle" (*The Criminal*, 68). Though otherwise revelling in physical anomalies and deviations, Ellis specifically footnotes this term and then proceeds to take issue with those who regard the notch "as normal" and who suggest that "with a little practice it might be discovered in nearly all ears." "This may well be," Ellis concedes, "but in its distinctly marked form it can scarcely be called normal" (68).

60. Darwin, *Descent of Man*, 21:19-20.

61. Darwin, *Expression of the Emotions*, 307; Wells, *The Island of Doctor Moreau*, 88.

62. Lombroso, "Atavism and Evolution," 46, 42.

63. On this subject, Lombroso wrote that genius, "besides displaying . . . a rapidity of conception above the average, presents us with a whole series of well-marked signs of retrogressive atavism: low stature, left-handedness, sterility, sub-microcephalism, omplete callousness extending even to moral insanity, deadened sensitiveness of touch and insensibility to pain, a restricted range of vision, sometimes . . . distorted sense of hearing, and in many cases an interchange of sexual characteristics (absence of beard, &c.), above all, very commonly perverse, degenerate, or ignorant children" ("Atavism and Evolution," 46).

64. Golding, *Lord of the Flies*, 12-37.

65. Gilbert and Sullivan, *Princess Ida; or, Castle Adamant*, in *Plays of Gilbert and Sullivan*, 273.

66. H. Ellis, *The Criminal*, 86.

67. Freud, "A Difficulty in the Path of Psycho-Analysis" (1917), in *Standard Edition*, 17:140-41.

68. Freud, *Civilization and Its Discontents*, in *Standard Edition*, 21:89.

69. Ibid., 21:86.

70. Chambers, *Natural History of Creation*, 248.

71. Freud, *Civilization and Its Discontents, Standard Edition*, 21:96.

72. G. Eliot, *Daniel Deronda*, 738.

73. Guy, "The Concept of Tradition," 253. In *The Importance of Being Earnest*, a play written and staged in the same midcentury year as that in which "A: B: O." appears to have been composed, Oscar Wilde drew mocking attention to his class's almost paranoid fear of revolutionary upheaval. The otherwise unflappable Lady Bracknell—a consort battleship of smug Victorian conservatism—responds with something akin to hysteria to Jack Worthing's admission that, lacking any definitive knowledge of his parentage, he can trace his ancestry back only as far as "a somewhat large, black leather hand-bag, with handles to it" discovered in a cloakroom in Victoria Station: "To be born, or at any rate bred, in a hand-bag, whether it had handles or not, seems to me to display a contempt for the ordinary decencies of family life that reminds one of the worst excesses of the French Revolution." When told of Bunbury's death—"he was quite exploded," Algernon announces—she declares that any unfortunate man expressing an interest in "social legislation" would have been "well punished" for the "morbidity" that made him "the victim of a revolutionary outrage" (*The Importance of Being Earnest*, in *Oscar Wilde*, 495, 528).

74. Morel, "Treatise on the Degenerations," 10:136.

75. Frazer, *Psyche's Task*, 4.

76. Pater, "Coleridge," in *Three Major Texts*, 431; Hawthorne, *House of the Seven Gables*, 2.

77. All Scripture quotations are from the King James Version.

78. Butler, "An Antiquary," in *Characters* and *Passages*, 42-43.

79. Plutarch, cited in H. Ellis, *The Criminal*, 91.

80. Fowler, *Hereditary Descent*, 19, 21, 80.

81. Carlyle, *The French Revolution*, 1:31.

82. Poe, "The Gold Bug," in *Collected Works*, 3:832, 843, 827 (hereinafter cited in the text).

83. Thomas Dunn English, cited in Poe, *Collected Works*, 3:799; Poe, "The Philosophy of Composition," in *Essays and Reviews*, 14-15.

84. Poe, *Eureka*, in *Poetry and Tales*, 1342.

85. Kempton, "The Gold/Goole/Ghoul Bug," 7. Legrand may instead be one of Poe's inspired *reasoners*,

like the German astronomer Johannes Kepler, whose intuition about "the imperishable and priceless secrets of the Universe" stemmed, as Poe surmised in *Eureka*, from "the conviction resulting from *deductions* or *inductions* of which the processes were so shadowy as to have escaped his consiousness, eluded his reason, or bidden defiance to his capacity of expression" (1270).

86. Pater, "Duke Carl of Rosenmold," in *Three Major Texts*, 311.

87. *The Second Prayer-Book*, 204 (hereinafter cited in the text).

88. W. James, *Varieties of Religious Experience*, 114, 126-35.

89. Darwin, entry 56e in "Notebook D," in *Charles Darwin's Notebooks, 1836-1844*, 350-51; Browne, *Religio Medici*, 26.

90. Müller, *The Science of Language*, 1:386.

91. Pater, "Conclusion," in *Three Major Texts*, 217. Like the line from Dugdale's speech that it undoubtedly helped to shape, Pater's line is paratactical and in its own way "decadent." In his study of the man of genius, Lombroso argued that certain inequalities of style, among them "the monotonous repetition of certain words or phrases, recalling the verses of the Bible or the suras of the Koran," were themselves indicative of the "pathologic and atavistic origin of many of the literary productions of the insane" (*The Man of Genius*, 174-75). Borrowing quite directly from Lombroso, Nordau cited those books that "[plagiarize] the Gospel in form and substance" and aim "at an external resemblance to the Bible and Koran" as exemplifying the "mysticism" that was itself "a cardinal mark of degeneration" (*Degeneration*, 466, 22).

92. Pater, "Conclusion," in *Three Major Texts*, 218-19.
93. Spivak, "Decadent Style," 233.
94. De la Mare, *Private View*, viii.
95. Review of *The Shadow of Death*.
96. Sir Max Beerbohm, cited in H. Jackson, *The Eighteen Nineties*, 102.
97. De la Mare, *The Eighteen-Eighties*, vii-viii.

3. Unsealing Sense in Henry James's *The Turn of the Screw*

1. Levine, "By Knowledge Possessed," 364.
2. Haggard, *The Annotated She*, 195; Stevenson, *The Strange Case of Dr. Jekyll and Mr. Hyde*, in *Works*, 6:70.
3. Wells, *The Island of Doctor Moreau*, 203; Lovecraft, "The Haunter of the Dark," in *Best of H. P. Lovecraft*, 223.
4. Poe, "MS. Found in a Bottle" (1833), in *Collected Works*, 2:145-46.
5. Poe, "A Descent into the Maelström" (1841), in *Collected Works*, 2:589; Conrad, *Heart of Darkness*, 69.
6. Wells, *The Definitive Time Machine*, 90, 38; Poe, "A Descent into the Maelström," in *Collected Works*, 2:578, 594; Haggard, *The Annotated She*, 196; Kipling, "The Man Who Would Be King," in *The Phantom 'Rickshaw*, 63; Stoker, *Dracula*, 371.
7. Levine, "Darwin, Nature, and Victorian Narrative," 364, 368, 373.
8. Ibid. 374. One finds a modern fictionalized rendering of Levine's synthesis in A.S. Byatt, *Possession* (1990), which at one point offers a series of nested citations—Edmund Gosse's commentary upon his naturalist father Philip's blunderings (the "fairy paradise has been violated, the exquisite product of centuries of natural selection has been crushed under the rough paw of well-meaning idle-minded curiousity") buried within Professor Mortimer P. Cropper's commentary upon Randolph Henry Ash's 1859 tramp through Yorkshire ("the poet in search as he put it of 'the origins of life and the nature of generation' was unwittingly, with his crashing boots covered with liquid india-rubber, as much as with his scalpel and killing-jar, dealing death to the creatures he found so beautiful, to the seashore whose pristine beauty he helped to wreck") (269)—each of the citations reflecting the nineteenth-century preoccupation with discovery and the confederate conditions of death, killing, and repossession.
9. H. James, "Preface to *The Aspern Papers*," in *The Art of the Novel*, 172 (hereinafter designated by "Preface" and page number in the text); H. James, *Turn of the Screw*, 197-98 (hereinafter cited in the text).
10. James heaps such critical contempt upon Baudelaire (in his guise as high priest of Decadence). But for the "almost ludicrously puerile view of" evil that he presents in *Les fleurs du mal*, James suggests, Baudelaire might otherwise "have been a great poet": "'Le Mal?' we exclaim; 'you do yourself too much honour. This is not Evil; it is not the wrong; it is simply the nasty!' Our impatience is of the same order as that which we should feel if a poet, pretending to pluck 'the flowers of good,' should come and present us, as specimens, a rhapsody on plumcake and *eau de Cologne*" ("Charles Baudelaire," quoted in Miller, *Theory of Fiction*, 306). In the end, however, James did not escape the similarly searing sights that H.G. Wells fixed upon Jamesian "motives," "novels," "relations," "gambits," and "sins," "irregular or . . . hinted at": "The thing his novel is *about* is always there. It is like a church lit but without a congregation to distract you, with every light and line focused on the high altar. And on the altar, very reverently placed, intensely there, is a dead kitten, an egg-shell, a bit of string." The preponderant style that James settled upon such deracinated topics and the "tales of nothingness" that contained them Wells mocks as "leviathan retrieving pebbles. It is a magnificent but painful hippopotamus resolved at any cost, even at the cost of its dignity, upon picking up a pea which has got into a corner of its den. Most things, it insists, are beyond it, but it can, at any rate, modestly, and with an artistic singleness of mind, pick up that pea" (*Boon*, 108-10).
11. H. James, *The Complete Notebooks*, 109.

12. Hawthorne, preface to *House of the Seven Gables*, 2-3; Edgar Allan Poe, "The Philosophy of Composition," in *Essays and Reviews*, 15; Pater, "Style," in *Three Major Texts*, 403.

13. H. James, *The Complete Notebooks*, 190.

14. H. James, "Mary Elizabeth Braddon," in *Henry James Literary Criticism*, 742. In his review of *Aurora Floyd* James edges closer to a definition of terms and features of the moder reincarnation of the "beautiful lost form" that (in typically Jamesian fashion) he never entirely identifies (either in his notebook jottings, or in his various reviews, or in his prefaces). Having dismissed Ann Radcliffe's mysteries as "romances pure and simple," he goes on to explain that the "good ghost-story, to be half as terrible as a good murder-story, must be connected at a hundred points with the common objects of life." Half of the force of the best sort of ghost story, he insists, derives "from its prosaic, commonplace, daylight accessories. Less delicately terrible, perhaps, than the vagaries of departed spirits, but to the full as *interesting*, as the modern novel reader understands the word, are the numberless possible forms of human malignity" (742). His definition helps somewhat to explain the nature of the underlying motive in *The Turn of the Screw*—to reveal that unsuspected depths of horror (whether psychological or supernatural) may coexist with the commonplace and the mundane in the realm of the "real." The title of his story may embody this theme: the turning screw moves simultaneously in the horizontal plane of the real while its "point" explores the axis of horror. In the horizontal plane, much of its visible motion—the motion of the familiar—revolves around the central axis, which by nearly imperceptible degrees steadily bores more deeply into the medium it penetrates. The conceit is an aptly Jamesian one.

15. M.R. James, cited in Jack Sullivan, "Psychological, Antiquarian, and Cosmic Horror 1872-1919," in Tymn, Zahorski, and Boyer, *Horror Literature*, 251.

16. Rousseau, *Emile*, 54.

17. Arthur Schopenhauer, cited in Chamberlain, *The Child and Childhood*, 379.

18. Sutherland, *The Oxford Book of Literary Anecdotes*, 190-91.

19. Ruskin, cited in Chamberlain, *The Child and Childhood*, 379.

20. The evolutionary trail leading from Wells's Eloi to many of the creatures featured in contemporary science fiction films is littered with alien beings whose superiority is expressed neotenously: in the babyish features with which they are physiognomically encoded. Thus, although the bodies of the beings featured in Stephen Spielberg's *Close Encounters of the Third Kind* (1977) are adultlike though somewhat attenuated and streamlined, their superiority is evidenced (appropriately enough) in their hairless, exaggerated crania and wide eyes. One of their progeny (so to speak), who makes its appearance some years later in *E.T.* (1982), bears a striking resemblance to an aged baby, with its bald, bulbous cranium, its great, blinking eyes, its distended stomach, and its diminutive limbs. Stephen Jay Gould has written engagingly of the similar process of reverse ontogeny—"a true evolutionary transformation," as he calls it—that Mickey Mouse (though his "chronological age never altered") has undergone since his inception roughly sixty years ago. In "A Biological Homage to Mickey Mouse," Gould notes that the Mickey who began as a distinctly ratlike, "rambunctious, even slightly sadistic fellow . . . became progressively more juvenile in appearance" (Gould, "A Biological Homage to Mickey Mouse," in *The Panda's Thumb*, 95-97). Gould's essay is the source for my definition of the term *neoteny*.

21. Chamberlain, *The Child*, 9, 32.

22. Byatt, *Possession*, 544.

23. Plotz, "A Victorian Comfort Book," 173.

24. W.B. Clark, *Asleep in Jesus*, 28-29.

25. John Kucich, "Death Worship," 59.

26. Dickens, *Dombey and Son*, 222 (hereinafter cited in the text).

27. Holubetz, "Death-Bed Scenes," 16.

28. Michener, "Memoir," in *Prose and Poetical Works*, 11.

29. Ibid., 12-13.

30. Choate, "To his Dear Brother."

31. Wheeler, *Death and the Future Life*, 30.

32. Bronfen, *Over Her Dead Body*, 77.

33. Plotz, "A Victorian Comfort Book," 178.

34. W.B. Clark, *Asleep in Jesus*, 28-30.

35. Wells, "The Door in the Wall" in *The Door in the Wall*, 6 (hereinafter cited in the text).

36. A. Huxley, "Vulgarity in Literature," in *Music at Night*, 333-34.

37. Kucich, "Death Worship," 59; Pater, "The Child in the House" (1878),in *Three Major Texts*, 234. Hawthorne stepped close to the edge of this same abyss when, turning aside from his mother's deathbed, he saw his daughter ("little Una of the golden locks, looking very beautiful; and so full of spirit and life, that she was life itself") at play, as coincidence would have it, in a cemetery. The vision left him feeling—if only temporarily—"dark and wretched, if there were nothing beyond"; as if it had been "a fiend that created us, and measured out our existence, and not God" (Hawthorne, *The American Notebooks*, 428-29).

38. Kucich, "Death Worship," 59.

39. Holubetz, "Death-Bed Scenes," 16.

40. Bronfen suggests that the "proximity of death provokes in the dying person a succession of images from that life which is about to end, along with one's interpretations of past occurrences, one's convictions, one's advice to posterity" (*Over Her Dead Body*, 80).

41. Ibid.

42. G. Stewart, "Thresholds of the Visible," 33-34.

43. G. Eliot, *Scenes of Clerical Life*, 67.

44. Van den Abbeele, "The Scene of Enlightenment Lucidity," 14.

45. Dickens, *The Old Curiosity Shop*, 654 (hereinafter cited in the text).

46. Professor David Cody made the initial observation that James might well have drawn upon the recently published *Dracula* as a precursor text; I am grateful to him for having shared his insight with me.

47. Stoker, *Dracula*, 486 (hereinafter cited in the text).

48. Bronfen, *Over Her Dead Body*, 78.

49. Most notable is Christopher Craft's "'Kiss Me with Those Red Lips': Gender and Inversion in Bram Stoker's *Dracula*," *Representations* 8 (fall 1984): 107-33. Other relevant studies include Nina Auerbach, "Magi and Maidens: The Romance of the Victorian Freud," *Critical Inquiry* 8, no. 2 (winter 1981): 281-300; Anne Cranny-Francis, "Sexual Politics and Political Repression in Bram Stoker's *Dracula*," in *Nineteenth-Century Suspense from Poe to Conan Doyle*, ed. Clive Bloom, Brian Docherty, Jane Gibb, and Keith Shand (London: Macmillan, 1988), 64-79; Regenia Gagnier, "Evolution and Information, or Eroticism and Everyday Life, in "*Dracula* and Late Victorian Aestheticism," in *Sex and Death in Victorian Literature*, ed. Regina Barreca (Bloomington: Indiana Univ. Press, 1990), 140-57; Marjorie Howes, "The Mediation of the Feminine: Bisexuality, Homoerotic Desire, and Self-Expression in Bram Stoker's *Dracula*," *Texas Studies in Literature and Language* 30, no. 1 (1988): 104-19; Philip Martin, "The Vampire in the Looking-Glass: Reflection and Projection in Bram Stoker's *Dracula*," in *Nineteenth-Century Suspense from Poe to Conan Doyle*, 80-92; Carol A. Senf, "'Dracula': Stoker's Response to the New Woman," *Victorian Studies* 26, no. 1 (autumn 1982): 33-49; Anne Williams, "*Dracula*: Si(g)ns of the Fathers," *Texas Studies in Literature and Language* 33, no. 4 (winter 1991): 445-63.

50. Stoker's choice of term may have originated with Dickens, who, in *Our Mutual Friend* (1865), hints that Bella Wilfer's physical beauty is a truer index of her spiritual goodness than her sometimes petulant and willful statements might otherwise imply. The dying boy, Johnny, whose sickroom Bella visits, knows her only as the "boofer lady"; he bequeaths a "kiss for the boofer lady" (382, 386). By the time Stoer introduces his variation of the epithet, such "bloofer" ladies as Lucy Westenra bring not aid and succor but infection and death.

51. Lombroso, *The Man of Genius*, 15-16.

52. Sandra Siegel, "Literature and Degeneration: The Representation of 'Decadence,'" in Chamberlin and Gilman, *Degeneration*, 202.

53. Wilde, *The Importance of Being Earnest*, in *Oscar Wilde*, 501; Ruskin, *Proserpina*, vol. 1, in *Works of John Ruskin*, 25:264.

54. Gustave Flaubert, cited in Turquet-Milnes, *The Influence of Baudelaire*, 67.

55. Examples in Victorian literature of such petrified immobilization abound. Browning's duchess, for example, is doomed perpetually to look "as if she were alive," while his bishop of Saint Praxed's Church feverishly contemplates the "great smooth marbly limbs" of his mistresses, whose charms he recalls in "marble's language." There is *Jane Eyre*'s Miss Temple, whose "face, naturally pale as marble," appears to assume in Mr. Brocklehurst's presence "the coldness and fixity of that material"—"her mouth closed as if it would have required a sculptor's chisel to open it, and her brow settled . . . into petrified severity"— although her pupil, who seems bounded by such immobilizing men, discovers at Thornfield the company of a man who does not leave her feeling "petrified" (Brontë, *Jane Eyre*, 73, 317). Then there is Edith Dombey's husband, who, "being a good deal in the statue way himself," delights to see his wife sit "like a statue" at her wedding feast (Dickens, *Dombey and Son*, 481-82); Gwendolyn Harleth, who, looking "like a statue into which a soul of Fear had entered," assumes in the context of a *tableau vivant* a role she will perform more realistically in the company of her husband (G. Eliot, *Daniel Deronda*, 54); and Trilby, who in Svengali's mesmerizing company looks "dazed and stupefied, as in a waking dream" (Du Maurier, *Trilby*, 372).

56. Poe, "The Man of the Crowd," in *Collected Works*, 2:506.

57. Conrad, *Heart of Darkness*, 25.

58. Ibid., 35, 29.

59. Pater, "Leonardo da Vinci," in *Three Major Texts*, 149; Conrad, *Heart of Darkness*, 57.

60. De Quincey, "System of the Heavens as Revealed by Lord Rosse's Telescopes," in *Essays in Philosophy*, 232-36.

61. Ruskin, *Modern Painters*, vol. 4, in *Works of John Ruskin*, 6:90.

62. Ibid., 6:89.

63. W.B. Clark, *Asleep in Jesus*, 19; Ruskin, *Modern Painters*, vol. 4, in *Works of John Ruskin*, 6:88.

64. De Quincey, "System of the Heavens as Revealed by Lord Rosse's Telescopes," in *Essays in Philosophy*, 238-39.

4. Articulating the Dead

1. H. James to Vernon Lee, April 27, 1890, in *Henry James Letters*, 3:277.

2. Ibi., 3:276; Lee, *Hauntings*, xi.

3. Lee herself eventually came to doubt the motives underlying his various "exchanges" with her, suspecting James of having found in her person as well as in her ideas his sources for characters and themes of his own fictions. If for no other reason (though she felt there were many more), his veiled allusion to her half-brother Eugene Lee-Hamilton (the suppressed subject of the passive-voice construction—"named to me"—thus indirectly introduced as his source of information concerning the model for Jeffrey Aspern) served as evidence of the material his association with her had afforded him. For the history and analysis concerning the "feud" between Vernon Lee and her once admired Henry James, see Merete Licht, "Henry James's Portrait of a Lady: Vernon Lee in *The Princess Casamassima*," in *A Literary Miscellany Presented to Eric Jacobsen*, ed. Graham D. Caie and Holger Nørgaard (Copenhagen: University of Copenhagen, 1988), 16:285-303; Adeline R. Tintner, "Fiction is the Best Revenge: Portraits of Henry James by Four Women Writers," *Turn-of-the-Century Women* 2, no. (winter 1985): 42-49; and Carl J. Weber, "Henry James and His Tiger Cat," *PMLA* 68, no. 5 (Sept. 1953): 672-87.

4. Brooks, "Notes on Vernon Lee," 456.

5. Shaw, "A Political Contrast," 758; Brooks, "Notes on Vernon Lee," 456.

6. Shaw, "A Political Contrast," 758.

7. H. James to William James, Jan. 20, 1893, in *Henry James Letters*, 3:402. James suggested to Thomas Sargeant Perry that although Lee was not *"great,"* she was nonetheless "a most astounding young female" possessed of "a monstrous cerebration" (H. James to T.S. Perry, Sept. 28, 1884, quoted in Gunn, *Vernon Lee*, 103).

8. Symonds to Henry Graham Dakyns, Nov. 27, 1882, letter 1308, Symonds to Violet Paget (Vernon Lee), April 4, 1884, letter 1382, in Symonds, *Letters*, 2:792, 898.

9. Max Beerbohm, cited in Gunn, *Vernon Lee*, 3.

10. Browning, "Inapprehensiveness," in *The Poems*, 2:886-87; Edith Wharton, cited in Colby, *The Singular Anomaly*, 281. One of Lee's late ghost stories, "The Doll," is featured in Jessica Amanda Salmonson, ed., *What Did Miss Darrington See? An Anthology of Feminist Supernatural Fiction* (New York: Feminist Press at CUNY, 1989), and although "Lady Tal" is not a supernatural fiction, Elaine Showalter considered it sufficiently "decadent" to include it in her collection of women writers of the fin de siècle, *Daughters of Decadence*. Articles devoted, in whole or in part, to Lee's supernatural fiction include Carlo Caballero, "'A Wicked Voice': On Vernon Lee, Wagner, and the Effects of Music," *Victorian Studies* 35, no. 4 (summer 1992): 385-408; Peter G. Christensen, "The Burden of History in Vernon Lee's Ghost Story 'Amour Dure,'" *Studies in the Humanities* 16, no. 1 (June 1989): 33-43; Peter G. Christensen, "'A Wicked Voice': Vernon Lee's Artist Parable," *Lamar Journal of the Humanities* 15, no. 2 (fall 1989): 3-15; Adeline R. Tintner, "Vernon Lee's 'Oke of Okehurst; or The Phantom Lover' and James's 'The Way It Came,'" *Studies in Short Fiction* 28, no. 3 (summer 1991): 355-62; and Martha Vicinus, "The Adolescent Boy: Fin de Siècle Femme Fatale?" *Journal of the History of Sexuality* 5, no. 1 (July 1994): 90-114.

11. Showalter, *Daughters of Decadence*, ix; Showalter, "Syphilis, Sexuality, and the Fiction of the Fin de Siècle," 109.

12. H. James to Grace Norton, Feb. 27, [1887?], in *Henry James Letters*, 3:166.

13. Shaw, "A Political Contrast," 758; Praz, "Vernon Lee," 568; H. James to Vernon Lee, April 27, 1890, in *Henry James Letters*, 3:276; Lee, "J.S.S.," 243. Although English by birth, Lee does not always credit herself with having had a characteristically "English" sensibility. She found that "the wonderful Oscar Wilde," at their first meeting in 1881, "talked a sort of lyrico-sarcastic maudlin cultschah for half an hour," and she wrote to her mother that she felt strongly that the English could not see that "the creature [was] clever, & that a good half of his absurdities [were] mere laughing at people" (Lee to Matilda Paget, June 20, 1881, in *Vernon Lee's Letters*, 65). She spoke on other occasions of the English as a race with whom she had little in common, and thus implicitly confirmed what others repeatedly claimed of her: that it was to Italy that she owed much of her own peculiar way of seeing and writing about the world. Her friend and associate Maurice Baring revealed that sightseeing in Italy with Vernon Lee was "sight-seeing indeed," for she not only knew highways and byways but "let you into secrets of Italian civilisation and history" and "showed you the meaning of Italian roads, stones, carts, barrels, wine-vats, wells, effigies, dolls, puppets, Catholic shrines and wayside pagan gods." She "had breathed that air all her life; it was native to her," he wrote: "She had worshipped the Lares and Penates of ancient Italy all her life, and knew the ritual and the respect that should be paid to them as well as to the Christian saints who had taken their place" (Baring, *Lost Lectures*, 69-70).

14. Ormond, "Vernon Lee as a Critic," 151.

15. Lee, *The Eighteenth Century in Italy*, 4; H. James to T.S. Perry, Dec. 12, [1884?], in *Henry James Letters*, 3:61.

16. Colby, *The Singular Anomaly*, 238.

17. Robbins, "Vernon Lee," 139; Reed, *Decadent Style*, 241; Baugh, *A Literary History of England*, 1477. Reed claims that Lee was incapable of responding to Wagner's music, because although she "sensed the suffocating emotion in this style," she could "not grasp its intellectual subtlety and rigor" (241).

18. Pater, "Vernon Lee's 'Juvenalia.'"

19. Lee, "J.S.S." 249, 247.

20. Lee, "Can Writing Be Taught?" in *The Handling of Words*, 300.

21. Lee, "Ruskinism," in *Belcaro*, 211.

22. Ibid.

23. H. James, "The Art of Fiction," in J.E. Miller Jr., *Theory of Fiction*, 42-43; Buchan, *Memory Hold-the-Door*, 159; Wilde, "Pen, Pencil, and Poison," in *The Complete Works*, 5:100; Lee, "Ruskinism," in *Belcaro*, 210.

24. Lee, "Ruskinism," in *Belcaro*, 206-7, 210.

25. Ibid., 211, 206. Three years later, with the publication of *Miss Brown*, Lee attacked the fleshly school. Anne Brown, the novel's heroine, develops an aversion to the aestheticism espoused by the young Pre-Raphaelite painter who releases her from her position as the servant of an English family living abroad in Italy and who educates and hopes to marry her. She finds that she is constitutionally incapable of subscribing to the philosophy of the aesthetes, "these individual excrescences" with whom she is forced to mingle: "For all her familiarity with the aesthetic world, in whose apprehension, as Thaddy O'Reilly's Yankee friend had quietly remarked, 'right or wrong don't exist,'—for all her habit of reading poems in which every unmentionable shamefulness was used as so much vermilion or pale-green or mysterious grey in a picturesque and suggestive composition,—Anne had retained a constitutional loathing for touching some subjects, which was like the blind instinctive horror of certain animals for brackish water or mud" (Lee, *Miss Brown*, 2:196-98). Anne comes increasingly to rail against the insipidities of the aesthetic movement, whose advocates "would let all the world rot away in physical hideousness rather than have that physical hideousness put before their eyes," and then to take real steps to eliminate or remedy the causes of such ills (ibid., 2:197). In *Miss Brown*, that is, the dram of puritanism that Pater discovered in Lee's discourses on beauty is represented as lacking in the writings of Pater's discples.

26. Lee, *Renaissance Fancies and Studies*, 251; Lee, *Gospels of Anarchy*, 140-41.

27. Lee, *Baldwin*, 230.

28. Gunn treats 1901 as a turning point in her career, noting that although she "lived on until 1935, much of the work which bears her peculiar stamp had been written, or the future shape of it foreseen, before the Queen's death in 1901 brought [the Victorian] age symbolically to a close" (*Vernon Lee*, 1).

29. Gregory, "The Romantic Inventions of Vernon Lee," in *Spirit of Time and Place*, 103.

30. Pater, "Style," in *Three Major Texts*, 452, 450.

31. Lee, *Hauntings*, viii-ix.

32. Lee, "Faustus and Helena," in *Belcaro*, 75.

33. Lee, *Hauntings*, x.

34. Lee, "Faustus and Helena," in *Belcaro*, 76-77.

35. Lee, *Hauntings*, ix-x.

36. Lee, "Faustus and Helena," in *Belcaro*, 80, 77.

37. Lee, "The Lie of the Land," in *Limbo*, 45.

38. ("Vernon Lee ebbe come pochi il genio di scoprire il ritmo segreto d'un paesaggio, d'una epoca, d'un'opera d'arte. L'unicità delle sue scoperte amava fissare in un nome, in un simbolo emblematico") (Praz, "Vernon Lee," 561).

39. Symons, "Decadent Movement," 859.

40. ("a speculare nelle sfumature") (Praz, "Vernon Lee," 561). See Praz for a discussion of Lee as a sort of pseudosymbolist artist whose "knowledge was based on the exceptional echo of some real experiences, of some verse of a poet, meditated so long that it finally becomes emblematic" ("sapere era basato sull'eccezionale eco di qualche viva esperienza, di qualche verso di poeta, a lungo meditato fino a divenire emblematico") (Praz, "Vernon Lee," 562).

41. Lee, "Faustus and Helena," in *Belcaro*, 75.

42. Ibid., 81. Lee's conception of the supernatural may have its origins in Immanuel Kant's description, in the *Critique of Judgement* (1790), of an "aesthetic attribute" and an "aesthetic idea," the latter of which is often precipitated by the former. According to Kant, aesthetic attributes represent not "what lies in our concepts of the sublimity and majesty of

creation, but rather something else—something that gives the imagination an incentive to spread its flight over a whole host of kindred representations that provoke more thought than admits of expression in a concept determined by words. They furnish an *aesthetic idea*, which serves the rational idea as a substitute for logical presentation, but with the proper function, however, of animating the mind by opening out for it a prospect into a field of kindred representations stretching beyond its ken" (Immanuel Kant, *Critique of Judgement*, cited in Robinson, *Poetry, Painting and Ideas*, 5).

43. H. James, cited in Edel, *Stuff of Sleep and Dreams*, 306.

44. Lee, cited in Cary, "Vernon Lee's Vignettes," 186.

45. Lee, cited in MacCarthy, "Vernon Lee," 21; Lee, *Hauntings*, vii.

46. Lee, "On Style," in *The Handling of Words*, 60.

47. Waters, "Vernon Lee," 221; Brooks, "Notes on Vernon Lee," 449; Burdett Gardner, *Lesbian Imagination*, 21; Symonds to Violet Paget (Vernon Lee, May 23, 1880, letter 1182, in *Letters*, 2:636.

48. Lee, "A Wicked Voice," in *Hauntings*, 197, 208 (hereinafter cited in the text).

49. Lee wrote "Winthrop's Adventure" in 1874, about two years after she and John Singer Sargent saw a picture at the Arcades of Bologna of the eigheenth-century soprano castrato singer Farinelli (Carlo Broschi). Lee was a great student and lover of music and was considered by many to be one of its most discerning critics. Her first major critical work, *Studies of the Eighteenth Century in Italy* (1880), and her last major critical work, *Music and Its Lovers* (1932), were both devoted to music, the first being in part a history of eighteenth-century Italian music, the last being her attempt to do with music what she had spent most of her life doing with language: that is, tracing the interrelationship between the cadences, tonalities, and movements of musical scores and the ideas or emotions generated thereby.

50. Lee, "Winthrop's Adventure," in *For Maurice*, 143 (hereinafter cited in the text).

51. Wilde, *The Picture of Dorian Gray*, in *Oscar Wilde*, 62, 74-75.

52. Wilde, preface to *The Picture of Dorian Gray*, in *Oscar Wilde*, 48.

53. John Clute, "Vernon Lee," in Bleiler, *Supernatural Fiction Writers*, 1:333.

54. Lee, "The Virgin of the Seven Daggers," in *For Maurice*, 97; Shiel, "Xélucha," in *Shapes in the Fire*, 7, 4.

55. Bleiler, ed., *Guide to Supernatural Fiction*, 454.

56. Gautier, "Une Notice," 17.

57. Wilde, *The Picture of Dorian Gray*, in *Oscar Wilde*, 83. For discussions of the association of the decorative with the feminine, see, for example, Bronfen, *Over Her Dead Body*; R.B. Gordon, *Ornament, Fantasy, and Desire*; Schor, *Reading in Detail*; and Saisselin, *The Bourgeois and the Bibelot*.

58. Felski, "The Counterdiscourse of the Feminine," 1094-97.

59. Gardner, *The Lesbian Imagination*, 21.

60. Bleiler, *Guide to Supernatural Fiction*, 302.

61. Lee, "The Doll," in *For Maurice*, 210 (hereinafter cited in the text).

62. Nordau, *Degeneration*, 27.

63. Baring, *Lost Lectures*, 69.

64. Lee, *The Eighteenth Century in Italy*, 391.

65. This work combines two of Lee's particular interests at this period in her life: puppets and fairy tales. In 1880, the same year that saw the publication of her *Studies of the Eighteenth Century in Italy*, Lee published an anthology of Italian fairy stories entitled *Tuscan Fairy Tales*. Her first professional literary endeavor, "Les aventures d'une piece de monnaie" (1870), published when she was just fourteen, was itself something of a fairy tale, telling the story of the travels of a Roman coin from the ancient world to the present. Lee studied artists such as Carlo Goldoni and Carlo Gozzi, both of whom were fascinated with fairy tales and fairy comedy; she also appropriated fairy tale motifs and structures for many of her own stories.

66. Gordon Craig, "The Game of Marionettes: Letters to a Friend, from Gordon Craig,"

Mask 5 (1912-13): 149; Yorick [P. Ferrigni, pseud.], "A History of Puppets," *Mask* 5 (1912-13): 119-20.

67. Conrad to R.B. Cunninghame Graham, Dec. 6, 1897, letter 3, in *Joseph Conrad's Letters*, 50.

68. Baudrillard, *Simulacra and Simulation*, 2 (hereinafter cited in the text).

69. Symons, "Decadent Movement," 858.

70. Yorick, "A History of Puppets," *Mask* 5 (1912-13): 115, 117.

71. Maurice Rollinat, cited in Nordau, *Degeneration*, 225; Hoffmann, "Automata," in *Best Tales of Hoffmann*, 81.

72. Ernst Jentsch, cited in Freud, "The 'Uncanny,'" in *Standard Edition*, 17:226.

73. Bronfen, *Over Her Dead Body*, 64.

74. Susan Gubar, "'The Blank Page' and the Issues of Female Creativity," in Pelensky, *Isak Dinesen*, 101.

75. S.S. Ellis, *Wives of England*, 30; Carpenter, *Love's Coming-of-Age*, 49.

76. Gordon Craig, "Gentlemen, the Marionette!" *Mask* 5 (1912-13): 95; Symons, "An Apology for Puppets," 55. Acting was not the only performative art for which the marionette became a sought-after subject. Claude Debussy composed scores featuring Harlequin, Columbine, Scaramouche, and Pulcinella, the precursors of the golliwogs and dolls of his 1909 piano piece, *The Children's Corner*, while decadent versions of the Pierrots and Pantalones and Pantomimes from the *Commedia dell'Arte* became the models for the colored waxwork dolls of the Munich artist Lotte Pritzel, whose effete dandies, chichettes, madonnas, and St. Sebastians—arrested in whorls of motion and langorous descents—seem to suffer the neurotic preciosity and attenuated sickliness characteristic of their turn-of-the-century milieu. Helen Appleton Read suggests that the peculiar allure of these celebrated works lay in the fact that they were "delicate orchids in human form, outgrowths of a neurotic mind": a mind that was fueled by "the same delicate and unhealthy preciosity which we find in the vision of Beardsley, who was a consumptive" (Helen Appleton Read, cited in Dijkstra, *Idols of Perversity*, 348). It is perhaps worth noting in light of the "unhealthy preciosity" with which her own creations were associated that Pritzel was a friend of Hans Bellmer, who, before the success of his *Die Puppe* (1934) persuaded him otherwise, relied on her assurances that his experiments with his Doll were not symptomatic of his own insanity.

77. Eleonora Duse, cited in Symons, *Studies in Seven Arts*, 336; Gordon Craig, "The Artist and the Über-marionette," *Mask* 1, no. 2 (April 1908): 5.

78. Craig, "Gentlemen, the Marionette!" 95.

79. Symons, "An Apology for Puppets," 55; Beerbohm, "The Best Scenery I Know," 217.

80. Saisselin, *The Bourgeois and the Bibelot*, 67; S.S. Ellis, *The Women of England*, 17.

81. Felski, "The Counterdiscourse of the Feminine," 1098; Saisselin, *The Bourgeois and the Bibelot*, 67-68; Spofford, *Art Decoration Applied to Furniture*, 224-25.

82. H. James, "The Altar of the Dead," 50-51, 5. In the conclusion to her *Studies of the Eighteenth Century in Italy* (1880), Lee suggests that, for her readership, the men and women of the Renaissance were little better than dead documents rather than living texts, their titles and subjects generally known but their meanings lost or inaccessible to readers who lacked the powers of sympathetic engagement that would allow them to conceive of the artists of the Renaissance as anything more vital or imperative than "a superior sort of mummy": "We buy their old garments to hang in our parlours, we knock against their old armour as we would knock against a brand new fender, we ransack their papers, their lives; we feel no scruple in handling their dead personalities; they are totally dried, embalmed, turned into something wholly different from ourselves; we cannot, by the greatest stretch of imagination, conceive that they like or dislike anything we do to them or say about them; it is so long since they lived that the very ghosts of them are dead" (*The Eighteeth Century in Italy*, 438). Her remarks serve both as a critique of her own increasingly dehumanizing culture and as an apologia for her self-appointed role as a humanist whose function is to recall these "mummies" to life by means of the palingenetic powers of the sympathetic imagination.

83. G. Eliot, *Mill on the Floss*, 24-25.

84. Gisèle Prassinos, cited in Webb, *Hans Bellmer*, 55-56; Hans Bellmer, cited in ibid., 34.

85. Bellmer, cited in ibid., 38; Symons, "An Apology for Puppets," 55; H. James, "The Altar of the Dead," 11.

86. Lee, cited in Gardner, *The Lesbian Imagination*, 311-12.

87. S.S. Ellis, *Women of England*, 48.

88. S.S. Ellis, *Daughters of England*, 43.

89. Adolf Furst, "A Note on Marionettes," *Mask* 2 (1909-10): 72.

90. Lee, "Faustus and Helena," in *Belcaro*, 77.

91. Lee, introduction to *For Maurice*, xviii, xvi.

92. Lee, "Faustus and Helena," in *Belcaro*, 78.

93. Ibid., 77, 80.

94. Carroll, *The Cult of the Virgin Mary*. 6-7. Marina Warner explains that during the late fourteenth century, with "the growth of the prosperous urban class, which permitted an exclusively domestic life to the wives of merchants and tradesmen," a "new domestic idealism was projected onto the Holy Family as part of the same movement that attributed the social customs of earth to heaven . . . , that disrobed the Virgin of her regalia, and exchanged typology and metaphysics for anecdote. The cult of humility, understood as female submissiveness to the head of the house, set the seal on the Virgin's eclipse as a matriarchal symbol" (*Alone of All Her Sex*, 185, 188). Warner emphasizes that, with the advent of this cult of humility, "the type of virtues decreed feminine degenerate easily: obedience becomes docility; gentleness, irresolution; humility, cringing; forbearance, long-suffering" (190).

95. Warner, *Alone of All Her Sex*, 49.

96. Lee, "The Virgin of the Seven Daggers," in *For Maurice*, 97-98. Lee probably encountered prototypes of her baroque Virgin in the course of her visit to Granada, where, while recovering from nervous exhaustion, she conceived of her story. It is interesting to compare her description of the accoutrements of the Madonna to a similar description contained in an essay by Henry James entitled "From Normandy to the Pyrenees" (1876). James encountered an avatar of the Virgin of the seven daggers in the village of San Sebastian, in Spain, of which he writes: "Here the local colour was richer, the manners more naïf. Here too was a church with a flamboyant Jesuit façade and an interior redolent of Spanish Catholicism. There was a life-sized effigy of the Virgin perched upon a table beside the great altar (she appeared to have been walking abroad in a procession), which I looked at with extreme interest. She seemed to me a heroine, a solid Spanish person, as perfect a reality as Don Quixote or Saint Theresa. She was dressed in an extraordinary splendour of laces, brocades and jewels, her coiffure and complexion were of the finest, and she evidently would answer to her name if you should speak to her. Mustering up the stateliest title I could think of, I addressed her as Doña Maria of the Holy Office; whereupon she looked round the great dusky, perfumed church, to see whether we were alone, and then she dropped her fringed eyelids and held out her hand to be kissed. She was the sentiment of Spanish catholicism; gloomy, yet bedizened, emotional as a woman and mechanical as a doll. After a moment I grew afraid of her, and went slinking away" (H. James, "From Normandy to the Pyrenees," in *Portraits of Places*, 179-80).

97. Lee, introduction to *For Maurice*, xix. Other late- nineteenth-century artists—Aubrey Beardsley, Fernand Khnopff, Emile Bernard, Carlos Schwabe, Gustave Moreau, Lucien Lévy-Dhurmer, for example—had a veritable field day with the image of the Madonna *diabolique*. Lotte Pritzel included a Madonna amid her collection of Pierrots and odalisques: an anorexic, haughty figure, bedecked in gauze and lace and topped by an ornate crown. Arrested in a whirl of motion, she lifts—uncomfortably, as though the action is strange to her, and brazenly as well—her child, who is a dandified savior.

98. Lee, "Faustus and Helena," in *Belcaro*, 102-3; Adams, *The Education of Henry Adams*, 384.

99. Adams, *The Education of Henry Adams*, 384.

100. De Lauretis, *Technologies of Gender*. 43-44. I am graeful to Robin Cody for suggesting the relevance of Courbet's painting in the context of Lee's story.

101. Connolly, *Enemies of Promise*, 107; Lee, introduction to *For Maurice*, xix.

102. Carlyle, *Reminiscences*, 329-30.

103. Virgil, *The Aeneid*, 89-90.

104. Furst, "A Note on Marionettes," 72.

105. Gayatri Chakravorty Spivak, translator's preface to Derrida, *Of Grammatology*, lxvi; Bellmer, cited in Webb, *Hans Bellmer*, 38.

106. Freud, "'The Uncanny,'" *Standard Edition*, 17:224-25.

107. George Egerton, "A Keynote to *Keynotes*," in Gawsworth, *Ten Contemporaries*, 58.

108. Gubar, "'The Blank Page,'" 114.

109. Frazer, *The Golden Bough*, 115.

110. Aristotle, *The Complete Works*, 2:2392.

111. Farnell, *The Cults of the Greek States*, 130.

112. Irigaray, *This Sex Which Is Not One*, 30.

113. Culler, *The Victorian Mirror of History*, 103.

114. Preston, "Vernon Lee," 220; Lee to Henrietta Jenkins, Dec. 18, 1878, in *Vernon Lee's Letters*, 59; H. James to William James, Jan. 20, 1893, in *Henry James Letters*, 3:402.

115. Woolf, "Women and Fiction," in *Granite and Rainbow*, 81.

116. Lee, "Faustus and Helena," in *Belcaro*, 85.

5. The Word Made Flesh

1. G. Eliot, *Daniel Deronda*, 477-78; Arthur Machen to P.J. Toulet, Jan. 1, 1899, in Reynolds and Charlton, *Arthur Machen*, 72-73.

2. Machen, *Hieroglyphics*, 58; Machen, "The Great God Pan," in *The House of Souls*, 170.

3. Machen, "Edgar Allan Poe: the Supreme Realist," in *The Glorious Mystery*, 81; Machen, "A Secret Language," in *The Glorious Mystery*, 74; Symons, *Symbolist Movement in Literature*, 2-3.

4. Machen, *Three Impostors*, 161 (hereinafter cited primarily in the text).

5. Wilde, *The Picture of Dorian Gray*, in *Oscar Wilde*, 116.

6. Machen, "A Secret Language," in *The Glorious Mystery*, 69-70. Characteristically, Machen suggests that the romantics were the first to divine the glorious mysteries bound up in the outward forms of nature, and he offers an exact date—1796—as that on which "men so much as approximated to the significance of the great sacrament of the world" (69).

7. Machen, "A Secret Language," in *The Glorious Mystery*, 70. Machen's language blends the empirical concerns of the physical sciences ("force," "energy," "matter") with those more abstract motives of religion, and, more specifically, British Catholicism, of his interest in which he made little secret, admitting that his artistic vision was shaped by an Anglo-Catholic sensibility: "I write of the arts from the Catholic standpoint: I see constant analogies between the two worlds of religion and art" (Machen, cited in Wesley D. Sweetser, "Arthur Machen: A Biographical Study," in Sewell, *Arthur Machen*, 24). In *Hieroglyphics*, Machen's acclaimed work of literary theory, one of his "voices," the hermit, declares that since "Catholic dogma is merely the witness . . . of the enduring facts of human nature and the universe," it is therefore "necessary to be, at all events subconsciously, Catholic" if one wishes to "make literature" (*Hieroglyphics*, 164). The unpardonable sin follows not from acts of murder or thievery—mere transgressions of social life and social laws—but from the pride that manifests itself in the "effort to gain the ecstasy and the knowledge that pertain alone to angels" and thus "to obtain something which was never [Man's]." Poets, sorcerers, and philosophers who suffer from "a lonely passion of the soul—or a passion of the lonely soul" (*Hieroglyphics*, 78) yearn for such knowledge and, in aspiring that far, repeat the fall. In Machen we find an intermingling of the very old—Christian legend—and the very new—nineteenth-century scientific speculations about what is older still, the organic processes of evolution, decay, and recapitulation. The archetypal and theological frameworks—the idea of the fall, of the tree of knowledge, of crucifixion and resurrection—retained their place, in Machen's estimation, in a modern soci-

ety seeking, through the historical and natural sciences, to lift the veils of nature and disclose its hidden designs. Although those patterns had remained relatively unchanged, the truths that they unmasked had become more threatening. For Machen, the peculiar conjunction existing between dogma and modern scientific theory helped to engender, if it did not fully capture, the sense of the metaphysical evil—to his mind, so persistent in the universe—that he sought, throughout the final decade of the nineteenth century, to impart to his reader. Others have explored Machen's interest in Catholic tradition and dogma more fully than I have done here, among them Cazamian, "Arthur Machen," and Sweetser, *Arthur Machen*.

8. Machen, *Hieroglyphics*, 39; *Oxford Dictionary of the Christian Church*, s.v. "sacrament."

9. Wilde, *The Picture of Dorian Gray*, 63; Machen, A Secret Language," in *The Glorious Mystery*, 71; Machen, *The Hill of Dreams*, 126-27.

10. T.H. Huxley, "On the Physical Basis of Life," 145 (hereinafter cited in the text).

11. Morley, *Recollections*, 1:90.

12. For a condensed but illuminating synopsis of the competing concepts of protoplasm that dominated scientific discourse from 1835 through 1861, see Geison, "Protoplasmic Theory of Life," 273-78.

13. Ibid., 279.

14. Beale, *Protoplasm*, 120.

15. Pater, "Conclusion," in *Three Major Texts*, 219 (hereinafter cited in the text).

16. "Study and Opinion in Oxford," 192.

17. Stevenson, "Pulvis et Umbra," in *Across the Plains*, 271.

18. Pater, "Coleridge," in *Three Major Texts*, 439-40.

19. Stevenson, "Pulvis et Umbra," in *Across the Plains*, 271.

20. Müller, *The Science of Language*, 1:474 n. 1 (hereinafter cited in the text).

21. Farrar, "Philology and Darwinism," 528.

22. Romanes, *Mental Evolution in Man*, 238, 359.

23. Schleicher, "On the Significance of Language for the Natural History of Man," in Koerner, *Linguistics and Evolutionary Theory*, 79-80.

24. Müller, "Darwin's Philosophy of Language," 529.

25. Ibid.

26. Müller critiqued Schlegel's tree metaphor as follows: "If language grows, it can grow on one soil only, and that soil is man. Language cannot exist by itself. To speak of language, as Frederick Schlegel did, as a tree sending forth buds and shoots in the shape of terminations of nouns and verbs, or, as Schleicher did, as a thing by itself, as an organic thing living a life of its own, as growing to maturity, producing offspring, and sheer dying away, is their mythology; and though we cannot help using metaphorical expressions, we should always be on our guard against being caried away by the very words which we are using" (*The Science of Language*, 1:47).

27. Franz Bopp, *Über J. Grimm's Deutsche Grammatik* (1827), cited in Nerlich, "Linguistic Evolution," 103. In his desire to observe the orthodoxies of scientific inquiry, Müller resists making explicit the premise upon which his central argument concerning the essential difference between beasts and men is predicated: namely, that human beings were made in the image of God, and that human consciousness, reason, and intellect are pale semblances of a divine omniscience. His repeated allusions to "one common source" and "one common origin of human speech" (*The Science of Language*, 1:458-61) suggest that he conceived of the primordial language out of which all other languages, dialects, and idioms had evolved as divinely inspired. Ralph Waldo Emerson toyed with a roughly analogous idea, which he stated as follows: "I am very much struck in literature by the appearance, that one person wrote all the books; . . . there is such equality and identity both of judgment and point of view in the narrative, that it is plainly the work of one all-seeing, all-hearing gentleman" ("Nominalist and Realist" (1844), in *Essays and Lectures*, 579). Emerson is clearly if rather coyly describing the same "author" whom Sir Thomas Browne, as we have seen, invoked in his *Religio Medici* when he wrote of Nature as a "universall and publik Manuscript" (its leaves inscribed with

"mysticall letters" and "common Hieroglyphicks") that had been created by God in his role as "Maker," "excellent Artist," and "skilfull Geometrician" (1:24-25).

28. Huysmans, *Against Nature*, 46.

29. Symons, "Decadent Movement," 859.

30. "As often, then, as man is excited by such external or internal impressions as demand no action (conflict, flight, adaptation), but reach his consciousness in the form of a mood, he relieves his nervous system of this excitation through some kind of artistic activity, either by means of the plastic arts or by music and poetry. . . . He creates the work of art, not for its own sake, but to free his nervous system from a tension. The expression, which has become a commonplace, is psycho-physiologically accurate, viz., the artist writes, paints, sings, or dances the burden of some idea or feeling off his mind" (Nordau, *Degeneration*, 324).

31. Huysmans, *Against Nature*, 46, 49.

32. Nordau, *Degeneration*, 300.

33. Machen, *Precious Balms*, 2.

34. Ibid., 12; Oscar Wilde, cited in Michael, *Arthur Machen*, 11; Oscar Wilde, cited in Cazamian, "Arthur Machen," 275.

35. Lovecraft, *Supernatural Horror in Literature*, 88.

36. Machen, "The Great God Pan," in *The House of Souls*, 236-37 (hereinafter cited in the text).

37. Machen, "Edgar Allan Poe: The Supreme Realist," in *The Glorious Mystery*, 85, 88.

38. Lovecraft, *Supernatural Horror in Literature*, 90. In "The Novel of the Black Seal," Mr. Phillipps, after hearing another tale of bodies degenerating into protoplasmic pulp, goes home, drinks too much tea, and proceeds "to sketch out the outlines of a little work" that bears this title. Twentieth-century audiences would not lose their taste for protoplasmagoria. Chayefsky's Edward Jessup portrays a scientist who regresses, at first stage by stage but later vertiginously, all the way back to the viscid compound forming the basis of life on Earth. Although he emerges, at an intermediate stage in his experiment, as "a finely furred creature barely four feet tall, . . . with definable human features except for a massive projecting ridge of bone above his eyebrows and a prognathic, chinless jaw, a somewhat flattened skull, a low brow; . . . and . . . feet not entirely arched yet" (*Altered States*, 113), his retrogression is not complete. In the final labors of his descent, he is poised between two antagonistic states f being: a "sharply outlined . . . human self" and "a pulsating mass of white substance," a "mass of substance . . . trying to assume a form," with stumps "of arms and legs, misshapen and misplaced," and "deformed snouts and bleeding eyes" (161).

39. Haggard, *The Annotated She*, 194-95.

40. Romanes, *Mental Evolution in Man*, 314, 329.

41. I intentionally invoke a grammar of music, and specifically terms that might be used to describe the sonata form, which (if only tentatively applicable here) provides a provocative means of conceptualizing what transpires structurally within the story. The opening section of "The Great God Pan" sets forth, from a conventionally omniscient perspective, an event that, however bizarre, is largely cohesive and scrutable and that moreover contains the germs and hints of what is to follow. The narrative structure, as I have already suggested, proceeds more or less madrigally from that point, with idiosyncratic voices emerging and subsiding into abeyance with little warning. The climactic scene of Helen Vaughan's death—which amounts in the end to merely another voice telling its story—is followed by an epilogue casting a backward glance to "origins." The sonata form also consists of a tripartite structure proceeding from an exposition to something rather innocuously called the sonata development, and finally to the recapitulation. The exposition sets the theme—actually, two contrasting themes, the thematic and the harmonic. What follows is an intermediate exploratory section in which tonic keynotes of the exposition are avoided, set aside in favor of tonal complexities, rhythmic variations, textual modulations, and melodic fragmentation in which the "composer breaks up his original material, recombining motives and themes, and building up a homogeneous body from the various and seemingly unrelated parts" (*The International Cyclopedia of Music and Musicians*, 567). A certain anxiety and tension are inherent in this passage,

born of the attempt to force a homogeneity in the midst of tonal and rhythmic discursiveness, spontaneity, and instability. The sonata development prepares the way for the "recapitulation," in which both the defining tonalities of the exposition reemerge, often with considerable modification. The differences are generally highlighted or exploited because the composer understands that the listener "will be subconsciously comparing what he is hearing with what he heard in the exposition" (*The New Oxford Companion to Music*, 1:704). So, although the original order and pattern of the tonal themes are resurrected, their "effect on the listener, however, is not the same. He hears them with new ears because he has lived through the revealing experience of the development" (*Encyclopedia Britannica*, 1967 ed., s.v. "sonata"). One cannot help but think how neatly the terms *development* and *recapitulation* conjoin the aesthetics and thematics that emerge in this species of horror fiction with its distinctive narrative structure and its obsession with biological retrogression and recapitulation. The swirling vortex of voices that suck the reader downward and inward toward the shocking denouement in which Helen, poised at the apex of evolutionary development, is swept vertiginously back in time to her "origins" also forces the reader, in a sense, to experience some portion of that retrogression. Already sufficiently unstable, given the wavering quality of the descent that traverses the space separating the "heights" from the "depths," Helen's passage through the various stages of evolutionary development is rendered all the more destabilizing by the reader's recollection of Helen's having been a woman "of the most wonderful and most strange beauty" (191): given the reader's having "lived through," that is, "the revealing experience of the development," both narrative and thematic.

42. The inscription reads: "To the great god Nodens (the god of the Great Deep or Abyss), Flavius Senilis has erected this pillar on account of the marriage which he saw eneath the shade" (241).

43. Romanes, *Mental Evolution in Man*, 421, 296.

44. For a discussion of the centrality of childhood—as metaphor, as paradigm, as actual evolutionary stage—to the theory of recapitulation, see Gould, "Measuring Bodies: Two Case Studies on the Apishness of Undesirables," in *The Mismeasure of Man*, 113-45, and Gould, *Ontogeny and Phylogeny*.

45. Haeckel, *The Evolution of Man*, 1:7.

46. Chambers, *Natural History of Creation*, 202.

47. Wells, *The Definitive Time Machine*, 49, 56.

48. Ibid., 46, 56. For all that he resisted the organic tropes and metaphors to which he continually returned, Müller provides us with an interesting philological perspective from which to consider Wells's evolutionary conceit. The languages of "highly civilised nations," Müller writes, show none of the restless changefulness and purposeful adaptability of younger, less fully evolved languages. Instead, they "become more and more stationary, and sometimes seem almost to lose their power of change" (1:35). Similarly, the bodies, the buildings, and the language of the Eloi constitute "the last surgings of the now purposeless energy of mankind before it settled down into perfect harmony with the conditions under which it lived—the flourish of that triumph which began the last great peace. This has ever been the fate of energy in security: it takes to art and to eroticism, and then come languor and decay" (Wells, *The Definitive Time Machine*, 51-52).

49. Romanes, *Mental Evolution in Man*, 416, 421. What Romanes referred to as "roots," Frederic William Farrar had called "speech-cells," an undeveloped germ in which "the rudiments of all special organs"—verbal, nominal, and nonverbal—"are implicitly *involved*, but in which they are as little *developed* as in the germinal vesicles which represent the earliest forms of animal and vegetable life" ("Philology and Darwinism," 529).

50. Machen, "The Novel of the Black Seal," in *Three Impostors*, 110.

51. Bourget, "Charles Baudelaire," in *Essais de psychologie contemporaine*, 1:19-20. This passage is quoted in "A Note on Paul Bourget," in H. Ellis, *Views and Reviews*, 51-52.

52. As Linda Dowling suggests in her *Language and Decadence in the Victorian Fin de Siècle*, Bourget's "pseudo-Darwinian vocabulary of 'laws' and 'organism' takes on its full significance only when we see that it represents no contrived metaphorical application of

Darwinian hypotheses to language. Rather, as August Schleicher had argued, just the reverse: language provided a founding analogy for and confirmation of Darwinian biology"
(133).

53. Chambers, "The King in Yellow," in *The King in Yellow*, 16-17.

54. Zola, *Nana*, 2:312, 336.

55. Ibid., 2:294, 336.

56. Morel, "Treatise on the Degenerations," 10 (Mar. 25, 1857): 136; 10 (April 1, 1857):
150.

57. "Impressionism in literature is an example of that atavism which we have noticed as
the most distinctive feature in the mental life of degenerates. It carries back the human mind
to its brute-beginnings, and the artistic activity of its present high differentiation to an embryonic state; that state in which all the arts (which were later to emerge and diverge) lay side by
side inchoate and inseparate" (Nordau, *Degeneration*, 485).

58. Machen, *Precious Balms*, 82, 81, 6-7.

59. Ibid., 18, 24.

60. Reynolds and Charlton, *Arthur Machen*, 52.

61. Kristeva, *The Powers of Horror*, 4.

62. Ibid., 4, 2.

63. Buchan, "The Grove of Ashtaroth," in *The Best Short Stories*, 1:112.

64. Stevenson, *The Strange Case of Dr. Jekyll and Mr. Hyde*, in *Works* 6:23-24.

65. De la Mare, "A: B: O.," in *Eight Tales*, 100; Stoker, *Dracula*, 28-29.

66. Wells, *The Island of Doctor Moreau*, 82, 88, 92; Wells, *The Definitive Time Machine*, 64, 67-68.

67. Poe, "The Facts in the Case of M. Valdemar," in *Collected Works*, 3:1240 (hereinafter cited in the text).

68. Freud, *The Aetiology of Hysteria*, in *Standard Edition*, 3:193-96.

69. Lovecraft, "Pickman's Model," in *Best of H. P. Lovecraft*, 43.

70. Darwin, *Expression of the Emotions*, 304.

71. "Das unheimliche" and "abjection" are obviously related terms. Like the condition
that it names, the "unheimliche" is an elusive term, developing "in the direction of ambivalence" (Freud mines several different languages in search of a strict definition of "this particular shade of what is frightening," only to find that none exists) and a composite term (with
some pleasure, Freud discovers that "among its different shades of meaning the word '*heimliche*'
exhibits one which is identical with its opposite, '*unheimliche*,' so that what "is *heimliche* thus
comes to be *unheimliche*") ("The 'Uncanny,'" in *Standard Edition*, 17:226, 221, 224). Where
Freud assigns, in psychoanalytic terms, a certain retrogressive quotient to the concept, involving "a harking-back to particular phases in the evolution of the self-regarding feeling, a
regression to a time when the ego had not yet marked itself off sharply from the external
world and from other people" (236), Kristeva assigns to abjection a certain quotient of uncanniness, inhering in the "massive and sudden emergence of uncanniness, which, familiar as it
might have been in an opaque and forgotten life, now harries me as radically separate, loathsome. Not me. Not that. But not nothing, either. A 'something' that I do not recognize as a
thing. A weight of meaninglessness, about which there is nothing insignificant, and which
crushes me" (*The Powers of Horror*, 2).

72. Freud, "The 'Uncanny,'" in *Standard Edition*, 17:223, 226.

73. Ibid., 17:241.

74. Todorov, *The Poetics of Prose*, 143.

75. Lovecraft, cited St. Armand, *The Fiction of H. P. Lovecraft*, 9; Freud, "The 'Uncanny,'" in *Standard Edition*, 17:220.

76. De Goncourt and de Goncourt, *The Goncourt Journals*, 15.

77. Wilde, replies to the *Scots Observer*'s 1890 reviews of *The Picture of Dorian Gray*,
reprinted in Mason, *Oscar Wilde*, 69-70.

78. Starrett, *Buried Caesars*, 12.

79. Lovecraft, *Supernatural Horror in Literature*, 90; Benét, "The Other That Hides."

80. Lovecraft, *Supernatural Horror in Literature*, 90. Although to someone like Dorian Gray the "very mystery" of "curious unpictured sins . . . lent them their subtlety and their charm" (Wilde, *The Picture of Dorian Gray*, in *Oscar Wilde*, 139), Benét objected to such significative reticence, remonstrating that "whatever inferences may be drawn from" the stories contained in a work titled *Ornaments in Jade* (1924)—an even more elliptical work than "The Great God Pan"—"would be inferences of the monstrous" ("The Other That Hides," 44). Dowling argues that Machen employs the technique of the "unutterability *topos*" in *The Hill of Dreams* (a book composed two years before *Ornaments in Jade*) as an ingenious way of critiquing the Decadent style. His veiled argument, she says, is that a solipsistic Decadence requires "a language so perfected in its private symbolism that it will no longer yield its meaning even to the select few, but only to the unique reader," who also happens to be the writer (*Language and Decadence*, 160). She reaches her conclusion, logically enough, from the fact that, having spent the duration of the novel reading about the decadent hero's painstaking attempts to create a story full of terrible beauty and mysticism, the reader discovers on the last page that Lucian's manuscript consists of sheets "covered with illegible hopeless scribblings; only here and there it was possible to recognize a word" (Machen, *The Hill of Dreams*, 247). In point of fact, of course, Machen's strategy is employed in order to hide the fact that the horror confronted in his stories is only a trope for something (the fear of sexuality, the fear of degeneration, the fear of dissolution) that he could not himself express, much less discuss openly even in the 1890s, and that he felt compelled, therefore, to mask, occult, and repress in his fictions. The emphasis on symbolism made it obvious that something was being encoded and must therefore be decoded.

81. Rickett, "A Yellow Creeper," in *Lost Chords*, 17, 19-21. I am indebted to Professor Margaret Stetz for bringing Rickett's work to my attention.

82. Ibid., 22-23.

83. Mallarmé to Charles Morice, n.d., in *Mallarmé*, 105.

84. Symons, "Decadent Movement," 866.

85. Maeterlinck, *Treasure of the Humble*, 18, 15, 3, 19.

86. Baltruaitis, *La stylistique ornementale*, 276.

87. Multatuli, "Décomposition," 685.

6. The Anatomy of Failure

1. Conrad, *Heart of Darkness*, 44. Subsequent references, cited parenthetically, are from this edition. The most frequently cited of Conrad's works have been assigned the following abbreviations:

> *CP: Conrad's Prefaces to His Works*
> *JCL: Joseph Conrad's Letters to R.B. Cunninghame Graham*
> *JCLL: Joseph Conrad Life and Letters*
> *LE: Last Essays*
> *NLL: Notes on Life and Letters*
> *PR: A Personal Record*

2. G. Stewart, "Lying as Dying in *Heart of Darkness*," 319.

3. Fletcher, "The 1890's: A Lost Decade," 346.

4. Joseph Conrad, cited in Ian Watt, *Conrad in the Nineteenth Century*, 139. As Patrick Brantlinger has pointed out, it "seems likely that much of the 'horror' either depicted or suggested in *Heart of Darkness* does not represent what Conrad saw" in the course of the voyage up the Congo River which he undertook in 1890 (*"Heart of Darkness,"* 367). The story's lack of specifics as well as Conrad's own admission to Cunninghame Graham that Roger Casement, whom he had met in the Belgian Congo, "could tell you things! Things I've tried to forget; things I never did know" (*JCL* 149) would seem to substantiate Brantlinger's claim. For a discussion of the extent to which details of Conrad's trip are transposed in or excluded from *Heart of Darkness*, see Watt, *Conrad in the Nineteenth Cetury*, 135-46.

5. Conrad did note that H.G. Wells captured one sort of reality when he contrived in his

fiction to "give over humanity into the clutches of the Impossible and yet . . . to keep it down (or up) to its humanity, to its flesh, blood, sorrow, folly." When Conrad designated Wells as the "Realist of the Fantastic!" (*JCLL* 1:259-60), he was, perhaps, returning a compliment that Wells had paid him some two years earlier, when, in 1896, he proclaimed, "Surely [*An Outcast of the Islands*] is the real romance—the romance that is real!" (review of *An Outcast of the Islands*, 510).

6. Machen, "A Secret Language," in *The Glorious Mystery*, 74, 69-70.

7. Machen, "Edgar Allan Poe, the Supreme Realist," in *The Glorious Mystery*, 86.

8. Leo Tolstoy, cited in W. James, *Varieties of Religious Experience*, 130; Lovecraft, *Supernatural Horror in Literature*, 85; Lovecraft, "Pickman's Model," in *Best of H. P. Lovecraft*, 49.

9. Symons, "Decadent Movement," 859.

10. Conrad to Edward Garnett, Sept. 29, 1898, in *Collected Letters*, 2:94-95.

11. See, for example, Hay, "Joseph Conrad and Impressionism"; Frederick Karl, "Joseph Conrad"; Joseph Martin, "Conrad and the Aesthetic Movement," *Conradiana* 17, no. 3: 199-213 (1985); Christopher S. Nassar, "Vision of Evil: The Influence of Wilde's *Salome* on *Heart of Darkness* and *A Full Moon in March*," *Victorian Newsletter* 53 (spring 1978): 23-27; A.M. Rose, "Conrad and the Sirens of Decadence"; Ian Watt, "Impressionism and Symbolism in *Heart of Darkness*," in Sherry, *Joseph Conrad*, 37-53.

12. Bleiler, *Victorian Ghost Stories*, 5. Conrad's "public" renunciation took the form of a rebuttal, nested in the preface to *The Shadow-Line* (1917), in which he responded to various unnamed critics who had suggested that he had tended to take his imagination "beyond the confines of the world of the living, suffering humanity." Conrad insisted that the "world of the living contains enough marvels and mysteries as it is," "marvels and mysteries acting upon our emotions and intelligence in ways so inexplicable that it would almost justify the conception of life as an enchanted state. No, I am too firm in my consciousness of the marvellous to be ever fascinated by the mere supernatural, which (take it any way you like) is but a manufactured article, the fabrication of minds insensitive to the intimate delicacies of our relation to the dead and to the living, in their countless multitudes; a desecration of our tenderest memories; an outrage on our dignity" (*CP* 173). In this and similar statements, Conrad publicly distanced himself from such writers of overtly "sensational" works as J. Sheridan LeFanu, M.R. James, or, in his own day, Arthur Machen, none of whom conceived of the supernatural in fiction as "a manufactured article," a "fabrication," or "a desecration." Not to be put off by the proclamation of a writer not generally recognized for consistency or implacability, Edmund Wilson, in his "Treatise on Tales of Horror," speculates that in the ideal anthology of horror stories "by really first-rate modern writers," Conrad's novella would serve as a companion piece to Melville's "Benito Cereno," "a more plausible yet still nightmarish affair" (*Classics and Commercials*, 175-76).

13. Scheick, *Fictional Structure in Ethics*, 114-15.

14. Gautier, "Une notice," 17.

15. Brantlinger, "*Heart of Darkness*," 374. It is important to point out that Brantlinger is concerned specifically with those Gothic romance conventions appropriatedby writers of imperialist adventures: "G. A. Henty, Rider Haggard, Robert Louis Stevenson, Conan Doyle, John Buchan, Rudyard Kipling, and Conrad among them." Although late-nineteenth-century adventure stories or quest romances seemed to serve officially as vehicles for imperialist propaganda, the most sophisticated of these romances (including Conrad's novella) "threaten to submerge or 'derealize' the critique of empire within their own more strictly esthetic project" ("*Heart of Darkness*," 374). I have appropriated Brantlinger's argument in a discussion that focuses on a distinct although closely related genre of horror literature. The social and intellectual forces that rekindled the popularity of the adventure story, however, were precisely those that revived a flagging Gothic tradition, and the questions dealt with most frequently in products of the former genre are very close—sometimes identical—to those that surface in horror stories.

16. G.R. Thompson has already noted that "The Fall of the House of Usher" "bears a

number of surprising similarities in theme, imagery, and structure to *Heart of Darkness*," although he identifies only the emphasis that both works place upon the "double, the skull motif, and theme of mental and moral collapse" ("Explained Gothic ['The Fall of the House of Usher']," in Eric W. Carlson, ed., *Critical Essays on Edgar Allan Poe* [Boston: G.K. Hall, 1987], 143, 151 n.1). My argument is that the extent and nature of internal evidence suggests that Conrad had Poe's story more or less consciously in mind as he conceived of and wrote *Heart of Darkness*.

17. Poe, "The Fall of the House of Usher," in *Collected Works*, 2:400 (hereinafter cited in the text).

18. See, for example, Fred L. Milne, "Marlow's Lie and the Intended: Civilization as the Lie in *Heart of Darkness*," *Arizona Quarterly* 44, no. 1 (spring 1988): 106-12; Reeves, "A Voice of Unrest"; Bruce R. Stark, "Kurtz's Intended: The Heart of *Heart of Darkness*," *Texas Studies in Literature and Language* 16, no. 3 (fall 1974): 535-55; G. Stewart, "Lying as Dying in *Heart of Darkness*," 319-31; G.R. Thompson, "Explained Gothic."

19. Conrad most probably had Nordau in mind when, in *Chance* (1912), he refers to John Fyne as having made sense of the apparent conflict between his father-in-law's artistic genius and unconventional behavior by seizing "with avidity upon the theory of poetical genius being allied to madness, which he got hold of in some idiotic book everybody was reading a few years ago. It struck him as being truth itself—illuminating like the sun" (*Chance* [New York: Doubleday, 1914], 194). That "idiotic book" is, in all likelihood, *Degeneration*, in which, working from the theories posited by his mentor, Lombroso, Nordau explores the manner in which the characteristics of retrogressive atavism might reveal themselves in the individual whose pronounced aesthetic sensibility or intellectual capacity—what Lombroso defined simply as "genius"—could be seen as an indication of neurotic degeneration.

With his "lofty frontal bone" and the impression he conveys of gigantic bodily stature, Kurtz bears the stigmata of the born criminal type. Nordau was careful to point out, however, that such a "genius" might not bear the physiognomic signs of his degeneracy; thus, more telling is Kurtz's behavior; when he is discovered crawling abjectly back to yet another midnight ritual, for example, he attempts to excuse his perversity by muttering something about having "had immense plans" (143). Somewhat later, as the steamer in which he lies crawls back toward "civilization," the delirious Kurtz demands that "kings meet him at railway-stations on his return from some ghastly Nowhere, where he intended to accomplish great things" (148). Nordau had argued that the degenerate man of genius "will employ his brilliant faculties quite as well in the service of some grand object as in the satisfaction of the basest popensities" (23).

Nordau did not number Conrad among the "higher degenerates" with whom he was concerned even though, ironically, Warrington Dawson notes that he admired Conrad's "sense of word values and coloring in English," which he elsewhere designates as one of the tell-tale mental stigmata of degeneration (Warrington Dawson, cited in Randall, *Joseph Conrad and Warrington Dawson*, 70 n. 24). Of the favor that *The Nigger of the 'Narcissus'* (1897) apparently found with Nordau, Conrad wrote that "Praise is sweet, no matter whence it comes"; the ambivalence of the response is explanation enough of Conrad's opinion of Nordau (*JCLL* 1:255.) Other critics have addressed in brief fashion the issue of Conrad's appropriation of Nordau's theories, among them Eloise Knapp Hay, *The Political Novels of Joseph Conrad* (Chicago: Univ. of Chicago Press, 1963); Martin Ray, "Conrad, Nordau, and Other Degenerates: The Psychology of The Secret Agent," *Conradiana* 16, no. 2 (1984): 125-40; John E. Saveson, "Conrad, *Blackwood's*, and Lombroso," *Conradiana* 6, no. 1 (1974): 57-62; C.T. Watts, "Nordau and Kurtz: A Footnote to 'Heart of Darkness,'" *Notes and Queries* 21, no. 6 (June 1974): 226-27.

20. G. Stewart, "Lying as Dying in *Heart of Darkness*," 326.

21. Marlow's narrative is similarly self-reflexive in the sense that although Marlow may not be able to express the inexpressible, as Jeremy Hawthorn suggests, he "is able to express its inexpressibility" (*Joseph Conrad*, 28). Watt reminds us that Henry James "did not much like *Heart of Darkness*," objecting to "'the narrator mixing himself up with the narrative.'"

Watt points out that "Marlow is certainly very different from the Jamesian central intelligence" and that, in introducing a narrator who functions both as subject and as object, "*Heart of Darkness* prefigures how the modern novel was to reject, much more fully than did James, the assumption of full authorial understanding" ("Impressionism and Symbolism in *Heart of Darkness*," in Sherry, *Joseph Conrad*, 51).

22. See, for example, David Abel, "A Key to the House of Usher," *University of Toronto Quarterly* 18, no. 2 (1949): 176-85; Maurice Lévy, "Edgar Poe et la tradition 'gothique,'" *Caliban* 5, no. 2 (1968): 35-51; G.R. Thompson, "Explained Gothic"; Leo Spitzer, "A Reinterpretation of 'The Fall of the House of Usher,'" *Comparative Literature* 4 (1952): 351-63.

23. G. Stewart, "Lying as Dying in *Heart of Darkness*," 323.

24. Specifically, *Heart of Darkness* was serialized in *Blackwood's Magazine* between February and April of 1899. Conrad was particularly pleased to find his story so reputably placed given that, as he rather aristocratically put it, "one was in decent company there and had a good sort of public" (cited in Watt, *Conrad in the Nineteenth Century*, 131).

25. Brantlinger approaches the crux of the issue when he argues that in the face of Kurtz's "heroism"—which consists largely in his "staring into an abyss of nihilism so total that the issues of imperialism and racism pale into insignificance"—details of impaled heads and indigens bedecked in animal skins "appear in Marlow's account like so many melodrama props" ("*Heart of Darkness*," 379). Brantlinger's important insight, however, falls short of fully explaining the peculiar sense of apparently irreferable yet insistent anxiety that the story engenders in its reader.

26. One is reminded, once again, of Henry James's response to Baudelaire's *Les fleurs du mal*. The disappointment of the reader with the quality of evil presented therein, said James, was exactly the same as the disappointment he would feel if, having been promised the flowers of good, he were presented with "a rhapsody on plumcake and *eau de Cologne*" (Henry James, "Charles Baudelaire," in Miller, *Theory of Fiction*, 306). The manner of anxiety with which Conrad's text is charged transcends that which a mere catalog of transgressions could provide.

27. Lovecraft, "Pickman's Model," in *Best of H. P. Lovecraft*, 43.

28. As the early-twentieth-century British author and biographer A[lphonse] Symons reminded the readers of his *Anthology of 'Nineties' Verse*, after anthropology had shown "the moral code to be no more than a time-serving expedient," and physical science had "disproved divinity," there remained, in the "twilit end of the nineteenth century," only a minority who, "despairing of truth outside itself, looked inward to the only verities that had not seemed to crumble while it watched: the cultivation of the self, the consolation of art." They discovered their "creed," he continued, in the conclusion of a book written twenty years earlier: "six explicit sentences" from that text, expressive of "the secret scepticism of [Walter Pater's] inner mind," became "the gospel of the men of the 'nineties" (xviii-xix).

29. In such a solipsistic world, matters of aesthetics necessarily prevail over questions of ethics and morality, if only because the former emphasize the primacy of the artist's feelings and ideas, whereas the latter suggest some sort of collective worldview. Perhaps unconsciously, Conrad echoed the Decadent aesthetic when he admitted to Edward Noble that his own view of life was one that "rejects all formulas, dogmas and principles of other people's making" (*JCLL* 1:184). Paradoxically, such an aesthetic program indicates how very committed the Decadents were to creating something of enduring value—to performing their own sort of "rescue work"—and to taking refuge upon an island of artificial splendor set in the midst of an impersonal, barren, and entropic wasteland.

30. Reed, *Decadent Style*, 15-16, 9.

31. Pecora, "*Heart of Darkness* and the Phenomenology of Voice," 1011.

32. George Washington Moon, *The Dean's English* (1868), cited in Dowling, *Language and Decadence*, 45.

33. Reeves, "A Voice of Unrest," 286, 304.

34. Dowling, *Language and Decadence*, 33, 104.

35. Said, "Conrad," 120.

36. Reeves, "A Voice of Unrest," 299. Recognizing, as Said had in 1974, that Conrad's "working reality, his practical and theoretical competence as a writer, was far in advance of what he was saying" ("Conrad," 116), critics have increasingly addressed *Heart of Darkness* as an exploration of matter linguistic, epistemological, and phenomenological. See, for example, William Bonney, *Thorns and Arabesques: Contexts for Conrad's Fiction* (Baltimore: Johns Hopkins Univ. Press, 1980); Peter J. Glassman, *Language and Being: Joseph Conrad and the Literature of Personality* (New York: Columbia Univ. Press, 1976); Hawthorn, *Joseph Conrad*; Pecora, "Heart of Darkness and the Phenomenology of Voice"; Sanford Pinsker, "Language, Silence, and the Existential Whisper: Once Again at the *Heart of Darkness*," *Modern Language Studies* 2, no. 2 (1972): 53-59; Reeves, "A Voice of Unrest"; Royal Roussell, *The Metaphysics of Darkness* (Baltimore: Johns Hopkins Univ. Press, 1971); Said, "Conrad," 116-32; Edward Said, "Conrad and Nietzsche," in Sherry, *Joseph Conrad*, 65-76; G. Stewart, "Lying as Dying in *Heart of Darkness*"; David Thorburn, *Conrad's Romanticism* (New Haven, Conn.: Yale Univ. Press, 1974); Eric Trethewey, "Language, Experience, and Selfhood in Conrad's *Heart of Darkness*," *Southern Humanities Review* 22, no. 2 (spring 1988): 101-11; White, *The Uses of Obscurity*.

37. In the sense that he is a manipulator and debaucher of language, Kurtz may also function as one possible mask for Conrad himself, as Arthur Symons may have intuited when he alluded to Conrad's correspondingly "unlawful soul." Arthur Symons idetified "ABNORMALITY" as the "keynote of Conrad's creative genius" (*Notes on Joseph Conrad*, 23). In his appreciation of Conrad, Symons imagines him "squatting like some Satanical spider in his web, in some corner, stealthily hidden away from view, throwing out—almost like *la Pieuvre*—tentacles into the darkness. At the centre of his web sits an elemental sarcasm discussing human affairs with a cynical ferocity: behind that sarcasm crouches some powerful devil, insidious, poisonous, irresistible, spawning evil for his own delight" (7-8). A "casuist of souls," Conrad would, in Symons's estimation, "drag forth some horribly stunted or horribly overgrown soul from under its obscure covering, setting it to dance naked before our eyes" (12). Writing in response to Symons's encomiums concerning *Heart of Darkness*, Conrad gently but firmly urged, "I did not know that I had a 'heart of darkness' and an 'unlawful' soul. Mr. Kurtz had, and I have not treated him with the easy nonchalance of an amateur" (*JCLL* 2:73).

Garrett Stewart makes nearly these very points when he argues that "Conrad quietly implicates England, and Marlow as Englishman, in Kurtz's European hubris and diseased idealism—and of course implicates himself, too, as British-educated master of nonnative English eloquence"; Conrad's story, he suggests, stresses "the risks and responsibilities of rhetorical power" ("Lying as Dying in *Heart of Darkness*," 321). I fail to find the sort of persuasive internal evidence in support of Stewart's claim that "Marlow realizes the double nature of language, its power to illuminate and ennoble but also to corrupt" (321). To my mind, *Heart of Darkness* seems to embrace a central premise of the Decadent movement: to wit, that, as the product of a civilization that had grown too complex, too specialized, and as a result had begun to break down, language necessarily embodies a "spiritual and moral perversity" (the phrase is Symons's from "Decadent Movement," 858). That which appears beautiful or ennobling, the practitioners of Decadent style would argue, is in fact merely a manifestation of what Symons termed its "disease of form" (859).

38. Gautier, "Une Notice," 17.

39. Wilde, "The Critic as Artist," in *The Complete Works*, 5:142.

40. Thus, Kurtz's painting (which, like those of Roderick Usher, stresses ideality) depicts a draped and blindfolded woman carrying a lighted torch that illuminates the impenetrable blackness enshrouding her. Critics have pointed out that since a torch replaces the traditional scales, the figure may represent wisdom rather than justice, as her blindfold might otherwise have suggested. Although her blindfold would enable her to render impartial judgments, in this context it merely impedes her effort to illuminate a world steeped in darkness; its presence therefore indicates that she performs her duties in an arbitrary, confused, and blind fashion. Furthermore, the torchlight that spills over onto her face reveals her sinister aspect, which suggests that her methods may be cruel, even unsound. Conrad clearly wants

us to recognize that Kurtz's picture is a self-portrait, and he establishes the relationship between the drawing and its creator in the course of Kurtz's deathbed scene. Marlow enters the dying Kurtz's cabin, and by the light of the candle that he carries he can see Kurtz's "ivory face," which, in the darkness, carries an expression "of sombre pride, of ruthless power, of craven terror—of an intense and hopeless despair" (68). Like the blindfolded woman, he entered a foreign land in a blind and reckless fashion and thus conducted his business with "'no method at all'" (61).

41. G. Stewart, "Lying as Dying in *Heart of Darkness*," 321.

42. Though superficially my argument in this respect seems to duplicate Stewart's, the difference that separates the two is substantial. Stewart suggests that, in the scene of the helmsman's death, we learn that "even untutored mortality has its voiceless eloquence," although the "nameless savage . . . has no English in which to voice the mysteries of his injury and his death" (G. Stewart, "Lying as Dying in *Heart of Darkness*," 322). I would argue that, in *Heart of Darkness*, a command of the English language is portrayed as being something of a liability rather than an advantage or virtue.

43. Pecora, "*Heart of Darkness* and the Phenomenology of Voice," 998.

44. Ibid., 1001.

45. Wells, *The Definitive Time Machine*, 88.

46. Wells, review of *An Outcast of the Islands*, 509; Leavis, *The Great Tradition*, 216, 218, 212, 219.

47. Said, "Conrad," 116; Mudrick, "The Originality of Joseph Conrad," 549, 552.

48. Reeves, "A Voice of Unrest," 289.

49. Conrad to Richard Curle, April 24, 1922, letter 89, in *Conrad to a Friend*, 142.

50. Dowling, *Language and Decadence*, 161.

51. Said, "Conrad," 129.

52. Reeves, "A Voice of Unrest," 303.

53. Conrad may very well have been guided in his treatment of the numerous images that go to make up *Heart of Darkness* by his own definition of "a work of art"—which, he claimed, "is very seldom limited to one exclusive meaning and [does] not necessarily [tend] to a definite conclusion." The nearer a work "approaches art," he believed, "the more it acquires a symbolic character": "All the great creations of literature have been symbolic, and in that way have gained in complexity, in power, in depth and in beauty" (*JCLL* 2:205).

54. To the extent that form establishes meaning in *Heart of Darkness*, Conrad's story reveals its nascent symbolist tendencies. For the symbolists, the idea that informs a work of art, although never subordinate to the form that clothes it, should not, as Jean Moréas put it, "make its appearance deprived of the sumptuous trappings of external analogies" ("Manifesto of Symbolism," cited in Milner, *Symbolists and Decadents*, 51). In other words, the form that works of literature or paintings take represents the embodiment of the artist's idea and is inseparable from it. According to Arthur Symons, Gustave Flaubert's theory of beauty was predicated on the notion that "form is a living thing, the physical body of thought, which it clothes and interprets" (*Symbolist Movement in Literature*, 139), while Flaubert, speaking for himself, insisted to his friend Louise Colet that one "cannot remove the form from the Idea, because the Idea exists only by virtue of its form" (Flaubert to Louise Colet, Sept. 18, 1846, in *Selected Letters*, 77).

55. Symons, *Notes on Joseph Conrad*, 37. Of Conrad's prose, in which he observes "a peculiar flavour, fiery and fervent," Symons has this to say: "The rarest subtlety in prose is its physiological quality; for prose listens at the doors of all the senses, and repeats their speech almost in their own tones. There is no form of art which is not an attempt to capture life, but to create life over again. . . . Prose fiction transforms, it cannot help transforming; but by its nature it is able to follow line for line in a way that verse can never do. . . . To the mystic who was Blake, and to the artist who was Conrad the whole world is mysterious" (22, 37). In seeking out its "physiological quality" and in detecting in it an attempt "to create life over again" and to transform it, Symons finds evidence in Conrad's prose of what he celebrated in Decadent literature in general: "that learned corruption of language by which style ceases to

be organic, and becomes, in the pursuit of some new expressiveness or beauty, deliberately abnormal" ("A Note on George Meredith," in *Studies in Prose and Verse*, 149).

56. Conrad to Richard Curle, April 24, 1922, letter 89, in *Corad to a Friend*, 142.

57. Stéphane Mallarmé to Eugène Lefébure, Mar. 20, 1870, letter 57, in *Selected Letters*, 90. One can compare this statement with that of Stevenson, who, in his dedication (to Sidney Colvin) of *Travels with a Donkey in the Cevennes* (1879), described every book as "in an intimate sense, a circular letter to the friends of him who writes it. They alone take his meaning; they find private messages, assurances of love, and expressions of gratitude dropped for them in every corner" (in *Works*, 1:147).

58. As Dowling points out, however, the fatal book is a "central Decadent *topos*"; it is typically a fiction. The syntax and rhythms of the prose that constitutes the fatal book embody the soul of, or the cult of, style. The author who employs this *topos* must approximate through his own ingenious, complicated prose the stylistic subtleties of such works as the talismanic book of love that Lucian labors to produce in Arthur Machen's *The Hill of Dreams* (1907), the corrupting yellow book that Lord Henry Wotton passes on to Dorian Gray, Lovecraft's *Necronomicon*, and Kurtz's report to the International Society for the Suppression of Savage Customs. Each is a poisonous, albeit fictional, text that is said to mesmerize the reader, who in turn responds to and acts upon the *expression* of the ideas, and not the ideas themselves, whose meaning is masked by the beauty of the form that cloaks them. Thus, Dowling argues, "the fatal book *is* fatal . . . not because of its power to kill outright, but because of its power decisively to change an individual life" (*Language and Decadence*, 164).

59. Dowling, *Language and Decadence*, 160.

60. See Hay, "Joseph Conrad and Impressionism," 137-44; Eloise Knapp Hay, "Impressionism Limited," in Sherry, *Joseph Conrad*, 54-64; Karl, "Joseph Conrad," 565-76. In this context, for example, Ian Watt draws an analogy between Conrad's literary experiments and Claude Monet's artistic ones: frustrated, as Conrad had been, by their obtuseness, Monet would dub his critics "Poor blind idiots," ridiculing them for their insistence that the viewer must be allowed to "see everything clearly, even through the fog" (cited in Watt, "Impressionism and Symbolism in *Heart of Darkness*," in Sherry, *Joseph Conrad*, 39). Watt points out that "the difficulty and the obscurity" of Conrad's story, as in the great impressionist's paintings, "are essential parts of what the artist is trying to convey" (39).

61. Poe, "Nathaniel Hawthorne," in *Essays and Reviews*, 572.

62. Hawthorne, preface to *House of the Seven Gables*, 2-3.

Conclusion

1. De la Mare, ed., *The Eighteen-Eighties*, vii.

2. Lovecraft, *Supernatural Horror in Literature*, 13.

3. Lovecraft, cited in St. Armand, *The Fiction of H. P. Lovecraft*, 9; Lovecraft *Supernatural Horror in Literature*, 13.

4. Lovecraft, "The Rats in the Walls," in *Best of H. P. Loveraft*, 16, 29.

5. My source of information concerning the classifications of early teratologists is Stephen Jay Gould's "Helpful Monsters," in *Hen's Teeth and Horse's Toes*, 187-88.

6. Pater, "Conclusion," in *Three Major Texts*, 217.

7. Ibid., 218; *Visuddhimagga*, cited in Borges, "New Refutation of Time," in *Other Inquisitions, 1937-1952*, 186.

8. Conrad, *Notes on Life and Letters*, 13.

9. Pater, "Conclusion," in *Three Major Texts*, 218; Derrida, "Speech and Phenomena" (1967), in *A Derrida Reader*, 13.

10. Chesterton, *George Bernard Shaw*, 247.

11. Edmond de Goncourt, cited in Symons, "Decadent Movement," 860.

12. Beerbohm, "A Defense of Cosmetics," 141.

13. Buckley, *William Ernest Henley*, 164-65.

14. Symons, "Decadent Movement," 859.

15. Ibid., 862; Beerbohm, "A Defense of Cosmetics," 144.

16. Beerbohm, "A Defense of Cosmetics," 140-44.

17. Ibid., 137, 141.

18. Burdett, *The Beardsley Period*, 89.

19. Wells, *The Story of a Great Schoolmaster* in *The Works of H.G. Wells*, 24:320; Wells, *The Definitive Time Machine*, 44, 53, 90.

20. Lovecraft, cited in St. Armand, "H. P. Lovecraft," 128.

21. Lovecraft, *Supernatural Horror in Literature*, 15.

22. Wilde, "The Importance of Being Earnest," in *Oscar Wilde*, 530; Dickens, *Dombey and Son*, 413, 416.

23. Beerbohm, "A Defense of Cosmetics," 139-40.

24. Lovecraft, *Supernatural Horror in Literature*, 14.

25. Calinescu, *Five Faces of Modernity*, 167.

26. Ibid., 174.

27. Orwell, *Nineteen Eighty-Four*, 403-4; Shiel, "On Panic," in *Science, Life and Literature*, 196.

28. Lem, *The Futurological Congress*, 103, 129 (hereinafter cited in the text).

29. Chesterton, *George Bernard Shaw*, 247; Beerbohm, "A Defense of Cosmetics," 145.

30. Beerbohm, "A Defense of Cosmetics," 139.

31. W. James, *Varieties of Religious Experience*, 119.

32. Shiel, "Xélucha," in *Shapes in the Fire*, 9-11, 17.

33. Borges, "New Refutation of Time," in *Other Inquisitions, 1937-1952*, 187.

34. It is worth noting that Eliot considered using Kurtz's dying cry—"the horror! the horror!"—as the epigraph to his poem. Had he chosen to do so, he would perhaps have seemed to undermine the very stylistic strategies that allow the text to become the thing it seeks to describe.

35. Symons, "Decadent Movement," 589.

36. Wells, "Zoological Retrogression," 253.

Bibliography

The Decadent Movement

Primary Works

Allen, Grant. "The New Hedonism." *Fortnightly Review* 55 (Jan.-June 1894): 377-92.

Bagehot, Walter. *Literary Studies, by the Late Walter Bagehot*. 3 vols. London: Longmans, Green, 1905.

———. *The Works and Life of Walter Bagehot*. 9 vols. London: Longmans, Green, 1915.

Baudelaire, Charles P. *Fatal Destinies: The Edgar Poe Essays*. Trans. Joan Fiedler Mele. Woodhaven, N.Y.: Cross Country Press, 1981.

———. *Les fleurs du mal*. Paris: Calmann-Lévy, [1868?].

Beardsley, Aubrey. *Letters from Aubrey Beardsley to Leonard Smithers*. Ed. R.A. Walker. London: First Edition Club, 1937.

———. *Under the Hill*. New York: Grove, 1959.

Beerbohm, Sir Max. "A Defense of Cosmetics." *Yellow Book* 1 (April 1894): 65-82.

———. "A Letter to the Editor." *Yellow Book* 2 (July 1894): 281-85.

Bourget, Paul. *Essais de psychologie contemporaine*. 2 vols. Paris: Plon-Nourrit, 1917.

Constant, Benjamin. "Les dessins de Victor Hugo." *La République française* (Paris), May 5, 1888.

Crackanthorpe, Hubert. "Reticence in Literature: Some Roundabout Remarks." *Yellow Book* 2 (July 1894): 259-69.

Cram, Ralph Adams. *The Decadent, Being the Gospel of Inaction*. N.p., 1893.

De Goncourt, Edmond, and Jules de Goncourt. *The Goncourt Journals: 1851-1870*. Ed. and trans. Lewis Galantière. Garden City, N.J.: Doubleday, Doran, 1937.

Fénéon, Félix. *Oeuvres plus que complètes*. Ed. Joan U. Halperin. 2 vols. Geneva, Switz.: Librairie Droz, 1970.

Gautier, Théophile. "Texte." In *Dessins de Victor Hugo*, by Paul Chenay, 7-27. Paris: Castel, 1863.

———. "Une Notice." In *Les fleurs du mal*, by Baudelaire, 1-75.

———. "Venté du mobilier de M. Victor Hugo." *La Press* (Paris), June 7, 1852.

Harrison, Frederic. "Art and Shoddy: A Reply to Criticisms." *Forum* 15 (1893): 718-26.

———. "The Decadence of Romance." *Forum* 15 (1893): 216-24.

Housman, Laurence. "The Zeit-Geist." In *Quarto: A Volume Artistic, Literary, and Musical* 4 (1898): 17-20.

Hugo, Victor. *Oeuvres complètes*. Ed. Jean Massin. 18 vols. Paris: Le club français du livre, 1967-70.

Huysmans, Joris-Karl. *Against Nature*. Trans. Robert Baldick. New York: Penguin, 1959.

———. *L'art moderne/certains*. Paris: Union Générale d'Editions, 1975.

———. "Les Dessins de Victor Hugo." *La Jeune Belgique* 9 (1890): 135-36.

———. "Instrumentum Diaboli." In *The Graphic Works of Félicien Rops*, by Lee Revens, 15-38. New York: Land's End, 1968.

Johnson, Lionel. "The Cultured Faun." *Anti-Jacobin*, no. 7 (Mar. 1891): 156-57.

Le Gallienne, Richard. *Retrospective Reviews: A Literary Log*. 2 vols. London: John Lane, 1896.

———. "What's Wrong with the Eighteen Nineties?" *Bookman* 54 (1921): 1-7.

Maeterlinck, Maurice. *The Treasure of the Humble*. Trans. Alfred Sutro. New York: Dodd, Mead, 1907.

Mallarmé, Stéphane. *Mallarmé: Selected Prose Poems, Essays, and Letters*. Trans. Bradford Cook. Baltimore: Johns Hopkins Univ. Press, 1956.

——. *Selected Letters of Stéphane Mallarmé*. Ed. and trans. Rosemary Lloyd. Chicago: Univ. of Chicago Press, 1988.

Marillier, H.C., ed. *The Early Work of Aubrey Beardsley*. New York: Dover, 1967.

Multatuli [Eduard Douwes Dekker]. "Décomposition." *La Revue blanche* 12, no. 96 (June 1897): 683-85.

Pater, Walter. *Walter Pater: Three Major Texts*. Ed. William E. Buckler. New York: New York Univ. Press, 1986.

Review of *The Shadow of Death*, by Stanislaus Eric Stenbock. *Pall Mall Gazette* (London), Mar. 1, 1894, 4.

Rickett, Arthur. *Lost Chords: Some Emotions without Morals*. London: A.D. Innes, 1895.

Rolfe, Frederick. *Chronicles of the House of Borgia*. New York: Dover, 1962.

Saltus, Francis Saltus. *Honey and Gall*. Philadelphia: Lippincott, 1873.

Stutfield, Hugh E.M. "Tommyrotics." *Blackwood's Magazine* 157 (Jan.-June 1895): 833-45.

Swinburne, Algernon Charles. *A Study of Victor Hugo*. London: Chatto and Windus, 1886.

Symonds, John Addington. *Essays Speculative and Suggestive*. London: Chapman and Hall, 1890.

——. *The Letters of John Addington Symonds*. Ed. Herbert M. Schueller and Robert L. Peters. 3 vols. Detroit: Wayne State Univ. Press, 1968

Symons, Arthur. "An Apology for Puppets." *Saturday Review*, July 17, 1897, 55-56.

——. *Confessions: A Study in Pathology*. New York: Jonathan Cape and Harrison Smith, 1930.

——. "The Decadent Movement in Literature." *Harper's New Monthly Magazine* 87 (Nov. 1893): 858-67.

——. "Editorial Note." *Savoy* 1 (Jan. 1896): 5.

——. *Studies in Prose and Verse*. London: Dent, 1922.

——. *Studies in Seven Arts*. London: Archibald Constable, 1906.

——. *A Study of Walter Pater*. N.p.: Norwood Editions, 1977.

——. *The Symbolist Movement in Literature*. New York: Dutton, 1958.

Vacquerie, Auguste. *Demi-Teintes*. Paris: Garnier Frères, 1845.

Verhaeren, Emile. "Les dessins de Victor Hugo." *L'Art Modern* (Brussels), June 3, 1888, 181.

Vicaire, Gabriel. *Les déliquescences, poèmes décadents d'Adoré Floupette*. Paris: Les éditions Henri Jonquières, 1923.

Wilde, Oscar. *The Complete Works of Oscar Wilde*. 12 vols. Garden City, N.Y.: Doubleday, Page, 1923.

——. *Letters of Oscar Wilde*. Ed. Rupert Hart-Davis. New York: Harcourt, 1962.

——. *Oscar Wilde*. Ed. Isobel Murray. Oxford: Oxford Univ. Press, 1989.

——. *Salomé*. London: Heinemann, 1957.

The Yellow Book: An Illustrated Quarterly. 13 vols. London: John Lane, 1894-97.

Zola, Emile. *Nana*. Trans. Victor Plarr. 2 vols. London: Lutetian Society, 1894.

Secondary Works

Adams, Elsie B. *Bernard Shaw and the Aesthetes*. Columbus: Ohio State Univ. Press, 1971.

Adlard, John. *Stenbock, Yeats and the Nineties*. London: Cecil and Amelia Woolf, 1969.

Aldington, Richard, ed. *The Religion of Beauty: Selections from the Aesthetes*. London: Heinemann, 1950.

Auchard, John. *Silence in Henry James: The Heritage of Symbolism and Decadence*. University Park: Pennsylvania State Univ. Press, 1986.

Balakian, Anna. *The Symbolist Movement: A Critical Appraisal.* New York: Random House, 1967.
——, ed. *The Symbolist Movement in the Literature of European Languages.* Budapest: Akadémiai Kiadó, 1982.
Balfour, Arthur. *Decadence.* Cambridge: Cambridge Univ. Press, 1908.
Bargainnier, Earl. "Images of 1890s." *Journal of Popular Culture* 12 (1978-79): 19-29.
Beckson, Karl. *Aesthetes and Decadents of the 1890's: An Anthology of British Poetry and Prose.* New York: Vintage, 1966.
——. *London in the 1890s: A Cultural History.* New York: Norton, 1992.
——. "A Mythology of Aestheticism." *English Literature in Transition* 17 (1974): 233-49.
Birkett, Jennifer. *The Sins of the Fathers: Decadence in France, 1870-1914.* London: Quartet, 1986.
Bloom, Harold. "Walter Pater: The Intoxification of Belatedness." *Yale French Studies* 50 (1974): 163-89.
Bradbury, Malcolm, and James McFarlane, eds. *Modernism, 1890-1930.* Atlantic Highlands, N.J.: Humanities, 1978.
Buckler, William E. "*The Picture of Dorian Gray:* An Essay in Aesthetic Exploration." *Victorians Institute Journal* 18 (1990): 135-74.
Buckley, Jerome Hamilton. *The Triumph of Time: A Study of the Victorian Concepts of Time, History, Progress and Decadence.* Cambridge, Mass.: Harvard Univ. Press, 1966.
——. *William Ernest Henley: A Study in the "Counter-Decadence" of the 'Nineties.* Princeton, N.J.: Princeton Univ. Press, 1945.
Burdett, Osbert. *The Beardsley Period: An Essay in Perspective.* New York: Boni and Liveright, 1925.
Calinescu, Matei. *Five Faces of Modernity.* Durham, N.C.: Duke Univ. Press, 1987.
Carter, A[lfred] E[dward]. *The Idea of Decadence in French Literature, 1830-1900.* Toronto: Univ. of Toronto Press, 1958.
Casford, E. Leonore. *The Magazines of the 1890s.* Eugene: Univ. of Oregon Press, 1929.
Cazamian, Madeleine L. *Le roman et les idées en Angleterre: L'anti-intellectualisme et l'esthétisme (1880-1900).* Paris: Société d'éditions: les belles lettres, 1935.
Cevaslo, G.A. *The 1890s: An Encyclopedia of British Literature, Art and Culture.* New York: Garland, 1993.
Chamberlin, J. Edward. "An Anatomy of Cultural Melancholy." *Journal of the History of Ideas* 42 (1981): 691-705.
——. *Ripe Was the Drowsy Hour.* New York: Seabury, 1973.
Charlesworth, Barbara. *Dark Passages.* Madison: Univ. of Wisconsin Press, 1965.
Chase, Cynthia. *Decomposing Figures: Rhetorical Readings in the Romantic Tradition.* Baltimore: Johns Hopkins Univ. Press, 1986.
Chesterton, Gilbert K. *George Bernard Shaw.* New York: John Lane, 1909.
Connolly, Cyril. *Enemies of Progress.* New York: Macmillan, 1948.
Davray, Henry D. "Lettres anglaises." *Mercure de France* 63 (Sept. 15, 1906): 302.
Dijkstra, Bram. *Idols of Perversity: Fantasies of Feminine Evil in Fin-de-Siècle Culture.* Oxford: Oxford Univ. Press, 1986.
Dowling, Linda. *Aestheticism and Decadence: A Selective Annotated Bibliography.* New York: Garland, 1977.
——. *Language and Decadence in the Victorian Fin de Siècle.* Princeton, N.J.: Princeton Univ. Press, 1986.
——. "Walter Pater and Archaeology: The Reconciliation with the Earth." *Victorian Studies* 31, no. 2 (winter 1988): 209-31.
Easton, Malcolm. *Aubrey and the Dying Lady.* Boston: David R. Godine, 1972.
Ellis, Havelock. *Affirmations.* Boston: Houghton, 1922.
——. *Views and Reviews.* 1st and 2d ser. Boston: Houghton, 1932.
Ellmann, Richard. *Edwardians and Late Victorians.* New York: Columbia Univ. Press, 1960.
——. *Oscar Wilde.* New York: Vintage, 1988.

Fass, Barbara. *La Belle Dame Sans Merci and the Aesthetics of Romanticism*. Detroit: Wayne State Univ. Press, 1974.

Felski, Rita. "The Counterdiscourse of the Feminine in Three Texts by Wilde, Huysmans, and Sacher-Masoch." *PMLA* 106, no. 5 (Oct. 1991): 1094-1105.

Fletcher, Ian. "The 1890s: A Lost Decade." *Victorian Studies* 4 (1960-61): 345-54.

———. *Walter Pater*. London: Longmans, Green, 1959.

———. ed. *Decadence and the 1890s*. London: Arnold, 1929.

Fraser, Hilary. *Beauty and Belief*. Cambridge: Cambridge Univ. Press, 1986.

Gagnier, Regenia. *Idylls of the Marketplace: Oscar Wilde and the Victorian Public*. Stanford, Calif.: Stanford Univ. Press, 1986.

Gawsworth, John [Terence Armstrong], ed. *Ten Contemporaries: Notes toward Their Definitive Bibliography*. Norword, Penn.: Norwood Editions, 1976.

Georgel, Pierre. *Dessins de Victor Hugo*. Paris: Maison de Victor Hugo, 1971.

———. *Drawings by Victor Hugo*. London: Victoria and Albert Museum, 1974.

———. "Le romantisme des années 1860: Correspondance Victor Hugo–Philippe Burty." *Revue de l'Art* [Paris] 20 (1973): 8-64.

Gerber, Helmut. "The Nineties: Beginning, End, or Transition?" In *Edwardians and Late Victorians*, ed. Ellmann, 50-79.

Goldfarb, Russell M. "Late Victorian Decadence." *Journal of Aesthetics and Art Criticism* 20 (1962): 369-73.

Gordon, Jan B. "'The Wilde Child': Structure and Origin in the *Fin de Siècle* Short Story." *English Literature in Transition* 15 (1972): 277-90.

Gordon, Rae Beth. *Ornament, Fantasy, and Desire in Nineteenth-Century French Literature*. Princeton, N.J.: Princeton Univ. Press, 1992.

Guy, Josephine. "The Concept of Tradition and Late Nineteenth-Century British Avant-Garde Movements." *Prose Studies* 13, no. 2 (Sept. 1990): 250-59.

Harris, Wendell V. "Fiction in the English 'Experimental' Periodicals of the 1890's." *Bulletin of Bibliography* 25 (1968): 111-18.

———. "Identifying the Decadent Fiction of the Eighteen-Nineties." *English Fiction in Transition* 5, no. 5 (1962): 1-13.

———. "John Lane's Keynotes Series and the Fiction of the 1890's." *PMLA* 83 (1968): 1407-13.

Hough, Graham. "George Moore and the Nineties." In *Edwardians and Late Victorians*, ed. Ellmann, 1-27.

Jackson, Holbrook. *The Eighteen Nineties: A Review of Art and Ideas at the Close of the Nineteenth Century*. London: Jonathan Cape, 1927.

Johnson, E.D.H. "The Eighteen Nineties: Perspectives." In *Wilde and the Nineties*, ed. Ryskamp, 25-30.

Jullian, Philippe. *Dreamers of Decadence: Symbolist Painters of the 1890s*. Trans. Robert Baldick. New York: Praeger, 1972.

———. *The Symbolists*. Oxford: Phaidon, 1973. Reprint, New York: Dutton, 1977.

Kingcaid, Renée A. *Neurosis and Narrative: The Decadent Short Fiction of Proust, Lorrain, and Rachilde*. Carbondale: Southern Illinois Univ. Press, 1992.

Kuryluk, Ewa. *Salome and Judas in the Cave of Sex*. Evanston, Ill.: Northwestern Univ. Press, 1987.

Mason, Stuart. *Oscar Wilde: Art and Morality*. London: J. Jacobs, 1908.

Maurois, André. *Victor Hugo and His World*. London: Thames and Hudson, 1966.

Milner, John. *Symbolists and Decadents*. New York: Studio Vista, 1971.

Munro, John M. *The Decadent Poetry of the Eighteen-Nineties*. Beirut: American Univ. of Beirut Press, 1970.

Murdoch, W.G. Blaikie. *The Renaissance of the Nineties*. London: Alexander Moring, 1911.

Nalbatian, Suzanne. *Seeds of Decadence in the Late Nineteenth-Century Novel*. New York: St. Martin's, 1983.

Nelson, James G. *The Early Nineties: A View from the Bodley Head*. Cambridge, Mass.: Harvard Univ. Press, 1971.

Ojala, Aatos. *Aestheticism and Oscar Wilde.* 2 vols. Helsinki: Finnish Academy of Science and Letters, 1954-55.

Ollinger-Zinque, Gisèle. *Ensor by Himself.* Trans. Alistair Kennedy. Brussels: Laconti, 1976.

Picon, Gaëtan, ed. *Victor Hugo Dessinateur.* Paris: Editions du Minotaure, 1963.

———, ed. *Victor Hugo, Dessins.* Paris: Gallimard, 1985.

Pierrot, Jean. *The Decadent Imagination, 1880-1900.* Chicago: Univ. of Chicago Press, 1981.

Praz, Mario. *The Romantic Agony.* Cleveland: World, 1965.

Reade, Brian. *Aubrey Beardsley.* New York: Bonanza, 1967.

Reed, John R. *Decadent Style.* Athens: Ohio Univ. Press, 1985.

———. "Mixing Memory and Desire in Late Victorian Literature." *English Literature in Transition* 14 (1971): 1-15.

Robinson, Alan. *Symbol to Vortex: Poetry, Painting and Ideas, 1885-1914.* London: St. Martin's, 1985.

Rosenblatt, Louise. *L'idée de l'art pour l'art.* Paris: Librairie Ancienne Honoré Champion, 1931.

Ryskamp, Charles, ed. *Wilde and the Nineties: An Essay and an Exhibition.* Princeton, N.J.: Princeton Univ. Press, 1966.

St. Armand, Barton L. "H.P. Lovecraft: New England Decadent." *Caliban* 12 (1975): 127-55.

Seiler, R.M., ed. *Walter Pater: The Critical Heritage.* London: Routledge and Kegan Paul, 1980.

Showalter, Elaine. "Syphilis, Sexuality, and the Fiction of the Fin de Siècle." In *Sex, Politics, and Science in the Nineteenth-Century Novel,* ed. Ruth Bernard Yeazell, 88-115. Baltimore: Johns Hopkins Univ. Press, 1986.

———, ed. *Daughters of Decadence: Women Writers of the Fin de Siècle.* New Brunswick, N.J.: Rutgers Univ. Press, 1993.

Silverman, Debora L. *Art Nouveau in Fin-de-Siècle France.* Berkeley: Univ. of California Press, 1989.

Spackman, Barbara. *Decadent Genealogies: The Rhetoric of Sickness from Baudelaire to D'Annunzio.* Ithaca, N.Y.: Cornell Univ. Press, 1989.

Spivak, Gayatri Chakravorty. "Decadent Style." *Language and Style* 7, no. 4 (fall 1974): 227-34.

Stokes, John, ed. *Fin de Siècle, Fin du Globe: Fears and Fantasies of the Late Nineteenth Century.* New York: St. Martin's, 1992.

Symons, A[lphonse] J[ames] A[lbert], ed. *An Anthology of 'Nineties Verse.* London: Elkin Mathews and Marrot, 1928.

Temple, Ruth Z. "Truth in Labelling: Pre-Raphaelitism, Aestheticism, Decadence, Fin de Siècle." *English Literature in Transition* 17 (1974): 201-22.

Thompson, C.W. *Victor Hugo and the Graphic Arts (1820-1833).* Geneva, Switz.: Librairie Droz, 1970.

Thornton, R.K.R. *The Decadent Dilemma.* London: Edward Arnold, 1983.

Turquet-Milnes, Gladys R. *The Influence of Baudelaire in France and England.* London: Constable, 1913.

Weintraub, Stanley, ed. *The Yellow Book: Quintessence of the Nineties.* New York: Doubleday-Anchor, 1964.

Williams, Roger Lawrence. *The Horror of Life.* Chicago: Univ. of Chicago Press, 1980.

Wilson, Angus. *The Naughty Nineties.* London: Eyre Methuen, 1976.

Wilson, Simon. *Beardsley.* New York: Dutton, 1976.

Literature of Horror

Primary Works

Barbey D'Aurevilly, Jules-Amédée. *The She-Devils (Les Diaboliques).* Trans. Jean Kimber. London: Oxford Univ. Press, 1964.

Blackwood, Algernon. *Tales of the Uncanny and Supernatural.* London: Peter Nevill, 1952.

Bleiler, E.F., ed. *A Treasury of Victorian Ghost Stories*. New York: Scribner's, 1981.
Buchan, John. *The Best Short Stories of John Buchan*. Ed. David Daniell. 2 vols. London: Michael Joseph, 1980.
Chambers, Robert. *The King in Yellow and Other Horror Stories*. New York: Dover, 1970.
Chayefsky, Paddy. *Altered States*. New York: Harper and Row, 1978.
Cox, Michael, and R.A. Gilbert, eds. *The Oxford Book of English Ghost Stories*. London: Oxford Univ. Press, 1986.
Cram, Ralph Adams. *Black Spirits and White*. Chicago: Stone and Kimball, 1895.
Crowley, Aleister. *The Strategem and Other Stories*. Freeport, N.Y.: Books for Libraries Press, 1971.
Gilchrist, R[obert] Murray. *The Stone Dragon and Other Tragic Romances*. London: Methuen, 1894.
Gilman, Charlotte Perkins. "The Yellow Wallpaper." New York: Feminist Press, 1973.
Golding, William. *Lord of the Flies*. London: Faber and Faber, 1954.
Hichens, Robert. *Tongues of Conscience*. New York: Frederick A. Stokes, 1898.
Hodgson, William Hope. *The Night Land*. 1912. Reprint, Westport, Conn.: Hyperion, 1976.
Hoffmann, E.T.A. *The Best Tales of Hoffmann*. Ed. E.F. Bleiler. New York: Dover, 1967.
Huneker, James. *Melomaniacs*. New York: Greenwood, 1969.
James, M.R. *More Ghost Stories of an Antiquary*. London: Edward Arnold, 1912.
———. *A Warning to the Curious and Other Ghost Stories*. London: Edward Arnold, 1927.
Kipling, Rudyard. *A Diversity of Creatures*. New York: Scribner's, 1917.
———. *The Phantom 'Rickshaw and Other Stories*. New York: Scribner's, 1913.
Le Fanu, J. Sheridan. *Best Ghost Stories of J.S. Le Fanu*. New York: Dover, 1964.
Lem, Stanislaw. *The Futurological Congress*. Trans. Michael Kandel. San Diego, Calif.: Harcourt, 1974.
Lovecraft, H[oward] P[hillips]. *The Best of H. P. Lovecraft*. Ed. Robert Bloch. New York: Ballantine, 1982.
Morrow, W.C. *The Ape, the Idiot and Other People*. Philadelphia: Lippincott, 1897.
Onions, Oliver. *Widdershins*. New York: Dover, 1971.
Orwell, George. *Nineteen Eighty-Four*. Oxford: Clarendon, 1984.
Peattie, Elia Wilkinson. *The Shape of Fear and Other Ghostly Tales*. Freeport, N.Y.: Books for Libraries Press, 1969.
Poe, Edgar Allan. *Collected Works of Edgar Allan Poe*. Ed. Thomas Ollive Mabbott. 3 vols. Cambridge, Mass.: Belknap of Harvard Univ. Press, 1978.
———. *Essays and Reviews*. New York: Literary Classics of the United States, 1984.
———. *Poetry and Tales*. New York: Literary Classics of the United States, 1984.
Shelley, Mary. *Frankenstein; or, The Modern Prometheus*. Ed. Nora Crook. London: William Pickering, 1996.
Shiel, Matthew Phipps. *The Best Short Stories of M.P. Shiel*. London: Victor Gollancz, 1948.
———. *Shapes in the Fire*. 1896. Reprint, New York: Garland, 1977.
Stenbock, Stanislaus Eric. *The Shadow of Death* and *Studies of Death*. 1893. Reprint, New York: Garland, 1984.
Stevenson, Robert Louis. *The Works of Robert Louis Stevenson*. 20 vols. London: Cassell, 1907.
Stoker, Bram. *Dracula*. Harmondsworth, Eng.: Penguin, 1993.
Sullivan, Jack, ed. *Lost Souls*. Athens: Ohio Univ. Press, 1978.
Walpole, Horce. *Hieroglyphic Tales*. Ed. Kenneth W. Gross. Los Angeles: Augustan Reprint Society, 1982.
Watson, H[enry] B[rereton] Marriott. *Diogenes of London and Other Sketches*. London: Methuen, 1893.
Wells, H[erbert] G[eorge]. *The Complete Short Stories of H.G. Wells*. London: Ernest Benn, 1966.
———. *The Definitive Time Machine: A Critical Edition of H.G. Wells's Scientific Romance*. Ed. Harry M. Geduld. Bloomington: Indiana Univ. Press, 1987.

———. *The Door in the Wall and Other Stories*. Boston: David R. Godine, 1980.
———. *The Island of Doctor Moreau: A Critical Text of the 1896 London First Edition, with Introduction and Appendices*. Ed. Leon Stover. Jefferson, N.C.: McFarland, 1996.
Wharton, Edith. *Ghosts*. New York: Appleton, 1937.
Wilde, Oscar. *The Picture of Dorian Gray and Other Writings by Oscar Wilde*. Ed. Richard Ellmann. New York: Bantam, 1982.
X.L. [Julian Osgood Field]. *Aut Diabolus aut Nihil and Other Tales*. London: Methuen, 1894.

Secondary Works

Apter, T.E. *Fantasy Literature: An Approach to Reality*. London: Macmillan; Bloomington: Indiana Univ. Press, 1982.
Ashley, Mike. *Who's Who in Horror and Fantasy Fiction*. New York: Taplinger, 1978.
Auerbach, Nina. *Our Vampires, Ourselves*. Chicago: Univ. of Chicago Press, 1995.
Barclay, Glen St. John. *Anatomy of Horror*. London: Weidenfeld and Nicholson, 1978.
Birkhead, Edith. *Tale of Terror: A Study of Gothic Romance*. London: Constable, 1921.
Bleiler, E.F., ed. *The Checklist of Science Fiction and Supernatural Fiction*. Glen Rock, N.J.: Firebell Books, 1978.
———, ed. *The Guide to Supernatural Fiction*. Kent, Ohio: Kent State Univ. Press, 1983.
———, ed. *Supernatural Fiction Writers*. 2 vols. New York: Scribner's, 1982.
Block, Edward, Jr. "James Sully, Evolutionist, Psychologist and Late Victorian Gothic Fiction." *Victorian Studies* 25 (1982): 443-68.
Bloom, Clive. *The "Occult" Experience and the New Criticism*. Totowa, N.J.: Barnes and Noble, 1986.
Briggs, Julia. *Night Visitors: The Rise and Fall of the English Ghost Story*. London: Faber, 1977.
Burke, Edmund. *A Philosophical Enquiry into the Origins of Our Ideas of the Sublime and Beautiful*. Ed. J.T. Boulton. London: Routledge and Kegan Paul, 1958.
Clover, Carol J. *Men, Women and Chainsaws: Gender in the Modern Horror Film*. Princeton, N.J.: Princeton Univ. Press, 1992.
Daniels, Les. *Living in Fear*. New York: Scribner's, 1975.
Day, William Patrick. *In the Circles of Fear and Desire*. Chicago: Univ. of Chicago Press, 1985.
Evans, Hilary, and Dik Evans, eds. *Beyond the Gaslight: Science in Popular Fiction, 1895-1905*. London: F. Muller, 1976.
Fleenor, Julian. *The Female Gothic*. Montreal: Eden, 1983.
Fleming, Peter. "The Stuff of Nightmares." *Spectator Literary Supplement* 18 (April 1931): 633.
Frank, Frederick S. *Guide to the Gothic*. Metuchen, N.J.: Scarecrow, 1984.
Gray, Jeffrey Alan. *The Psychology of Fear*. London: Weidenfeld and Nicholson, 1971.
Hammacher, A.M. *Phantoms of the Imagination*. New York: Henry N. Abrams, 1981.
Heler, Terry. *The Delights of Terror: The Aesthetics of the Tale of Terror*. Urbana: Univ. of Illinois Press, 1987.
Hugo, Victor. "Preface to *Cromwell*." In *Prefaces and Prologues to Famous Books*, 337-87. New York: Collier, [1910?].
Hume, Robert D. "Gothic versus Romantic: A Revaluation of the Gothic Novel." *PMLA* 84, no. 2 (Mar. 1969): 282-90.
Jackson, Rosemary. "Shades of Gothic in Victorian Literature." *Minnesota Review* 13 (1979): 98-112.
Jarrett, Derek. *The Sleep of Reason*. London: Weidenfeld and Nicolson, 1988.
Joshi, S.T. *H. P. Lovecraft: Four Decades of Criticism*. Athens: Ohio Univ. Press, 1980.
Kalikoff, Beth. *Murder and Moral Decay in Victorian Popular Literature*. Ann Arbor: UMI Research Press, 1986.
Kayser, Wolfgang. *The Grotesque in Art and Literature*. Trans. Ulrich Weisstein. New York: McGraw-Hill, 1966.

Kempton, Daniel. "The Gold/Goole/Ghoul Bug." *ESQ* 33, no. 1 (1987): 1-19.
Kerr, Howard, John W. Crowley, and Charles L. Crow, eds. *The Haunted Dusk: American Supernatural Fiction, 1820-1920.* Athens: Univ. of Georgia Press, 1983.
Kierkegaard, Søren. *The Concept of Anxiety.* Princeton, N.J.: Princeton Univ. Press, 1980.
Kristeva, Julia. *The Powers of Horror: An Essay on Abjection.* New York: Columbia Univ. Press, 1982.
Lea, Sydney L.W., Jr. *Gothic to Fantastic: Readings in Supernatural Fiction.* New York: Arno, 1980.
Lévy, Maurice. *Le roman "gothique" anglais, 1764-1824.* Toulouse: Association des publications de la faculté des lettres et sciences humaines de Toulouse, 1968.
Lovecraft, H[oward] P[hillips]. *Supernatural Horror in Literature.* New York: Dover, 1973.
Messent, Peter B. *Literature of the Occult.* Englewood Cliffs, N.J.: Prentice-Hall, 1981.
Penzoldt, Peter. *The Supernatural in Fiction.* New York: Humanities, 1965.
Prickett, Stephen. *Victorian Fantasy.* Bloomington: Indiana Univ. Press, 1979.
Punter, David. *The Literature of Terror.* New York: Longmans, 1980.
Rabkin, Eric. *The Fantastic in Literature.* Princeton, N.J.: Princeton Univ. Press, 1976.
Ringe, Donald A. *American Gothic: Imagination and Reason in Nineteenth-Century Fiction.* Lexington: Univ. Press of Kentucky, 1982.
Robert-Jones, Philippe. *Beyond Time and Space: Non-Realist Painting in the Nineteenth Century.* Oxford: Oxford Univ. Press, 1978.
Scarborough, Dorothy. *The Supernatural in Modern English Fiction.* New York: Putnam's, 1917.
Scarry, Elaine. *The Body in Pain: The Making and Unmaking of the World.* New York: Oxford Univ. Press, 1985.
Scheick, William J. "Exorcising the Ghost Story." *Cahiers Victoriens et Edouardiens* 17 (April 1982): 53-62.
Schlobin, Roger C. *The Aesthetics of Fantasy Literature and Art.* Brighton, Eng.: Harvester, 1982.
Scott, Sir Walter. "On the Supernatural in Fictitious Composition; and particularly on the Works of Ernest Theodore William Hoffman [*sic*]." *Foreign Quarterly Review* 1 (1827): 60-98.
Sedgwick, Eve. *The Coherence of Gothic Conventions.* New York: Methuen, 1986.
Siebers, Tobin. *The Romantic Fantastic.* New York: Cornell Univ. Press, 1984.
St. Armand, Barton L. "H.P. Lovecraft: New England Decadent." *Caliban,* no. 12 (1975): 127-55.
———. "Poe's 'Sober Mystification': The Uses of Alchemy in 'The Gold Bug.'" *Poe Studies* 4, no. 1 (June 1971): 1-7.
———. *The Roots of Horror in the Fiction of H.P. Lovecraft.* Elizabethtown, N.Y.: Dragon Press, 1977.
Sullivan, Jack. *Elegant Nightmares.* Athens: Ohio Univ. Press, 1978.
———. *The Penguin Encyclopedia of Horror and the Supernatural.* New York: Viking, 1986.
Thompson, G.R., ed. *The Gothic Imagination.* Pullman: Washington State Univ. Press, 1974.
Todorov, Tzvetan. *The Fantastic.* Ithaca, N.Y.: Cornell Univ. Press, 1975.
Tracy, Ann B. *The Gothic Novel, 1790-1830: Plot Summaries and Index to Motifs.* Lexington: Univ. Press of Kentucky, 1982.
Twitchell, James B. *Dreadful Pleasures: An Anatomy of Modern Horror.* New York: Oxford Univ. Press, 1985.
Tymn, Marshall B., Kenneth J. Zahorski, and Robert H. Boyer, eds. *Fantasy Literature: A Core Collection and Reference Guide.* New York: Bowker, 1979.
———, eds. *Horror Literature: A Core Collection and Reference Guide.* New York: Bowker, 1981.
Varma, Devendra P. *The Gothic Flame.* New York: Russell and Russell, 1957.
Varnado, S.L. *Haunted Presence: The Numinous in Gothic Fiction.* Tuscaloosa: Univ. of Alabama Press, 1987.

Wilt, Judith. "The Imperial Mouth: Imperialism, Gothic and Science Fiction." *Journal of Popular Culture* 14, no. 4 (spring 1981): 618-28.

Zizek, Slavoj. "Grimaces of the Real, or When the Phallus Appears." *October* 58 (fall 1991): 45-68.

Nineteenth-Century Science and Philology

Primary Works

Beale, Lionel Smith. *Protoplasm; or, Life, Matter, and Mind.* 2d ed. London: J. Churchill, 1870.

Booth, William. *In Darkest England and the Way Out.* New York: Funk and Wagnalls, 1890.

Chamberlain, Alexander Francis. *The Child: A Study in the Evolution of Man.* London: Walter Scott, 1906.

Chambers Robert. *Vestiges of the Natural History of Creation.* New York: Wiley and Putnam, 1846.

Charcot, J.-M. and Paul Richer. "Note sur l'anatomie morphologique de la région lombaire: Sillon lombaire médian." *Nouvelle Iconographie de la Salpêtrière* 1 (1888): 13-26.

Darwin, Charles. *Charles Darwin's Notebooks, 1836-1844.* Ed. Paul H. Barrett, Peter J. Gautrey, Sandra Herbert, David Kohn, and Sydney Smith. Ithaca, N.Y.: Cornell Univ. Press, 1987.

———. *The Descent of Man and Selection in Relation to Sex.* Vols. 21 and 22 of *The Works of Charles Darwin,* ed. Paul H. Barrett and R.B. Freeman. New York: New York Univ. Press, 1987.

———. *The Expression of the Emotions in Man and Animals.* Chicago: Univ. of Chicago Press, 1965.

———. *The Foundations of* The Origin of Species: *Two Essays Written in 1842 and 1844.* Ed. Francis Darwin. New York: Kraus, 1969.

———. *More Letters of Charles Darwin, A Record of His Work in a Series of Hitherto Unpublished Letters.* Ed. Francis Darwin. New York: Appleton, 1903.

———. *On the Origin of Species.* Ed. Ernst Mayr. Cambridge, Mass.: Harvard Univ. Press, 1964.

"Degeneration and Genius." *Psychological Review* 2 (1895): 287-92.

Duchenne de Boulogne, Guillaume-Benjamin. *The Mechanism of Human Facial Expression.* Ed. and trans. R. Andrew Cuthbertson. Cambridge: Cambridge Univ. Press, 1990.

Ellis, Havelock. *The Criminal.* London: Walter Scott, 1897.

———. *The Problem of Race Regeneration.* London: Cassell, 1911.

Farrar, Frederic W. "Philology and Darwinism." *Nature* 1, no. 21 (Mar. 24, 1870): 527-29.

Ferri, Enrico. *Criminal Sociology.* New York: Appleton, 1900.

Fowler, Orson S. *Hereditary Descent.* 1848. Reprint, New York: Garland, 1984.

Freud, Sigmund. *The Standard Edition of the Complete Psychological Works of Sigmund Freud.* Ed. James Strachey. 24 vols. London: Hogarth Press, 1955.

Galton, Sir Francis. *Hereditary Genius.* 1892. Reprint, Gloucester, Mass.: Peter Smith, 1972.

Haeckel, Ernst. *The Evolution of Man: A Popular Exposition.* 2 vols. New York: Appleton, 1896.

———. *The History of Creation: Or the Development of the Earth and Its Inhabitants by the Action of Natural Causes.* 2 vols. London: Henry S. King, 1876.

His, Wilhelm. *Anatomie menschlicher Embryonen.* 3 vols. Leipzig: Vogel, 1882.

Huxley, T[homas] H[enry]. *Evolution and Ethics.* Ed. James Paradis and George C. Williams. Princeton, N.J.: Princeton Univ. Press, 1989.

———. *Lay Sermons, Addresses, and Reviews.* New York: Appleton, 1870.

———. *Lectures and Essays.* London: C.A. Watts, n.d.

———. *Life and Letters of Thomas Henry Huxley.* Ed. Leonard Huxley. 2 vols. New York: Appleton, 1901.

——. *Man's Place in Nature and Other Anthropological Essays.* New York: D. Appleton, 1896.

——. "On the Physical Basis of Life." *Fortnightly Review* 11, no. 26 (Feb. 1, 1869): 129-45.

——. *Social Diseases and Worse Remedies.* London: Macmillan, 1891.

Kelvin, William Thomson. *Mathematical and Physical Papers Collected from Different Scientific Periodicals from May, 1841, to the Present Time.* 6 vols. Cambridge: Cambridge Univ. Press, 1882-1911.

Lombroso, Cesare. "Atavism and Evolution." *Contemporary Review* 68 (July 1895): 42-49.

——. *The Man of Genius.* 1910. Reprint, New York: Garland, 1984.

Lombroso-Ferrero, Gina. *Criminal Man, according to the classification of Cesare Lombroso.* With an introduction by Cesare Lombroso. Mountclair, N.J.: Patterson Smith, 1972.

Marshall, Charles F. *Syphilology and Venereal Disease.* New York: William Wood, 1906.

Maudsley, Henry. *Physiology and Pathology of the Mind.* Ed. Daniel N. Robinson. 1867. Reprint, Washington, D.C.: University Publications of America, 1977.

Morel, B[énédictin] A[ugustin]. "An Analysis of a Treatise on the Degenerations, Physical, Intellectual, and Moral, of the Human Race, and the Causes Which Produce Their Unhealthy Varieties." Trans. Edwin Wing. *Medical Circular* (London) 10-11 (1857).

Morison, Alexander. *The Physiognomy of Mental Diseases.* 1843. Reprint, New York: Arno, 1976.

Müller, F. Max. "Lectures on Mr. Darwin's Philosophy of Language." *Fraser's Magazine* 7-8 (May-July 1873): 525-41, 659-79, 1-24.

——. *The Science of Language.* 2 vols. 1891. Reprint, New York: AMS, 1978.

——. *The Science of Thought.* New York: Scribner's, 1887.

Nida, William Lewis. *Ab, the Cave Man: A Story of the Time of the Stone Age.* Chicago: A. Flanagan, 1911.

Nisbet, John F. *The Insanity of Genius and the General Inequality of Human Faculty Physiologically Considered.* 1900. Reprint, Folcroft, Penn.: Folcroft Library Editions, 1973.

Nordau, Max. *Degeneration.* New York: Appleton, 1895.

Romanes, George. *Mental Evolution in Man.* London: Kegan Paul, Trench, 1888.

Shaw, George Bernard. *The Sanity of Art: An Exposure of the Current Nonsense about Artists being Degenerate.* London: New Age Press, 1908.

Spencer, Herbert. *Education: Intellectual, Moral, and Physical.* Paterson, N.J.: Littlefield, Adams, 1963.

Stewart, Balfour. *The Conservation of Energy.* London: H.S. King, 1873.

Talbot, Eugene S. *Degeneracy: Its Causes, Signs, and Results.* London: Walter Scott, 1898.

Tyndall, John. *Heat a Mode of Motion.* 6th ed. New York: Appleton, 1883.

Wells, H[erbert] G[eorge]. "A Story of the Stone Age." In *The Famous Short Stories of H.G. Wells.* New York: Literary Guild of America, 1937.

——. "Zoological Retrogression." *Gentleman's Magazine,* Sept. 7, 1891, 246-53.

Secondary Works

Aarsleff, Hans. *The Study of Language in England, 1780-1860.* Princeton, N.J.: Princeton Univ. Press, 1967.

Asker, D.B.D. "Wells and Regressive Evolution." *Dutch Quarterly Review of Anglo-American Letters* 12 (1982): 15-29.

Beer, Gillian. *Darwin's Plots.* London: Routledge and Kegan Paul, 1981.

——. "The Emotion of Fear in the Evolution of Theory and Victorian Narrative." *Cahiers Victoriens et Edouardiens* 15 (1982): 39-49.

Benson, Donald R. "'Catching Light': Physics and Art in Walter Pater's Cultural Context." In *One Culture: Essays in Science and Literature,* ed. George Levine, 143-63. Madison: Univ. of Wisconsin Press, 1987.

Blinderman, Charles S. "Huxley, Pater, and Protoplasm." *Journal of the History of Ideas* 42, no. 3 (July 1982): 477-86.

Boime, Albert. "Portraying Monomaniacs to Service the Alienist's Movement: Géricault and Georget." *Oxford Art Journal* 14, no. 1 (1991): 79-91.

Brantlinger, Patrick, ed. *Energy and Entropy: Science and Culture in Victorian Britain.*
    Bloomington: Indiana Univ. Press, 1989.
Chamberlin, J. Edward, and Sander L. Gilman, eds. *Degeneration: The Dark Side of Progress.*
    New York: Columbia Univ. Press, 1985.
Dowling, Linda. "Walter Pater and Archaeology: The Reconciliation with Earth." *Victorian
    Studies* 31, no. 2 (winter 1988): 208-31.
Geison, Gerald L. "The Protoplasmic Theory of Life and the Vitalist-Mechanist Debate." *Isis*
    60, no. 3 (fall 1969): 273-92.
Gibbons, Tom. *Rooms in the Darwin Hotel.* Nedlands, W. Australia: Univ. of Western Austra-
    lia Press, 1973.
Gilman, Charles. "Stolen Paradigms: Stammbaum to Black Box." In *Papers in the History of
    Linguistics,* ed. Hans Aarsleff, Louis G. Kelly, and Hans-Josef Niederehe. Amsterdam:
    Benjamins, 1987.
Gilman, Sander L. *Disease and Repreentation: Images of Illness from Madness to AIDS.*
    Ithaca, N.Y.: Cornell Univ. Press, 1988.
Gould, Stephen J. *Ever Since Darwin.* New York: Norton, 1977.
———. *Hen's Teeth and Horse's Toes.* New York: Norton, 1984.
———. *The Mismeasure of Man.* New York: Norton, 1981.
———. *Ontogeny and Phylogeny.* Cambridge, Mass.: Harvard Univ. Press, 1977.
———. *The Panda's Thumb: More Reflections in Natural History.* New York: Norton, 1980.
Haley, Bruce. *The Healthy Body and Victorian Culture.* Cambridge, Mass.: Harvard Univ.
    Press, 1978.
Hayles, N. Katherine. *The Cosmic Web: Scientific Field Models and Literary Strategies in
    the Twentieth Century.* Ithaca, N.Y.: Cornell Univ. Press, 1984.
Henkin, Leo J. *Darwinism in the English Novel, 1860-1910.* New York: Russell and Russell,
    1963.
Hurley, Kelly. "Hereditary Taint and Cultural Contagion: The Social Etiology of *Fin-de-Siècle*
    Degeneration Theory." *Nineteenth-Century Contexts* 14, no. 2 (1990): 193-214.
Inman, Billie Andrew. "The Intellectual Context of Walter Pater's 'Conclusion.'" *Prose Stud-
    ies* 4, no. 1 (May 1981): 12-30.
Jeffords, Susan. "The Knowledge of Words: The Evolution of Language and Biology in Nine-
    teenth-Century Thought." *Centennial Review* 31, no. 1 (winter 1987): 66-83.
Keefe, Robert. "Literati, Language, and Darwinism." *Language and Style* 19, no. 2 (spring
    1986): 123-37.
Kingcaid, Renée A. *Neurosis and Narrative: The Decadent Short Fiction of Proust, Lorrain,
    and Rachilde.* Carbondale: Southern Illinois Univ. Press, 1992.
Knoll, Elizabeth. "The Science of Language and the Evolution of Mind: Max Müller's Quar-
    rel with Darwinism." *Journal of the History of the Behavioral Sciences* 22, no. 1 (Jan.
    1986): 3-22.
Koerner, Konrad, ed. *Linguistics and Evolutionary Theory: Three Essays by August
    Schleicher, Ernst Haeckel, and Wilhelm Bleek.* Amsterdam: Benjamins, 1983.
Kuhn, Thomas S. *The Structure of Scientific Revolutions.* Chicago: Univ. of Chicago Press,
    1964.
Leps, Marie-Christine. *Apprehending the Criminal: The Production of Deviance in Nineteenth-
    Century Discourse.* Durham, N.C.: Duke Univ. Press, 1992.
Levine, George. *Darwin and the Novelists: Patterns of Science in Victorian Fiction.* Cam-
    bridge, Mass.: Harvard Univ. Press, 1988.
———. "By Knowledge Possessed: Darwin, Nature, and Victorian Narrative." *New Literary
    History* 24 (1993): 363-391.
Loos, Adolf. "Ornament and Crime." In *The Architecture of Adolf Loos: An Arts Council
    Exhibition, Great Britain,* trans. Y. Safran and W. Wang, 100-103. London: Arts Coun-
    cil, 1985.
Martindale, Colin. "Degeneration, Disinhibition, and Genius." *Journal of the History of Be-
    havioral Sciences* 7, no. 2 (April 1971): 177-82.

Morton, Peter. "Biological Degeneration in H.G. Wells and other Late Victorians." *Southern Review: Australian Journal of Literary Studies* 9 (July 1976): 93-112.
——. *The Vital Science: Biology and Literary Imagination, 1860-1900.* London: Allen, 1984.
Myers, Greg. "Nineteenth-Century Popularizations of Thermodynamics and the Rhetoric of Social Prophecy." In *Energy and Entropy*, ed. Brantlinger, 307-38.
Nerlich, Brigitte. "Linguistic Evolution." *Lingua* 77, no. 2 (Feb. 1989): 99-112.
Norris, Margot. *Beasts of the Modern Imagination: Darwin, Nietzsche, Kafka, Ernst, Lawrence.* Baltimore: Johns Hopkins Univ. Press, 1985.
Nye, Robert. "Degeneration and the Medical Model of Cultural Crisis in the French *Belle Epoque*." In *Political Symbolism in Modern Europe: Essays in Honor of George L. Mosse*, ed. Seymour Drescher, David Sabean, and Allan Sharlin, 19-41. New Brunswick, N.J.: Transaction, 1982.
Paradis, James, and Thomas Postlewait, eds. *Victorian Science and Victorian Values: Literary Perspectives.* New Brunswick, N.J.: Rutgers Univ. Press, 1985.
Pick, Daniel. *Faces of Degeneration: A European Disorder, c. 1848-c. 1918.* Cambridge: Cambridge Univ. Press, 1989.
Schiller, Andrew. "Order and Entropy in Natural Language." In *Language Topics: Essays in Honour of Michael Halliday*, ed. Ross Steele and Terry Threadgold, 315-31. Amsterdam: Benjamins, 1987.
Skultans, Vieda, ed. *Madness and Morals: Ideas on Insanity in the Nineteenth Century.* London: Routledge and Kegan Paul, 1975.
Turner, Frank. *Between Science and Religion: The Reaction to Scientific Naturalism in Late Victorian England.* New Haven, Conn.: Yale Univ. Press, 1974.
Tytler, Graeme. *Physiognomy in the European Novel.* Princeton, N.J.: Princeton Univ. Press, 1982.

Miscellaneous

Primary Works

Adams, Henry. *The Education of Henry Adams: An Autobiography.* Boston: Houghton, Mifflin, 1961.
Ainsworth, William Harrison. Review of *Moby-Dick. New Monthly Magazine* (London) 98 (July 1853): 307-8.
Aristotle. *The Complete Works of Aristotle.* Ed. Jonathan Barnes. 2 vols. Princeton, N.J.: Princeton Univ. Press, 1984.
Ashbee, Henry Spencer. *Forbidden Books of the Victorians.* London: Odyssey, 1970.
Baring, Maurice. *Lost Lectures: or, The Fruits of Experience.* New York: Knopf, 1932.
Beerbohm, Sir Max. "The Best Scenery I Know." *Saturday Review*, Aug. 28, 1897, 217.
Blanc, M. Charles. *Grammaire des arts du dessin.* 2d ed. Paris: Jules Renouard, 1870.
Borges, Jorge Luis. *Other Inquisitions, 1937-1952.* New York: Simon and Schuster, 1965.
Brontë, Charlotte. *Jane Eyre.* Ed. Jane Jack and Margaret Smith. Oxford: Clarendon, 1969.
Browne, Sir Thomas. *The Letters of Sir Thomas Browne.* Ed. Geoffrey Keynes. London: Faber, 1946.
——. *Religio Medici.* Vol. 1 of *The Works of Sir Thomas Browne*, ed. Geoffrey Keynes. Chicago: Univ. of Chicago Press, 1964.
Browning, Robert. *Robert Browning: The Poems.* Ed. John Pettigrew. 2 vols. New Haven, Conn.: Yale Univ. Press, 1981.
Buchan, John. *Memory Hold-the-Door.* London: Hodder and Stoughton, 1954.
——. *Scholar Gipsies.* London: Bodley Head, 1896.
Butler, Samuel. *Characters and Passages from Note-Books.* Ed. A.R. Waller. Cambridge: Cambridge Univ. Press, 1908.
Byatt, A.S. *Possession.* New York: Vintage International, 1991.
Carlyle, Thomas. *The French Revolution: A History.* 2 vols. London: Dent, 1914.

——. *Reminiscences*. Ed. James Anthony Froude. New York: Scribner's, 1881.

——. *Sartor Resartus*. London: Dent, 1916.

Carpenter, Edward. *Love's Coming-of-Age: A Series of Papers on the Relations of the Sexes*. New York: Mitchell Kennerley, 1911.

Chamberlain, Alexander Francis. *The Child and Childhood in Folk-Thought*. New York: Macmillan, 1896.

Chesterton, G[ilbert] K[eith]. *George Bernard Shaw*. New York: John Lane, 1909.

Choate, John. "To His Dear Brother." Aug. 7, 1784. Author's private collection.

Clark, W.B. *Asleep in Jesus: or, Words of Consolation to Bereaved Parents*. London: T. Nelson, 1856.

De Quincey, Thomas. *Essays in Philosophy*. Vol. 9 of *The Works of Thomas De Quincey*. Boston: Houghton, Mifflin, 1876-77.

Dickens, Charles. *Dombey and Son*. Oxford: Clarendon, 1974.

——. *The Old Curiosity Shop*. Harmondsworth, Eng.: Penguin, 1972.

——. *Our Mutual Friend*. Harmondsworth, Eng.: Penguin, 1971.

Doyle, Arthur Conan. *The Complete Sherlock Holmes*. Ed. Christopher Morley. New York: Doubleday, [1960].

Du Maurier, George. *Trilby*. New York: Harper, 1894.

Eliot, George. *Daniel Deronda*. Oxford: Clarendon, 1984.

——. *The George Eliot Letters*. Ed. Gordon S. Haight. 9 vols. New Haven, Conn.: Yale Univ. Press, 1955.

——. *Middlemarch*. Harmondsworth, Eng.: Penguin, 1981.

——. *The Mill on the Floss*. Ed. Gordon S. Haight. Oxford: Clarendon, 1980.

——. *Scenes of Clerical Life*. Ed. Thomas A. Noble. Oxford: Clarendon, 1985.

Eliot, T.S. *Selected Essays*. New York: Harcourt, 1950.

Ellis, Sarah Stickney. *The Women of England: Their Social Duties, and Domestic Habits; The Wives of England: Their Relative Duties, Domestic Influence, and Social Obligations; and The Daughters of England: Their Position in Society, Character, and Responsibilities*. 3 vols. in 1. New York: J. and H.G. Langley, 1843.

Emerson, Ralph Waldo. *Essays and Lectures*. New York: Literary Classics of the United States, 1983.

Flaubert, Gustave. *The Selected Letters of Gustave Flaubert*. Trans. and ed. Francis Steegmuller. New York: Farrar, Straus and Young, 1953.

Gilbert, William S., and Arthur S. Sullivan. *The Complete Plays of Gilbert and Sullivan*. New York: Norton, 1976.

Goethe, Johann Wolfgang von. *Selected Poems*. Ed. Christopher Middleton. Trans. Michael Hamburger. Cambridge: Suhrkamp/Insel Publishers Boston, 1983.

Grand, Sarah. *The Heavenly Twins*. New York: Cassell, 1893.

Haggard, H. Rider. *The Annotated She*. With an introduction by Norman Etherington. Bloomington: Indiana Univ. Press, 1991.

Hardy, Thomas. *Tess of the d'Urbervilles*. Ed. Juliet Grindle and Simon Gatrell. Oxford: Clarendon, 1983.

Hawthorne, Nathaniel. *American Notebooks*. Columbus: Ohio State Univ. Press, 1972.

——. *Hawthorne: Tales and Sketches*. Ed. Roy Harvey Pearce. New York: Literary Classics of the United States, 1982.

——. *The House of the Seven Gables*. Columbus: Ohio State Univ. Press, 1971.

——. *The Scarlet Letter*. Columbus: Ohio State Univ. Press, 1962.

Herford, Oliver. *An Alphabet of Celebrities*. Boston: Small, Maynard, 1899.

Hogarth, William. *The Analysis of Beauty*. Oxford: Clarendon, 1955.

Huxley, Aldous. *Music at Night and Other Essays*. London: Chatto and Windus, 1949.

James, William. *The Varieties of Religious Experience*. Cambridge, Mass.: Harvard Univ. Press, 1985.

Joyce, James. *Selected Letters of James Joyce*. Ed. Richard Ellmann. London: Faber, 1975.

Macaulay, Thomas Babington. *Critical and Historical Essays Contributed to* The Edinburgh Review. 3 vols. London: Longman, Brown, Green, and Longmans, 1843.

The Mask: A Quarterly Journal of the Art of the Theatre (Florence, Italy). 15 vols. (1908-29).

Melville, Herman. *Pierre; or, The Ambiguities; Israel Potter: His Fifty Years of Exile; The Piazza Tales; The Confidence-Man: His Masquerade; Uncollected Prose; Billy Budd, Sailor (an Inside Narrative).* New York: Literary Classics of the United States, 1984.

"Melville's *Moby Dick.*" *Southern Quarterly Review* 5 (Jan. 1852): 262.

Michener, Fannie L. *The Prose and Poetical Works of Fannie L. Michener.* Philadelphia: Lippincott, 1884.

Morley, John. *Recollections.* 2 vols. New York: Macmillan, 1917.

Nietzsche, Friedrrich. *The Will to Power.* Ed and trans. Walter Kaufman. New York: Vintage, 1967.

Orwell, George. *The Collected Essays, Journalism and Letters of George Orwell.* Ed. Sonia Orwell and Ian Angus. 4 vols. New York: Harcourt, 1968.

Otto, Rudolf. *The Idea of the Holy.* Trans. John W. Harvey. London: Oxford Univ. Press, 1981.

Petronius. *Works.* Trans. Thomas Addison. London: J. Watts, 1736.

Pritzel, Lotte. *Das Puppenbach.* Berlin: Erich Reiss, 1921.

Rolfe, Frederick [Baron Corvo, pseud.]. *Chronicles of the House of Borgia.* New York: Dover, 1962.

———. *In His Own Image.* London: John Lane, 1900.

Rousseau, Jean-Jacques. *Emile.* London: Dent, 1911.

Ruskin, John. *The Works of John Ruskin.* Ed. E.T. Cook and Alexander Wedderburn. 39 vols. London: George Allen, 1903-12.

The Second Prayer-Book of King Edward VI. London: Griffith, Farran, Okeden, and Welsh, 1891.

Shiel, M[atthew] P[hipps]. *Science, Life and Literature.* London: Williams and Norgate, 1950.

Spofford, Harriet Prescott. *Art Decoration Applied to Furniture.* New York: Harper, 1878.

Stevenson, Robert Louis. *Across the Plains: With Other Memories and Essays.* New York: Scribner's, 1907.

———. *Essays in the Art of Writing.* London: Chatto and Windus, 1919.

Strachey, Lytton. *Eminent Victorians.* New York: Putnam's, 1918.

"Study and Opinion in Oxford." *Macmillan's Magazine* 21 (Dec. 1860): 184-92.

Tennyson, Alfred. *Idylls of the King.* In *Tennyson's Poetry,* ed. Robert W. Hill Jr., 288-431. New York: Norton, 1971.

———. *In Memoriam.* In *Tennyson's Poetry,* ed. Robert W. Hill Jr., 119-95. New York: Norton, 1971.

Virgil. *The Aeneid of Virgil.* Trans. J.W. Mackail. London: Macmillan, 1937.

Waite, Arthur E. *Shadows of Life and Thought.* London: Selwyn and Blount, 1938.

Walpole, Horace. *Horace Walpole's Correspondence with Madame du Deffand and Mademoiselle Sanadon.* Vol. 5 of *Horace Walpole's Correspondence,* ed. Wilmarth S. Lewis, 48 vols. New Haven, Conn.: Yale Univ. Press, 1937-81.

Wells, H[erbert] G[eorge]. *Boon, The Mind of the Race, The Wild Asses of the Devil, and The Last Trump.* New York: George H. Doran, 1915.

———. *The Famous Short Stories of H.G. Wells.* New York: The Literary Guild of America, 1937.

———. *The Works of H.G. Wells.* 28 vols. London: T. Fisher Unwin, 1924-27

Woolf, Virginia. *Granite and Rainbow: Essays.* New York: Harcourt, 1958.

Wordsworth, William. *Selected Poems and Prefaces.* Ed. Jack Stillinger. Boston: Houghton, 1965.

Yeats, William Butler. *The Collected Works in Verse and Prose of William Butler Yeats.* 8 vols. Stratford-on-Avon, Eng.: Bullen, 1908.

Secondary Works

Altick, Richard D. *The English Common Reader: A Social History of the Mass Reading Public, 1800-1900.* Chicago: Univ. of Chicago Press, 1957.
———. *The Presence of the Present.* Columbus: Ohio State Univ. Press, 1991.
Baltrusaitis, Jorgis. *La stylistique ornementale dans la sculpture romane.* Paris: Librairie Ernest Leroux, 1931.
Baudrillard, Jean. *Simulacra and Simulation.* Trans. Sheila Faria Glaser. Ann Arbor: Univ. of Michigan Press, 1994.
Baugh, Albert C., ed. *A Literary History of England.* New York: Appleton-Century-Crofts, 1948.
Batho, Edith, and Bonamy Dobrée. *The Victorians and After.* London: Cresset, 1938.
Bergonzi, Bernard. *The Turn of a Century: Essays on Victorian and Modern English Literature.* New York: Barnes, 1973.
Brantlinger, Patrick. *Bread and Circuses: Theories of Mass Culture and Social Decay.* Ithaca, N.Y.: Cornell Univ. Press, 1983.
———. *Rule of Darkness: British Literature and Imperialism, 1830-1914.* Ithaca, N.Y.: Cornell Univ. Press, 1988.
Bronfen, Elisabeth. *Over Her Dead Body: Death, Femininity, and the Aesthetic.* New York: Routledge, 1992.
Brooke-Rose, Christine. *A Rhetoric of the Unreal.* Cambridge: Cambridge Univ. Press, 1981.
Buckley, Jerome Hamilton. *The Victorian Temper: A Study of Literary Culture.* New York: Vintage, 1951.
Carroll, Michael P. *The Cult of the Virgin Mary: Psychological Origins.* Princeton, N.J.: Princeton Univ. Press, 1986.
Cecil, Robert. *Life in Edwardian England.* London: Batsford, 1969.
Chapman, Raymond. *The Sense of the Past in Victorian Literature.* New York: St. Martin's, 1986.
Cody, David. "Invited Guests at Hawthorne's 'Christmas Banquet': Sir Thomas Browne and Jeremy Taylor." *Modern Language Studies* 11, no. 1 (winter 1980): 17-26.
Culler, A. Dwight. *The Victorian Mirror of History.* New Haven, Conn.: Yale Univ. Press, 1985.
Daiches, David. *Some Late Victorian Attitudes.* London: Andre Deutsch, 1969.
De la Mare, Walter, ed. *The Eighteen-Eighties.* Cambridge: Cambridge Univ. Press, 1930.
DeLaura, David J. *Hebrew and Hellene in Victorian England: Newman, Arnold, and Pater.* Austin: Univ. of Texas Press, 1969.
De Lauretis, Theresa. *Technologies of Gender: Essays on Theory, Film, and Fiction.* Bloomington: Indiana Univ. Press, 1987.
Derrida, Jacques. *A Derrida Reader: Between the Blinds.* Ed. Peggy Kamuf. New York: Columbia Univ. Press, 1991.
———. *Of Grammatology.* Trans. Gayatri Chakravorty Spivak. Baltimore: Johns Hopkins Univ. Press, 1976.
Dictionary of Philosophy and Psychology. Ed. James Mark Baldwin. New York: Macmillan, 1928.
Eagleton, Terry. *Marxism and Literary Criticism.* Berkeley: Univ. of California Press, 1976.
Edel, Leon. *The Modern Psychological Novel.* New York: Grosset and Dunlop, 1964.
———. *Stuff of Sleep and Dreams: Experiments in Literary Psychology.* New York: Harper and Row, 1982.
———. *Writing Lives: Principia Biographica.* New York: Norton, 1984.
Ellenberger, Henri F. *The Discovery of the Unconscious.* New York: Basic, 1970.
Ellmann, Richard, ed. *Golden Codgers.* New York: Oxford Univ. Press, 1973.
Farnell, Lewis Richard. *The Cults of the Greek States.* 5 vols. Oxford: Clarendon, 1907.
Foucault, Michel. *The Order of Things.* New York: Vintage, 1973.

Frazer, James George. *The Golden Bough: A Study in Magic and Religion.* New York: Macmillan, 1963.
———. *Psyche's Task.* London: Dawsons of Pall Mall, 1968.
Gerber, Helmut, ed. *The English Short Story in Transition 1880-1920.* New York: Western, 1967.
Gose, Elliot. *Imagination Indulged: The Irrational in the Nineteenth-Century Novel.* Montreal: McGill-Queen's Univ. Press, 1972.
Harris, Wendell V. "The Beginnings of and for the True Short Story in England." *English Literature in Transition* 15 (1972): 269-76.
———. *British Short Fiction in the Nineteenth Century: A Literary and Bibliographic Guide.* Detroit: Wayne State Univ. Press, 1979.
———. "English Short Fiction in the 19th Century." *Studies in Short Fiction* 6 (1968): 1-93.
———. "Vision and Form: The English Novel and the Emergence of the Short Story." *Victorian Newsletter* 47 (1975): 8-12.
Hicks, Granville. *Figures of Transition: A Study of British Literature.* New York: Macmillan, 1939.
Holubetz, Margarete. "Death-Bed Scenes in Victorian Fiction." *English Studies* 67, no. 1 (Feb. 1986): 14-34.
Homans, Margaret. *Bearing the Word: Language and Female Experience in Nineteenth-Century Women's Writing.* Chicago: Univ. of Chicago Press, 1986.
Hynes, Samuel. *The Edwardian Turn of Mind.* Princeton, N.J.: Princeton Univ. Press, 1968.
The International Cyclopedia of Music and Musicians. Ed. Oscar Thompson. 11th ed. New York: Dodd, Mead, 1985.
Irigaray, Luce. *This Sex Which Is Not One.* Trans. Catherine Porter. Ithaca, N.Y.: Cornell Univ. Press, 1985.
Kucich, John. "Death Worship among the Victorians: *The Old Curiosity Shop.*" *PMLA* 95, no. 1 (Jan. 1980): 58-72.
Lauterbach, Edward S., and W. Eugene Davis. *The Transitional Age: British Literature, 1880-1920.* Troy, N.Y.: Whitston, 1973.
Leavis, F.R. *The Great Tradition.* Garden City, N.Y.: Doubleday, 1954.
Lester, John A., Jr. *Journey through Despair.* Princeton, N.J.: Princeton Univ. Press, 1968.
Loke, Margaret. *The World As It Was, 1865-1921: A Photographic Portrait.* New York: Summit, 1980.
Marcus, Steven. *The Other Victorians.* New York: Basic, 1966.
McConnell, Frank. *The Science Fiction of H.G. Wells.* New York: Oxford Univ. Press, 1981.
McLaren, Angus. "Abortion in England, 1890-1914." *Victorian Studies* 20 (1977): 379-400.
Miyoshi, Masao. *The Divided Self: Literature of the Victorians.* New York: New York Univ. Press, 1969.
The New Oxford Companion to Music. Ed. Denis Arnold. 2 vols. Oxford: Oxford Univ. Press, 1983.
Orel, Harold. *The Victorian Short Story: Development and Triumph of a Literary Genre.* Cambridge: Cambridge Univ. Press, 1986.
Oxford Dictionary of the Christian Church. Ed. F.L. Cross and E.A. Livingstone. 2d ed. London: Oxford Univ. Press, 1974.
Pearsall, Ronald. *Public Purity, Private Shame.* London: Weidenfeld and Nicolson, 1976.
———. *The Worm in the Bud: The World of Victorian Sexuality.* London: Pimlico, 1993.
Pelensky, Olga Anastasia. *Isak Dinesen: Critical Views.* Athens: Ohio Univ. Press, 1993.
Plotz, Judith A. "A Victorian Comfort Book: Juliana Ewing's *The Story of a Short Life.*" In *Romanticism and Children's Literature in Nineteenth-Century England,* ed. James Holt McGavran Jr., 168-89. Athens: Univ. of Georgia Press, 1991.
Read, Donald, ed. *Documents from Edwardian England, 1901-1915.* London: Harrap, 1973.
Reed, John R. *Victorian Conventions.* Athens: Ohio Univ. Press, 1975.
Rose, Michael. "Late Victorians and Edwardians." *Victorian Studies* 17 (1974): 319-26.

Rothenstein, William. *Recollections, 1872-1900.* Vol. 1 of *Men and Memories.* New York: Coward-McCann, 1931.

Saisselin, Rémy G. *The Bourgeois and the Bibelot.* New Brunswick, N.J.: Rutgers Univ. Press, 1984.

Sartre, Jean-Paul. *What Is Literature?* Trans. Bernard Frechtman. New York: Philosophical Library, 1949.

Scheick, William J. *Fictional Structure in Ethics: The Turn-of-the-Century English Novel.* Athens: Univ. of Georgia Press, 1990.

Schor, Naomi. *Reading in Detail: Aesthetics and the Feminine.* New York: Methuen, 1987.

Starrett, Vincent. *Buried Caesars: Essays in Literary Appreciation.* Chicago: Covici-McGee, 1923.

Stewart, Garrett. "Thresholds of the Visible: The Death Scene of Film." *Mosaic* 16, nos. 1-2 (winter/spring 1983): 33-54.

Stone, Norman. *Europe Transformed 1878-1919.* Glasgow: William Collins Sons, 1983.

Street, Brian V. *The Savage in Literature: Representations of "Primitive" Society in English Fiction, 1858-1920.* London: Routledge and Kegan Paul, 1975.

Sutherland, James, ed. *The Oxford Book of Literary Anecdotes.* London: Oxford Univ. Press, 1975.

Temple, Ruth Z. "The Ivory Tower as Lighthouse." In *Edwardians and Late Victorians,* ed. Ellmann, 28-49.

Thompson, Edward P. *The Making of the English Working Class.* New York: Vintage, 1966.

Tindall, William York. *Forces in Modern British Literature, 1885-1956.* New York: Vintage, 1956.

Todorov, Tzvetan. *The Poetics of Prose.* Ithaca, N.Y.: Cornell Univ. Press, 1977.

Trudgill, Eric. *Madonnas and Magdalens: The Origins and Development of Victorian Sexual Attitudes.* London: Heinemann, 1976.

Van den Abbeele, Georges. "Sade, Foucault, and the Scene of Enlightenment Lucidity." *Stanford French Review* 11, no. 1 (spring 1987): 7-16.

Van Vechten, Carl. *Peter Whiffle: His Life and Works.* New York: Knopf, 1927.

Vicinus, Martha. "Dark London." *Indiana University Bookman* 12 (1977): 63-92.

Warner, Marina. *Alone of All Her Sex.* New York: Knopf, 1976.

Watson, E.W. *Life of Bishop John Wordsworth.* New York: Longmans, Green, 1915.

Webb, Peter. *Hans Bellmer.* London: Quartet, 1985.

Wheeler, Michael. *Death and the Future Life in Victorian Literature and Theology.* Cambridge: Cambridge Univ. Press, 1990.

Wilson, Edmund. *Classics and Commercial.* New York: Farrar, Strauss, 1950.

Joseph Conrad (1857-1924)

Primary Works

The Collected Letters of Joseph Conrad. Ed. Frederick R. Karl and Laurence Davies. 5 vols. Cambridge: Cambridge Univ. Press, 1983-86.

Conrad to a Friend: 150 Selected Letters from Joseph Conrad to Richard Curle. Ed. Richard Curle. London: Sampson Low, Marston, 1928.

Conrad's Prefaces to His Works. With an introduction by Edward Garnett. New York: Haskell House, 1971.

Heart of Darkness. Ed. Robert Kimbrough. 3d ed. New York: Norton, 1988.

Joseph Conrad: Life and Letters. Ed. G. Jean-Aubry. New York: Doubleday, 1927.

Joseph Conrad's Letters to R.B. Cunninghame Graham. Ed. C.T. Watts. Cambridge: Cambridge Univ. Press, 1969.

Last Essays. With an introduction by Richard Curle. London: J.M. Dent, 1926.

Notes on Life and Letters. New York: Doubleday, Page, 1923.

A Personal Record. New York: Doubleday, Page, 1923.

Secondary Works

Bender, Todd K. "Conrad and Literary Impressionism." *Conradiana* 10, no. 3 (1978): 211-24.

Brantlinger, Patrick. *"Heart of Darkness:* Anti-Imperialism, Racism, or Impressionism?" *Criticism* 27, no. 4 (fall 1985): 363-85.

A Conrad Memorial Library: The Collection of George T. Keating. New York: Doubleday, 1929.

Crews, Frederick. "The Power of Darkness." *Partisan Review* 34, no. 4 (fall 1967): 507-25.

Gillon, Adam. "Conrad and James: A World of Things beyond the Range of Commonplace Definitions." *Conradiana* 15, no. 1 (1983): 53-64.

Hawthorn, Jeremy. *Joseph Conrad: Language and Fictional Self-Consciousness.* London: Edward Arnold, 1979.

Hay, Eloise Knapp. "Joseph Conrad and Impressionism." *Journal of Aesthetics and Art Criticism* 34 (winter 1975): 137-44.

Hunter, Allan. *Joseph Conrad and the Ethics of Darwinism.* London: Croom Helm, 1983.

Jean-Aubry, G. *Joseph Conrad, Life and Letters.* 2 vols. New York: Doubleday, 1927.

Johnson, Bruce. "'Heart of Darkness' and the Problem of Emptiness." *Studies in Short Fiction* 9, no. 4 (fall 1972): 387-400.

———. "Names, Naming, and the 'Inscrutable' in Conrad's *Heart of Darkness.*" *Texas Studies in Literature and Language* 12, no. 4 (winter 1971): 675-87.

Karl, Frederick R. "Joseph Conrad: A *Fin de Siècle* Novelist—A Study in Style and Method." *Literary Review* 2, no. 4 (summer 1959): 565-76.

McCarthy, Patrick A. *"Heart of Darkness* and the Early Novels of H.G. Wells: Evolution, Anarchy, Entropy." *Journal of Modern Literature* 13, no. 1 (Mar. 1986): 37-60.

Miller, J[oseph] Hillis. *Poets of Reality: Six Twentieth-Century Writers.* Cambridge, Mass.: Harvard Univ. Press, 1965.

Mudrick, Marvin. "The Originality of Joseph Conrad." *Hudson Review* 11, no. 4 (winter 1958-59): 545-53.

O'Hanlon, Redmond. *Joseph Conrad and Charles Darwin.* Edinburgh: Salamander, 1984.

Pecora, Vincent. *"Heart of Darkness* and the Phenomenology of Voice." *ELH* 52, no. 4 (winter 1985): 993-1015.

Randall, Dale B.J. *Joseph Conrad and Warrington Dawson: The Record of a Friendship.* Durham, N.C.: Duke Univ. Press, 1968.

Reeves, Charles Eric. "A Voice of Unrest: Conrad's Rhetoric of the Unspeakable." *Texas Studies in Literature and Language* 27, no. 3 (fall 1985): 284-310.

Renner, Stanley. "The Garden of Civilization: Conrad, Huxley, and the Ethics of Evolution." *Conradiana* 7, no. 2 (1975): 109-20.

Rose, Alan M. "Conrad and the Sirens of Decadence." *Texas Studies in Literature and Language* 11, no. 1 (spring 1969): 795-810.

Said, Edward. "Conrad: The Presentation of Narrative." *Novel* 7, no. 2 (winter 1974): 116-32.

Sherry, Norman. *Joseph Conrad: A Commemoration.* London: Macmillan, 1976.

Stewart, Garrett. "Lying as Dying in *Heart of Darkness.*" *PMLA* 95 (May 1980): 319-31.

Symons, Arthur. *Notes on Joseph Conrad: With Some Unpublished Letters.* London: Myers, 1925.

Watt, Ian. *Conrad in the Nineteenth Century.* Berkeley: Univ. of California Press, 1979.

———. *"Heart of Darkness* and Nineteenth-Century Thought." *Partisan Review* 45, no. 1: 108-19.

[Wells, H(erbert) G(eorge)]. Review of *An Outcast of the Islands,* by Joseph Conrad. *Saturday Review,* May 16, 1896, 509-10.

White, Allon. *The Uses of Obscurity: The Fiction of Early Modernism.* London: Routledge and Kegan Paul, 1981.

Walter de la Mare (1873-1956)

Primary Works

Eight Tales. Ed. Edward Wagenknecht. Sauk City, Wis.: Arkham House, 1971.
Introduction to *They Walk Again: An Anthology of Ghost Stories,* ed. Colin de la Mare.
     London: Faber, 1931.
On the Edge. New York: Knopf, 1931.
The Picnic and Other Stories. London: Faber, 1941.
Private View. London: Faber, 1953.
The Riddle and Other Tales. New York: Knopf, 1923.
The Wind Blows Over. New York: Macmillan, 1936.

Secondary Works

Bonnerot, Luce. *L'oeuvre de Walter de la Mare: Une aventure spirituelle.* Paris: Didier, 1969.
———. "Walter de la Mare ou la transgression fantastique: Deux textes." *Caliban* 16 (1979): 17-
     26.
Brain, Russell. *Tea with Walter de la Mare.* London: Faber, 1957.
Cecil, David. *Walter de la Mare.* London: Oxford Univ. Press, 1973.
Clark, Leonard. *Walter de la Mare.* London: John Lane, 1960.
Hopkins, Kenneth. *Walter de la Mare.* London: Longmans, Green, 1953.
Jacobsen, Josephine. "The Masks of Walter de la Mare." *Sewanee Review* 86 (1978): 549-56.
Mégroz, R[odolphe] L[ouis]. *Walter de la Mare: A Biographical and Critical Study.* London:
     Hodder and Stoughton, 1925.
Reid, Forrest. *Walter de la Mare: A Critical Study.* London: Faber, 1929.

Henry James (1843-1916)

Primary Works

"The Altar of the Dead." In *The Novels and Tales of Henry James,* vol. 17, 3-58. New York:
     Scribner's, 1909.
The Art of the Novel: Critical Prefaces. With an introduction by Richard P. Blackmur. New
     York: Scribner's, 1934.
The Complete Notebooks of Henry James. Ed. Leon Edel and Lyall H. Powers. New York:
     Oxford Univ. Press, 1987.
Henry James: Stories of the Supernatural. Ed. Leon Edel. New York: Taplinger, 1970.
Henry James Letters. Ed. Leon Edel. 4 vols. Cambridge, Mass.: Belknap of Harvard Univ.
     Press, 1980.
Henry James Literary Criticism. New York: Literary Classics of the United States, 1984.
Portraits of Places. London: Macmillan, 1883.
The Turn of the Screw. Vol. 11 of *The Bodley Head Henry James.* London: Bodley Head,
     1974.

Secondary Works

Schleifer, Ronald. "The Trap of the Imagination: Gothic Tradition and 'The Turn of the
     Screw.'" *Criticism* 22 (1980): 297-319.

Vernon Lee [Violet Paget] (1856-1935)

Primary Works

Baldwin: A Book of Dialogues on Views and Aspirations. Boston: Roberts Brother, 1886.

The Beautiful: An Introduction to Psychological Aesthetics. Cambridge: Cambridge Univ. Press, 1913.

Belcaro. London: T. Fisher Unwin, 1887.

Euphorion. London: T. Fisher Unwin, 1885.

For Maurice: Five Unlikely Stories. London: John Lane, 1927.

Gospels of Anarchy and Other Contemporary Studies. New York: Brentano's; London: T. Fisher Unwin, 1909.

The Handling of Words and Other Studies in Literary Psychology. New York: Dodd, Mead, 1923.

Hauntings: Fantastic Stories. London: John Lane, 1906.

"J.S.S.: In Memoriam." In *John Sargent,* by Evan Charteris, 233-55. New York: Scribner's, 1927.

Laurus Nobilis, Chapters on Art and Life. London: John Lane, 1909.

Limbo, and Other Essays. London: John Lane, 1908.

Miss Brown. Ed. Ian Fletcher and John Stokes. 3 vols. in 1. 1884. Reprint, New York: Garland, 1978.

Pope Jacynth and Other Fantastic Tales. London: John Lane, 1907.

The Prince of the Hundred Soups: A Puppet-Show in Narrative. London: T. Fisher Unwin, 1883.

Renaissance Fancies and Studies. London: John Lane, 1909.

Studies of the Eighteenth Century in Italy. London: T. Fisher Unwin, 1907.

Supernatural Tales: Excursions into Fantasy. London: Peter Owen, 1955.

Vanitas. Leipzig: Bernard Tauchnitz, 1911.

A Vernon Lee Anthology. Ed. and with an introduction by Irene Cooper Willis. London: John Lane, 1929.

Vernon Lee's Letters. Ed. Irene Cooper Willis. N.p., 1937.

Secondary Works

Baring, Maurice. "Vernon Lee: An Appreciation." *Times* (London), Feb. 15, 1935, 19.

Brooks, Van Wyck. "Notes on Vernon Lee." *Forum* 45 (1911): 447-56.

Cary, Richard. "Vernon Lee's Vignettes of Literary Acquaintances." *Colby Library Quarterly* 9, no. 3 (Sept. 1970): 179-99.

Colby, Vineta. *The Singular Anomaly: Women Novelists of the Nineteenth Century.* New York: New York Univ. Press, 1970.

Gardner, Burdett. *The Lesbian Imagination (Victorian Style): A Psychological and Critical Study of "Vernon Lee."* New York: Garland, 1987.

Gregory, Horace. *Spirit of Time and Place: Collected Essays of Horace Gregory.* New York: Norton, 1973.

Gunn, Peter. *Vernon Lee: Violet Paget, 1856-1935.* London: Oxford Univ. Press, 1964.

MacCarthy, Desmond. "Vernon Lee." *Bookman* (London) 81 (Oct. 1931): 21-22.

Manocchi, Phyllis F. "'Vernon Lee': A Reintroduction and Primary Bibliography." *English Literature in Transition* 26, no. 4 (1983): 231-67.

Ormond, Leonee. "Vernon Lee as a Critic of Aestheticism in *Miss Brown.*" *Colby Library Quarterly* 9, no. 3 (Sept. 1970): 131-200.

Pater, Walter. "Vernon Lee's 'Juvenalia.'" *Pall Mall Gazette* (London), Aug. 5, 1887, 5.

Praz, Mario. "Vernon Lee." *Pan* (April 1, 1935): 560-69.

Robbins, Ruth. "Vernon Lee: Decadent Woman?" In *Fin de Siècle, Fin du Globe: Fears and Fantasies of the Late Nineteenth Century.* Ed. John Stokes. New York: St. Martin's, 1992.

Shaw, George Bernard. "A Political Contrast. *Satan the Waster:* A Philosophical War Trilogy." *Nation* (London) 27 (Sept. 18, 1920): 758-60.

"Vernon Lee." *Literary World* (Boston) 15 (Nov. 1, 1884): 373.

"Vernon Lee." *Times* (London), Feb. 14, 1935, 17.

Waters, Harriet Preston. "Vernon Lee." *Atlantic Monthly* 55 (Feb. 1885): 219-27.

Welleck, René. "Vernon Lee, Bernard Berenson and Aesthetics." In *Friendship's Garland*, ed. Vittorio Gabrieli. 2 vols., 2:233-51. Rome: Edizioni di Storia e Letteratura, 1966.

Arthur Machen (1863-1947)

Primary Works

The Autobiography of Arthur Machen. With an introduction by Morchard Bishop. London: Richards, 1951.
The Children of the Pool and Other Stories. New York: Arno, 1976.
The Glorious Mystery. Chicago: Covici-McGee, 1924.
Hieroglyphics: A Note upon Ecstasy in Literature. London: Martin Secker, 1923.
The Hill of Dreams. London: Martin Secker, 1923.
The House of Souls. London: Grant Richards, 1923.
Ornaments in Jade. New York: Knopf, 1924.
Precious Balms. London: Spurr and Swift, 1924.
Tales of Horror and the Supernatural. New York: Pinnacle, 1971.
The Three Imposters. London: Martin Secker, 1923.

Secondary Works

Benét, William Rose. "The Other That Hides." *Saturday Review of Literature* (New York) 1 (Aug. 16, 1924): 44.
Carter, John. "Mr. Machen Goes A-Journeying within Himself." *New York Times Book Review and Magazine*, Oct. 12, 1924, 12.
Cazamian, Madeleine L. "Arthur Machen." In *Le roman et les idées en Angleterre: L'anti-intellectualisme et l'esthétisme (1880-1900)*, by Cazamian, 246-84.
"Confessions of a Lotus-Eater." *Times Literary Supplement* (London), Sept. 14, 1922, 581.
"Current Literature." *Nation* 85 (July 11, 1907): 37.
Gorman, Herbert S. "Arthur Machen Pursues His Mystic Way." *New York Times Book Review*, Jan. 16, 1927, 5.
"The Great God Pan." *Literary News* 16 (Feb. 1895): 44.
Hecht, Ben. "The Satyr-Machen: A Diagnosis of the Last Pagan." *Chicago Literary Times* 1, no. 3 (April 1, 1923): 3.
Krutch, Joseph Wood. "Tales of a Mystic." *Nation* 115, no. 2984 (Sept. 13, 1922): 258-59.
Lynch, Helen. "Arthur Machen." *Sewanee Review* 47 (July-Sept. 1939): 424-26.
Michael, David Perry Martin. *Arthur Machen*. Cardiff: Univ. of Wales Press, 1971.
"New Novels." *Athenaeum* 1 (Mar. 16, 1907): 317.
"Our Literary Table." *Athenaeum* 2 (Aug. 4, 1906): 129.
Reynolds, Aidan, and William Charlton. *Arthur Machen: A Short Account of His Life and Work*. Philadelphia: Dufour Editions, 1964.
Sewell, Brocard, ed. *Arthur Machen: Essays by Adrian Goldstone, C.A. and Anthony Lejeune, Father Brocard Sewell, Maurice Spurway, Wesley D. Sweetser, Henry Williamson*. Llandeilo, Wales: St. Albert's, 1960.
Sweetser, Wesley D. *Arthur Machen*. New York: Twayne, 1964.
———. "Arthur Machen: A Bibliography of Writings about Him." *English Literature in Transition* 11 (1968): 1-33.

Index

CPSIA information can be obtained at www.ICGtesting.com
Printed in the USA
LVOW10*1823210416

484697LV00012B/176/P